THE SOCIAL ECONOMY
OF FREEDOM

First published 2011
Pascal Blanqué
The Social Economy of Freedom
ISBN 978-2-7178-6097-9

Pascal BLANQUÉ

THE SOCIAL
ECONOMY
OF FREEDOM

☐☐ ECONOMICA

49, rue Héricart, 75015 Paris

For G. & descendants

Homo economicus is an individual Subject, who is a free conscience and whose freedom is merged with the action directed at and over the world. This Subject is confronted with the Other in its relationship with the world and in its action design. But above all, *Homo economicus* is a man who remembers and forgets. ***Homo memor (economicus)***.

« *Those who want one canonical understanding of the "true" nature of freedom may underestimate the very different ways in which ideas of freedom and non-freedom can enter our perception, assessment and evaluation* [...] *When it comes to distinct concepts, a thousand may be difficult to manage, but there should be no great difficulty in being able to see several different aspects of freedom as being complementary rather than competitive.* »

Amartya Sen, *The Idea of Justice*

« *It has become a common practice to disparage freedom of action by calling it "economic liberty". But the concept of freedom of action is much wider than that of economic liberty, which it includes; and, what is more important, it is very questionable whether there are any actions which can be called merely "economic" and whether any restrictions on liberty can be confined to what are called merely "economic" aspects. Economic considerations are merely those by which we reconcile and adjust our different purposes, none of which, in the last resort, are economic.* »

F.-A. Hayek, *The Constitution of Liberty*

« *When people speak of a "social conscience" as against mere "conscience", they are presumably referring to an awareness of the particular effects of our actions on other people, to an endeavor to be guided in conduct not merely by traditional rules but by explicit consideration of the particular consequences of the action in question. They are in effect saying that our action should be guided by a full understanding of the functioning of the social process and that it should be our aim, through conscious assessment of the concrete facts of the situation, to produce a foreseeable result which they describe as the "social good".* »

F.-A. Hayek, *The Constitution of Liberty*

GENERAL INTRODUCTION

This book provides a theory of the economic Subject (Part I) and offers a general analysis of the theoretical and practical issues of economic freedom (Part II).

The appearance of homo economicus *coincides with the modern advent of economics, namely that of the Subject. The first part of the book advances a theory of* homo economicus *as Subject, i.e. as imaging and acting consciousness. The economic action process develops within a specific space-time reference frame, which is structured by duration and memory: the conception of image-objects, which contain the projects and the anticipations; the selection and valuation of such image-objects on the financial market; action and impact within the real world. Within this process, which clarifies the concept of risk, the economic Subject projects itself and acts as if it remembers and forgets: it is* homo memor economicus.

The economic Subject is not alone in the world. The presence of others plays an essential role in its constitution and in numerous notions (beauty contest, consensus, conflict, uncertainty...).

Within this general framework, the work establishes the conditions for a possible economic and financial norm and, consequently, for regulation. It also shows how the question of a moral code within economic and financial action can be approached.

Finally, it is emphasised that a certain number of economic and financial phenomena, which are misunderstood and therefore attributed to strange "animal spirits", can be apprehended and incorporated within a general theory of the economic Subject and of action.

The second part of the book first introduces the philosophical foundations for the modern idea of economic freedom and shows that this is based on the fundamental identity which links the Subject as consciousness with action and freedom. This identity develops under the inspection of others and therefore constitutes a logic of interdependencies.

It is explained, inter alia, *that the question of economic freedom is, to a great extent, that of the collective forms of freedom, which accompany the development of the action process. Such collective forms contain, in particular, the conditions for a norm and therefore for regulation in the face of conflicts. The concept of freedom does not contain,* ex ante, *the concept of justice, and freedom is even faced with a paradox, that of representing the principal risk both for itself and for the Subject.*

PART I

THEORY
OF THE ECONOMIC SUBJECT

INTRODUCTION

§ 1.   If modern economics provides a "legitimate" feeling that it exerts the full strength of the central economic Subject, which is simultaneously creative and destructive, in the relationship established with the world and in the definition and determination itself of values or value, it is because the modern moment coincides with the event, the installation and the ascension of a Subject described simultaneously as consciousness (of) and as pure freedom. We will be discussing this line of reasoning in detail (the reference frames of the imaging and acting forms of consciousness; the action process of the economic and financial transformation, an overall process). The centrality of the economic Subject, defined as pure consciousness and complete freedom, means, fairly logically, that the value or values move from the Subject towards *everything else,* which is understood to mean a group of concepts such as the world, physical reality or that which is real. The whole global economic and financial process leads to what we call the impact with (on) *everything else* and this impact contains value, while also creating value through the impact itself. This progression of value will be analysed in the next few paragraphs. We will then demonstrate that the centrality of the Subject may be overcome and that the means of determining value may therefore in turn be partly decentralised.

Before we do so, it is necessary to bear in mind the path for the creation of value in the global process of economics. The word "creation" is used intentionally since the (economic and financial) value is closely connected to anti-matter, an essential element of the specific reference frame of the imaging consciousness, a formative negativity of that which is projected, imagined or anticipated. At this stage of the process, this first pillar or first dimension which we have already discussed (imaging consciousness and associated form of the Stock Market, the financial market and of finance, since the market replicates, organises, selects and values the image-objects produced by the imaging consciousness) incorporates the concept of value essentially through the construction of image-objects. As we stated, there are image-objects which are products of the capture-perception of what is real (where unreality creeps in for the amount of time required by the perception-capture, but without much more, i.e. without a *prior* distortion of the object targeted in the world); there are image-objects which are constructed with much more anti-matter, and therefore negativity and unreality, based on an *analogon*, a real, existing object which is projected within an act of transformation which is an anticipation; based on "nothing" in the sense that, at least so it would seem, (on the assumption of a structured unconscious which we will come back to, since the unconscious constitutes an important question for the reference frame of the image-objects which we have described; this reference frame is the product of a consciousness, does it leave space for an unconscious subworld which, while passing through the consciousness, forms part of the DNA of the image-objects?) the image-object seems to appear as a reference from nowhere, as pure imagination, a pure creation of illusions, which sometimes correspond to real objects which have been dreamt and which are projected forcefully within time and space.

§ 2.   The value is constituted at two levels within this first dimension of image-objects. The principal dimension is very much the "trough" of negativity, the anti-matter layer of unreality, non-being, being in a state of non-being (not-yet-being) which are present to some extent in any economic project, in any anticipation. At the start of the whole economic action process, a form of consciousness places the world at a distance by projecting it in anticipation, which represents a transformation. This negativity of the project, the anticipation and the projection is the first definition of value at the earliest stage of the process. Established by the economic Subject in its act of capture and action – a projection into the world, the value emerges as that which is in a state of non-being, as that which, in the project phase at first, will structure anticipations, produce "visions" which can be seen reflected on the financial markets, as if in a mirror: there, as if in a sifter, the image-objects which contain a rough version of the value which is still mixed and unrefined, will be refined, organised and "enhanced" (the negativity of the planned anticipation will be converted into monetary units). At this stage, finance (especially the markets) essentially plays the role of identifying, sorting, estimating and directing the image-objects and therefore the value located within the negativity of the image-objects. The process then continues within the second dimension (acting consciousness; the path of impact with the world, reality, physical reality). The acting consciousness, as we have seen, extends the refinement of the image-objects up until the immediate pre-impact: the value is still negativity in substance (it is still anti-matter and is governed by the characteristics of the space-time reference frame of the consciousness). When the impact with the world occurs, the project is *completed*, a product of *reality*, the non-being fills up and the value will acquire the form of that which has been accomplished at the end of the economic action process (to a greater or lesser extent, more or less well): the value will to some extent become fixed and will *be*, since the project becomes appropriate for its objective, the design dissolves and merges with its target, they become one and the same. This does not mean that other transformations are impossible but, at the point of impact, the value changes dimension (from non-being to being), but not its nature (the value remains the product of the economic action process for which the conscious Subject is the central driving force).

§ 3.   We stated earlier that in the first pillar (imaging consciousness; financial markets), there were two dimensions of value. We described the principal one (negativity as a mode of being of the image-object in its capacity as a formative support for the project and the economic anticipation and which is "borne", reflected and driven by the form of finance). The second dimension corresponds to the image-objects of the capture-perception of real objects. Such image-objects only contain a small amount of unreality, a low dose of negativity: they essentially contain a replication of that which *is*, and are therefore very distinct from the other image-objects which structure economic projects, actions and anticipations. If we add to this description of value in the first pillar that which we stated above in respect of the second pillar (imaging consciousness; impact), we have three dimensions of value within the process: value as a mode of being (capture-perception of reality); value as negativity and non-being of the economic action and anticipation (the core of the economic and financial value in the prior, gestation phase of the economic action); value as being within the project's impact on the world and physical reality (completion of the transformation). This third dimension refers back to the first, since once the action is fixed/formed by the impact, another real object will once again be the target of capture-perception containing the value of that which *is* (in the manner of being perceived). There is both that which *is* and that which is to come; these are the two sources of value, governed by the Subject and its consciousness, in particular the fact that what *is* is that which has been (physically) transformed and at the very least perceived, which is a form of appropriation.

We have therefore defined levels of value within the global economic action process comprising two pillars or sequences (even if it is not strictly speaking a chain of events). There is what *is*, i.e. that part of the world which has not been transformed and which the consciousness perceives (capture-perception) and that which has been transformed as a result of the global economic process, as described (that which comes just after the impact, in completion of the project).

There is also that which is in a state of non-being, i.e. all the forms which contain the project, the anticipation or the action, first within the reference frames of the imaging consciousness and on the financial markets and then in the preparation of the action and its implementation in physical reality.

These value levels have a common thread; they are all governed by the economic Subject within the Subject's identity = consciousness. That which is is that which has been targeted (through perception, and especially through transformation) by the economic Subject. And that which is is to a certain extent less important than that which is to come, that which is in a state of non-being = not-yet-being. Since the essential structure of all modern economics, and more generally all modern economic/ political systems, where the economic Subject represents the central point (whether personal/individual or collective, as in economic authoritarianisms of all types), is the project and, consequently, the projection, action and anticipation, which intersect with the action, are intended to be transformed. This essential structure is borne by the Subject, which is defined – individually or collectively – by the global economic action process of transformation, and this essential structure is inhabited by the anti-matter of the economic Subject's consciousness, i.e. the negativity. This essential structure is intended to produce value or values in the same proportion as the anti-matter, which is itself produced in the form of image-objects within the reference frames of the consciousness, which will simply be referred to on the Stock Market as "anticipations", "forecasts", "business plans", etc.

§ 4.   Value is above all anti-matter, pure negativity. It has indeed been seen that the projection reference frame interacted with the reality which is or is in the process of being formed or transformed, but the economic (and therefore financial) value (since the financial value is a stage/sequence of the gestation of the global economic action process, a stage of the gestation of the image-objet, a stage which is accordingly an integral part of economics in a wider sense) lies in the distancing of reality, of that which is, in order to project through unreality, through negativity. The value is a negative of the world. Consequently it is not surprising that the innermost structure of the concept of economic value is made up of the very elements of the specific space-time reference frame within which the image-objects are created, develop, die and grow until they encounter the reality within which the image-objects are therefore consolidated. Like the image-object, the value is anti-matter; its temporality is discontinuous and relies on duration, memory recall and lapse. However, the value is not the image-object. The value is contained in the density, the intensity of an image-object in terms of the project, the negativity/unreality which creates, imagines, sees otherwise, differently. This goes hand in hand with the essential principle that the value is ultimately benchmarked in accordance with the impact on physical reality, reality, the world, i.e. at the end, after the outcome of the global economic action process. There is accordingly a form of strength of memory of the impact, which will determine whether the project has transformed the internal energy borne by the image-objects which structured it. Thus, on the one hand, the value is defined on the basis of the density of negativity (of projection), and on the other there is also, as part of the reasoning of the process of impact of the world and reality which is basically economics, a test of reality, as it were, where that which is is brought closer to that which has essentially been in a state of non-being during the whole process. It can indeed be submitted, as we indeed will, that the value may, to some extent, be "isolated" within the pure negativity of the project (that which presents the highest density of projection, the negative of the world, arguably has value), independently of any assessment of the final impact – this second, important pillar of the global process of economics which is the action process – it could then possibly be thought that the value is retained by that which is pure imagination or illusion. This is possible for, and indeed true of, a work of art, whose density of negativity is enough to assess the value within a process which is precisely not that of the economic process, since it stops at the first pillar, at the production of image-objects. Since economics (and finance) are not the only domains, far from it, – nor indeed the Subject's only means of action with regard to the world and reality... – and there are many other means of action whose common starting point is the production of object-images by the consciousness. This is true of art, painting and activities of "pure" imagination. Economics is also based on the production of image-objects and on what we have called the domain of financial imagination[1], which sustains finance in various forms, the main one being the financial market. However, and herein lies the difference, economics are defined by a global action process. *Global* is understood to mean a group of sequences running from the reference frames of image-objects of the imaging consciousness up until the impact of action on physical reality, passing through the selection and preparation of the image-objects which will be involved in the impact. By *action*, we mean that the very meaning of economics, as compared to many other forms of relationship between the Subject and *everything else* (the world, reality...), is contained within the development of an action

---

1. *La dynamique boursière* (Stock Market Dynamics), Economica, 2009.

process. It is therefore normal that the strictly economic value should be the pure negativity (the project, the image-object) which will impact the world, and such impact will have a feedback effect on the image-object. This forms the very foundation of the special nature of economics. It may be regretted or indeed criticised but this is how it is. One might as well argue from the viewpoint of what economics really are and what the many other forms of activity effected by the Subject with regard to the world will never be.

§ 5. We will now consider the structure of value. We have seen that value as inexistence was lodged within the image-objects, such image-objects themselves moving within the reference frame of the imaging consciousness. Value is accordingly inexistence, part of the economic Subject's ability to obliterate (render unreal, not-real) reality, the world or physical reality in order to project itself towards another or towards a different environment/object. The value therefore lies within the desire to transform from the point of view of the actual action, but is initially in the anticipation, the alternative vision. Without prejudging the limits or framework which enclose this act of projection – and which raise an important issue regarding the capacity of economics and finance to self-regulate, to regulate – the value for the economic Subject is created from a production of anti-matter (negativity, the capacity to deny the world in order to (re)create it, to transform it) which will follow the path of the action up until its impact with materiality. The dual nature of the economic act bears witness to its two origins, which are closely associated. The economic act is the vision of projection and anticipation of the consciousness (the imaging consciousness) for the purpose of an impact with reality (the acting consciousness). The sole task of the imaging consciousness is to generate object-images, as compared to the acting consciousness, which selects and finalises, i.e. identifies the object-images which are intended for impact.

The structure of value is therefore anti-matter (negativity) "constituted", like all anti-matter of the object-image's core, of duration as the major substance (and also of memory/ forgetfulness). We have shown that anti-matter was duration, that the negativity of the effort of projection, anticipation and action was based on a flow/stock of duration, the fundamental temporality of projection. This means that the anticipation essentially contained in the consciousness's image-object – and which can be found in the Stock Market or on the financial markets in general – is made up of pure duration, together with an M/F (memory/forgetfulness) erosion factor. One projects in the same way one remembers and one forgets (unitary identity of memory and forgetfulness, two faces of one and the same mirror). One anticipates, one remembers/forgets: in the same manner as the economic Subject's consciousness, which is based on the platform of duration. This ultimately means that value is made up of duration, in the sense that the anti-matter which structures projection, action and anticipation is essentially duration, which is given form/distorted by the impulses of the consciousness and also by the M/F (memory, forgetfulness) pair.

Economic value is therefore essentially linked to the economic act which brings it into being. This is understood, first, to be the act of the Subject's consciousness which structures the anti-matter (the duration) by giving it the initial form of the image-object in the same way that one sculpts a piece of clay. Certain image-objects are intended for a project and impact, and will go further in the process, estimated (by the financial market) and then steered towards the materiality of the act of transformation. The economic value is a certain density of duration. This density of duration provides a greater or lesser degree of energy (speed) for the project which represents the internal core of the image-object. We have shown in this work, in continuation from *Fondements de la dynamique boursière*, that duration constituted, as it were, the nuclear reactor for the specific space-time reference frame of economics and finance; that the discontinuous dynamic of leaps was driven by memory recalls and lapses, since the pure duration which theoretically makes up the core of the image-objects is in fact neither complete nor absolutely pure, since it is always exposed to a certain degree of erosion by *M/F*; that the energy and speed within the mental/psychological reference frame of the image-objects were a function of the initial density of duration allocated to the image-object (which we have called the first section of duration, in the manner of a block of wood, a slab of stone, a soil sample), and also of the memory and forgetfulness dynamic which gives form to/distorts the raw material of duration. Economic value is a function of the density of duration, contained within the image-object's core, which forms the basis of the initial project and is reflected and "shaped"– in the same way one refines and sculpts a stone – on the financial market or in the Stock Market. The deeper and more dense the initial section cut from the unrefined duration (dense time), then the more important, the richer and more compact the "matter" of the image-object's core of projection/anticipation/action will be and the greater the economic value (although, as we have stated, this does not prejudge later processes experienced by this value and by the image-object in general, up until the impact, which will determine the total and complete economic value at the end of the global economic action process).

§ 6.   The initial, fundamental, economic value (initial in the sense that it is produced in the first pillar, together with the image-objects of the imaging consciousness during the prior sequence of the global economic action process) is a function of the density of duration. It is also a dynamic function of the distortion of this primary duration, boosted by the discontinuous and asymmetrical movements of memory and forgetfulness. The fundamental, economic value (as stock, reserve of value) will be said to be provided by the image-object's heredity, the generic card defined by the section or block cut out of duration: it is the image-object's genome, it is provided at the outset, as it were, and remains, for the most part, a point of reference throughout the global, economic process. It is possible to estimate it. That said, this static vision of value operates in conjunction with a dynamic since, throughout the process, the genome undergoes distortions and changes, which range from mere erosion due to forgetfulness (a phenomenon which is not necessarily linear) or to more significant mutations, related for example to powerful memory recalls, extensions of the slots of duration and memory which fall within the genetic heritage discussed – or contractions which may sometimes be sudden – through to implosive fractures which radically alter, or quite simply destroy, the image-object.

Our principal aim is therefore to estimate this initial, fundamental, economic value, the block cut out of duration, which will serve as the reference point for the analysis throughout the global economic process which we have described. The genetic heritage contained within the image-object will be the central focus for the estimation of the value on the financial markets, which play an essential role of organising and estimating the image-objects. However, this fundamental value will undergo non-linear fluctuations and leaps which are triggered, as we have stated, by the distortions of the space-time reference frame, which are in turn driven by the dilations and contractions of both memory and forgetfulness. It is these distortions which drive the financial markets and the genetic form of the Stock Market (see our description in *Fondements de la dynamique boursière*) with the pronounced special features which are often discussed (apparently unpredictable meaning, leaps and interruptions which are understandable in their own reference frame). These distortions, which form the very existence of the financial markets, are essentially those of memory/duration. This explains in particular why the movements of the financial markets react much more to that which has taken place and which, more precisely, forms part of duration and memory, than to the immediacy of continuous information. That said, there are permanent interactions between the block of duration/memory – and its distortions – and the immediate information which is, occasionally, significant enough to trigger *by itself* distortions of the heritage (as compared to movements of memory and forgetfulness which respond to an internal logic of the image-object without any, as it were, "external" stimulation). Without going so far, reality/the world/physical reality have a permanent feedback effect on the reference frame of the image-objects, either because the said reality contains or delivers information which relates more or less directly to the project and the genetic heritage of some or other image-object, or because some or other project contained in some or other image-object (or rather some element of some project contained in such an image-object) reaches the point of impact in the described process: the element of a project, projection or anticipation experiences a test of physical reality, of assessment of the action, information which has a feedback effect (such as, for example, the publication of quarterly results and the announcement of predictions for the year) on and in respect of the projects (in the sense of a group or chain of image-objects) of which they form particular, individual elements. Accordingly, there is continuous interaction between the upstream (imaging consciousness) and the downstream (impact) parts of the process within a unitary and integrated framework. The financial market is a form of intermediation, an interface in this chain between the two major upstream and downstream sequences. Accordingly, the economic value, as we have stated, draws continuously from its two sources, the image-object and the impact, the dual nature of a unitary phenomenon maintained by the continuous interaction between the two segments of the process which produces the global economic action.

The economic value is duration made up of anti-matter within the formation of the image-objects which inhabit the psychological reference frame of the Subject's consciousness, and a process which progresses in a unitary fashion from the image-objects of the imaging consciousness up until the impact, with permanent interactions between the two centres of the global economic action process. This economic value has no status of a purely static kind. On the contrary, this global economic value, emerging from a global process, will follow a path of formation and distortions, and therefore a dynamic which is implied by the path itself. The path of formation passes through the various sequences of the two pillars which we have described (imaging consciousness and financial market; acting consciousness and impact). This path means that the economic value will never be reduced to the sole genome of the original image-object but will have to incorporate a gestation stage within the strictly financial market phase and then later and simultaneously (since the action process advances by means of individual elements of impact which provide information by means of feedback or interaction, as it were, to the more complex, overall chain of multiple image-objects which may be individually even more complex) within the sequence of impact on the world. The economic value accordingly emerges from an apprenticeship or formation which, in brief, intersects the image-object and the impact within physical reality. Next to the formation are the distortions, which we have described above as being the result of unique processes of the duration-memory/forgetfulness matter, feedbacks/boosts of reality which keep pace with the developments of materiality which occur within this real world and direct boosts from the economic Subject's consciousness. Accordingly, the economic value, which is defined from the outset by a genetic and hereditary heritage of duration, a veritable section of time borne as genomic heritage within the image-object's core, ultimately emerges from a fairly complex process of repetitions between the mental reference frame of the consciousness and the traces of materiality left in the real world on impact.

The distortions of the original economic value i.e. that which literally represents the image-object's core (the anti-matter, the negativity), form part of an economic value process on a learning path, which can be described as "natural". However, these distortions regularly give rise to the phenomena of over- and under-valuation. These phenomena reflect particular diversions from one or more reference points which are sufficiently stable to act as points of reference: the points of reference are provided by the raw material of duration which constitutes and structures the hard core of the image-object within which the economic action project in its preliminary phase is contained. The distortions of this original economic value may result in the estimation being very far above or below the said points of reference or equilibria which we have described as "relative" or "limited", from *Théorie* onwards. It is the financial markets (the Stock Market) which record these extreme points, which form an integral part of their role in assessing the image-objects. Here can be found the source of the "imbalances" found in the financial markets, which are more often the rule than the exception, as we have seen, but which remain conceivable as the limit of the variations and leaps (that which we call a crisis is the expression of this limit, and its resolution is a return to a "normality", as defined by a rule of variations, discontinuities and leaps). These reference points, these foundations of relative or limited equilibria enable forms of regulatory standards to be founded, as we have shown.

The economic value, to put a temporary end to the discussion, establishes and secures the meaning within a global economic and financial process which is traversed by a form of temptation of fate. It also introduces the purpose or aim within the object-image's core, within the financial imaginative world and the economic act, which will steer the global economic action process like a story, rescuing economics as it passes from absurdity or pure contingency.

§ 7.   The economic value, during its emergence process, can therefore be broken down into two main dimensions. First, there is an act of pure and free consciousness which establishes image-objects which have a link of varying strength with "reality" (real object) and the essence of the value lies in the projection and anticipation, a creative negativity and anti-matter which we have seen is made up of duration. Second, there is practical-materiality, i.e. the impact which produces feedback and interaction with physical reality and the world, within the context of the act which extends the phase of imaging consciousness (i.e. acting cons-ciousness and impact). The structure of the economic value therefore includes negativity and practical-materiality, in a fundamental frame-work which is based, as we have seen, on duration and undergoes an "information process" together with dynamic distortions driven by memory and forgetfulness, memory recalls and lapses. There is therefore a permanent tension between the voluntary projection (or a projection which includes the unconscious - we will come back to this later) of the economic Subject in its capacity as free and pure consciousness, and, second, that which *is* which is real, which is part of physical reality, the world, which presents a permanent factor of opposition or resistance and which is specific to what we have called "practical materiality". The result of this tension is, first, that the economic Subject cannot, at least on a long-term basis, be a pure and to some extent disembodied consciousness (the economic value cannot be reduced *purely* to the object-images and the *pure* universe of the specific space-time reference frame which we have described). As such, as we have stated, the strictly economic act separates and distinguishes itself from the Subject's other human activities (the economic Subject is not the Subject in all the activities which the latter may have to perform). Secondly, this tension means that the economic Subject is permanently involved in a confrontation with practical materiality, which can easily turn into a battle of strengths: taking control of the world, of reality, of physical reality, of all that we have summarised under the term "practical inertia" consequently threatens to lead to that which, literally, has no limits, and here lies the core of many contemporary questions regarding the Subject's unlimited destruction or transformation of the world – certain such questions are not posed as they should be – questions which cross-refer to something which could define limits and, beyond that, to a form of moral approach. We will come back to this later. Matters which are not identical – economics and morality – should not be confused. And yet it is from an intimate understanding of economics (and of finance, since the two are unfailingly linked) that a possible opportunity may arise of identifying *limits* or the basis for such limits – since, in principle, nothing exists which notifies economics of *a fortiori* moral limits and an order that they should apply in suspension may undoubtedly enable one to acquire a good conscience but at the price of increased confusion.

The economic Subject can only be a pure consciousness producing object-images. And the economic act, economics itself in general, must not be seen as pure concepts, since their very nature is to mix the pure reference frames with both the imaging consciousness and practical materiality. The history of modern economics is contained within the emancipation of the economic Subject as pure consciousness, in the manner we have described, and within the tension with practical materiality which has, accordingly, acquired a semblance of an examination of reality which is worrying for some, and is in any event striking, since it raises, at the very least, the issue of the limits of such a fate, as we discussed above. The fatal nature of this process seems to be an established fact but one cannot swear to the same. Practical materiality could also revolt.

The social utility of the institutional form represented by the financial market (the Stock Market) lies, as we have seen, in the interface and the intermediation between the reference frame for the imaging consciousness (object-images containing the project and the anticipation) and, at the other end of the process, "reality", the impact and practical materiality. The utility, within the global process, as we have shown, is also contained within the practical extension given to the imaging consciousness which produces the object-images: these object-images are consolidated and organised on the financial market, assessed and sorted. Accordingly, we already have two functions of utility: the institutional form of consolidation, of the processing of the image-objects produced by the economic Subject's consciousness; the intermediate point of the determination of the economic value between the mental/ psychological form of the representations of the pure cons-ciousness directed at the structure of the economic project (anticipation, projection) and the practical-material form of the act of impact within physical reality where the project becomes an economic act (fact, event). This form, in many respects intermediate, is therefore unsurprisingly a point of tensions resulting from the friction of the plates containing the up- and downstream universes of the global economic action process which, although different, are parties to a unitary dynamic. This form is also a point of expression or reflection of the multiple distortions described above and, therefore, also unsurprisingly a point of imbalances or diversions from the standards of value (under- and over-valuations). There is nothing surprising about this, if one tries to understand the key roles played by finance and the form of the financial market within economics; and if one agrees not to reject the possible regulation of the financial markets, which first implies the need to accept that economics and finance are indeed very specific phenomena and reference frames (discontinuities, variations and leaps are the rule rather than the exception or abnormality) but are comprehensible – i.e. they contain meaning, even if their appearance is unpredictable – if one uses the reference points within their own specific reference frames, reference points which define the relative or limited equilibria for a fundamental, economic value which is informed and distorted – possibly in so significant a manner that abrupt changes or crises ensue, whether temporary or of entire economic or micro-financial systems; these reference points, relative equilibria and fundamental economic value provide an opportunity for possible regulation. Since it would be quite contradictory to state first that the financial markets are incomprehensible and governed purely by chance and second that their regulation is absolutely necessary. More specifically, the possibility of regulation depends upon the possibility of defining a relative equilibrium, based upon a concept of economic value. This is the task to which our work has been dedicated; demonstrating that it was, indeed, possible within the specific reference frames of economics and finance. The initial task is to create a reference frame for understanding economic and financial phenomena which can be most closely observed – and observation shows very clearly that the most traditional reference frames of clock time and playing fields, of linearities and abnormalities-exceptions do not describe what is happening. It also shows that they do not take adequate account of the fact that the economic acts and phenomena are the product of an economic Subject within a mental or psychological reference frame, which is that of a consciousness, which projects and anticipates in order to act, and that this mental reference frame is made up of an innermost structure, the essence of which is time, in this case duration, and whose distortions stimulate economics and finance, within a psychological space which governs all economic and financial anticipations, which contain the essential structure of the economic projects which will, or will not, in turn give rise to action or economic acts, with greater or lesser degrees of success.

§ 8.   All that has been said up to now regarding the economic and financial value was considered within a certain context, as stated at the outset. This context, essentially that of modern economics, views the process of the creation and application of the economic value as being entirely governed by the economic Subject, which establishes the value by bringing it within the world's practical materiality, i.e. by transforming the world.

Chapitre 1

STRUCTURES
OF THE CONSCIOUSNESS (I)
THE ECONOMIC AND FINANCIAL
IMAGINATIVE WORLD [1]

§ 9.   Finance, and especially stock market finance, organises the exchange and trade of images. These images, which are produced by expectation and projection, represent the very "way of being" of a Subject, Subject-investor or *homo economicus*. It is the nature of finance to base itself, unlike the majority of other sciences, on projects, i.e. on that which forms part of nothingness and not on objects or simply on facts and events alone. The presence of what will come to pass, together with the project, forms the very essence of finance. This means that negativity constitutes the principal (non-)matter of the space-time of finance, the Stock Market and numerous sections of the economy. This non-matter or negativity which inhabits the projected objects, the expectations, within this space-time, is the result of the interplay of the Subject-investor's consciousness. By means of projection, this ultimate product of non-matter or oblivion therefore effaces and deletes that which effectively is but simultaneously calls something else into nothingness. This effacing capacity lies at the heart of any economic theory of the Subject, which remains to be constructed.

Finance and the Stock Market therefore organise the circulation of foreign objects and images, which stem from an imagination, that of the Subject and a domain of imagination, that of the consciousness. The constitution of the conscious Subject projecting itself into the world, i.e. an understanding of the Subject as being that which allows the world

---

1.   These developments were discussed in an earlier publication in *La dynamique boursière – Les fondements,* Economica, 2009.

both to make itself present and be transformed, this modern understanding of the Subject make it possible for finance to appear in the form in which we now know it. The creation of (financial) objects which are in a state of not-yet-being can only be made possible by the appropriation of the world by a Subject who becomes aware (i.e. surpasses, imagines) and as a result seeks to transform. The trade of (financial) images is therefore inconceivable without a theory of the Subject based on the Subject's effacing consciousness.

The trade of images is not unconnected to that of commitments and credit, given the extent to which economic and financial space-time is occupied by projection and expectation, i.e. the way in which a Subject-consciousness surpasses itself, each effort involved therein producing images and projects.

The very nature of finance is to describe that which does not exist, to try and capture that which floats, undoubtedly fragile images which are embodied and known but which are essentially inhabited by non-matter or, perhaps more correctly, by anti-matter since the consciousness produces images by secreting anti-matter, i.e. from the domain of imagination. The space-time specific to finance and in particular to the Stock Market is inhabited by, constituted of anti-matter and imagination in proportion to the capacity of the Subject and its consciousness to efface perception and projection or to create images.

Accordingly, no modern finance can appear or be formed without a theory of the Subject and a space-time for such Subject, a space-time of consciousness and its capacity to produce a world of imagination. It is this same space-time, the nature of which is sometimes described as "psychological" and certainly as "mental", which, far-removed from clock-time, from the known linearities of our "real" world of objects, facts and events, concentrates contractions and dilations of matter (anti-matter) which is contorted at whim in sudden accelerations and makes the energy centres of this space travel more or less quickly throughout this strange reference frame, depending upon the extent to which they are stimulated (as discussed in our other works, this stimulation of energy is linked in particular to memory).

Finance is accordingly based on anti-matter which constitutes its basic space-time. As such, finance is filled with nothingness, since, at any given time, it concerns what will come to pass and what remains to be done or accomplished, in respect of which the financial market effectively tries to assess the contours, risk and price. The essential part of the measure or standard will consequently be prospective in nature, attempting to apprehend a future result and assess the future impact of an action. The financial market is, effectively, seeking to allocate a price to an action, which will efface the world or part of it, in order to recreate, transform or alter it. The financial space-time is therefore specific on two counts. It does not contain real objects but only images; the said images (commitments, projections…), which represent future real objects which will, or will not, literally "take place", are projections or representations of an acting Subject's consciousness.

§ 10.   The conscious acts of the Subject directed at the world are all financial objects, which float within the financial or market space-time. Such objects are not virtual, since they may become reality after completion of the project which they embody and which they contain; they may also, as such, i.e. as pure financial objects, have an impact on what is real and possibly modify it. Market finance structures the reception, the confrontation, the real life of this space-time of objects which are in a state of non-being. To an extent never seen before, market finance has physically organised a scene of action, namely a confrontation of the targets of the consciousness, of intentions and designs, aimed like arrows at objects which exist or do not exist, since the targeting seeks to modify or destroy and often creates the object while moving towards it.

Modern finance, by creating the market institution, has given a practical form to the aim of the Subject's consciousness, the nature of which is imaginary. This practical form makes the action visible by institutionalising it and accommodates within the real world a space-time which may seem real but which in fact borrows its features, its workings and its energy from its source Subject. This practical, open externalisation of the aim of the action introduces a potentially conflictual joint existence of at least two reference frames of time and space, one formative the Subject's method of thinking and acting and the other constructing the linearities of the real world. These two parallel dimensions, which may however be superimposed or even intersect, play a profound role in the structure of the two main spheres at work in economics, namely the real and financial spheres. The essential distinctions now made from observation of clock-time and other specific spatio-temporal forms refer back to these two dimensions, as do the descriptions of finance as virtual, albeit with a significant lack of understanding and criticism.

It is not that no "finished" financial objects exist since, being the result of a process, they may to some extent be observed or described after completion of the work of construction, constitution and emergence; however, the financial object will always be worked upon, driven, distorted, contracted and extended by the project which contains its energy and the structures of consciousness, memory recall and lapse which form the anti-matter, always slightly more remote than might appear, stretching out towards the target which it will never reach, permanently uncompleted and with no prospect of ever being self-sufficient.

By providing economics and finance with a theory of the Subject, defining the Subject as a form of consciousness and design which effaces and therefore creates, one can take into account not only the modern context which hastens economics in the sense of appropriation by a Subject who is now central, but also – consequently – the emergence of a specific spatio-temporal reference frame which is, for the most part, that of the acting consciousness itself. This acting consciousness, which only exists, strictly speaking, by extricating or removing itself during the action which constitutes its way of being, will manufacture imaginary objects (and, more generally, an imaginary space-time) which give physical form to the target in the same way one lights a track at night, but are absolutely not the actual point of impact with the world. This space-time which comes between us and the world, as soon as the action plans appear, is essentially that of economics and finance. By coming between the Subject and the world, this space-time is both the form through which the world is effaced (creator/destructor) and the form through which the world appears.

§ 11.   We are trying to demonstrate that the financial space-time is structured like a world of imagination, that the objects which inhabit and drive this reference frame are images which are separate from real objects, that such images are produced by an imaging consciousness of the Subject and that such objects are present-absent, since they render present something real which is absent. Within the financial universe, and specifically the financial securities market, we are therefore interested in mental images. Such images, in our mind, inhabit the reference frame of expectations and projections which form the very means by which the Subject's consciousness and action open up to the world. This projection focuses on the real object by means of creative negativity. The real object is effaced and then left behind during the ensuing projection towards something which is in a state of non-being. Accordingly, this projection is accompanied by (produces) mental images, which represent a certain way in which the object can be absent within its very presence. Within the Stock Market sphere, and more generally the sphere of finance and economics, the vast majority of concepts and indicators which are presumed to be useful are intersected by expectation, i.e. a form of effacement of the real object which is intended to be appropriated (results, company cash flows, growth…), and this effaced form constitutes the image which is, effectively, traded and negotiated. The real objects are not themselves discussed or traded: but rather the projections, i.e. the mental images which make the real object present to some extent, even though this real object is in a state of non-being (not-yet-being) because it is not there, because it is projected into the future. When I try and imagine what the growth, prices or activity of some or other sector will be, or the geo-political environment, I am focussing on a series of real objects which are not yet in a state of being, because I am projecting myself into the future, or which are, quite simply, in the present but on which I am focussing through an imaging consciousness. Both real contemporary objects which exist or future anticipated objects – which are the dominant means of organising financial structures – pass through the imaging consciousness and mental image, a form of *analogy* by means of which, or through which, the real targeted object – whether existing or projected – will appear (make itself present) to the consciousness.

The mental image of a company, its resources, organisation or results, the mental image of oil and gas resources, of prices, political and military tensions, there are mental images of objects X which can be described as real, in the sense that they inhabit the normal reference frame of clock time and standardised space, whether present or future. Real objects are transformed into mental images by the imaging consciousness and it is in this form that they come to the market. When we consider the determining elements of the financial market, we do not have access to the real object as such but to images. The mental images of real objects called X cannot be confused with the real object X itself, which is to some extent a reduced model. One must overcome the illusion of inherence in order to state clearly that the financial and market reference frame (which can be extended to include economics) is not a reference frame of real objects, whether existing or projected, but a reference frame of mental images governed by its own temporality and spatiality, the phenomena of memory, *continuum*, belief, memory lapse, by non-linearities and sudden contractions and dilations. This reference frame, which we have described within the context of market dynamics and the particular features of the space-time, stems from the way in which the Subject's consciousness operates (whether that Subject be economic, an investor or *homo economicus*). It is an effacing consciousness, which takes possession of the world and of its real objects by leaving them behind (thus by rendering them absent, literally by imagining them) and is simultaneously imaging, since an image corresponds to each effacing and creative design of the consciousness. It is a mental universe lined with (mental) images, which will constitute the fundamental framework for the financial and market action and dynamics, a universe of anti-matter which reflects the transforming action plan, within the real world.

The images which inhabit the space-time reference frame of the Stock Market and of finance are "filled" with knowledge, to differing degrees. These forceful images of expectations, which are more or less remote and which are specific to this reference frame, are what they are, no more or less. They summarise a certain depth of knowledge, rather than constituting an additional or new dimension. Since the mental image (and by "mental" we include everything which refers, in literature, including our own literature, to a "psychological" dimension, to the effects of memory recall and lapse, to everything which expresses the intricate existence of a particular spatio-temporal dimension which is specific to economic, financial or market phenomena), is to some extent "charged" (recharged) by present and past knowledge, where blocks of time-matter perform their role by means of permanent tensions between memory recall and lapse, the whole within a *continuum* of duration. This is where the link between the act of imaging consciousness and the constitution of a financial imagination is formed. It is based on a structure of time-matter and spatial speeds, which is determined by the various states of duration, its accelerations and contractions, duration being understood to mean the time-matter which contains the knowledge discussed above and which will foster the mental image.

§ 12.   The domain of the economic, financial and market imagination results from the relationship between the object and a consciousness. This relationship constitutes the essential form of understanding of modern economics, confronted by tension, acquisition and transformation as between the Subject and the (real) world. The mental image, as we have described it, is the manner in which the real object appears within the specific space-time reference frame, where the financial dynamics are formed. More precisely, the (real) object is targeted – one considers all the objects of discussion, trade and calculation which drive the financial markets throughout the day – in a form, an overall packaging of tangible and perceptible elements which have been perceived (a particular company and its directors, its brand, its building, this knowledge of memory recall and lapse which mixes everything which has been perceived in respect of a company, which surrounds the company, these mysterious blocks of duration and time-matter which will procure, within the mental image at a particular time, that some or other elements, which are past or present concretions, become fixed; which will procure that an image becomes fixed in the same way as one momentarily freezes knowledge); since expectation is a mental image which fixes a state of time-matter; to this static vision should be added the dynamic dimension, where the time-matter will be stimulated by memory, extended by memory lapse, or shortened, compressed by one or the other.

To expect is to imagine and one imagines in the same way one forgets or remembers. The real object targeted by the imaging consciousness and delivered by the mental image is a summary which compresses within itself a layer of duration. It is within this layer that the various temporal and spatial strata for one and the same object lie (the same company five years ago, ten years ago, in a particular area for a particular market or product) and will be put into play, set in motion, from memory recall to lapse, from deletion to juxtaposition. The real targeted object only rarely appears in its pure and most immediate present. The real economic, financial or market object always appears to the consciousness surrounded by an obscure halo, mixing various archaeological layers, and the face which it presents to the imaging consciousness may, often, be that of another clock time or, more often, a mix of several faces. Memory recall and lapse will, as discussed, have the power to move these strata at great speed and therefore these images as well, within the space-time reference frame.

The consciousness of the economic Subject, the Subject-investor, and the *homo economicus*, targets an object whose contents are directly or indirectly linked to the financial matter, targets an object through its image and is not therefore the consciousness of a targeted image. It is the object itself which is targeted (the company, the director, the product...) and which will accordingly make itself present from the point of its absence, since the act of targeting it brings into being the absence of the object, which will be represented by the image. The object as an undifferentiated *whole* is targeted by the consciousness of the economic and financial Subject, the image therefore assuming an undivided nature. The image is one and is fixed, saturated with the knowledge that the consciousness has injected it with (this static vision then makes way for a set of dynamics of mental images, since the economic, financial and market dynamics are fundamentally a set of dynamics of mental images within a space-time reference frame structured by the Subject's imaging consciousness and whose imagination is structured in similar form to anti-matter, which is stimulated, stretched and contracted by the "knowledge" of memory and duration, and also by memory lapse). The financial image presents itself as an undivided whole with distinct properties; this is how the *object image* appears to the economic Subject's consciousness and/or Subject-investor. However, this undivided appearance which is the very form of the mental image conceals within it certain blocks of time-matter and space representing the archaeological strata of knowledge, which constitute, "charge" or "recharge" the mental image: these fundamental unitary elements, which borrow heavily from that which has been and continues to endure, are grouped together to some extent by the consciousness in the undivided form adopted by the image.

§ 13.   Belief constitutes one of the essential structures of the imaging consciousness, within the space-time reference frame of economics and finance. By this one means that it is through belief that one accepts the idea that the real object X is targeted (and therefore appears to the consciousness) *through* the layers and strata of time which are compressed or stretched to a greater or lesser degree. The said strata certainly imprison a spatio-temporal variant of X but, also, as with the layers excavated by archaeologists, numerous other elements within the direct or indirect environment. This evocation of layers of earth which contain the principal trace (by principal one means that of the primary representation or theme of the targeted object, in the same way that oil production cannot be directly confused with the theme of inflation or that the results of an aircraft manufacturer cannot be directly confused with the exchange parity of the dollar or the Arab-Israeli conflict), is of the same nature as the blocks of time-duration-memory, affected by a certain degree of memory lapse, cut out of a long duration and summoned or dismissed within a mental space-time reference frame. We discussed these blocks in *Théorie* and again in *Les Fondements*.

The financial object – whether real and existing, inexistent or absent within time or space – which is targeted and which will give rise to the production of a (financial) object-image by overtaking and effacing the reality, which is then captured as a generalised whole, becomes present in the sense that it appears to the consciousness which targets it and consequently makes it present but only insofar as such object is distanced within its own reality, captured and effaced and therefore literally rendered absent. This presence (of the financial object-image) – absence (of the real financial object), which is the foundation for the operation of the financial and market space-time reference frame, is made possible by the phenomenon of belief which incorporates the idea of a complete and spontaneous adherence but also, and especially, the idea of memory which provides the bases for the adherence.

The real object of financial analysis and interpretation in the daily operation of finance and the markets, which is therefore targeted by a consciousness, becomes the object-image and the essential element for the structure of the market reference frame. The transformation or change of the real object of financial analysis (e.g. the "true" activity of a company) into an image incorporates the whole of an experience, duration or a memory. It relates to the experience of the targeted object and that of its direct or indirect environment. It also relates to the experience of the economic Subject, Subject-investor or *homo economicus*, which effects the targeting, since the imaging consciousness is always effected from a particular point of view. Without ignoring any difference which may exist between imagination and memory (or recollection), we maintain that the structure of the world of imagination, which is that of the space-time reference frame of finance and the Stock Market, is charged, "recharged" and nurtured by memory. One imagines in the same way as one remembers, within the reference frame which is the subject of our study. This means inter alia that the leaving behind of what is real and the conversion into an image, the distancing, rendering absent and projection are of the same nature as the act of remembering, particularly when the image as a total object (complete summary) is full of anti-matter (oblivion), driven by the flows of memory and duration. Memory-duration is anti-matter (oblivion) in the leaving behind of what is real and the constitution of the financial object-image.

§ 14.   The fundamental identification of the memory and imagination through the mechanics of imaginary projection-creation, recollection and, it should be added, discounting of the future (one expects, imagines and remembers in accordance with processes of a homogenous nature within the financial and market space-time reference frame), this very identification of the acts of memory, expectation and imagination of the consciousness and the Subject (we are now distancing ourselves somewhat from Sartre's theories on the world of imagination, which are in other respects so useful) would not be complete without the integration of memory lapse: since one forgets in the same way as one remembers, expects and imagines. The constitution of the financial object-image by means of effacement cannot ignore the extent to which it is memory lapse which renders absent or inexistent and which can introduce a form of oblivion. However, we will have to distinguish between that which results from the same operation of nature (expectation, memory recall, memory lapse, imagination; from this point of view, memory recall and lapse are the same type of phenomena within the financial and market space-time reference frame) and that which seems similar, at first sight (to forget and to efface, to assume that what is real is absent or inexistent and to forget it). Does one imagine in the same proportion that one forgets? It would seem not. One imagines in the same proportion as the memory which nurtures the creation of the world of imagination and which constitutes the essential background for the game of finance, the financial markets and the Stock Market. This is one of our fundamental theories: duration and memory structure the "psychological", "mental" reference frame of anti-matter or oblivion which targets by rendering absent and which renders present a transcended, inexistent or absent reality in the form of an image. Memory lapse is more the coefficient of erosion of the axis of duration and memory than the dominant factor of this process, despite appearances which can easily make it seem similar to oblivion. Imagination, expectation, memory lapse and recall constitute the essential structures of the economic Subject's consciousness and Subject-investor, of the psychological forms.

We have demonstrated that the financial and market space-time reference frame was characterised by an imaginary structure and essence. Therefore there exists a category of objects of the Subject's consciousness, which analyses and participates in financial and economic matters (is it not accordingly wider, more general than we would like to believe?): it relates to imaginary objects which populate finance (and, as we have just stated, potentially all worlds, since any object of the consciousness is eligible for the processes described here). It relates to financial object-images, unitary elements of the mental or "psychological" financial reference frame within the sense used by Allais. The objects exist *sui generis*, are presented once and for all, as if set in static by the summary of reality which has suddenly been effected, and this is enough to characterise finance by means of this function, which is to some extent a mental one. These objects are moreover contained within a set of dynamics driven by the consciousness, within the group which such consciousness may form from such unitary object-images and within the memory recall or lapse of some or other unitary object-images. This is where the sudden accelerations are formed, which contract space and time or, inversely, the dilations. Everything takes place and is played out in accordance with the Subject's consciousness and it is in this way that all these developments constitute a theory of the economic and financial Subject.

The financial object-image targeted by the consciousness by leaving behind the real object is unitary, a general summary, and as such is always something other than the sum of its elements. This object-image is always located beyond that which seems to be attainable, and each new image moves the perspective further away. This enables one to understand in passing why the Stock Market and the markets may often seem unattainable, since the image, of its very nature, is what is in reality unattainable, since located at a distance and permanently overtaking. Moreover, although the image is always a general summary, which is fixed at the moment of appreciation, it generates its own variants, namely other images, which will bring into play the effects of memory recall and lapse, experience and belief, in the same way as one operates valves or a sail. However, the images which have already been produced will continue to exist within the reference frame as created: the financial object-images will not die within the financial and market space-time reference frame; they continue to float like planets in space, sometimes they are forgotten and confined within another dimension or another galaxy and sometimes they return. The mental world of finance and its imaginary objects is expanding.

Reflection, in finance (in the wider sense), produces images to the same extent as the Subject-consciousness' focus on the world (on companies, businesses and, more generally, the world of facts and events) affirms the appearance of the (real) object as a form of possession. The real object, as we have stressed, must be distinguished from the object-image which is unreal, even when it relates to targeting and appropriating financial or economic contents which are not yet in a state of being, which are only a projection. The object-image is unreal either because it refers to contents or a real object which forms part of nothingness (this negativity is unavoidable), or because it refers to "future" contents, in which case the negativity is even more unavoidable. The financial object-image is in a state of non-being and negativity constitutes its way of being.

Finance, the Stock Market, and economics in general, work and reason within a field of *unreal elements*, a field of object-images which express the extent to which such reflections are based on projection and appropriation. However, the Subject, because it only produces object-images, will always remain at a distance from what is real, placed in front of or behind the window of the image, and this distance cannot be eliminated. Financial or market sciences only deal with what is real behind the window of mental object-images. It is these mental images which, in various forms (analyses, forecasts, projected results, professional strategy, macro-economic or sectorial assumptions, risk scenarii, possible sociological developments...), constitute what is called *the market*, or rather the regulated financial market as we know it; a place where all these forms of unreality (negativity), all these *images* are traded, confronted and sold. The consciousness of the economic Subject and Subject-investor produces projects and plans for the appropriation and transformation of the world: these projects and plans take the form of unreal object-images which take material form (thus endowing them with a certain reality) within the enclosure of the market, a sort of external form of the imaging consciousness.

The economic and financial Subject uses the imaging consciousness because economics and finance are essentially based on desire and consequently on the various forms of shortcoming (negativity). This is indeed the relationship established with the world in the economic and financial context, as was amply demonstrated in *Tractatus* or in *Généalogie*.

§ 15.   By assuming that finance – and in particular the financial market – is inhabited by mental, and therefore unreal, object-images (and the same is true of economics as a whole to a certain extent), one also assumes that the determining factors of time and space which govern the real targeted object (whether existing or "future", projected or expected), are the result of such unreality, i.e. the space-time reference frame is absolutely specific. Time and space cannot have the same character or same substance within an imaging reference frame, within a field of object-images. It was demonstrated, in *La Dynamique boursière*, that time-matter acquires an alternative substance, which is more suited to the expansions and compressions; that space acquires a meaning which is more qualitative, to some extent, provided by time itself and speed in particular. The economic, financial or market space is a mental space of mental object-images, where such objects move around by means of stimulations of time-matter moulded by duration (the mental object-images having a complete form, including, inter alia, spatial characteristics). There are accordingly, and this is important, two dimensions, two levels of understanding and analysis: the level of the financial object-image, an enclosed whole, which is to some extent closed into itself (e.g. the forecasted results for a particular company in the coming year; the scenario of sales of products in America; the impact of a 20% rise in the dollar, of a 15% drop in the price of petrol on the net results, on the stock price); each of these options corresponds to what we will call a financial object (mental image), an object for which and within which external relations no longer exist between elements (there is henceforth pure internality and the spatio-temporal dimensions are fixed, without any parts, without any possible segmentation, within the financial object). Moreover, there is a second level, that of the enclosure within which all these object-images evolve, move around, the mental "place" where external spatio-temporal relations are established between these object-images, relations which cannot be those of the world of clock time. This is why it can be said that the time of the consciousness of the image is not that of the object-image.

We therefore assume that all the financial proposals (and, in general the economic proposals), and in particular all the expectations in any form whatsoever, together with all the representations of economic and financial reality (one can therefore distinguish, within that which is transformed into an image, between the representation of the "existing" reality and the expectation-forecast, neither of which differs to the extent that the unreality viewed by the imaging consciousness describes them all together), that all such acts of the conscious reflection of the economic and financial Subject who produce object-images, *are* all object-images.

Each financial or economic object-image, i.e. each unitary element (since one can segment and reduce to an almost-primary element all the complex chains which are represented and expected and which take the form of a specific language of the space-time reference frame of finance and the Stock Market), each block is therefore made up of time-matter which is compressed, reduced or contracted duration. In line with the fundamental theories presented in our earlier works, the pure block or the more complex chains are sections of time, of the time and are therefore presented as intertemporal summaries of sequences, particular lengths of time-matter. It is within this layer of duration that the mental object-image, whose referrer or correlative is the existing real object or the projected object, is cut out and constructed. This means that the block, as described, possesses its own spatio-temporal DNA, which is produced once and for all (and as such the object-image is a closed whole like an oyster closes itself up) and its own energy, which may be released once the memory recall or lapse stimulate this essential matter.

The DNA of financial object-images (an expectation of results, for example) therefore contains a specific structure of duration, a summary of events and facts, which is intertemporal. The time of the financial object-image (the block, the chain), like the time in which all the mental economic, financial or market object-images are steeped, this time of unreality is unreal in the sense that it does not really pass, that it can dilate, unfurl or, on the contrary, contract, at will, in a reversible manner which is specific to the unreality of its structure. The consciousness of the economic Subject or Subject-investor, whose structure is different, remains at a distance from the unreal object.

The financial object-images which we have presented, unitary blocks or more complex chains, have a specific spatio-temporal structure: each financial proposal, representation or expectation creates its own time and space, in fact literally carries it along with it, once taken from the section cut out of the dense duration, i.e. the complete intertemporal summary of specific durations, in the same way one bores into the ground. This particular spatio-temporality provides the object-image with its independence but that does not mean a constant inertia or immobility. The mental object-image of finance and the Stock Market is not a frozen, dead image. An autonomous generality is provided suddenly but the consciousness will maintain a relationship of high or low tension with the object-image by driving the memory recall or lapse. It is these impetuses which make the image appear and disappear and, within the object-image, particular sequences or slices of duration appear and disappear, the whole of which contributes to the discontinuous and erratic nature of the object-image itself and to the link of tension between the subject-consciousness and the object-image which remains at a distance.

Saturated with anti-matter, the mental financial, economic or market object-image is a strange form of anti-world through which, paradoxically, the world appears and ultimately exists with regard to an economic Subject.

§ 16.   The object-image which is produced by the consciousness of a *homo economicus*, the Subject-investor or mere Subject is filled with that which is absent (which is literally not there, whether in terms of geographical remoteness, distance in time or any other form of absence expressed by reference to a space-time reference frame whose two dimensions foster negativity, nothingness), with what is inexistent (not yet, maybe, never, from probable to probabilised, such as a scenario of an increase in sales, in growth, in prices, a true illusion, that which will never be real but will live from time to time within unreality). Filled with anti-matter or anti-world, in the sense used above, the space-time reference frame of finance and the Stock Market, which is psychological in form, cannot mix with real objects. In order to target the existing (present) reality and also that which does not exist ("future" illusory project) – a targeting which will place the two dimensions on the same level of unreality –, the consciousness of the economic and financial Subject will for this purpose travel through the past, since the targeting, which makes the existing, absent or non-existent reality unreal, mobilises the past by making an intertemporal summary (in fact thousands of summaries) of sections of duration, which we have called individual durations. The act of consciousness which gives rise to the object-image is an act which both constitutes the object by transferring knowledge to it, knowledge of intertemporal summary, of duration and memory; and, more probably, by stimulating the block of the past which is already cut out and which constitutes the finance-object, such stimulation coming inter alia from memory recalls and lapses which are specific to the dynamics of the space-time reference frame of finance; in any event, by driving to some extent the dynamics of the spatio-temporal reference frame, once the object-images are created, by stimulating and distorting the dimensions of time and space.

All the processes and acts of appropriation, representation and expectation of the real world for economic and financial purposes, all such processes target real, existing, absent or inexistent items by means of knowledge constituted beforehand by the intertemporal summary of durations, and therefore by means of psychological (mental) contents. The matter of this mental image, which backs all the economic-financial thinking and projects, is necessarily already constituted as a target for the consciousness, a matter which has been shown to be "knowledge" cut out of the dense duration accumulated in space-time. The consciousness will create the object-image from this matter, which will, in order to exist in unreality for the imaging consciousness, have to acquire the substance or structure of anti-matter.

The imaging consciousness of the economic and financial Subject contains the psychological contents of the target, including the dynamics of memory recall and lapse. However, these contents, located at the (transcendental) level of the Subject's consciousness, and which represent, expect and appropriate, cannot contain or incorporate the appreciable characteristics and qualities of the item, whether temporal or spatial, and such characteristics and qualities can only be represented and not possessed. The item which is represented and targeted remains external and alone, since the transcendental position of the cons-ciousness cannot be assimilated to any exteriority. Here can be seen the possible illusion of inherence referred to by Sartre.

§ 17.   Economic and financial (market) matters are structured like domains of imagination. There is a fundamental analogy between memory and imagination. One remembers and forgets in the same way one expects or imagines. These are the essential assumptions of our work.

The financial, market or economic object-image constituted by the targeting of the consciousness contains nothing other than that which we have placed in it, i.e. the summarised intertemporal knowledge which we have called a block of duration – which is itself segmented *ad infinitum* into individual durations –, as one whole, which is the financial object-image, a unique, summarised whole. The fact that one only finds within the financial image what one has placed in it is certainly a sign that the essential structure of the financial object-image is inadequate – the same is true of all images, of any image – but it would be accurate if one were only to see a fixed and frozen object, since if it can only contain what we have placed in it, this matter experiences a life driven by memory recall and lapse. When it is stated that one can only find what one has *placed* there, this relates to an initial *placing* of a complete memory by the Subject who will, later, forget or remember.

The proposals, representations and appropriations which inhabit economics and finance are essentially structured by intentions which express the targeting relationship between the economic or financial Subject and a world of existing reality or of absent or inexistent reality. All that is stated in analyses of finance and of the financial markets in particular, translates an intention which creates an unreal object, namely the object-image, a mental form resulting from knowledge (duration), which is worked and sculpted by memory recall and lapse. Each intention presupposes a certain depth of knowledge accumulated by the consciousness of the Subject-investor or Subject – the *homo economicus*. The Subject will, within the relationship with the world, which is formed in the economic act, mobilise or lead to some extent and will include a whole body of knowledge, all sorts of layers of learning, an inheritance of conscious or unconscious duration, whether or not forgotten, whether in whole or in part but which, at any given time, will constitute the space-time matter for the operation of the financial and market reference frame. It is not readily established that each Subject investor, that each individual *homo economicus* possesses, as its spatio-temporal reference frame, all the infinite fields of knowledge, facts and events embraced by human history. Although, in theory, it can be assumed that each individual Subject individually includes a field of duration and knowledge, which is that of human history, each still has to place an individual filter of a specific history and journey from its slice of human life in the world as it is. In a similar vein, the question is raised whether, in the relations between the conscious Subject and the world, which constitutes the fundamental structure of economics, finance or the Stock Market, there exists a conscious section and unconscious section within the space-time reference frame, which we have described, since the Subject only represents as an object-image that which it actually knows in some way or another, which it has perhaps forgotten or repressed, in order to use the terminology of the unconscious. Memory recall and lapse are therefore the formative axes of the mental space-time reference frame, which should be intersected with the conscious and unconscious dimensions. The strictly individual time of the knowledge accumulated by the said Subject should be expanded to include all implied human knowledge (duration).

§ 18.   Let us return to the structure of the image of financial "objects" which circulate in economic and financial thinking, in financial practices and markets. Our assumption (theory) is that economic and financial matters – finance and the financial markets – are structured like domains of imagination and inhabited by object-images produced by the consciousness of the Subject actor (investor, consumer, etc.). It is the financial market as an essential, contemporary form which is the place of circulation, trade, confrontation, creation and destruction of object-images, going so far as to assume itself, in a certain manner, the form of a collective consciousness by incorporating, extending or dispersing the production of images from billions of individual unitary consciousnesses. It is to the same extent as economics and finance are traversed by negativity, i.e. the projection towards that which is in a state of non-being (the project, the action), the calculating and imagining expectation, that the object-image constitutes the fundamental form of such methods of relating to the worlds represented by these two disciplines, since the object-image is nothingness. This is where the intimate relationship with time is situated, in the gap of negativity which structures the act of consciousness (and action), since the projection towards that which is in a state of non-being is an action towards what will come to pass (future) within a total, general summary constituted by the image-producing act of consciousness, which goes strictly hand in hand with the action. Economics and finance are traversed by absence and nothingness: that which is in a state of non-being or not-yet-being, will not perhaps be, that which is promised (promise, trust, credit), foreseen, projected, expected, agreed for the future (the contract), invested, all these formative dimensions of the action. Since economics and finance are based on the idea that the Subject forms of the world and of the transformation which it can make it experience or undergo, since there is accordingly a degree of hindsight or distance on the part of the consciousness which forms such an idea, the object-image emerges from this creative act of the consciousness. There is at the very least a symmetry and often an identity between the creative act of the consciousness which produces the object-image and what is called "action" at the heart of economics and finance.

The financial markets in their contemporary form are therefore devices for dreaming, imagining, creating (and destroying), a physical form and the location of a total (and general) collective consciousness. In this place of object-images which have a price, there is a certain relationship with time, that of the consciousness, and space, that of the consciousness as well, and therefore a space-time reference frame, within which the temporality of unreal objects targeted by the consciousness is itself unreal, in the sense that it cannot relate to the temporality of clocks as we know it but, on the contrary, a time-matter which may contract and/or dilate, extend, accelerate, slow down, reverse or jump steps at will, while always remaining the same; a time-matter fostered by duration and stimulated by memory recall and lapse, a layer of knowledge which always precedes the constitution of the image, a pre-existing layer specific to each consciousness and its past but which will experience some sort of change in the process of creation of the image (cut out of the layer of duration; discontinuities and ruptures in memory recalls and lapses). Within the structure of the financial object-image, this mental production of the consciousness, there therefore exists a spectrum of determinants – specifically those determinants which we are aware of, which is finished (static, when a financial or economic image is provided) and unstable (dynamic, when the object-image experiences internal transformations or external shocks, in the same way as free electrons may collide with each other). Within this structure of the image, there are discontinuities, which result from the very special relationship between the financial image and its object, within a space-time reference frame which is specific to a mental universe of economics and finance structured by the conscious and acting Subject. The image of the object targeted by the consciousness of the Subject investor, consumer (...) is not the real object, either because the real object exists but is kept at a distance by the act of consciousness, or because this real object is committed to a transformation (which will come to pass and which is therefore absent), or finally because the object is inexistent and will remain so. In any event, there is a structure of unreality in the sense of negativity, which conceals within itself either the definitive inexistence (the illusion) of a real object (however the unreal object will, itself, exist) or the departure of a real object or its transforming projection (however the mere capture by the act of consciousness is already a form of transformation).

§ 19.   The image of the real object refers to, is fostered by a duration, by knowledge, by a time-matter of duration, memory recall and lapse (e.g. the economic or financial results of ten years ago or a turbine project from thirty years ago, at the other end of the world...) which means that the real object, which is in turn situated within a "normal" space-time reference frame (which is linear, that of clocks with regard to temporality, that of linear movements with regard to space), is targeted by the consciousness of the Subject investor, consumer (...) through a specific prism, within a different space-time marked by the special features discussed above (temporal and spatial discontinuities; speeds which depend upon memory recall and lapse). Within this mental reference frame of the economic and financial imagination, the object of the image is defined within time and space in a different manner from the real object targeted by the act of consciousness. In particular, one moves more or less quickly within the space of the financial image depending upon whether one remembers or forgets to a greater or lesser degree.

The primary object of the financial matter, which is the financial image, results from the targeting of a real object within today's clock time and within space, as it appears to me today. This targeting is effected by mobilising a whole layer of duration and memory, linked to the real object, whether directly or indirectly, a mobilisation which will transform/transport the real targeted object into a different space-time reference frame. The real object, once targeted, becomes something else. This is true of a simultaneous targeting (I visualise today what the markets for some or other company are today). This is even truer for a future targeting, provided that I am trying to visualise what the said real object will become (I visualise today what the markets for such company will be). The real targeted object will undergo a trans-formation within the projection, a projection which goes beyond it (a negativity which makes the object "absent" from itself, part of nothingness) which will mobilise a whole layer of duration and memory which will in turn, like a dynamic concretion, foster and drive the future object. This future object is a transformation of the real object which seems reasonable, especially since the future object bears within it a mark of its origin and of the past. This future object (what the markets for such a company will be) is "inexistent" in the sense that it is not yet in a state of being but already contains a certain intensity of truth. This "inexistence" is therefore relative to some extent, i.e. relative to a mark of origin, memory and duration. However, it can also relate to an absolute inexistence, in the sense that the object transformed by the targeting does not contain any direct or indirect connection with a real object which exists today and which can therefore be the subject of some form of transforming continuity. The same is true of the attempt to imagine what might happen to such a company in fifty years when extreme, climate, geopolitical or socio-economic risks have materialised. This inexistence is not yet absolute, since a link persists with the real object and it is not an illusion. The extreme imaginative projections (what will a company become in a hundred years?) may become closer to such inexistences, where the financial object-image is a black hole of negativity and almost an illusion.

§ 20.   These object-images which circulate and are traded on the financial markets therefore contain various, variable degrees of time-matter connecting them by means of duration and memory to real objects of the present day and the past, with variable densities of duration and memory, a variable negativity (which should be seen as anti-matter, almost as a black hole which hollows out the object-image from the inside) and which is all the greater, the stronger the "inexistence" of the projected object. The differences in density and their variability have some link to the determination of value and prices. Finance (and more generally economics) should be seen as a world of representations (in relation to a consciousness, a Subject), and therefore as unitary object-images, true primary elements of a system which we have called a "reference frame" of a specific space-time, which undergo trans-formations as we have just seen, which can also constitute chains, groupings and consolidations, chains of value and, at the same time, chains which form language.

The spatio-temporal reference frame for economics and finance is inhabited by primary elements, which are all unitary object-images produced by an infinite multitude of individual consciousnesses. Each primary element is characterised by a density of duration and memory (which contains the link between time-matter and value) and by a density of negativity or anti-matter (which contains the intensity of projection towards that which is not yet, which is not, which will never be, in a state of being, this space of what is possible and impossible, which is subject to gradations and segmentations). Such primary elements are in absolute and relative movement. Absolute, i.e. as compared to themselves and stimulated by the conscious Subject (memory recalls and lapses), within an internal set of dynamics of the discontinuous modification of the layers of duration and knowledge. Relative, i.e. of some as compared to others, once again stimulated by the conscious Subject, when the primary elements collide, consolidate into a chain, merge into each other and are, as a result, transformed. A transformation results from such relative movements, in addition to the internal movements which are specific to the primary elements, the whole of which forms the dynamics of the financial, and specifically the market, space-time reference frame. These mental physics of the primary object-images, that of the consciousness of the Subject investor, the consumer or, in general, of the *homo economicus*, are the basis for the dynamics and the language of economics and finance in the modern age.

§ 21. Any unreal object-image brings with it a specific space-time reference frame, its own time and space, in proportion to the spatio-temporal references of the imaging consciousness which produced it. One of the important accepted facts of our work is the unavoidably specific or special nature of object-images, which attain a form of independence and inhabit the mental market universe: the anti-matter or anti-world, which forms the essential structure of market dynamics and finance. It will also be remembered that the constitution of the financial, market or economic object-image (pre)supposes a certain knowledge, that the imaging consciousness of the Subject investor (financial or economic player) is responsible for learning, since the consciousness which will produce the financial object-image can only visualise as an image – this image or images which inhabit the space-time reference frame and which foster the market dynamics – that which it already knows and/or remembers after having perhaps first forgotten. By being responsible for learning and knowledge, the imaging consciousness is only carrying out its task of accumulating and producing *duration*, which is the raw, primary time-matter driven, given form or distorted by memory recall and lapse, in a process which is literally that of market dynamics (it was demonstrated in *Théorie* that this process lay at the heart of economic dynamics); this layer of duration, which has been compressed and squashed, will be transferred to the financial/market object-image and will constitute its substance and structure, a summary of multiple times, of various temporal sequences, an intertemporal summary of various, individual durations. This compression of duration is not fixed and will not remain passive, since the impetus from the Subject's consciousness, represented by the memory recalls and lapses, will be responsible for dilating, re-compressing, informing and distorting, or will produce other images from which the spatio-temporal DNA has mutated. Contrary to agreed opinion, nothing prevents an internal form of life of the image from being placed within a spatio-temporal reference frame of duration which is driven, like electricity disseminated in a basin, by the phenomena of memory recall and lapse. Equally, nothing prevents one assuming, in addition to the primary, pure units represented by the images within the financial and market space-time reference frame, the existence of more or less complex chains of market object-images, which form a structure and language which mutate, develop or disappear or the existence of complex financial images which form one with an aggregation or chaining (there would accordingly be a category of fundamental, primary object-images, certain of which would perhaps have a given, stable spatio-temporal DNA and a category of complex images of groups of primary images);

in any event, discussion on this spatio-temporal market reference frame, made up of simple elements and more complex elements, remains open. Finally, learning, knowledge and therefore duration, which contribute to the constitution of the market or financial object-image, undergo a modification, initially during the memory of an intertemporal section of individual durations, and then within the dynamic life of this structure, which is granted as a legacy, within the DNA, to the nucleus of the financial image. This is because the mobilisation and modification of duration within those space-times, which are specific to the mental universes structured by the imaging consciousness of the Subject investor (*homo economicus*), remain at the heart of market, financial and economic dynamics.

Chapitre 2

STRUCTURES
OF THE CONSCIOUSNESS (II)
THE IMAGINE CONSCIOUSNESS
AND THE ACTING CONSCIOUSNESS

§ 22. There are two levels, that of the acting consciousness and that of the imaging consciousness. The two levels are connected (ultimately there is a consciousness which acts on, in, towards the world because the consciousness has the capacity to produce images). The acting consciousness targets the world and this very targeting brings about a transformation. For the economic Subject, being conscious of the world requires from the outset a relationship of modification, alteration and transformation. The economic Subject's acting consciousness is consciousness (of), i.e. (literally) awareness of the world which is a free expression of a negativity (when the economic Subject becomes aware (of) it places at a distance and "imagines" an "alternative" object, even if this final object is not intended for a particular transformation: it is already involved in an alteration process). The nature of the economic act lies within this very capture, the act of consciousness being prolonged or not by the transformation of the object. The economic act produces the transforming point of contact with the world, and therefore produces the economic fact. There is accordingly an economic act, which itself includes the act of (imaging) consciousness and the extension towards reality, which we will call action in the strict sense of the word. At the point of impact with the world, an economic fact appears. The economic object may have two meanings: first, an image-object, product of the imaging consciousness within a specific mental space-time reference frame and, second, an object-element of the world before the transforming action (the object is not transformed, the economic fact is transformed, it is the very name of the transformation).

§ 23.   The imaging consciousness, as we saw in *La Dynamique boursière* is the capture of real objects (and this very capture itself brings about an alteration of the object and its structure within the mental reference frame) which produces object-images; but also the pure creation of object-images without real referents (right up to the illusion which stems from pure imagination). This imaging consciousness founds or begins the action process (acting consciousness) up until the impact with reality and the world of real objects. In the world, there are objects [elements of reality which have (not yet) been transformed by action] and facts (meeting point and point of impact of the process of the acting consciousness and the real world). The objects in the world are only apparent to me through a targeted perception and representation of the (imaging) consciousness of the economic Subject. This means that the economic Subject does not have access to the real object in the world itself (in its essence) since the world is captured by the consciousness which, as a result, manufactures an object-image which resembles the object in the world but is different in both structure and essence. There are accordingly two types of transformation: the transformation which leads to the very design of perception and representation of the imaging consciousness and the transformation of the object itself in the world (the economic "fact"). The economic Subject is therefore essentially structured on the basis of a pool of image-objects which form a specific mental reference frame, and such objects produced by the imaging consciousness are not of the same type as the objects in the real reference frame of space and time, certain object-images maintaining a connection with the real object (capture by the imaging consciousness with a greater or lesser degree of original alteration and later distortion, since the object-image has a life and dynamic of its own), or no connection at all (an autonomous, independent object-image, only referenced within the mental space-time of the imaging consciousness; which does not in any way prevent such object-images, which are to some extent illusory, finally sustaining the acting consciousness and the act of the economic Subject towards the world with impact. Quite the contrary, in our view. The act and anticipation stem from an essential negativity, i.e. from the capacity of the economic Subject's consciousness (creation, imagination) to obliterate, which explains why the act often results from a pure, illusory negativity, which drives many object-images which do indeed inhabit the Subject's mental space-time reference frame and also, rather more interestingly, the physical expression represented by the financial market itself.

We have therefore stated that within the world there are objects and facts. Within the economic Subject, there is an imaging consciousness and an acting consciousness; there are object-images, which are pure forms of the mental reference frame of the imaging consciousness, imaging perception or pure imaginations (anticipations); within this living reference frame of object-images (or image-objects, the two expressions serve the same purpose and will be used indifferently), a certain number of image-objects (object-images) will enter a specific process, channelled towards a real target which is to be modified or created (possibly from nothing), a specific process of the acting consciousness which will establish a link between the mental reference frame of certain image-objects and the physical action on the real object within the world. The form of the financial market, of the Stock Market, plays several roles: it is a physical expression, a materialisation of the image-objects or certain image-objects which inhabit the reference frame of the imaging consciousness, as we have emphasised on many occasions; it is also the place where certain image-objects are channelled towards the real world for the purposes of transformation. This place in the market or the Stock Market is a place of restitution (of reflection in the way that a mirror reflects) of the mental reference frame of image-objects (the reflection is one too), and a place of elimination of certain image-objects (or of greater or smaller modifications to such image-objects), finally and above all of the selection of certain image-objects directed at the real world. Unsurprisingly, references to the world of the consciousness and to a specific space-time will coexist in this place, together with references to a real world of clock time and playing fields. At this stage of the process, which ultimately leads towards the action, or which does not lead there (this is essential), as many elements remain virtual as ultimately real within the process chain, (virtual in the sense of image-objects which retain that status).

§ 24.   Accordingly, this chain, which is also a process, contains, from the outset: the economic Subject's imaging consciousness, which produces and manages a pool of image-objects which may or may not have a link of representation (of perception) with the real world, a pool which has its own dynamic and a specific (this imaging consciousness is reflected in the physical form of the financial market and the Stock Market), psychological or mental reference frame (it does not matter which, we are seeking to name that which characterises the activity of the consciousness); the acting consciousness, which selects, steers a certain number of image-objects towards the real world, at the cost of possible transformations and the specific space-time reference frame described in the situation where the imaging consciousness remains the same (this acting consciousness structures the physical form of the financial market and the Stock Market in a dominant fashion, in the sense that the market is an important link in the action process which leads images towards the actual impact; but the space-time reference frame remains that of the consciousness which produced and drove the image-objects and not that of clock time and football stadiums, and part of that universe of image-objects is self-referenced and does not, whether in a definitive or temporary manner, have a prospect of impact, the extension of impact towards reality). This explains both errors which may affect the comprehension of the special form of the financial market and the Stock Market: confusion between two space-time reference frames; confusion between that which is connected to reality (process of the acting consciousness and action up until impact with the world and until the "fact") and that part of the imaging consciousness which remains within the reference frame and which is called "virtual". These two dimensions exist in the financial market. The final stage is the phase of the transforming impact in and on the real world, in the same way as a meteorite rains down upon a planet. One is then dealing with economic "facts", in the manner we have described, multiple points of impact with the world's surface, the final phase of the manifestation of the image-object which stems form the consciousness, the crystallization phase where, almost literally, a specific structure, stemming from the reference frame of consciousness, which is liquid and which can be distorted as we have shown in *La Théorie* and *Les Fondements de la dynamique boursière*, acquires solid form in the same way as water or sand may create stone or sand-roses. One is now in the presence of "facts", of crystallized phenomena, of more solid forms of image-objects. These "facts" (points of impact) become fairly quickly in reality forms of new objects, which will in turn have a feedback effect on the consciousness, in the same way that, at the original stage of the process which we have described, there is a consciousness which captures real objects by creating pure unrealities (whether transitory or definitive), in both instances image-objects, certain of which will remain autonomous and to some extent virtual (whether temporarily or definitively) whilst others will sustain the process of impact with reality.

There is accordingly a circle of creation traversed by a dynamic which produces unreality and reality at each end of this axis with continuous actions (feedbacks) from one upon the other.

§ 25.   That which is called finance directly intersects the phases of the process which involve the imaging consciousness, the financial market and the acting consciousness. That which we call economics in turn directly intersects the phases of the acting consciousness and of impact on the real world (the "facts"). The two intersections of one and the same process interact and, in certain respects, share a certain number of points in common. However, it is not fortuitous that it was felt necessary to give a certain number of processes, or segments of processes, the name of "finance" after giving other sequences the name of "economics". We have shown that the two dimensions are indispensable in order to see and understand the chain of manufacture of unreality and reality in the modern age. These two dimensions are essentially connected to each other; there is no point in opposing economics and finance, since both form part (are indeed the two main pillars) of the relationship between the economic Subject and the world in the modern age. It can indeed be seen that finance shows a tendency to become independent, since the segments of the global process to which it lends its name themselves show a tendency to become independent. It can as a result also be seen that economics is perceived as living at the risk of finance since, and it is not untrue to say so, economics describes more particularly that which is of the world and that which transforms or is transformed at the end of the Subject's action process. However, more profoundly, even though it is always possible to separate and distinguish between the various sequences, it should be stated even more forcefully that the complete (or global in the sense used in *Théorie*) understanding of the relationship between the Subject and the world requires an understanding of the two pillars and the links between the two and that, ultimately, economics acquires a new structure in the modern age, which includes finance, thus representing a body which is both internal and external, both dependent and independent.

§ 26.   A certain number of distinctions are thus drawn and sections cut out as between the real world of object-things and the financial reference frame of object-images. We demonstrate that the dimensions of space and time are not the same but that, at the same time, all that we known of the real world depends upon a perception or representation of the consciousness, the very nature of which is no different from the financial reference frame of image-objects which we have just discussed. The world of real things is indeed real and accessible but we do not acquire direct access to it. This means that a distinction can indeed be drawn between economics and finance which would be supported by the distinctions between clock time and the spaces of playing fields on the one hand and the time and mental space of a non-linear universe on the other. However, it is always and throughout the same economic Subject-consciousness which captures and manufactures mental objects. The most real economy will always ultimately be dependent upon the dynamics of a Subject's reference frame, since it is only reality for an economic Subject and, once that is established, everything else follows. Everything else is in particular the fact that every real thing includes a dose of unreality, if the conscious Subject places it at a distance in order to conceive, perceive, project or transform it. This dimension of unreality connects, even in part, the universe of the "real" economy to bits of mental reference frames which derive from those which we have described for the financial markets, finance and the Stock Market.

§ 27.   The imaging consciousness thus irrigates the whole process of capture of the world and action on the world. Economic reality is inconceivable without the unreality of the economic Subject's consciousness which perceives, projects and transforms. Economics cannot be imagined without the financial world. And the action cannot be imagined without the reflective and imaging consciousness. This necessary connection leads, in the modern age, to positioning the financial market as an intermediate structure between the economic Subject (consciousness) and the world, and as a "real" structure (in the sense of an institution), and therefore an institutional form, of consciousness. Finance and the market are the major, modern forms of the consciousness of the world, of the intermediation of the relationship between the (economic) Subject and the world. In fact, as was shown in *Tractatus* or *Généalogie*, "economics" is the name given to this link to the modern world between the Subject and the world. The means of appropriation and transformation of the world, through the very role played by negativity (imaging and acting, since the links are profoundly necessary between each), the means of imagination – and by that is meant anticipation, projection and creation – form part of the modern forms of finance in the real expressions of the phenomenon, data from the consciousness within the dynamics of the production of economic and financial objects – which are still derived from images – data based on negativity. Since, in order to act, one has to think "not".

Acting is confused in economics with imagining and it is this imagination, understood as a capacity to create that which is not or is not yet, which sustains the phenomenon of finance itself. In truth, once the projection, anticipation, the intention to modify and the change creep within the economic discipline, i.e. a negativity linked to the economic Subject's approach, once economics accommodates time as a breach for projection and for distancing (capture) in order to transform, then finance starts to develop within economics itself, in order little by little to become independent until it becomes a practical external form represented by the financial market (the Stock Market).   Since the manufacture and exchange of image-objects, i.e. of that which is not or is not yet (which is in a state of non-being), acquires in the modern age considerable importance and significance, over and above the production and circulation of goods and services. One of the most essential features of the modern age, of the economic market process and capitalism in general lies in the fact that that which is not or is not yet tends to be more important than, or of a different importance to, that which simply is. This is a forceful phenomenon of modern economics and finance. Since the project and the action structure the field of modern economics, borne by a Subject-consciousness whose means of projection within that which is not (or is not yet) is based on a negativity injected into object-images which inhabit the (real) project and its representations, in particular on the financial market, whose role is to organise, sort and drive the said representations and also to allocate them a price.

The image-object cohabits with the real object-thing, superimposes itself upon it to some extent. As we have seen, the real object remains inaccessible for the economic Subject which only has access to the product of the capture through consciousness of that which is (the thing, the object which I see in the real world). This product of the capture is an image-object which, although not betraying the truth of the real thing (real object), contains within it a special nature, a specific structure, the injected negativity, introduced by the consciousness in the very act of survival. We mean that the first dimension of image-objects is constituted by the economic Subject's consciousness, using the product of the capture of the real world as it is. Our approach draws a distinction between this dimension and another, second dimension inhabited by image-objects which are produced directly by the consciousness without an essential reference (i.e. without reference to a capture by the economic Subject, through perception or representation, of some or other real object in the world) in the world of real things and objects. These image-objects may stem from the real world, may for example inspire an image-object which does not itself have an exact counterpart in the real world, or may not seem to stem from the real world (special, diffuse links may exist, which may even be unconscious for some) and therefore form part of what is commonly called pure imagination or creation.

1. THE THREE DIMENSIONS OF THE IMAGE-OBJECT

§ 28. The distinctions are not easy to draw but on first analysis one can see pure product image-objects (pure in the sense of the photographic result of a targeted objective) resulting from the capture by the Subject's consciousness (the Ural sea, the Sahara desert); within this class of image-objects which are pure products of the capture, a distinction can be drawn between the image-objects which refer to that which is in a pure sense, i.e. which has not been transformed by the Subject, *homo economicus*, *homo faber*, etc. (water, earth, those things which are commonly called the "elements", although we should clarify exactly what such "elements" are), and, second, the image-objects which refer to that which, already, contains the trace of the Subject's action (a universe in infinite expansion); this distinction enables one to segment that which, already, within its DNA, its structure, contains an action or project dynamic, which may sooner or later be revived (one intends in this way to capture and follow the dynamic of the image-object which stems from memory recall or lapse); the image-objects maintain a link with an action or project which will be characterised by a specific, relevant reference frame, the very one which gave birth to the design for the action and the project, and which, within the dynamic life of the image-object will constitute the source and reference point for the dynamics, trajectories and transformations marked by the contractions and dilations of a mental space-time of duration, memory recall and lapse; it is not that the image-objects of pure perception cannot undergo a mutation (in the sense that a DNA may mutate), or cannot be linked to complex chains of image-objects, cutting bits of DNA, for example, as with a pair of scissors in order to stick them together, a piece of a real, pure untransformed thing, a piece of a project and action which has already been effected or which is still part of pure imagination, it is not therefore that this cannot be but rather that it must remain limited, the intended purpose of an image-object of pure-capture being to retain such pure suitability with regard to the untransformed object of capture; that said, and we will complete our review of this first class of image-objects with this, image-objects of pure capture (untransformed elements of the real world or transformed elements of the real world and which already contain the influence of an action) – which are as such an initial alteration of an inaccessible reality, like a photographic film placed on the world as it is, i.e. the untransformed elements, and the world as it will be, the "facts" as we have defined them as points of impact of the action within the world – such image-objects of pure capture may experience processes of additional alteration, transformation and mutation within the very unit which each constitutes or as between themselves after reconciliations, hybridizations and divisions; these image-objects of pure capture experience a dynamic, which is all the stronger since it does not (yet) relate to real objects transformed, since that which already bears the trace of the economic Subject's action will provide a heritage of identity and a DNA of duration and it is memory and forgetfulness which will be responsible for allocating to the latter its own existence.

The pure image-objects, i.e. of pure capture of the real world whether or not (yet) transformed accordingly constitute the first dimension of the space-time of image-objects stemming from the imaging consciousness, a consciousness which will also be acting once the image-object is directed by the action and becomes the structure of a project intended to impact the world.

§ 29.   The second dimension is made up of image-objects stemming from the imaginative creation of the consciousness, without any direct reference to the real world in the sense that these are not products which are conceived (but which may contain one or more bits of films captured from within reality, whether or not such reality has been transformed), innumerable creations or injections of negativity which are inexistent, within real referents which already exist (transforming projection, pure imaginative illusion, from a project in the economic sense up to a creation which seems to be quite insane, one covers a large range from the economic action project through to a project which is strictly artistic), or within the referents which, almost literally, do not exist other than within reference frames which are already constituted of image-objects without a reference frame, illusions and insanities, unconsciousness and pure bubbles of inexistence. This second dimension has been described analytically in *Les fondements de la dynamique boursière*, and restated in this *Théorie du Sujet économique*. It will be noted that this reference frame of image-objects is the most extensive (by comparison with the other two dimensions, that of image-objects of the pure capture of the consciousness, and that which we will look at in further detail below, which is already a chosen embryo of a project, racing like a rocket towards the planet of the real world, where it will leave a trace on impact – the impact leaves a trace, a duration which summons forgetfulness and memory). This reference frame of image-objects is extensive, i.e. it accommodates various densities of negativity, ranging from that which denies something in existence by projecting it into a transformation (I decide to construct new buildings on a site which is to be destroyed or transformed) through to that which no longer seems to refer to the real world (I launch a tool, which is the first to consolidate multiple functions, performs that which has never been performed before…) while retaining the property, the capacity to mutate into an image-object which structures a project and an action impacting the world. However, and above all, within this reference frame there are image-objects which have to some extent switched to the side of the action and the real project by structuring it (by means of a transfer from the imaging consciousness to the acting consciousness), and others which have not (yet) switched (because the image-object, a living object, has not reached the stage of maturity which will make the link with the real project) and yet others which will never switch. Chance and necessity, which ensure that certain image-objects, and not others, that certain chains joining bits of DNA of multiple image-objects of pure capture, of transforming reflection, of pure imagination, will turn out to form the structure of a real project with a transforming impact, and such chance and necessity constitute a mystery which we will revert to later. For all that, this process of selection, emergence and gestation within the departure room from the incubation laboratory, incubator or operating theatre, which takes place within the extensive reference frame of image-objects is the result of multiple transactions which we have introduced and presented (the evolution and mutation processes of unitary image-objects, of more or less complete mergers of unitary image-objects and of more or less complex transplants between image-objects). The population which results from this unpredictable and necessary selection process constitutes the third dimension.

§ 30.   The third dimension therefore contains image-objects which structure projects in the course of action. It is this third dimension which constitutes and structures the financial market and the Stock Market, in the practical form of the consciousness which we are aware of. This third dimension structures the action and therefore the acting consciousness. At this stage and for this dimension, the imaging consciousness becomes acting. There are accordingly three dimensions (the pure capture of the real world, the creation to a certain extent of image-objects from nothing and the formative steering of certain of such image-objects towards the action and the project). There are two modes of consciousness, imaging and acting (the consciousness is unique and there is a unique act of consciousness). There are three types of image-objects (pure capture of reality, whether or not transformed; transforming reflection-projection and pure imagination). The first type inhabits what has been called the first dimension; the second type inhabits the third dimension, that of the acting consciousness of the economic Subject's project and of the pre-impact and impact phase with the world; the second and third types inhabit the second dimension, that of the infinite reference frame-laboratory which not only has its own existence but sustains within it the small number of dynamics which will ultimately modify reality.

§ 31.   Reality in turn enters into relations with these various dimensions in several ways. What is real, the real world, reality are made up of object-things (which we have called "elements") and of economic facts. The real object-things (as compared to object-images) are what is in the world, of the world, prior to any action by the economic Subject. This dimension of unitary elements and these object-things are captured by the consciousness which produces in counterparty a class of image-objects which we have described as being of the first dimension. The economic facts are the product of the real world and of the Subject's action, i.e. a point of impact, whose structure contains both an image-object, manufactured by the consciousness and selected to intersect with reality within a project (acting consciousness), and a part of reality where the impact will take place (these are object-things which are captured by the consciousness, and are accordingly primary, rudimentary forms of image-objects). The economic facts, after a form of sedimentation process, assume the nature of object-things, which are part of reality even if the latter is in this instance the product of a transformation or mutation.

Reality settles like a film within the image-object which captures it, i.e. perceives it. Reality settles but the image-object remains at a distance from the captured object-thing, a flaw which is indeed modest but essential, a flaw of negativity, a siphoning-off of being which is barely perceivable but which heralds a much larger share of negativity within the image-objects of the second dimension (complete and extended imaging consciousness) and the third dimension (acting consciousness). Everything occurs as if the internal cellular dynamic of the entity represented by each image-object became stronger the more significant the place filled by negativity. Accordingly, the first generation image-object, produced by the capture, is fairly extensively saturated by the real object-thing, which leaves a limited space for negativity and therefore for the dynamics of change and of action (the counterpart of action, seen from an external viewpoint, is an internal dynamic resulting from the anti-matter which represents the negativity resulting from the projection – from the perception up until the project-changing action). Conversely, the image-objects which we have called "pure imagination", including the much-vaunted illusions, are in turn saturated with negativity and such negativity provides a strong internal energy and a large number of internal mutations and movements, which may lead to a form of instability and also to forms of cracks and implosions. The proportion of negativity within the internal structure provides the potential intensity of the dynamic.

The negativity sustains an internal energy of the cellular entity which is the image-object, which is more or less pronounced according to the fraction of negativity which is originally included on creation of the image-object (the image-objects, the capture-perception are low in negativity, are replicative and only slightly differentiated from the real object-thing which acts as a benchmark, and hence represent a limited independent energy, which does not prevent one imagining more pronounced dynamics of more complex groups, which combine unitary blocks of a more or less simple nature, including blocks of capture-perception).

Reality is accordingly at work in the consciousness's capture-perception process and the production in passing of first dimension image-objects. However, that is not all. Within the image-objects which inhabit and drive the vast second dimension which we have described, the fraction of negativity increases considerably within the central core of the unit constituted by each image-object. This means that the reference reality (a point of existence which is more or less confused, cut, segmented or transformed), when indeed one exists (the illusion, but more generally, the imagination-projection, the dream, which may lead to the transformation of reality; like the project for a bridge which stretches across several valleys, like a veil), or even therefore the lack of reference within reality, open up an infinite field of cellular units (image-objects) pierced, as it were, or hollowed out in proportion to the decline of being (negativity) which constitutes them. The cellular units are made up of anti-matter and therefore of anti-reality, in the sense that they project a change of reality or even another reality within designs which may seem illusory but which are not *a priori* disqualified from aspiring, effectively, to modify reality.

The fraction of anti-matter (negativity), which grows where reality has been expelled, governs, as we have seen, the dynamic of the unitary cell constituted by the image-object (conversely, the image-object which results from the capture-perception only possesses a low level of dynamic, or indeed none at all; inertia dominates, the image-object is provided at the outset and, without exception, will remain practically unaltered). This characterises the internal dynamics of the cellular units represented by the image-objects. However, and this is an essential point, the internal dynamics (i.e. which stem from the original determining factors specific to each cell and therefore to each image-object) are not the only dynamics. The cellular units or image-objects, move within a specific space-time reference frame, are attracted by each other, repel each other, collide with each other, are broken and reconstructed in an infinite number of possible genetic equations.

The forces of movement, attraction, repulsion, trajectories of collisions, of explosion and reconstruction which are at work within the mental space-time reference frame which we have described in *Les*

Fondements de la dynamique boursière, obey certain laws which provide their dynamic. This is how we demonstrated some remarkable properties of the mental or psychological reference frame within which the image-objects move, a reference frame of anti-matter in the sense of a photographic negative of reality (negativity of the imaging consciousness), of anti-matter "made up" of duration and driven by the discontinuities of memory recall and lapse. One moves – the image-objects move – within this reference frame more quickly (key concept of speed) the more strongly one remembers or forgets. Distance is a function of memory and forgetfulness within an anti-matter of duration. Since the matter of the psychological reference frame is an anti-matter, duration. Duration is that which is within the reference frame and maintains a link with negativity. The negativity, anti-matter which makes up the image-object (or, rather which reveals the anti-matter), "summons" duration as a form of stability within the decline of being represented by negativity (to be in a state of non-being). The duration, itself, is. The anti-matter established by the design of negativity of the economic Subject's consciousness, ultimately reveals duration as being that which is within the economic Subject's mental and psychological reference frame.

§ 32.   Before returning to these essential aspects of the dynamic constitution of the imaging *and* acting mental/psychological reference frame (in the sense of a product of the consciousness' process), let us note at this point that the processes which we have demonstrated are characteristic of a creative emancipation of the (imaging or acting) economic Subject, a process of emancipation which names the modern phase of liberalism and political freedom. Since that which the economic Subject feels in connection with the imaging creation (imaging as an element of a wider action process (imaging consciousness, acting consciousness, impact on the real world), that which it feels within the experience of negativity which fills reality with anti-matter in order to found the project, is liberty. This experience, which cannot be sufficiently perceived, founds the modern period of the Subject, of the economic action (the identity between the Subject's action and the economic action) and, above all, of market finance since the financial market, as has been shown, emerges from the consideration of the projection and the active anticipation, in relation with the project, and therefore emerges from a reference frame of mental or psychological projections of an economic Subject endowed with an imaging and, therefore, acting consciousness. What we are trying to say here is that finance, the financial market and the Stock Market are only conceivable on the basis of the modern emancipation of the economic

Subject and the constitution of a reference frame of image-objects which structure the projects to modify reality, and the financial market and the Stock Market will become within this process practical, institutional forms of this reference frame at work. Moreover, within this very process, the economic discipline progressively incorporates the dimension of that which is in a state of non-being, the dimension of emancipation and, in general, of the active projection. Accordingly the modern process of achievement of a certain fate of economics is said to be connected to finance, which is largely that of an emancipated, central and infinitely free, economic Subject, or at least it seems to be posed in this way. We described this modern process clearly in *Tractatus*, *Généalogie* and *Valeur et Temps*. We demonstrated its limits in terms of its very achievement. Demanding that one be able to consider economics, as we said, "over and beyond the Subject". Divest economics from the Subject, reduce the Subject's hold over the manner in which economics are considered, which, in passing, can only lead to considering finance in another way which, as we have seen, developed in proportion to the autonomy and emancipation of the economic Subject and its consciousness. It is not a question of considering economics without or as against the Subject but rather as "beyond" the Subject, which keeps intact the possibility of an active and effective freedom – which as it happens allows that which is to come towards the Subject in order to found that which must form part of the action and the project, by departing from the unilateral protocol within which the Subject unilaterally targets the world in order to transform it. We will come back to this since *Théorie du Sujet économique* is the exploration of the foundations of modern economics and finance – and therefore of the central role of the economic Subject – in order to attempt a form of transcendence. Within this transcendence, in particular, the value reverts to that which is in the world and moves towards an economic Subject which welcomes such an approach, a value which is almost exclusively, and fatally, fixed in the modern era within the Subject's obliterating projection directed at the world (the project of transformation of reality, the image-object which pierces the fraction of reality within negativity and anticipation, which are in a state of non-being). The reversal must have serious implications on the way in which the economic value and, more generally, economics are considered.

The conscious structures of the economic Subject, of economics, or, formulated slightly differently, of the structures of the economic Subject's consciousness (imaging consciousness, acting consciousness) therefore contain the transformation of the real object-thing in the world, on the occurrence of an event which produces an economic fact.

The economic fact is that which results from the encounter between a design-project attached to one or more image-objects and the world, within an impact which is an event. The economic event is therefore (has therefore become) that which results from the Subject's project and the image-objects which structure them when this device collides with the real world (it is accordingly not that which is in the world and which approaches the Subject, which the Subject in turn accommodates, takes in; and accordingly a possibility of reversal which we will return to later).

The transformation is carried by the imaging consciousness and the acting consciousness, attached to a mental reference frame of image-objects whose matter (anti-matter, structure of negativity) is duration, a temporality of the consciousness which completely and radically eludes any form of spatialization of time and which, on the contrary, is governed by discontinuities, extensions and compressions, asymmetrical speeds, accelerations and dilations which we described in *Théorie* and later in *Dynamique boursière*. This transformation of object-things in the real world produces events which generate economic facts. This transformation reveals the creative function of the Subject's freedom, which moves within a domain of financial imagination (by that we mean that the financier names the transformation projects which find a material form within the institutionalisation of the models represented by the financial market or Stock Market). This transformation process, which results from an emancipation of the economic Subject, founds the modern version of political and economic freedom in terms of purpose (we mean by this that the process created in the modern period follows an objective up until the extinction of its dynamics and until it reaches the limits which trigger transcendence or reversal; we have perhaps not witnessed the complete realisation of this objective, even though we may have the feeling that it is already well-advanced in many respects, although not necessarily the most commendable ones).

The transformation process (of the object into the event and into the fact) advances from the imaging consciousness up until the impact of action on reality through the acting consciousness – a complete chain which we have called action, since action does indeed commence prior to the action, or strictly speaking the impact; it commences with the capacity to produce anti-reality (the project), a photographic negative, an act of freedom, a creative act which summons the action, in the same manner as a hole summons matter or light. The transformation process is therefore that which we must call economic action (economics name the action in the modern age). This process is initiated by the consciousness which produces images and modifies them; which interprets, which produces anti-matter. These three functions are placed into interrelation and interaction with the level where the object, fact and event are continuously located. The notion of risk must be captured and understood within this interaction (interrelation), through the function of interpretation, in particular. We will come back to this point shortly.

2. REALITY

§ 33.   For the moment, we return to the essential implications of the transformation process governed by the economic Subject, which we have described. We have seen that the modern theory of the economic Subject (the economic Subject is confused with the sudden emergence of the modern age) establishes that the world seems to be (which is true, in a certain sense) but that the economic facts (and before the economic facts, the image-objects which structure and support the anticipations and projections) are pierced with negativity. This involves trying to distinguish that which, in reality, *is*, from that which – an immense and increasing population – simply bears the mark of the Subject's active design and, accordingly, retains within its innermost structure a negativity or distance where the action (and the freedom) may slip in for better or worse. Since, if a reality exists which we have described as "untransformed" (the "pure" elements which *are*,) the immense majority of occurrences form part of what should be called economic reality (and there one can find in particular the economic fact and event, the transformed object). This economic reality is at all times and throughout the product of the economic Subject's action and of the imaging and acting structures of the consciousness. The only reality lies in the name and the semblances of substance: it is in fact pierced right through by the negativity which inhabits the Subject's economic design in the manner of anti-matter. Even the reality which seems *to be* over and beyond (or prior to) the human transformation is itself only the product of a capture which alters but does not transform. It is for this reason in particular that there is a need to found reality on something beyond the Subject, i.e. a place where reality may be considered authentically on the basis of what *is*. However, is it therefore possible to go beyond the design of the economic Subject's consciousness? What is real and reality approach the economic Subject with a considerable "virtual" dimension, and by "virtual" we mean what results from the projection directed at that which is not or is not yet (anticipation). We use the word "virtual" intentionally here, since it is the dimension which dominates, from among the impressions or indeed even the convictions (even the most critical) with regard to modern economics – and the finance which constitutes such economics. What dominates there is the feeling of unreality, of promises, therefore the most usual forms of the negativity which structures the economic project and also the feeling of a distancing from the reality which is the closest in physical terms (the untransformed object-thing which we described above), the feeling of an anti-matter. Contained within this feeling, which sustains criticism and a certain moralising posture, there are two underlying dimensions which should be distinguished. First, there is the idea that the reference frame of image-objects with which the whole of the economic process is associated, from the conception of the project up to the impact of the action on reality, is a pool of negativities, of total or partial unrealities, the reality of which is "future" but is not yet in being, that the reference frame is therefore a set of promises which bind the Subject, the future and also reality, since such promises will have an impact on the real world within a transformation process. The promises stem from image-objects produced by the economic Subject (consciousness) certain of which, selected to some extent, will follow a path of action towards impact with reality (acting consciousness). There is accordingly an idea, which is correct, of a reference frame of promises which are exchanged within the practical form of the reference frame represented by the financial market and the Stock Market. Thus far, the reasoning is not unsettling. There is also the idea that this reference frame contains promises which are not kept, which cannot be kept, which will never be kept, all sorts of degrees (from pure and total unreality, the image-object which will prove on impact with reality to be very far removed from that which it seemed to be...). Finally, there is the idea, which is popular and populist in times of crises, that the reference frame of image-objects and therefore of the projects which structure the economics of reality through finance of the negativity, a finance which one encounters in real time in the quotation of promises, that this reference frame may therefore find itself cut out of reality, self-referenced, that the dimension of negativity specific to the structure of any projection, anticipation and therefore specific to any economic action project (to be in a state of non-being (not-yet-being)) sometimes threatens an unreality or virtuality such as the destination towards reality (impact) – which forms an essential part of the image-object's project – or is threatened by a failure to perform, but also that this fraction of unreality misunderstands, assaults or ignores reality within the transformation project which it bears, which explains this barely moral form of judgement made with regard to the virtualities of the universes of finance. Finance, including modern economics which operates together with finance, is defined by negativity, unreality, a certain virtuality which themselves define the project to transform reality. Once the link between the image-object and the process of the project to impact reality slackens or is radically transformed, breaks (sending the image-object back to the reference frame and to a form of self-referencing), a certain vigilance is required.

The first dimension is therefore linked to unreality and the promise, and therefore to the risk that the promise is not kept. The second dimension lies within the distance from the most immediately material or physical reality. Once again, excessive criticism seeks only to see in finance a radical break with the world, which is in contrast physical and real. It can be seen that the two dimensions are connected and that, in both cases, it should be shown that economics and finance, "reality" and negativity (unreality, virtuality) are the same two faces of a single process of the Subject's project and action with regard to the world. Once again, one can understand the starting point, not so much a matter of criticism but instead due to incomprehension. The action project is sustained by anti-matter, by unreality (it is the very structure of the image-object and anticipation). Materiality is therefore absent at the process' starting point, since the process will develop from anti-matter, which retains a dynamic and a manner of functioning which are specific to *a* reference frame, governed by the laws which are unique to that mental universe, laws which are not those of the real world. However, the process of the impact on reality will commence with certain image-objects and continue up until the action on the matter which will end up transforming the image-object into a "real" object-thing. There is naturally a risk of a definitive isolation of the image-object within its original reference frame. This is the object of the criticism of the "virtual" world which is aimed at finance, a criticism which may be applied in a few instances but which cannot be generalised since, rightly, it is the very nature of finance itself to produce, organise, select and value the negativities, unrealities or virtualities without which – the paradox is only on the surface – the real world could not be transformed. The amendments of the matter of the real world stem from the dynamics of the anti-matter propelled by the economic Subject within a specific reference frame of exchanged promises and valued projects, a reference frame whose physical form is the financial market. The anti-matter may remain trapped to some extent within the original reference frame, developing autonomies in such a way that they eventually inflate (become bubbles) without a relevant link or without any link at all with reality, with matter. This is one of the sources of the economic and financial imbalances, namely here the poor conception or mutation of an image-object and its structure or its DNA. The main financial, and therefore economic, disruptions are often caused by the image-objects, i.e. the projections, representations and anticipations which constitute the bases for the promises exchanged in respect of future action plans.

§ 34.   The distinction between economics and finance seems to intersect the distinction which might in principle exist between the category of the action and the category of the image. To a certain extent, the two categories each incorporate specific elements but, and this is the reason for our precaution, the image *and* the action form part of one and the same process, in the same way that economics and finance are incorporated within the same process which in the modern age is that of the Subject's transforming act, which can be described for reasons of simplicity as "economic" if one bears in mind that it encompasses both economics *and* finance (this is one of the points of application of a truly *global* Theory, as we have demonstrated, see *Théorie globale de l'intérêt, du cycle et de la mémoire*).

Let us go back to these two points. Let us distinguish economics and finance, as if the separation of the two were effective.   Economics governs the category of the action, finance the category of the image; the imaging consciousness echoes the former's acting consciousness; image-objects (or object-images) correspond to the object-things of the real world and to economic facts (impact of the design on the real world); the real world on the one hand, the financial market on the other; a temporality which is spatialized to a large extent (the time is that of the project, the action, in relation to a reference frame, or object-thing) compared to a non-linear space-time reference frame; a world of the image-object whose structure is anti-matter (negativity), a real world of matter; clock time within the real world, duration and its passing, speeds and non-linear peculiarities within the reference frame of the image; a real world which seems to contain values within itself, the progression of a Subject establishing values within the world through active projection.

These distinctions are artificial to a fairly large extent, not because each element as such is false, but rather that there are no connections between the two poles. It is indeed one and the same integrated process. We have already discussed this point, although not exhaustively. Economic action cannot be considered without the category of the image (therefore of the negativity) which distances the world in order to transform it through the project and finance contains the category of the image (image-object as we have defined it). The action is the name of the whole process, whose driving force is the imaging consciousness, which produces trans-real and unreal representations (which *change* reality), image-objects, certain of which will be used as a basis for the project's impact on the world (the fact): the imaging consciousness is incorporated as a principal driving force within the acting consciousness and the forms of consciousness are themselves incorporated within the global action process. Furthermore, as we have seen, the so-called "real" world is made up of conscious (and unconscious) perceptions, and therefore of operating modes which may be closer than one thinks to those of the specific space-time reference frame of image-objects. In all, the two individual categories form one single category within a unified economics where the Subject, world and the production of projects (or images, which amounts to the same thing) are integrated, whose operating modes and regulation are officialised and organised by finance.

In order to understand the whole process of economics, a process which is confused with the economic action in the modern age (as we saw in *Tractatus*, *Généalogie* and in *Valeur et Temps*, this identity could be questioned and overcome in order to reflect on economics elsewhere and in a different manner), one is advised to start with anti-matter and follow the river down to matter, to start with the conscious economic Subject (*homo economicus*) and travel down to the materiality of the object-thing within the material scope of the real world. By so doing, sterile clashes between a reality of authentic matter (economics do not lie) and unreal and virtual games of the financing of a project intersected by projects. Economics are sustained by projections, finance makes them visible in the same way in which a mirror reflects the economic Subject's consciousness which conceives and organises them.

Similarly, the distinction or conflict between clock time of the real world (or quite simply of economics for some) and the discontinuous space-time of the mental reference frame of the image-objects of finance, undoubtedly possess a certain legitimacy and utility. However they come up against certain limits. Although it is established that the space-time of the financial reference frame is different from that of clocks and playgrounds (see *Les Fondements de la dynamique bour-sière*), the very existence of a time of clocks and a space of football pitches within the economy (as compared to finance) and within the world, which is said to be "real" (as opposed to that of the negativity and unreality of the project) is far from being established. Quite the opposite – it is the very essence of the global action process, which we have described as economics – which includes and incorporates finance – which is generally governed by the dynamics of the mental or psychological space-time reference frame. Since the much-vaunted "real" world, like the mechanisms, principles and dynamics which are described as purely economic (once again by artificial comparison with finance) are all carried out, at all times and throughout, under the constructive eye of the economic Subject's consciousness (whether imaging or acting), which, from the very start of the process, imposes a specific reference frame. The most primitive real matter is always "in relation to" a Subject and the dynamics of the project and action which leads to its transformation (i.e. the very definition of economics) advances within this specific space-time reference frame of the Subject.

§ 35. Economics and finance are closely connected, as we have seen, within a unitary, global process which indeed contains several quite distinct sequences which we have described on the path which leads to the real world and the impact left there by the so-called economic action, but whose underlying unity is provided by the Subject's consciousness, which governs this process by driving a space-time reference frame, an essential anti-matter (duration) and the determining factors of a dynamic of speeds and dilations provided by memory recall and lapse, throughout all the sequences. The innermost structure of the economic Subject's consciousness which governs the process of economic action – and which structures the operation of financial markets – is time, a temporality based on a permanent flow which in certain aspects resembles a stock (duration), a flow/stock which is driven by the properties of the imaging consciousness (producer of image-objects which are exchanged and valued on the financial markets or on the Stock Market), since the imaging consciousness is a consciousness which remembers and forgets, memory and forgetfulness which in fact drive the movement.

Duration is on the side of that which *is*, which is set in non-linear motion by the memory recall or lapse driven by the economic Subject's consciousness. The temporal reference frame is not that of a spatialization of time nor that of clock time. The economic Subject is therefore consciousness, a consciousness whose structure is time. The innermost "matter" of this consciousness is the duration (which *is*) but whose precise status is more akin to that of anti-matter since, as we have seen, such anti-matter sustains and structures the negativity of the consciousness which projects, anticipates and places at a distance the real object or the inexistent object (imagination, unreality, illusion), a negativity which is the very essence of the economic project and action and the very essence of the image-objects and representations of that which is to come and which accordingly does not yet exist, which can be found in the Stock Market or in finance, with the uncertainty and risk which characterise the same. Certain image-objects will go further towards the impact with the real world, with feedback effects.

The essence of the consciousness is therefore in a state of non-being (not-yet-being), since the economic Subject's consciousness projects and places at a distance in view of a future event which is a transformation process.

The economic Subject is therefore consciousness, whose essential structure is that of duration, which is given form and distorted by the forces of the Subject's memory and forgetfulness. The economic Subject is therefore in a relationship with duration, which constitutes the most solid basis of the whole economic and financial process. Duration is a means of existing, it is the most solid anchorage for all the formative forces of the economic and financial process. However, the economic Subject does not attain complete access to it, since the essence constituted by duration is distorted, pierced, slowed down or accelerated by memory and forgetfulness. The negativity which forms the basis of the economic projection, action and anticipation is accordingly based on the undoubtedly solid support of duration but it is also partial and distorted by much more volatile forces, including memory and forgetfulness. An economic and financial process which is entirely based on duration would probably have no dynamic.

§ 36.   Accordingly several levels can be seen to emerge at this stage of our study. There is a level made up of the structures of the economic Subject's consciousness: the imaging consciousness, which produces image-objects, whose dynamics are propelled by the properties of the said consciousness which remember and which forget; the acting consciousness, which will convey certain image-objects within the sequence of practical impact with the real world. There is the level of institutional forms: of the acting consciousness, with the various practical forms of the decision to act within reality, from economic policy to the most material forms of action; more generally, there is the overall level of economics, which includes finance within an integrated process where the economic Subject's consciousness digests, modifies and produces reality, a reality which it is vain and misleading to wish to oppose in a sterile fashion to that which is not (the image-object, finance), since the process produces unreality (the consciousness) in order to transform reality – that is the very essence of the economic act, the unity of the process being provided by the space-time reference frame based on duration, memory and forgetfulness. Finally, there is the level of economic freedom, since the process of an economic and financial transformation, governed by the conscious, economic Subject, is a process of freedom, in the sense that the act of projection-creation and the project's creative and imaging negativity – this founding act of the economic Subject, represents the very content of an emancipating freedom, which is indeed not without limits, traps or illusions; the fact remains that there is a complete conformity between the emergence of the economic Subject as an imaging and acting consciousness at the heart of the modern economic and financial process, *and* the emergence of the concept of modern economic and political freedom; changes to one cannot be considered without changes to the other.

§ 37.   Mathematisation within economics and finance provides useful tools but does not enable physical reality to be satisfactorily understood and, more particularly given our approach, leaves us with a characterization of the consciousness of an object which is not physical reality. In the process which we have described, there is consciousness of an object which raises the question of the category of that object. As we have seen, this object is not and will never be physical reality itself, with regard to the object which is directly referred to within such physical reality; since the targeting-capture by perception, even if one keeps as close as possible to the targeted object within physical reality (the real world), remains at some distance (since, in order to capture, some distance is required, even if close). The real object within physical reality which is targeted becomes, once targeted, "another" object, an image-object (or object-image), which is very close to the object itself but which includes a dose of negativity (distance), a trace of the design. This new object will evolve within a specific reference frame, which is not that of physical reality (but that, whether mental or psychological, of the Subject's consciousness) and will follow the rules which are accordingly specific and unique to a space-time which is altogether different from that which seems to reign within physical reality (clock time, standardised spaces of playgrounds). However, the economic Subject's consciousness is capable of something quite different: the transforming targeting of a real object within physical reality; the creative targeting of a new object within physical reality which is inspired in part by one or more existing real objects (or a mix of real and unreal objects), or which literally imagines an "unreality", a "virtuality" which will nevertheless finally impact the real world (i.e. physical reality, the two expressions are used indiscriminately). All these targetings, which go beyond the mere targeting of capture-perception and can be described as "replicative", which share the common feature that they include a high dose or density of negativity or anti-matter which support the projection and anticipation which are essential to the fundamental structure of any economic action, all therefore correspond, each in turn, to image-objects. The reference frame of image-objects accordingly includes the targetings of explanatory capture (perception) and all the transforming targetings which are for the most part directed towards action and a high degree of negativity. All the image-objects have an identical nature and it is the degree of negativity and the indexation to a process of impact on the real world (physical reality) over two dimensions which enables a distinction to be drawn between the image-objects.

In any economic (and financial) process, one is accordingly faced with a dynamic of an economic Subject's consciousness of an object, which is real or real in part, or unreal, an object which is not physical reality but which instead brings the *significance* into play. We have seen in this work and also in *Les Fondements de la dynamique boursière*, that an image-object was constructed by the economic Subject by means of the contribution and deposit of *fragmented* layers of knowledge (duration and memory play an essential role). This fragmented nature raises the issue of the significance of certain events or occurrences and therefore of risk. Forgetfulness is the principal force of erosion which weakens the capacity to understand and which affects the significance: the notion of risk is based on this erosion of the potential significance, which depends upon the dynamics of memory and forgetfulness. In other words, it is the meaning of an economic and financial event which makes up the risk, in particular at the tails of distribution laws, which are not in fact known: even though the object targeted by the consciousness remains the same, a mutation/alteration/reorientation of certain connections or the emergence of a new dimension mean that the risk changes, since the meaning of the event has changed.

3. RISK

§ 38.   Risk in economics and finance (but in other concepts as well) forms part of the *interpretations* of object-images whose structure (duration which is given form and distorted by memory recall and lapse) is incomplete and cannot form part of the traditional expectations of a mathematical process based on numbers. Risk is closely linked to the imperfections, and thus the dynamics, of the image-objects produced by the economic Subject's consciousness. As we have seen, the image-object is made up of anti-matter (a negativity which is specific to the transforming projection, to the anticipation), of a base (flow/stock of duration) and of dynamics driven by memory and forgetfulness: the image-object is made up of layers of knowledge taken from the flow/stock of duration by memory; this knowledge of memory is not entirely stable, since it is exposed to the instability of the movements of the memory and its lapses (forgetfulness). The phenomenon of risk is fully complete within the fluctuations of memory and forgetfulness, in relation to a given object of the consciousness, whether more or less real, more or less unreal, since what will change is not the object targeted within the real world but the image-object whose structure can be suddenly distorted in discontinuous fashion (a mental or psychological space-time reference frame); it is the distortion of the image-object which will, more often than not, require an interpretation, most commonly because the real object may experience a distorting event in the real world (i.e. in physical reality) which has a feedback effect on the image-object.

It is particularly on the financial markets that this work of interpretation, re-interpretation, of new connections, the construal in fact of the unitary elements of the mental/psychological reference frame resulting from the economic Subject's consciousness prior to the global, transforming, economic action process, must be conducted since, as we have stated, the financial market gathers together, organises, values, develops and eliminates the image-objects produced by the economic Subject's consciousness, since the financial market (the Stock Market) embodies the modern, physical, institutional force of this mental reference frame of representations, projections and anticipations (i.e. the image-objects) without which there is no economic action (and, therefore, in the modern era, no economics at all). Consequently, it can be understood that risk forms an integral part of the very nature of the financial market, of the Stock Market, of finance in general, since the very role of the financial market is to gather the image-objects for the purposes of exchange, which presupposes an assessment of the various image-objects and of how they are distorted. The assessment and interpretation of the distortions (of the dynamic) of the image-objects is, as such, the task of interpreting the risk. "Risk" is understood to be that within the dynamics of an image-object (or of a chain of image-objects within the meaning given by us to this concept of a chain) which requires an interpretation, because the determining factors of the image-object's dynamic create a different situation, because the object targeted by the consciousness changes or is modified, because the very structure of the image-object, made up of memory recall and lapse, undergoes a mutation, because the environment of the image-object transforms or is transformed (shocks, reconstitutions which involve several image-objects; new coordinates to some extent of the space-time of the mental/psychological reference frame). Risk does not appear in addition to something else in the operation of the financial markets: the very nature of the financial market is risk within the meaning of the interpretation of the objects-images' dynamics.

This is what is meant when it is said that there is an interpretative process which is never completed. Something constantly emerges from this interpretative process in the same way that the famous wax, to which we have often referred, is given form and distorted. The connection is made at this juncture between the structure of the space-time reference frame of finance (which is that of the consciousness; duration, memory recalls and lapses) and its dynamic. Consequently it can be seen how risk is linked to time but, more specifically, to the distorted duration (i.e. the duration which has been compressed, stretched, accelerated or slowed down) by the – incomplete – memory recall and lapse, distortions which require the interpretation of fresh readings. The debates on the measures of VAR (value at risk) tell us no more than that it is hard to "fix" the temporality of a reference frame which undergoes distortions of memory recall and lapse and must continuously be adjusted and interpreted in accordance with the *events* or shocks which have occurred and which also modify the space and time pairing which lies at the heart of the reference frame's workings.

Risk is one of the main names of the reference frame's dynamic. Risk is (within) the capture by the economic Subject's consciousness of a slice of reality (or unreality), or that which is not yet real, within a reference frame whose structure is provided by duration, memory and forgetfulness. Once a new interpretation is provided, a new construal is made, such new construal or interpretations create in turn new *risks* which are only correctly appreciated by those who can understand them. To interpret or construe the dynamic of the reference frame and the image-objects which it is composed of, is to name the risk as a new risk, i.e. a mutation of the dynamic, of its determining factors (which are internal to the consciousness or are external, i.e. are within physical reality), or indeed the most fundamental part of the mental/ psychological reference frame (the calibrations of the space-time references, i.e. the system of the reference frame). Understanding the dynamic of the system represented by the space-time reference frame of image-objects and understanding the risk are one and the same thing.

Risk is perception-targeting by the consciousness (this may change, if for example "there is a bubble"). For a certain time, it can be said that "the risk is not perceived" (the two to three years preceding the burst of the real estate and credit bubble in 2007). For a certain time, the financial markets, through the use of premiums, send the message that the risk seems to have disappeared, that it is not or no longer perceived. A change has occurred, which, as we have stated, calls for an inter-pretation. The apparent paradox is that the change (false disappearance of the risk) is not really a change and that the true change to be perceived is in fact that there is no fundamental change (the risk has not disappeared), and that an inevitable adjustment will take place. The risk is perception of the risk, a product of the economic Subject's consciousness. As such, each image-object produced by the Subject, and later placed within the reference frame of the financial market, bears an initial trace imprinted by the consciousness, which will evolve and be subject to a dynamic.

§ 39.   The risk is perception of the risk and the risk is also lodged within the perceived risk. The true risk materialises within a *fresh* perception of the consciousness, which causes an outdated perception to expire. With regard to risk, much is a matter of perception; this is clearly highlighted by the relevant vocabulary ("the perceived risk", "the appetite for risk shows that investors' perception of risk has reduced", etc.); the construction and evolutions of so-called risk premiums, including the well-known *spreads*, shows a significant dimension of perception, of the consciousness (of). At any one time, the economic Subject's consciousness perceives and this perception is incorporated within the image-objects of the mental/psychological reference frame, and also that of the financial market which transfers it to the practical world. This consciousness can change at any time; it is when the change begins that the risk is revealed. The said change will render unconscious, after the fact, that which did not seem unconscious, a typical observation of periods of bubbles and manifestations of crises. As such, the manifestation of the risk itself lies within what is called awareness. The risk is the re-capture of the consciousness (awareness) at the time of new elements which shed new light and introduce an alternative interpretation (the change of regime). Anything which is not a risk or risky may, in the same way, become a risk/risky within an alternative parameter of environmental connections, from a literal point of view (that of the economic Subject's consciousness in this instance). As such, risk is a concept which forms part of the frameworks of relativity (whether absolute or limited) which we defined and used in *La Théorie*. Risk is defined at any one time in relation to the image-object or image-objects which are relevant for the object of the risk, within a more general mental reference frame where all the image-objects are located, a reference frame which constitutes the benchmarking point (reference point) for all the elements of the global economic and financial process. This reference frame constitutes, in numerous respects, a regime within the meaning given to such word in *Les Carnets* and in *La Théorie*. The change of regime (alteration or mutation within the reference frame) hastens the (new) awareness which is a new perception of the risk. In fact, the only risk which can really be appreciated lies within a change which implies a new interpretation. The risk only appears as a dynamic (of the economic Subject's consciousness, the image-object and the reference frame), the risk is not visible and does not exist in static form. This is why one of the ways, if indeed one exists, of preparing for the occurrence of the risk is undoubtedly to study the distortions or possible changes to the image-objects (of the consciousness, of perception) within the mental space-time reference frame. In passing, one should take time to reflect upon the possible determining factors, since directly contemporaneous events, although not negligible, are only of limited significance compared to the powerful effects of memory and forget-fulness which proper observation should identify. On the other hand, devoting time and resources to the study of the contemporaneous and immediate data regarding the risk, and the premiums attached to it, may indeed keep one busy but prove of little interest.

When it is said that the risk is identified with the dynamic dimension (change, mutation, alteration... there are various gradual stages, depen-ding upon the intensity of the questioning of the very foundations of the mental or psychological reference frame which shelters the image-objects produced by the economic Subject), it is not said – although it might be, and indeed often is, tempting to do so – that this dynamic of the delta (irrespective of its intensity) is an exception, an aberration, in a word, a distribution tail; it is said that this dynamic is continuously present within the universe of image-objects and the space-time reference frame which shelters them. Certain alterations may indeed be of such intensity that they threaten to break the very regime of the reference frame (as such, they may be exceptional forms), but the dynamic movements must be studied as generalities. As such, the dynamic of the objects of the consciousness cannot be evacuated in the distribution tails, since what we call distribution "tails", occurring at the end of an arrangement which ignores reality, is not an aberration but the generality. There is not, on the one hand, a known, linear quantity and, on the other, an unknown, non-linear quantity, it is easy to separate the two. By evacuating the dynamic of the objects of the economic Subject's consciousness in the distribution tails, by treating it as an exceptional aberration, one would quite simply be adopting a straight-forward, formal construction which would fundamentally ignore the way in which things happen within the real world, within physical reality and within the economic Subject's mental space-time reference frame. This would effectively mean that the reference frame and the interaction with the economic Subject and the world is frozen, and therefore that the very idea of the dynamic is denied, which makes no sense.

The distribution tails are accordingly not an aberration but the generality, which means that there are no distribution tails: there is instead a dynamic and regularities – above and beyond chance and contingency – which can be discovered, other than those of the formal interplay of thick distributions. There are no distribution tails, accordingly there are only (distribution) tails within an interpretative process as we have emphasised, based on the essential flows of the economic Subject's consciousness (duration, memory recall and lapse). It is a question of discovering the *aspects* (connections, details, perspectives…) of the world which we were not conscious of (we return to the idea of re-capture, of awareness). This is where the link between the economic Subject and the world can be established or re-established.

§ 40.   If the dynamic of the object-images of the economic Subject's consciousness cannot be isolated within distribution tails as aberrations but constitutes, on the contrary, a general form, one is faced with processes which may appear to be unpredictable, contingent and thus devoid of any meaning, if one can easily accept, which is not the case here, that meaning and chance are mutually exclusive and that only chance can cancel out meaning by creating something new and a *leap* within an unpredictable, non-linear process. We will devote some time to this essential point. If one accepts that the dynamic of the object-images of the consciousness is general and not a distribution tail, one presumes the existence of a process, which, as a general rule, incorporates non-linear, discontinuous leaps and trajectories. Such trajectories which introduce leaps may understandably seem unpredictable and the leaps which are a common feature thereof may, at least on first analysis, seem uncertain. One would be dealing with phenomena which might or might not be on an indifferent basis. The novelty which requires interpretation and creates the risk, which we refer to above, would be introduced by a contingent leap within an unpredictable, non-linear process – in fact, the leap and the "novelty" in the sense defined above are identical –, unless the leap demonstrates a form of necessity (within an overall process which remains unpredictable), or unless, ultimately, the process and the leap both present a necessary or determinist form, which does not prevent discontinuities or non-linearities within the process.

One is therefore attempting to characterise meaning *and* chance, meaning *or* chance, within the reference frame of image-objects and within their own dynamic which, as we know, is essential to the understanding of the financial markets and, in general, the global-economic process which incorporates finance. We know that we are faced with a global, non-linear process which evolves by means of leaps. An initial approach, which can be described as "pure chance", may consider that chance is that which can, on its own, wipe out meaning by means of a new factual breach (the leap). The reference frame therefore undergoes a process where meaning is wiped out by means of breaches/jumps, which call for an interpretation of what is learnt about a novelty which the economic Subject was, quite literally, unaware of. If one adopts such an approach, the leap completely wipes out the DNA, creating a sort of clean slate which excludes hereditary phenomena in two ways: the leap as such has no ascendance, no "reason", is not the result of reasoning or trajectories which are present within the structure of the image-object or image-objects, the leap has no reason, is absurd, is meaningless; accordingly, it is not even certain that the structure of the image-object has any depth at all, since duration, memory recall and lapse are no longer in circulation – the image-object is an empty shell and, on the financial markets or the Stock Market, chance permanently wipes out any attempt at meaning within a reference frame of chance and contingency which leaves no place for necessary forms. There is little need to state that we are uncomfortable with this approach. To conclude our comments on this approach, we note that the hereditary phenomena are excluded once again, since the leap leaves no trace (there is no memory recall or lapse with regard to the leap).

§ 41. A variation which can be devised as part of a second approach will always be able to describe the unpredictable element of a determinist or necessary design. It accordingly concerns events (leaps, discontinuities,…) which are both unpredictable and determinist, meeting a need which it is pointless to try and understand, since its determining factors completely elude both the conscious economic Subject and the elements which constitute the said need (duration, memory recall and lapse, in particular). The need for this risk is located over and beyond the Subject and the elements of consciousness which govern both the reference frame and its dynamic as we have presented the same.

There is a remaining approach which is of more interest and which can interpret the perceived risk within financial and economic phenomena as being linked to the fact that we do not know or do not yet know, to the fact that we have forgotten. Chance, if we pursue this approach, becomes a temporary form in theory, which might disappear once the conscious economic Subject, when producing image-objects, acquires access to a pure and perfect memory which is completely in line with duration. We know that this is not the case and that the human nature of the economic Subject's consciousness in fact goes hand in hand with the holes, imperfections, memory recalls and lapses which are the very nature of non-linear leaps. The fact remains that this is a plausible interpretation of these discontinuous leaps which manages to preserve a necessity, a meaning: these non-linear leaps form the very regime of the temporality of the economic Subject's consciousness and moreover of the space-time reference frame of finance and economics, characterised, in the context of duration, by the sporadic appearances of memory and forgetfulness. These leaps of memory and forgetfulness are not a matter of chance, it is they who give financial and economic phenomena an appearance of chance but this appearance has a meaning, which follows the laws of the dynamic of memory recall and lapse within a specific, mental reference frame. Moreover, the meaning may always arise from a memory, an aim of forgetfulness, from new layers of knowledge which may be added to the reference frame of image-objects, triggering the "novelty" and the need for interpretation which we discussed at the start of this discussion. It is neither a pure nor a determinist risk but meaning borne by duration and memory, which may be concealed and then suddenly revealed by a non-linear leap, like a clap of thunder in a clear sky. It is therefore essential to bear in mind the fact that the dynamic which is propelled within the space-time reference frame of the consciousness and, consequently, within the whole of the economic and financial process, is not a matter of pure chance but, on the contrary, contains meaning provided by memory and forgetfulness (and concealment and revelation drive the dynamic by means of leaps); that the distribution tails are a generality and not an aberration in the understanding of economic and financial phenomena; that the risk is (lies within) the novelty, i.e. the leap which reveals or conceals, creates a new or alternative situation, which calls for an alternative inter-pretation and not a projected, probability prognosis formulated in advance; that, consequently, there is no point trying to prepare a probability model since it will only include the distribution tail as a generality; that moreover it is not possible to model all the interpretations – which lie at the heart of the dynamic of the economic and financial reference frame and of the risk in particular – as required by the mathematisation of risks, since it involves all the relations between the economic Subject and the world as established by the consciousness, a dynamic which cannot allow itself to become fixed: when one states that it means leaving room for new understandings, one is in fact saying that one cannot fix the dynamic of the economic Subject's consciousness with regard to the world, and that this vital energy which is unique to the Subject-consciousness which drives it cannot be reduced and framed by a mathematisation of the risks, or probability modelling, without excluding the economic Subject, as do numerous approaches of this type to a certain extent, without realising it (but they are then discussing a completely different economic and financial process, which is not the one which we have described nor, especially, the one we can actually see during our observations).

§ 42.   Let us return for a moment to the matter of risk since this notion is defined, within economics and finance, on the basis of the dynamic of the mental or psychological reference frame which we have described and whose importance we have demonstrated: in fact, the distortion (of the reference frame) *is* the risk. There is a similarity between the information/distortion process of the reference frame (which triggers the new interpretation) and the notion of risk.

We have insisted upon the fact that risk is not that which comes to pass, is not a notion of "future events" which represents a fixed state of the economic and financial reference frame, is not a prepared notion "in anticipation of"; risk is not what comes to pass but what has occurred (or the impact of what occurs on the past as it has occurred): occurred in the distortion of the reference frame or the image-object, a leap which requires interpretation; occurred in the sense that a sequence of past (duration) has been recalled or forgotten, sources of concealment or disclosure which, as we have seen, explain the leaps and unpredictable appearance which they may acquire (whether more or less temporarily). Risk is consciousness of risk, literally the awareness of a triggering event which calls for a (new or alternative) interpretation; a triggering event which corresponds most of the time to what we have called a block of duration (see *Théorie*; see *Fondements de la dynamique boursière*) driven by the memory recall or lapse; the purely contemporaneous event may act as a trigger but only insofar as it leads to a new interpretation of blocks of duration/of the past which have been memorised and also forgotten to a greater or lesser extent, since as such it has no impact, it is even a non-event.

§ 43.   The risk is consciousness of the risk, the risk is awareness of the risk, an awareness which maintains a strong link with memory recall: the risk can be seen (materiality, awareness of the risk) within the memory recall, which may be sudden or violent; the risk rises, in terms of its potentiality, within forgetfulness; we have shown that the cycle could be interpreted on the basis of forgetfulness and the return to memory, which drive a specific dynamic (see *Théorie*). The risk is therefore a certain value given to time by the imaging consciousness of the economic Subject, within the specific space-time reference frame which structures the mental/psychological field of projects, anticipations and actions – and therefore within the time of the financial markets –, which also structures the real field of projects, anticipations and actions (from the imaging consciousness to the acting consciousness, from finance to economics).

§ 44. The risk is a certain value given to time by the economic Subject's consciousness. The risk is the nature or posture of the economic Subject's consciousness thrown (forwards) towards that which is not (yet) (i.e. is unreal, not yet real), which underlies the structure of non-being (negativity) and the imaging production of the consciousness (object-images, anticipations). The risk inserts itself within the open field of the Subject's project, anticipation, action and therefore refers back to a negativity, a space-time reference frame which is that of image-objects, whose distortions form events which require inter-pretation (the materiality phase of risk). A "certain value given to time" is understood to be both a posture of the consciousness turned towards that which is not yet (negativity which is the very structure of the project) and a becoming aware (one is said to "realise"), which means inter alia to recall, and to interpret (to reveal once again) a distortion of the updated reference frame. The two axes concur very closely since, from the point of view of the value given to time by the Subject's consciousness, that which is not yet and that which is recalled, together with a certain factor of forgetfulness, are one and the same process within a specific space-time reference frame structured by duration, memory and forgetfulness.

§ 45. Risk occupies an infinite field. Risk occupies the field of unreality in the sense that its essential determining factors are located within the reference frame of image-objects produced by the economic Subject's consciousness (it is formed within the distortions of the image-objects and the reference frame which require a new interpretation of that which has occurred in the same way as an awareness or memory recall), therefore within the reference frame which is of a similar type to that of the financial markets (the Stock Market), without forgetting the feedback effects of reality (i.e. the event within the real world, within physical reality) on the reference frame of image-objects. The spe-cifically financial risk is always linked to an information/distortion (mutation, alteration) of one or more image-objects – which may go so far as to form a distortion of the space-time reference frame itself – and requires a new or alternative description not only of that which is but especially of that which is not yet (project, anticipation, the fraction of unreality which is essential to the operation of the reference frame of the consciousness). The specific financial risk is therefore a change to the reference frame of the imaging consciousness or to one of the elements thereof. It is a risk of the same type which is noted on the financial markets. The specific economic risk, in turn, follows the reasoning of what has been stated above, linked to a distortion of certain image-objects selected by the acting consciousness, from within a separate sequence to that of the imaging consciousness but which is deeply incorporated within it, selected image-objects which are involved in the phase which leads to the impact with the real world and physical reality. A change which occurs to such image-objects, which are consequently close to reality but are not yet physical reality, a change which calls for a new interpretation, produces the risk in its economic materiality. In the same way that economics encompass finance, and in the same way that the acting consciousness and the imaging consciousness are incorporated within a global process which is that of the economic action, the economic risk encompasses the whole of a financial part (which is deeply linked to the mode of operation of the imaging consciousness and its reference frame) and a part which can more strictly be called "economic" (even if we continue to use the term economic in its more general sense), which is linked to the changes to the image-object which has been selected by the acting consciousness, when the said image-object draws closer to the real world or physical reality and/or collides with it (impact). The most visible and strongest points of materiality of the economic risk are those which appear at the point of impact with physical reality. However, this economic risk will always include within its genesis, its heritage, an origin linked to the imaging consciousness and its reference frame, like an original DNA created by the consciousness at the start of the global economic process. The alterations to the DNA may go way back within such process and may produce their effects right up until the moment of impact with physical reality.

§ 46.   At this stage, a few salient points can be deduced from our investigation. We have seen that each image-object, which appears within the economic and financial space-time reference frame or which circulates on the financial markets, incorporates an interpretation, in the sense of one or more states of memory and forgetfulness (static), together with a dynamic process of distortion of such inheritance or heritage. Accordingly, there is at any one time a state of (relative) equilibrium within a space-time reference frame which is itself determined and defined, which corresponds to that which is remembered and forgotten. This relative (or limited, in the sense in which this notion was defined in *Théorie*) state of equilibrium corresponds more generally to the states of limited, financial equilibrium (financial markets, Stock Market, financial variables) and economic equilibrium (real variables). In the state of limited equilibrium there are image-objects which possess a certain genetic heritage (that which is held in the memory and that which is forgotten for a certain given number of real or unreal objects). There is moreover a certain state of the body of image-objects, i.e. a certain number and a certain arrangement of image-objects which are each defined, as we have just stated by a state of memory and forgetfulness with regard to their own specific purpose. The map of all the image-objects defines, on a larger scale, the space-time reference frame which, by summarising the image-objects, may be defined, at any given time, by a certain genetic heritage (summary of all the image-objects) – i.e. memory, forgetfulness, duration – and, also, a certain mental/psychological spatiality in the sense in which we have defined this notion (for example, the speed of movement within the reference frame which, as we know, corresponds to a certain rhythm of the memory recall or lapse). In (limited) equilibrium, there is accordingly a situation which is defined by a state of that which is remembered and/or forgotten. It is a situation which we can describe as static in the sense that it represents a state at a given moment in time.

The dynamic scenario is provided first by the distortions of the genetic heritage of the image-objects and second by those of the structure of the reference frame, since these two types of distortions are connected. The dynamic of distortion stems, genetically, from the variations in value allocated to time by the economic Subject's consciousness, in this instance from the speed at which the economic Subject remembers or forgets (which contracts or dilates the distances within the mental or psychological space). This dynamic will distort the internal structure of the individual image-objects, and will therefore distort the DNA and the genetic heritage; this dynamic will bring some or other image-object or groups of image-objects closer together or push them further apart; this dynamic will therefore distort both the individual units (the structure of the image-object) and the general reference frame (spatio-temporal structure of all the image-objects); this will accordingly take place within the dynamic process of duration, given form and distorted by memory recall and lapse, in interaction with the real world and physical reality which may accompany, accentuate or more rarely trigger only the movements of memory and forgetfulness discussed above. This dynamic may lead to the fracture of the internal units of image-objects (a sort of implosion-disappearance or implosion-integration leading to a reconstitution which takes elements from several genetic heritages), and can even lead to the fracture of the reference frame if the contents, the structure of the arrangement and movement of the image-objects undergo profound change, i.e. when the data of duration, memory recall and lapse which govern the reference frame and therefore the psychological space-time pairing become deeply shaken, disturbed or transformed. This is indeed what is known externally as a crisis, whether it is a financial crisis (a bubble bursting), a more general economic crisis (recession, deflation or depression) or a more complete form of crisis of an economic regime (capitalism, communism or socialism...). A crisis is a normal process in the distortion of the genetic heritage (i.e. memory and forgetfulness) of the image-objects produced by the Subject's consciousness and the mental space-time reference frame which contains and projects them within the finance of the markets and physical reality, a form of normal process which is suddenly no longer normal. The abnormality which enables one to distinguish a crisis from more normal dynamic situations lies largely within the different types of velocities of memory recalls and/or crises of forgetfulness: a crisis is a violent distortion, in one sense or another, of the speeds of memory recall and/or lapse, and therefore a violent alteration (whether temporary or more lasting) or a deeper revision of the value given to time, which is responsible for determining at all times and in all places the manner and the speed at which one imagines, projects or anticipates and at which one moves within the space-time reference frame provided by the structure of the economic Subject's consciousness.

§ 47.   It can be noted from among the other salient points, which we will not consider on an exhaustive basis, that the financial market (the symbolic form of the Stock Market) is or may be seen as a physical externalisation of the imaging consciousness, together with an empowerment of its institutional form. This means that there are two major levels incorporated within the global economic action process, the unitary structure which exercises its reasoning and dynamic starting from the economic Subject's consciousness and continuing up until impact and the trace left within physical reality. The term *global* is used intentionally in the sense which we gave to it in *Théorie globale de l'intérêt, du cycle et de la mémoire* and which is in our view important, of the unitary integration of parallel structures and levels; it has the same sense when one states that there is a unitary economic process, therefore incorporating all forms of levels, including that which is called finance.

The first level is that of the imaging consciousness and the financial market, both being closely connected since everything takes place as if, at least, the operating mode (i.e. the space time reference frame and the image-objects which make up the same) were the same for each, and as if, very probably, the financial market were to give some form of face to the imaging consciousness within physical reality (since the financial market is indeed a real form), registered within physical reality, but since it is at the same time of a similar nature – means of operating, reference frame – to that of the imaging consciousness, an ambiguity is created, which causes a suspicion of harmful virtuality. This first level [imaging consciousness – financial market] is the finance level. This level has its own reasoning and its own dynamic, that of the imaging consciousness and its reference frame, but this level is also only part, to some extent the initial part, of a global economic action process. If one is trying to understand an economic action process, there is no alternative but to start with the Subject and, by so doing, one falls fairly quickly upon the fact that the whole action-projection-anticipation process is indeed overhung by the structure of the Subject's consciousness. This is fundamental, when one considers economics in the context of the Subject (*homo economicus*) and of action (the two are linked since the Subject-consciousness is projection-action). This is the modern context and it is within this context that we place ourselves in order to describe, to understand and in order to overcome.

The second level is that of the acting consciousness and of physical reality, the initial period of time moving towards the creation of the image-objects within the completion phase of the project, i.e. the preparation of its materiality, the second constituting the phase of impact. Unlike the first level, the second level does not implement the interplay of mirrors and continuity as against acting consciousness and physical reality. Physical reality is not – strictly speaking – the tracing within reality of the image-objects selected by the acting consciousness (the primordial task of this consciousness is to sort what will go towards the materiality of impact), even if the possible definition of the real world or physical reality is the incarnation of the projects contained within certain image-objects selected by the acting consciousness. Physical reality is the *impact*, i.e. the point and the moment when certain image-objects produced by the economic Subject's consciousness meet a practical materiality formed both from what *is*, i.e. what is not transformed and from what has been (transformed), containing a trace of duration, memory and possibly forgetfulness.

4. ACTION

§ 48.   Action – The global economic process is expressed as an economic action, i.e. the projection/anticipation of the economic Subject within and towards a physical reality – is first to create object-images (the first complete pillar, and also work of the acting consciousness), and second to fill with matter, establish the materiality (which an image-object will never have, whether it is purely mental or even projected like a shadow theatre, onto the financial markets) of an image-object and in the impact with physical reality.

There is not accordingly on the one hand a consciousness which produces images but which is incapable of thinking and inserting itself within reality, and, on the other hand, an acting consciousness which, in turn, has a true access to reality and possesses an effective materiality. In fact, reality, i.e. physical reality, is conceived and created in a certain manner and appropriated with effect from the interplay of the consciousness: there is no acting consciousness without imaging consciousness and no materiality impact with the world without both, each linked to the other. In particular, it is what we have called the acting consciousness which is most able to come close to physical reality and, without such acting consciousness the action project, in its purest form of materiality, has little chance of succeeding, and yet it retains a conscious posture, at a distance, still in creative projection, making the final selections of the image-objects which have already experienced a mutation to physical reality and materiality. What is called a *practical sense*, someone who is said to have a *practical mind* is endowed, above all, with an acting consciousness and it is this consciousness which is behind the work of this type of mind.

What more can be said about physical reality, this real world, which is the fourth axis of the global process and which supports the second pillar? We define it as *impact* and we link it very closely to the acting consciousness. By impact, we mean that it is the level of physical materiality which informs or distorts the idea which is driven for the most part by the imaging consciousness and which is refined and armed by the acting consciousness for the contact which is looming. Reality is constructed by means of the idea and the imaging/acting consciousnesses, both by the design of capture-perception of reality by the consciousness (physical reality and therefore economic reality only exists for a conscious Subject) and by means of the projection within that which is not yet and which will, for those ideas which are definitively projected by the acting consciousness, be that real part of the project, that physical reality of the project which mixes the physical materiality which we perceive (and whose imaging consciousness incorporates the image-objects of capture-perception) – and within such materiality there lies a history, a memory and forgetfulness –, with, also, a pyschic/pyschological/mental materiality, this energy of the imaging and acting consciousnesses, the energy of their reference frames which propels speeds and gives life to the projects. The fundamental basis of this mental form of materiality is also duration, memory and forgetfulness. These two forms of materiality are merged on impact to form one: this matter which we call reality, economic reality: a block of duration resulting from the Subject's experience, from its capacity to produce unreality (projection, anticipation), from its capture-perception of physical reality; a block of duration accompanied by memory and forgetfulness which inform and distort the block in the same way one sculpts stones or alters a piece of wax (see *Théorie*; see *Dynamique boursière*).

§ 49.   The acting consciousness is not faced with reality, the physical world of objects and humans like the imaging consciousness is faced with image-objects projected into the financial markets, image-objects which are the innermost structure of the consciousness and of the financial markets, the start of reality within the global economic action process which we are describing. The *economic reality*, which we distinguish from *physical reality*, is a product of the impact, and therefore of the information/distortion of blocks of duration, which are memorised or forgotten to a greater or lesser extent, and a product of the action and therefore a product of ideas of the reference frame of consciousnesses on such matter. The economic matter is duration. The economic reality is consciousness in respect of (of) such matter. The economic matter is duration. The economic reality is matter given form/distorted by the impulses of memory and forgetfulness on the hereditary sequences of matter and duration, which, in economics, tend to concur in terms of meaning.

Therefore we arrive at: $Ea = f[(Ci; MKtFi); (Ca; Realp)] \, M/F = Reale$

Where: Ea = economic action
Ci = consciousness (image; imaging/imagining)
Ca = consciousness (action; acting)
$Realp$ = physical reality
$Reale$ = economic reality

and: M/F = memory/forgetfulness

§ 50.   The links and bridging between the four main sequences of the economic action process are not always made, whether correctly or at all. Many economic and financial situations can be described, including the most extreme ones – especially the most extreme ones – by means of dysfunctions between these four dimensions, forms of embolisms, over- or under-representations of such a dimension, up until the imbalance which summons the crisis in order to restore a new regime and, therefore, a new (limited) equilibrium. These difficulties form part of the interplay from the outset. Accordingly, the imaging consciousness produces unreality which will never, strictly speaking, be real – although certain image-objects will end up producing an impact which informs and distorts physical reality, in order to update what we call *economic reality* –, which may lead to a situation (set of events) within which the unreality produced by the imaging consciousness in the upfront phase of the global action process and pure projection/ imagination/anticipation phase, is not selected by the acting cons- ciousness in the programme of impact with physical reality – which is a very normal regime – but which may to some extent degenerate by means of bulges of unrealities (bubbles). One can also imagine situations where the acting consciousness to some extent fails to select image-objects and lets in pure unrealities which will remain thus (illusions) and which will therefore not mutate into projects of impact and of transformation of physical reality. However, the impact will take place and the projects which such unrealities have structured will implode, will explode into reality, and will occasionally contaminate it, creating situations of economic crises like rejected transplants or impossible couplings. Many other combinations are possible, where some ingredient or other is missing from the necessary quantities or activities.

Therefore we arrive at:

$$Ea = \text{Real}e = f(x\ Ci + y\ MKt\ Fi + z\ Ca + w\ \text{Real}p)\ M/F$$

§ 51.   The form of time in the financial markets and within economic phenomena is spatialized (the playing field, echoing clocks in terms of temporality) and masks the dynamics of duration. A large part of the effort therefore quite simply involves making the dimensions of space and time which are specific to the economic and financial reference frame more apparent.

The forms of time and space which are specific to the reference frames of the economic Subject's consciousness, of the financial markets, and also of the reasoning and dynamic of the final action on physical reality (one cannot over-stress the fact that this is the same reference frame) constitute a substantial working axis which we have updated. Numerous structural questions remain. Those of the image- object: both internal structure (the hard core [duration, memory/ forgetfulness] and dynamic); and external (the dynamic of the financial markets; the dynamic of the alteration and mutation of image-objects, both individual *and collective*); the structures of the reference frame in relation to the specific forms taken by space and time; the structures of reality and unreality with, first, the production of object-images based on the negativity of the economic Subject's consciousness (unreality) and, second, a *physical reality* which is captured/perceived but also constructed by the acts of consciousness (whether imaging or acting) and an *economic reality* resulting from that which we call the global economic (action) process – information/distortion of a specific space-time reference frame based on the trinity of duration (being), memory and forgetfulness (dynamic) and which is that of the consciousness of the economic Subject which projects/anticipates and acts, the said information/distortion sustains the dynamic of the economic action and project up until the point of impact where the image-object meets physical reality in order to produce economic reality itself.

§ 52.   The link between the object-image and the real object constitutes an important question to which we have already devoted a certain amount of discussion. Let us return to the matter briefly. Something which transforms reality (therefore into an object) is economic. A distinction therefore needs to be drawn, as we have done, between reality which has not or not yet been transformed (that which is), reality which has been transformed (by the Subject's conscious design), its project of anticipation and the trace which it ends up imprinting in physical reality at the end of a process which includes the imaging production and its projection in market finance and then the refinement of image-objects into projects for the transformation of physical matter, which we call economic reality emerging from the extremely close contact between mental (psychological) matter in the particular reference frame and physical matter which receives the former's print and mark in a fairly extensive manner (act of transformation). There is accordingly an initial distinction between reality which has or has not been transformed. Reality which has not been transformed is that which is over and beyond human action, accordingly pure matter which has its own history, its density of duration and which may in a certain fashion be seen as raw, unrefined matter of the economic transformation process; it is also, as the transformation progresses, that which *is*, and therefore constitutes a reserve of value. A second distinction is added, between the real object and the object-image, which is very structured and which we have discussed in detail. It should be noted that the object-image is at the very least a representation and a transformation (and an interpretation) whose structure is unreal, which will sustain the action (there is therefore a connection between the object-image/reality and impact) or which may remain a pure object-image (an illusion or uncompleted design).

The economic act must consequently be seen as a design which either affects or fails to affect the world, which produces image-objects (which constitute the design). These image-objects form a specific, mental space-time reference frame whose physical material form is the financial market. The image-objects contain a transformation of the world. Their structure is temporal, more specifically duration which is given form by a consciousness which remembers and forgets.

The economic value is consequently that which will actually be transformed within reality (impact, transformed reality), and therefore also within the object-image which contains the design and to which a price will be given on the financial market. There is a link between the first and second point. The value is, in this sense, a structure of unreality (structure of the project) until the project has been completed. It is this structure of unreality to which the financial market will try and allocate a price. It is the value which will change, will become something different within the reality which I am targeting, which is not yet, which is in a state of non-being, which will be exchanged (on the market) because it will change (within physical reality): it is unrealities which are exchanged on the financial market. This act of creation is akin to the economic act of the so-called artistic imagination, their structures are the same with regard to a free, conscious Subject. The value emerges from the inexistence contained within the Subject's intended action; however, the value continues to look towards that which is; negativity and being are the two poles of tension between which the economic and financial value is determined and must be contained.

The act of economic transformation, or simply economics, are sustained by negativity, i.e. by the projection/anticipation of that which is not yet in a state of being. It is therefore unrealities, as we have said, which are exchanged on the financial markets and finance plays this key role of carrying, organising and valuing these unrealities. These unrealities are essential to the structure and development of economic projects and, ultimately, to the economic act. One can see that it may be easy to criticise these unrealities on the basis that one can see only sterile or indeed harmful virtualities, and yet the form of the financial market and more deeply of finance itself are there to perform a function which dominates and rules them, which stems from the economic Subject's consciousness itself: to make projects, to imagine, create and anticipate. Without the form of finance and of the financial market which we know, this function would remain and would be exercised. That does not mean that each form does not need rules and regulations. However, it can be seen how and why it is difficult to devise and implement what will for convenience here be called "regulations", to summarise all that may contribute to a monitored respiration of finance and its practical forms (the financial markets): for the most part, the difficulty lies in the coexistence of a specific, mental space-time reference frame which we have described by showing that it operates by means of sudden, indeed violent, interruptions, by leaps (and the distributions of occurrences of the operation of this reference frame with thick tails have hardly any significance since thick tails are a generality within this universe) and, on the other hand, a body of regulations which, on the contrary, is designed to try to set restrictive linearities, historical consistencies which can be erected as parapets, limits and points of reference. The search for regulation will not fail to take into account the historical dimension, the density of duration nor the phenomena of memory (with greater attention paid to memory than forgetfulness since, in the majority of cases, regulations are pushed through straight after crises), but the regulations will not see the interruptions, the leaps, the particular way of operating of the space-time reference frame of finance, the speeds which mean that the benchmark image-objects move within the Subject's mental reference frame and within that of the markets and the Stock Market more or less quickly the more one forgets or remembers, forgetfulness, the corrosive power which will progressively erode regulation and which is largely forgotten by the regulations. It seems to us that the policies for the regulation of the markets and finance, in the same way as economic policies (the act of economic policy) designed to create efficiency and quite simply conceptual consistency (see *Théorie*), must incorporate the essential features of their subject matter (which we have noted with regard to the reference frame and its leaps) and take account thereof when determining solutions. A limit does not have the same meaning and is not manufactured in the same way depending upon whether it is intended to apply to a continuous, linear phenomenon or, on the contrary, to unpredictable leaps.

§ 53.   We know that it is unrealities which are exchanged on the financial market and that the path which leads to the transformation of the real world, of physical reality – which is specifically the economic act – passes through unreality in the formation of the project. A certain number of object-images will never establish a link with reality (impact), because they are maintained in the state of illusions, remaining blocked within the mental reference frame and on the markets as well – which are the reflection thereof. Without ceasing to exist, such object-images take on an independent life of their own outside the action (the action is a necessary chain linking the image-object to reality), circulating like ghosts beyond the initial design which gave rise to them – they can in fact be seen attaching themselves to a new design as if to a second chance.

Moreover, the action is a chain and we have continuously stressed that economics (the economy) should be thought of and expressed as a global process of the consciousness with an impact on physical reality which produces the economic reality, after passing through the productions of the imaging consciousness which are valued on the markets and are then to some extent taken over by the consciousness in its acting form towards the impact. It can also be noted that reality has a feedback effect (creates an event) on the space-time reference frame and therefore on the nature of the designs which produce the object-images. We have demonstrated the mechanics of this. Finally, the value is also that which *is*, i.e. that which pre-exists the action, the virgin reality of the world; we say "also" because we know that the value accepts another covering, another sense, the project in its creative and imaginative negativity and which has been allocated a price by the market or the calculation of finance, i.e. a non-being of projection which establishes *in advance* the value after the event (that which *will be*), after the impact of transformation; the economic Subject sets the values, states the value by its (economic) act in the world, whilst in the first definition the value to some extent comes to the Subject, towards the Subject, which must take it into account, take responsibility for it. If one adopts the approach where the value is set by the Subject, within the world and through the action, value *is* once the transformation has been effected and it will join the second mode of being of value (one returns to the classification of transformed reality and untransformed reality), but the dominant mode of value in the economic process is inexistence (the promise). Finally, the specific reference frame which we have described produces value by means of the image-objects which contain the negativity of the project or at least of anticipation.

There is, accordingly, value, which is in a state of being, and this mainly relates to untransformed reality and transformed reality, but also – which is more difficult to define – to certain contents of the reference frame of the consciousness, in particular the foundation which is constituted by duration, as we have seen, i.e. a total and complete flow and not a spatialized segmentation of time which is specific to the idea that we have of the Subject's act and, upfront, of the determination of the project leading to the action. Within this pillar of value which is in a state of being, the contents of the reference frame, while assuming a mode of being (like duration), still retain a dimension of projection and therefore of negativity from the background of negativity in which they were steeped. Furthermore, within the second pillar, one finds value and values which are in a state of non-being (negativity), present within the structure of the object-images, within that of the financial markets (the

Stock Market), within that of the acting consciousness, i.e. within the structure of the project in its terminal phase of gestation, when it has become a project and is ready for impact, when it has almost entered into the material form of physical reality. One pillar (to be in a state of non-being) involves the Subject to such an extent that it is the result of the act; this pillar of the value is closely linked to the Subject's action as a central point of economics, of everything. The other pillar requires that we go and see what may be constructed over and beyond the Subject which allows that which lies beyond or below its own action to approach it, and in what manner.

5. BEYOND (WITH) THE SUBJECT

§ 54.   By constructing an economic and financial theory over and beyond the Subject, without eliminating the Subject (it cannot be the Subject, since it is in play) and while preserving the field of the consciousness and the reference frame, one makes it a point of reception (and action) rather than simply the point of action on the world. The critical issue is to move the approach discussed in our theory of the Subject off-centre to some extent (a Subject which allows what *is* to approach it, rather than, simply and in one sole direction, a process which transforms reality, the world and physical reality which is also a process for determining value or values); to do so whilst also preserving what has been acquired by the description made of the modes of operation and structure of the consciousness (duration, memory and forgetfulness) and of the financial markets. In fact, one is trying to clarify – if indeed it is possible to do so? – the essential elements of the global economic and financial process as described, the sequences (imaging consciousness/ market and finance; acting consciousness/physical reality and aspect), the key concepts of the reference frame. To preserve this acquisition while considering *action* and the determination of *value* in a different manner. This is the critical issue: can the economic Subject which has been introduced by the modern era, as central and with infinite power, be surpassed (which is not the same as being eliminated)? How should one consider the (economic) act and therefore the economic process of transformation, projection and anticipation, by moving the Subject somewhat off-centre (which means giving less importance to the project of negativity, i.e. of transformation of reality by the Subject's design) and therefore giving slightly more importance to the world, to physical reality, to that which *is*, even before the Subject's intervention? By giving slightly more importance as well to that which, within the Subject's intervention (impact), means that the action – and ultimately the economic reality which emerges from the global economic process as we have stated – falls within a perspective of entirety and plenitude of that which is, over and above the sole, continuous and infinite quest for transformation. To save both the economic Subject *and* the reality of that which is; to bring the global process of economics and finance (resulting from the consciousness and its reference frames, extended or rather projected onto and by the financial markets, ultimately led by the imaging consciousness towards the impact with physical reality and the world for its transformation which assumes the status of economic reality), within a possible regulation, i.e. a regulation which includes and therefore takes into account the particular features of the key elements of this process as we have described it, a regulation which places the economic Subject in a more balanced relationship with the world, with reality, physical reality, and also with the object/objects of its designs so that the resulting economic reality may find another balance, a regulation which tries to show the perspectives or indeed the limits to the essential processes of the production of image-objects, of anticipations, of projections, ultimately of the project itself in its pre-material form prior to impact, which accordingly tries to show the perspectives to finance and to the financial markets (the form of the Stock Market in general) and therefore to the processes of organisation, valuation and selection of the image-objects, which constitute the tasks of finance, to show the perspectives for the preparation of value, understood as that which will come to be in the modern process (that which will be changed or transformed by the Subject).

The theory of the Subject still remains that of the ascent and the empowerment of the Subject in the modern age, as we have shown in *Tractatus*, *Généalogie* and *Valeur et temps*. The taking over of the control of the world by the conscious Subject defines modern economics (economics is indeed the very name of this movement). This means that any theory of the economic Subject is drawn into this framework which defines it. This also means that this theory must however try to tear itself away from this modern approach and determination in order to establish economic reality as a product of a global economic action process which includes finance, and establish this beyond the Subject as an absolute central issue and point of unilateral constructions, but together with the Subject – in particular based on the use of the acts of consciousness which constitute a mental or psychological world which we have called a reference frame and whose features of space and time are established.

§ 55.   Although it can be seen quite clearly what the phrase "together with the Subject" may mean – by adopting the essential paths of the process which we have described from the interplay of consciousnesses prior to the process – it is less clear in the case of the dynamic elements which move the Subject away from the centre, "beyond" the Subject. It is however a path which should still be favoured and which we should try to take: to identify, describe, determine the modes of being which dominate and which approach the Subject (as compared to a central Subject which approaches the object, whether or not such object has been constituted, i.e. real or still unreal, in order to imprint its trace of value on it) by constituting the same structure of the economic Subject and its project. These modes of being may be found within the reference frame of the consciousness, within physical reality, whether or not the latter has been transformed. It is a question of establishing that the project which structures the economic act, from the unitary cells of the image-objects which structures the start of the process up until impact, includes something other than transforming anti-matter (inexistence, the negativity/liberty which sets the value), that there is space within the genesis of the economic action dynamic for the integration of that which is. And this has to occur without eliminating the freedom of capacity to imagine, project, create and act which are concealed by the consciousness and its negativity. To integrate, when possible, such modes of being within a process which is essentially – i.e. in its essence – marked by negativity, must enable economic and financial processes which may seem to be delivered to the Subject or to themselves to be ascribed to contingency and chance, to ascribe perspectives (meanings, which may also be limits to that which the economic action may achieve and also the Subject).

§ 56.   The modes of being provide above all an opportunity to create *standards* for economics and finance. On what bases should one establish the principles of regulation (the limits of meaning, which are also limits on action) if not on that which underlies the action of the conscious Subject beyond that which the Subject is? The monetary or market standards cannot ignore – within the context of an effective regulation – the structure, the key elements, the operation of specific reference frames which are not those of clock time or of playing fields (football pitches), by way of example, which are not those of logical reasoning in the form in which we present it: the monetary and market standards cannot ignore them and, quite to the contrary, must include such specific features (for example, the discontinuities which are specific to the mental space/time pairing) and certain of their concepts (such as duration, memory, forgetfulness). This can only be conducted on the basis of an understanding of the mechanisms which highlight the underlying sources of the phenomena (duration, memory, forgetfulness...), the processes by which the financial and real dimensions, the volumes of activity and price are established, and the imbalances which may be a feature of such phenomena and processes. This is what we showed in *Théorie*. Ignoring the above can lead to excesses which cause imbalances. When the regulation is clearly understood, one should be able to determine the standards on the basis of such phenomena and processes, by targeting the determination and preservation of relative equilibria (in the sense in which we have defined this important concept) which are defined in relation to the dimensions which are characteristic of the specific phenomena and processes which have been discussed and which we have described.

The apparent economic, and especially, financial (market) disorder – which is not only a matter of appearance – should not discourage one from seeking solid bases for standards which preserve a series of equilibria which are at least relative (i.e. as compared to a certain number of regularities which order the phenomena of economics and finance). The apparent disorder indeed highlights regularities which have been inadequately researched and used for the purposes of regulation. The greater part of the resources for research and analysis are exhausted as a result of the unproductive reliance on phenomena which are not relevant (see *Fondements*); since they produce very poor results, this serves as a pretext for the deduction that disorder and lack of comprehension – therefore the impossibility of introducing standards and of regulating – are in fact inevitable.

However, it is possible to base regulation on standards which are themselves tied to operating modes which can be described and identified and which are located at the heart of what can be called a regime. This is possible provided that observation accepts what we have demonstrated above and in earlier works (*Théorie, Fondements*), namely that the immediacy of a phenomenon and the pure, immediate, contemporary data only contain a small amount of information which, in turn, is located in a temporal dimension which is structured by duration, memory and forgetfulness and a mental, spatial dimension where the speed depends upon memory and forgetfulness; namely that there are mental or psychological reference frames which have a specific manner of operating and which contain image-objects which possess DNA, an identity of information relating to time (duration, memory, forgetfulness and the mental space discussed). These two axes may provide references on which regulation can be based.

There is a difficulty. It can be seen, as we have emphasised above, that regulation seems to necessitate, require a rule, a regularity and the term "standard" itself refers to this. However, the economic and financial phenomena highlighted in our works are based on operating modes which include interruptions and leaps. Consequently, it seems impossible to base regulation on "regularity" within a universe of variations. This difficulty must and may be overcome by the essential fact that the economic and financial modes of operation described in our works *form a regime* in the sense that the variations or discontinuities recur in a meaningful manner, even if such meaning may seem unpredictable. It is possible to describe such reference regimes. Moreover, the importance given to duration or to memory presents a wide field of blocks of duration which are more or less strongly or completely memorised and which contain references, almost regularities. The variation is memorised and its memory ends up having certain similarities with a form of regularity. Good knowledge of these reference regimes, of what we have called the reference frames, is a requirement for anyone who wants to found rules, including where such regimes are based on significant discontinuities.

§ 57.   It should be stated that balances, at least relative balances, exist, which are based on a better understanding of the phenomena and their workings. Given this, a "normative" approach on which regulation may be based becomes possible, and such a "standard" incorporates the variations and recurrences – which may be unpredictable – of an economic and financial regime for which this is the rule. It is a delicate exercise, since to state the Stock Market is irrational or incomprehensible or simply unpredictable/contingent, and then to state that it calls for a "normative regulation" are two contradictory statements. This is why, first, the *meaning* of the financial (and more generally, the economic) world must be preserved, i.e. as we relentlessly tried to do (see, in particular, *Théorie, Fondements*), by showing that there are paths and angles of comprehension of the Stock Market and of economics provided that one uses the special reference frames which are not the usual points of reference, nor those of clock time or the playing fields as we have often stated. By preserving the *meaning* of the financial world, one also preserves the possibility of regulating it, and this is true of economics in the global sense of the Subject's relationship with the world and physical reality, which encompasses finance. Also by demonstrating, which is a second difficulty, that meaning and a certain form of chance may coexist in this specific universe, that what is irregular or discontinuous may constitute the norm and not an aberration and may, therefore, be incorporated within a normative search process.

Variations or abnormalities represent such numerous recurrences that we have shown that they were not aberrations but inverted quasi-regularities, i.e. "normal" regimes which describe the financial reality, and more generally the economic reality, in a credible manner. Variations, discontinuities and leaps form an integral part of the mode of operation of the reference frames resulting from the imaging and acting consciousnesses and are present within the whole of the economic action process from the financial phase up until impact with physical reality. This means that the regulation must be based on these realities and extract from the same the quasi-regular or recurrent forms or forms which can be located: these are the forms which may provide pillars of reference.

That said, although variations, discontinuities and leaps constitute the DNA of economics and finance (we mean by this one or more structures which include an identity and operating method), they are also, at least in part, the product of practices by the various actors which, by themselves, or of themselves, created the variation or added to it. "Practices" are understood to mean all the decision-making modes relating to economics and finance (valuation, regulation, simulation…), ranging from the individual decision relating to a market of goods, shares or services up to the collective act of general, economic policy. Certain such practices, or indeed many, have ignored, or continue to ignore the underlying workings of the financial world (financial markets) and economics which we have analysed and the impact of such practices, which often fails to achieve its objective, creates a commotion. This means all initiatives such as a regulatory policy (monetary, budgetary policy, body of macro-economic policies) based on tools and indicators, which bear witness to a true consideration of the various dimensions, which we have advanced (reference frames, duration, memory, forgetfulness…), an analysis of the financial markets (see *Fondements de la dynamique boursière*) which does likewise and runs counter to the usual practices which use up resources in research which is inadequate, inappropriate or inexistent and an identification and construction of indicators of this type within all the fields of finance and economics, may hope to reduce the degree of variation, leaps or discontinuity to a lower level, which can be described as "natural".

Furthermore, there are reference points within the reference frame itself of variations and discontinuities. The two propositions are not incompatible. Such reference points, as we have seen, often stem from the density of duration and the phenomena of memory which enable a relative balance to be defined for some or other economic or financial variable referring to a block of duration which is more or less stable. Provided that the reference frames of economics and finance are structured on the basis of such dimensions, it is possible to determine points of reference. In the same way, the discontinuities in speeds of circulation (of the image-objects, anticipations and money...) – which depend upon the rates of memory and forgetfulness, and the link between the mental space and psychological time – may be understood and certain assumptions regarding the reference dimensions may be made, which will be used to determine relative points of balance for the regulatory acts.

It is by first accepting the idea that the variation is the rule and the abnormal the norm on the financial markets (or finance) in particular and economics in general, that one can then show the modes of operation of these atypical universes – i.e. essentially the meaning which drives them –, and that one can finally construct rules which, *inter alia*, will have the effect of reducing the number of variations with discontinuities, and even eliminate certain of them.

§ 58.   Let us return to the question of what a theory of the economic Subject over and beyond the Subject actually means. It may mean, within the field of economic and financial phenomena, identifying that which – even though the force of the Subject's will seems to triumph completely over the world which sets the image-objects, the action, the transformation – nevertheless forms an inevitable part of this consciousness of the Subject, that which approaches the Subject (which, in turn, seems to move towards everything which has an insatiable appetite), because it forms part of that which *is* and therefore progresses towards the Subject, and that which is in a state of non-being.

This means that the description or understanding of the manners of appreciating the economic Subject's consciousness do not exhaust the question of what determines and directs the economic Subject: there is over and above the consciousness but, at the same time, within its innermost structure, a matter of being which continues to overhang the Subject's specific means of action. It is on the basis of such modes of being at work within the development of the conscious, economic Subject and within a profound understanding of the economic, financial and market phenomena that the work of drawing up standards (to standardise the abnormal, as we have seen, is the name of the exercise as we have seen it) and regulation becomes possible.

To accept without a fight the economic Subject's complete monopolization – which is an abandonment rather than a historical necessity since reflection shows that the economic Subject itself gives in to the modes of being which overcome it – is not only an intellectual renunciation for the reasons which we have just stated but an acceptance that it is impossible to standardise that which one continuously criticises as being "phenomenal". It should be asserted that economics and finance are in fact governed by the mental/psychological reference frames, together with a global process leading up to the economic act, which are characterised by variations, discontinuities and leaps which are so recurrent that they constitute the norm and not an aberration or exception. It should be asserted that such reference frames and this global process of economics and the financial world can be understood, described and appreciated by an appropriate analysis and are ruled by specific modes of operation (space/time, duration/memory/forget-fulness, image-objects...) which are not incomprehensible (variations and discontinuities are not necessarily incomprehensible). It should be asserted that such variations and discontinuities, once replaced and understood within the context of the reference frames where they appear, form *regimes* (a certain number of elements, links and principles which form a temporary "system"), where limited or relative forms of equilibria exist which are governed by a few reference variables which can be assessed and therefore standardised. It should be asserted that the "phenomenal" can be standardised. And the main functions of macro-economic regulation (monetary policy, budgetary policy, etc.) cannot ignore such references, if they are to achieve their own objectives in full and take part in the regulation of the forms which intermediate their acts like the financial markets. Finally, other functions apart from these macro-economic functions are also involved (and remain essential, in particular monetary regulation, since this controls in particular the passage of the imaging consciousness to the financial markets within and by means of the production of image-objects of projection and anticipation, all within the global action process of economic transformation described above).

§ 59.   The analysis of the structures of the economic Subject's cons-ciousness has shown that the temporal and spatial reference frame, within which takes place the interplay of the consciousness, over-determines the Subject's interplay. The economic Subject is expressed within a context of imagination and action whose determining factors and foundations overcome it, traverse it and irrigate it. The determining factors which are beyond the Subject proceed within what we have called the "reference frame", such determining factors being the modes of being and therefore the foundations for the reference frames and, in general, for the global economic action process.

Determining elements *approach* the economic Subject, like duration. In our work, memory and forgetfulness are in turn the levers for the distortion of the essential, spatio-temporal matter which is duration. However, at the same time, memory is, for example, also matter which is given form by the Subject's direct consciousness. Time-matter is given form by the economic Subject's immediate consciousness (space/ time-matter to be more precise). The fundamental and final space/time-matter is duration. Duration may be *given form* (that which is given form is distorted, there lies the origin of the economic and financial dynamic through the information/distortion of mental *reference frames* which act as a matrix for practical forms such as the financial markets or the macro-financial regimes or economic regimes), and duration may therefore be given form by the consciousness. In this context, memory and forgetfulness may be considered as forms of stimulation/ information of the consciousness or as elements of the space/time-matter which are given form by the consciousness. Memory and forgetfulness have this dual status within our work which reflects their role as flow/stock, as a point of passage for electricity within the process. That said, it should be borne in mind that memory and forgetfulness are one and the same from the point of view of space-time matter: there is a unitary reality with two facets, one remembers in the same way one forgets, one anticipates and one projects in the same way one remembers and/or forgets, one moves within the reference frame of image-objects (structures which contain the projected, anticipated forms of the economic act) more or less quickly depending upon how deeply one remembers or forgets. There is a unitary reality of memory/ forgetfulness (*M/F* as noted in our work) which is both matter, given form/distorted by the immediate designs of the consciousness, and an influx of information/distortion directed towards duration. *M/F* is an intermediary form between space-time matter and the pure consciousness of the economic Subject.

Chapitre 3

THE OTHER

§ 60.   Up until now we have presented the Subject as a reference frame of an individual consciousness, a specific reference frame from the point of view *inter alia* of the dimensions of space and time, within an economic and financial action process of the individual Subject, proceeding from the production-conception of image-objects, passing through the place of work, selection and preparation-gestation of the image-objects (financial market phase), up until the ultimate phase of impact with the world – a set of things which are provided and others which are the result of a series of impacts – an impact which itself has a feedback effect on the production-conception of future image-objects, thus coming full circle.

We have therefore presented the individual Subject as a unique and solitary consciousness. However, the purely individual economic Subject is, at all times, subject to the structuring viewpoint of the Other. The economic Subject cannot be considered independently from the Other and, henceforth, the discipline of economics and finance cannot ignore, in its theory of the Subject, the fundamental dimension of otherness, a dimension which structures the consciousness itself (all consciousness is consciousness *of*, a projection-anticipation which is based on the negativity which represents the contents of the project since it always involves imagining, conceiving that which is in a state of non-being). We stressed this point in *Tractatus* and in *Généalogie*.

§ 61.   The Subject, which is to some extent solitary and pure, as we have seen, adopts at least two faces within economics and finance: the individual Subject; the collective Subject (i.e. the institution, the organisation, the community). These two forms of the economic and financial Subject constitute the dominant figures (on the one hand *homo economicus*, the economic agent and the market trader; on the other the government and the central bank, for example). These two forms of the Subject are watched over by the Other, which is a universe of other individual or collective consciousnesses. There are therefore two axes from the point of view of the consideration of the dimension of the Other within the structure and operation of the economic Subject: each economic Subject is consciousness (whether the said Subject is individual or collective as we have just seen) and in this respect is otherness (the project mode, which is stretched out towards that which is not, or is not yet, tearing the economic Subject out of itself, within the economic action process as discussed above); each economic Subject is immersed in a universe (which we will describe as a reference frame of otherness) inhabited by other forms of consciousness, whether individual or collective which each emit one or more signals at the end of their own economic action processes.

The Other introduces a relative dimension within the reference frame of forms of consciousness, a reference frame which gathers each consciousness as such and which may at the same time represent, in whole or in part, an aggregate or collective consciousness (accordingly, when one speaks *of the* market, one is referring in a certain manner to this reference frame-universe of multiple individual forms of consciousness in the sense in which we have defined them, i.e. in the two forms of the individual-person and the collective entity, i.e. the two main sources of the decision-making and economic action processes).

The Other therefore introduces a relative dimension, i.e. relative to that which the Other thinks. The act of the economic Subject, and consequently any economic and financial action process is structured and proceeds *in a relative fashion* to what the Other thinks. Economics and finance thus proceed within a reference frame of forms of consciousness which is ordered by relativity and driven by a dynamic which is specific to the reference frame. This specific dynamic of the reference frame of forms of consciousness constitutes the dimension which we currently intend to introduce to the overall diagram which we have presented. The Other is both a dimension of additional structure within the mode of operation of the economic Subject-consciousness and, above all, a dynamic resulting from the interplay within what we have called the reference frame of forms of consciousness. Our point here is that our overall diagram of the economic Subject is enriched by the otherness of an essential dimension but, above all, that the economic and financial dynamic cannot be fully reconstructed without taking into consideration the interactions and conflicts within the reference frame of forms of consciousness. The economic and financial dynamic is a relative dynamic of the forms of consciousness-Subjects.

Under the Other's gaze, the conflict erupts, which is an essential source of the economic dynamic. It concerns the conflict of the forms of consciousness in their two genetic forms, whether purely individual or collective (a person against the community, person against person, communities between themselves, in the sense that these two notions have been defined above). Since the project of any consciousness, which of its own motion moves out towards the project within the economic action process, will potentially intersect, use, hinder or destroy other projects-projections which come from other forms of consciousness within the reference frame. The Other is pure consciousness itself which is projected forwards of its own motion within the economic act, it is also what will hinder the project, will on the contrary be necessary for its completion (interaction and conflict of economic forms of consciousness), and is also, finally, as a strong form of the Other's viewpoint, known as value, that which counts or not or a little and how and for whom (the existence of a reference frame of forms of consciousness as we have described provides additional support for the conviction that value is fundamentally *relative*).

What is called the "economic Subject" must always either be assessed in relation to a reference frame of forms of consciousness or even be brought back and fully identified with this reference frame of forms of consciousness. The conflict of the forms of consciousness (of the economic Subject) is a conflict of projects, projections, states of non-being (negativity) which lie at the heart of the dynamic of the economic action process, starting with the conception of image-objects. The conflict of forms of consciousness, which is involved in the economic Subject's dynamic, is a conflict of image-objects. This means that the Other is either that which may enter in advance the structure of an image-object which is intended for a project and therefore supports the economic action or it is the *other* image-object, the image-object which acts as support for the project and for the action which enters into conflict with a support for the action stemming from a different consciousness.

§ 62.   In our general theoretical diagram, we have shown that finance, and particularly the form of the financial market, were places (in the physical sense but also in the sense of a moment of the Subject's consciousness within the economic action process) of confrontation, sorting, gestation and assessment of the image-objects. Such a definition is invaluable since it shows that finance can be explored as a form and institution (place) where the conflicts of the forms of consciousness of economic Subjects gathered. This gathering is symbolic since the financial market organises the management of conflicts of the individual forms of consciousness as an efficient phase within the economic action process, as a symbolic form which distances material violence, as an objectification-decision of the conflict of the Subjects-forms of consciousness without which the economic action process cannot proceed. The financial market is the symbolic place of management for image-objects which are in conflict, and accordingly for conflicts between forms of consciousness.

1. *BEAUTY CONTEST*, CONSENSUS

Consequently one is not surprised by the general importance of beauty contests in the consideration of the operation of financial markets and, in general, of economics. It is not, as Keynes suggested, a matter of understanding the substance of things but the relative dimension constituted by the image-object which is conceived for or around the things in question. And an infinite number of image-objects are produced by an infinite number of forms of consciousness within the reference frame which is being discussed. The beauty contest is the management of the conflict between forms of consciousness through the image-objects. Moreover, together with the beauty contest, the more serious concept of anticipation is also involved, which lies at the heart of the economic and financial dynamic. Anticipation is always a certain accumulation of the anticipations of others. If anticipation is also (especially on the financial markets) anticipation of what others anticipate (beauty contests), or at least the confrontation of each individual anticipation (i.e. each unitary consciousness) in a place of conflict management, then the financial market appears in its role of structuring the management of conflicts between forms of cons-ciousness, which are the conflicts between image-objects and therefore between anticipations.

The volatility of the financial markets and, in general, the volatility of the economic variables and elements, which are based upon anticipation, or the image-object as support for the action, can consequently all be explained by the fragmentation of the forms of consciousness, the impossibility of a pure and unitary vision of the Subject, which is always outside itself and in conflict with the projects of others, confrontations organised by the financial market and which brand the economic event or economic action. As such, one would be right in thinking that volatility or commotion, which are often criticised for their irrationality and excess, with regard to the financial market and economics, are perhaps ultimately only an "abnormal" form of nor-mality which is specific to economics and finance: the process of managing conflicts between the forms of consciousness corresponds to an underlying logic, although its progression may be preceded or accompanied by apparently irrational commotions, excess and forms. If the Stock Market gives such an impression; it is because it is the Stock Market which is tasked with the selection-improvement of the image-objects and conflicts. However, there are no conflicts without commotions. This is perhaps one of the origins of Stock Market commotions. There is therefore a link between the economic and financial dynamic and, second, the identification of a reference frame of the individual and collective forms of consciousness, which is specific and relative in nature, a dynamic of interactions and conflicts within the reference frame and numerous aspects of volatility and of "abnormal" distribution of events. The apparently unorganised, irrational and incomprehensible nature of the financial and economic phenomena may consequently become coherent and logical within the dynamic of the reference frame of forms of consciousness.

§ 63.   We have stated how closely the figure of otherness, of the Other, in economics and finance, was integrated with anticipation (when we say closely, this means the very structure of the economic Subject's consciousness, which is anticipation-negativity of projection), and that this anticipation was not only mixed together with the anticipations of other Subjects (adopting purely individual or collective forms) within a reference frame, but also led to anticipate that which the other forms of consciousness anticipate or may anticipate and that which constitutes a way of posing the issue of conflict between forms of consciousness; the latter often takes the economic and financial form of a beauty contest, a conflictual market of valuation and selection of image-objects (the principal support for the anticipation within the economic action process managed by the Subject-consciousness), a definition, when all is said and done, of the financial market and of finance in general.

The whole interplay, which is important in economics and finance, of the identification of "consensus" (this theme leads us beyond, towards the more political form of contemporary society, which we are not considering here), consists of integrating the Other, of anticipating anticipation, i.e. specifically of designing the image-objects which have (had) access to the production-conception of the Other's image-objects, have (had) access to what the Other thinks. The form of the *Market* is to a fairly large extent the symbolic place where one finds what the Other thinks, from a static viewpoint. "Consensus" is itself a collective form of the Subject which aims to make a Subject of the *Market* as such, a unitary (the only?) form which emerges with some difficulties and contradictions from the reference frame of forms of consciousness. The emergence of the Market as a symbolic, unitary form also constitutes an attempt to manage conflicts which are fundamentally specific to the multipolar structure of the fragmented reference frame of forms of consciousness. This management creates a commotion, which lies at the very core of the observation of economic and financial phenomena, the counterparty of a largely symbolic management of violence (the image-objects of economic and financial space-time are in a state of non-being, pure negativities in the state of anticipation and of projects, and not yet firm or solid objects and events). Finance organises a form of management of the appeasement of conflicts between forms of consciousness; in any event, it constitutes a unitary formalisation and objectification of the reference frame of forms of consciousness of economic Subjects and of their conflicts, in a symbolic and peaceful fashion (it is the internalisation of violence), at the stage of image-objects where the *impact* with the world is being prepared.

§ 64.   From a static viewpoint, the market is that which the Other thinks (the *form* which is taken by that which the Other thinks, which may be available in an infinite number of series of anticipations of anti-cipations [...]). At the same time, the market is the Other, for each individual consciousness (i.e. the consensus, *the* market, the trend, etc.). The language of economics and finance includes numerous terms referring to this.

Two dynamic reasonings can be imagined. The first will be called cellular dynamics, in the sense that a cellular organism (i.e. the individual consciousness, whether of a person/individual or a com-munity, as we have stated) is, as it were, attacked from outside (having entered under the Other's notice). This external attack sets in motion a dynamic of conflictual interaction within an extended reference frame of forms of consciousness whilst the original reference frame of the individual consciousness, i.e. (the *cell*), itself enters a process of dis-tortion, dilation and contraction which may, among other issues, lead to the rejection of that which constitutes an external DNA, to the integration of such DNA within the first cell together with mutation of the first DNA, to the destruction of the cell by that which appears afterwards, a form of virus. Such distortion processes are temporal processes (non-linear contractions/dilations within a specific space-time) and create commotion (volatility, unexpected interruptions and magnitudes which are accompanied by accelerations). Our point here is that the very special features of space-time and commotion which we have emphasised with regard to financial, market or, in general, economic phenomena, depend in particular (i.e. can be explained in part by) the irruption of the Other within the field of the economic Subject's individual consciousness, this Other, as we have shown, being another individual consciousness (i.e. another person or another community), an individual economic Subject (the individual, the person) or collective economic Subject (the State, the government, the central bank, the IMF, etc.), or the whole of the reference frame of forms of consciousness (the whole of the Other for each individual consciousness), i.e. what is often called *the* Market.

§ 65.   The fundamentally specific features of finance and economics, of space-time and commotion, are strongly linked to the consideration of the Other within the field of the economic Subject's individual consciousness. A proper understanding of economic and financial phenomena is obtained through awareness of the radical limits of an economic Subject which is alone in the world and so pure that it does not exist; by expanding the specific reference frame to all forms of consciousness, while accepting the idea that the cellular structure itself of each individual consciousness (its DNA, i.e. all the image-objects which we have seen are essential to the action process and that inhabit the financial market) is subject to the Other's viewpoint and the design. This is the price for a better knowledge of the phenomena.

The distortion process of the original cellular organism once it enters the Other's "action" field is destabilising and creates commotion; there is an imbalance until a new equilibrium (which is relative, limited in the sense in which we defined this type of equilibrium in *Théorie*) develops or is established, therefore opening up at least two options.

The relative, limited equilibrium is established, temporarily, with the determination of the "consensus", from among the terms which are most frequently used in the operation of the financial markets, which bestows a certain stability on the cellular organisms which we have discussed above, after a phase of external pressure and attack from the Other (i.e. from the other individual cells which are present within the reference frame of forms of consciousness). This particular moment of the economic and financial cycle when one talks of consensus, which vanishes as soon as one pronounces the word and perhaps even before that, represents a point of relative stability, a point which is elusive and fragile where, within the reference frame of forms of consciousness (individual economic Subjects), after a phase of conflicts and interactions which are more or less aggressive and which we have described (distortions-mutations phase of unitary cells and their DNA), therefore after a phase of pronounced economic and financial *dynamics* (the dynamic becomes identified with the conflictual interactions between unitary cellular organisms within the reference frame of forms of consciousness), there is a calmer, more linear period, which is scarcely a point, since this point is in turn rapidly attacked, thus creating a fresh imbalance, a new dynamic within the reference frame of forms of consciousness-economic Subjects, up until a new evasive point (of consensus) is reached, and so on. Such small evasive points are micro-moments when a semblance of linearity (the perception of linearity, of equilibrium, of stability which accompanies consensus and which is experienced as such) may reign within a universe which is however governed, as we have seen, by imbalance and discontinuities.

The relative, limited equilibrium may, also, be restored or established, not by the, to some extent normal, interaction of forces within the reference frame of the forms of consciousness-economic Subjects, but by the intervention of economic policy as a result of the act of a Subject which intervenes (State, central bank, for example). It may be necessary for the economic policy action to set the DNA of some or other unitary cellular organism (or some group of unitary cellular organisms), or to stabilise. This objective, to anchor generally such an individual or group consciousness, which lies within the global reference frame of the forms of consciousness (of economic Subjects) is all the more justified at such a moment in the cycle, since, if left to itself, the market can only attain the cellular stability of forms of consciousness and therefore of the various forms of the economic Subject on an exceptional basis.

§ 66.   The stabilising anchorage of forms of consciousness within the global reference frame of the figures of the economic Subject may take various forms when it forms the objective of the economic policy action (for example, the *anchoring of anticipations*, a generic and essential term of economic policy actions, and particularly of monetary policies, corresponds to the stabilisation objective of that which we have called the DNA of the reference frame of a conscious economic Subject, namely a set of image-objects which form the projection-conception of that which is to come and which supports the action).

The anchoring objective of the economic policy action is an objective for the alignment of the forms of consciousness (of economic Subjects), which opposes the freedom of forms of consciousness. The economic policy action can only achieve a form of stabilisation within the reference frame of forms of consciousness at the cost of a norm which, in one way or another, involves limiting the freedom of forms of consciousness or of such a consciousness, the regulation of an existing conflict which itself already drastically reduces the capacities for the conception of images-projects, of projection and anticipation, thus hampering both the action process and freedom.

The dynamic of the economic Subject which intervenes (State, central bank) in the determination of the norm, results in the identification and then the acceptance and imposition of a common DNA for all the individual forms of consciousness (persons and communities), i.e. one or more groups of image-objects which, as we have shown, can always be reduced to blocks of duration and memory cut out of the reference frame of forms of consciousness-Subjects and affected by a factor of forgetfulness.

2. SUPRA-CONSCIOUSNESS, THE MARKET

§ 67.   The market is accordingly that which the Other thinks (in the sense that the anticipations and image-objects of forms of consciousness may be accumulated and expressed, forming what we have called a reference frame of forms of consciousness) but which may be normalized by a collective consciousness (State, central bank...). We have also seen that the capacity to accumulate and express all the individual anticipations within the reference frame, therefore to make known the existence of a "consensus", is extremely limited by the persistence of the conflict as a fundamental form of the interaction between the individual forms of consciousness (individual or collective entities): the "consensus", the alignment of forms of consciousness, as has been stated, is an absolute exception, an evasive point of impossible equilibrium in a certain manner, an equilibrium which cannot be maintained; consequently, the existence of *an* anticipation of the market, more generally of *a* unitary consciousness of the reference frame of forms of consciousness which we would call "the market", such an existence may legitimately form the subject of serious doubts, over and above the methodological utility which it may procure. The imposition of the norm acts as a point of unification (a stitch) on a divided canvas, the solidity of which will be a function of the unification's capacity to use a solid structure (i.e. a matrix of variables listed within the duration-memory and forgetfulness which is specific to the reference frame) to confront the underlying destructive forces which are permanently at work within the reference frame of economic Subjects.

The market is the Other, an Other which is tormented by the continuous conflicts which constitute the mode of being and the operating mode of the reference frame of forms of consciousness. If the truth of the economic Subject is ultimately the multiplicity of the individual forms of consciousness, then the Other can only adopt a unitary face (*the* market) on an exceptional basis, since the conflict of free forms of consciousness immediately and continuously takes back the upper hand, within a dynamic of endless imbalance. In the same way, the imposition of the norm comes up against contrary forces which can only be frustrated for a time by anchoring the norm to that which, within such forces, comes from the remotest and deepest part of that which lasts within them and which is remembered by the individual forms of consciousness to a greater or lesser extent (forgetfulness).

Finally, although the theoretical possibility of a unitary supra-consciousness established as a total or totalising economic Subject remains problematic, in particular due to the constant conflict with the freedom (in the sense of the essential capacity to conceive image-objects and of projection-anticipation within the action process) of the individual forms of consciousness, assuming that such a total, unitary consciousness is conceived, then the said unitary consciousness-economic Subject, called "market", would undoubtedly be haunted by an unconscious (i.e. all that which is buried within duration-memory, forgotten to certain extents and which eludes the clear consciousness, at least on a provisional basis). There is an analogy between the unconscious and that which has been forgotten, since the initial duration, but which continues to produce its effect and to follow its path (and any individual consciousness is undoubtedly aware of this concealed area where that which has been forgotten but nevertheless continues to last, remains masked, representing the paradoxical status of the economic Subject's unconscious consciousness).

The market can be seen as a unitary supra-consciousness or as being unconscious of the individual forms of consciousness (the Other of the Other), two extreme visions. Modern reality, at least that of perceptions, fluctuates between the personalisation of the market, a totalising consciousness which cannot fail ("the market is always right"), which is without doubt the origin of the theory of efficiency and the market as the great "Id", a grey zone of irrationality and the unconscious which offers a specific reference frame of space-time, nature and operating mode to human consciousness, in the manner of an inverting and distorting mirror. One cannot help but be struck by the switch between the identity established in the first instance, "market = right", and the obscurity and incomprehensibility of the second, a theory which is no less popular than that of efficiency and which refers the market, often at times of crises, back to the public obloquy of that which, literally, cannot be imagined, cannot therefore be expressed or therefore normalized.

In short, one retains the idea of an attempted constitution of the market as a unitary, collective consciousness (i.e. a unity of the reference frame of forms of consciousness) (i.e. that which the Other thinks), a paradoxical consciousness since, at the same time, there is a form of unconscious of the market, a negative of the world, which reveals itself with a degree of commotion and within a very specific reference frame. The market may be seen, in a certain manner, as the place where a certain unconscious, a set of facts, things, objects, events and image-objects which, as we have seen, structure economics and finance, (i.e. the economic action process from the function of financial imagination (production-conception of image-objects) up until the impact with the world), is rendered visible, legible or more comprehensible, whether in whole or in part, surrenders to a consciousness, to an awareness; the market as a process of awareness of that which is buried or forgotten but which has not ceased to be there within duration.

We can recognise our essential points and axes: duration, memory and forgetfulness for the specific space-time reference frames, whether in relation to the individual consciousness or the reference frame of forms of consciousness, a much larger universe for which the market *could* constitute the unitary form, together with the limits, interrogations and paradoxes which we have just discussed.

§ 68.   We have shown that the "beauty contest", which is often referred to by theoretical writers, could be analysed on the basis of the conflictual interaction of the individual forms of consciousness whose fundamental support is the anticipation, understood as the set of image-objects conceived by the financial and economic imaginary world of the economic Subject's consciousness and which forms the basis of the projection within the action process. The conflictual interaction of the forms of consciousness-economic Subjects is the interaction of anticipations (*inter alia* to anticipate the anticipation) which, as we have seen, can at all times and in all places, be reduced to that which remains, in the present, of a block of past memory traversed by forgetfulness. During the "beauty contest", when one anticipates what the other forms of consciousness are thinking or anticipating (negativity of negativity), one in fact identifies, collectively within the general interaction, that which each and every one remembers and also that which has been forgotten, the block of duration shared by all the individual forms of consciousness, participants in the process within what we have called the reference frame of forms of consciousness. The market may consequently be understood as the place where that which lasts (and is therefore forgotten) is established as a general reference frame (hence the conflictual interaction of the forms of consciousness-economic Subjects, which helps explain the volatility, commotion and special features of space and time).

§ 69.   We have up until now tried to show how the Other fits into the economic Subject's action process and, in particular, how it fits into the interplay of the Subject's specific reference frame. We have not tried to describe the interrelation which is created between the forms of consciousness which form the genetic economic Subject, whether from a psychological, behavioural or moral viewpoint. A certain number of works on so-called behavioural finance have tried to ascribe words and concepts to certain interrelations. This is true of "the human demand for fairness" function. Such approaches – which are of interest, since they attempt to incorporate the Other in a fundamental manner within a reference frame of forms of consciousness and modes of interrelation, which are no longer those of a pure economic Subject, alone in the world – tend, however, with some degree of haste, to mix without any great sorting process or explanation that which may actually form part of the reference frame of a moral code (which, as we have stated, we distinguish from the norm, although a convergence is conceivable; we will come back to this later), of an act of conduct which is more or less secured to a long, settled practice or of a psychological feature which is supposed to describe *homo economicus* from time immemorial, at least within the reference frame where the action occurs.

Without challenging the relevance of such possible approaches, the mixed nature of the presentations which are made (moral, behavioural or psychological) creates a pronounced ambiguity and a real problem in identifying the issues and in constructing a global analysis matrix which will apply to all the potential depictions of interrelations in the interaction created between the forms of consciousness and between "*homo economicus*" in the plural sense since, as we have seen, a large part of the economic and financial dynamic stems from the fact that *homo economicus* is not alone in the world and, even if he were, like Robinson Crusoe on his island, he would continue to be haunted by the Other.

This is true of the function named "the human demand for fairness" attributed by Schiller and others to the famous animal spirits which we have already discussed, which advances a seductive explanation of the inflexibilities in the reduction of nominal wages (the wage is a function of that which is deemed to be equitable – fair – by the employee) and, consequently, of unemployment, if the wage is for this reason set below the wage which is said to represent an equilibrium. It is not clear whether it is a question of morality or conduct (global conceptual framework) nor how the relationship with the Other within this framework, which may be conflictual, is structured (structure of the interrelation of the forms of consciousness – economic Subjects).

3. THE OTHER'S VIEWPOINT, DURATION, *HABITUS*

§ 70.   Leaving aside, for the moment, the moral question, without denying the same, we advance the proposition that the global framework which governs the classification of the interrelations within the reference frame of forms of consciousness is based on what can be named *"habitus"* which, in our approach, is essentially defined by a trace of duration and memory which is more or less deep-set and which is accompanied by a dynamic (memory recalls and lapses). This *habitus*, which is a form of bodily sedimentation of practice, facts, events and objects (the blocks of duration on which we have founded our analysis) governs a form of classification of the interrelation of forms of consciousness (here being equity, fairness). All the classifications may fall within this principle of government but each interrelation presents an insurmountably specific aspect linked to the habitus which is unique to each individual consciousness, the individual or interpersonal reference frames within which such consciousness evolves (the unique nature of the DNA of each economic Subject-consciousness).

There is accordingly a representation of the fairness of a wage, a form of *habitus*, a section cut out of duration together with a memory which is itself accompanied by a factor of (slow) change and also of forgetfulness. This function of duration, memory recall and lapse expresses an interrelation within the reference frame of economic forms of consciousness (there is a certain level of wage *for everyone*, which corresponds to a certain definition of a task and which satisfies an appropriate criterion of fairness, both for the individual consciousness and for the others). The consideration of the Other as guarantor of a *habitus* (it is subject to the Other's view and the view of all the others that the idea may emerge that, within duration and memory which can be mobilised or is mobilised at the time the question is raised, there is a link between the level of a nominal wage and fairness).

The description of interrelation is therefore based on a *habitus* of duration, memory recall and lapse, as well as on a symbolic function adopted by an instrumental variable (here, in this case, the wage). In our example, the wage contains the symbol of fairness. It will be said that since the interrelation of the forms of consciousness-economic Subjects may be governed by a *habitus* of fairness corresponding to a certain regime-reference frame of duration, memory recall and lapse (which in principle shows a certain inertia, but which evolves and may experience sudden interruptions and discontinuities), it is possible that this regime may explain the inflexibility in the reduction of certain wages; the duration which is unique to *habitus* dominates the purely rational reasoning which would lead one to accept reductions in order to avoid an increase in unemployment (the inflexibility occurs in the name of all, of the others even if it ends up producing negative effects for everyone, in this instance for unemployment). The "extra-wage" of those who retain their job in times of crisis, and which increases the overall unemployment, may however come within another description of interrelation; rather than fairness, the egotistical protection of he who knows himself to be lucky not to have been affected by the crisis may also explain inflexibilities in wages and the rise in unemployment in times of crisis without a possible adjustment by the wage which is said to represent equilibrium. Here we have a conflictual version of the interrelation of forms of consciousness where the Other is the one which threatens the wage and the job: the conflict between forms of consciousness then explains the imbalance on the employment market and the incapacity of the wage to resolve it. The symbolic, instrumental variable of the wage is in this instance no longer the apparently positive otherness of fairness but rather the otherness of conflict. In both cases, we exclude the moral qualification and instead try to show that it is the form of the *habitus* which is at work (i.e. of the duration, memory recall and lapse which manage, at any given time, to fix a representation, behaviour or judgement by producing an economic effect). In both cases, the relationship with the Other, in what we have named the reference frame of forms of consciousness, is an interplay whether it relates to the description of fairness or to the more conflictual egoism.

§ 71.   Economics and finance are structured by the interrelations of the forms of consciousness-Subjects. These interrelations, over and beyond the behavioural, psychological or moral forms and expressions which they may possibly adopt and which are in particular given to them, ultimately come within the regimes of *habitus*, the stability of which is not a given, DNA embedded in the dense sections of time (i.e. of duration, memory and forgetfulness). *Homo economicus* is completely involved in its relations with the Other from which it inherits (duration, memory) before anything else, i.e. before being possibly able to modify it. This reality precedes any psychological, behavioural or moral description, within the economic Subject's mode of being.

Any economic action and, consequently, any economic fact, object or event is carried out subject to the Other's inspection. As such, the idea of a pure economic Subject alone in the world is a vision of the mind. As a result, any serious work must report on what is effected subject to the Other's inspection and which, as it were, originates from the Other. Since, as a result of this inspection by the Other, it must be possible to describe that which seems to lead, direct or determine the economic action process and which originates from the interaction with other individual forms of consciousness. It is therefore a matter of describing that which seems to govern the economic phenomena, like a set of laws resulting from the interaction and more generally from otherness. Such fragile recurrences seem to stem from some trait of human nature, occasionally running counter to what reason would recommend (as in the example of nominal wage inflexibilities), hence the temptation to read into it perpetual laws of psychology, behaviour or morality. We believe that such (fragile) recurrences structure the fields or reference frames of economics and finance and in this respect play a determining role in the action processes of the economic Subjects which are involved. Such recurrent structures of relations with the Other are made up of underlying time, i.e. of duration. This innermost matter within which, for each regime, field or reference frame, the economic facts, events and objects, the action processes which have already been effected or have already occurred subject to the Other's inspection, have been imprinted in the same way one remembers or forgets, means that there is, with regard to one and the same event, for example the attitude to wages and employment in time of crisis, the possibility of resorting to a function of fairness or, on the contrary, to a function of uncertain satisfaction in order to explain the existence of an "extra-wage" for those who retain a job and who resist: mobility, but at the same time, the observation of a certain recurrence of the characteristic as if it came from far away, a habit. This *habitus*, whose innermost matter is duration, forges what seem to form the laws for an economic Subject's action, and which, like all fields and reference frames of economics and finance, are relative to a certain number of elements whose stability and continuity are not established for all times and all places.

The blocks of raw duration which form the innermost, essential matter of economics and finance, are "given form" by memory (and by forgetfulness) in respect of all the relations with the Other, and these relations have left traces which are more or less pronounced within the wax of such blocks of duration, which memory and forgetfulness alternatively reheat or cool down. The economic Subject's relationship with the Other is engraved, like DNA, within the matter-duration which forms the innermost structure of the reference frame of economic and financial action, apparently recorded in the same way as a law. The economic Subject acts, at all times and places, subject to the Other's inspection and the structure of its action always contains a trace, like DNA, of the memory of the relations between the forms of consciousness, whether peaceful or conflictual. This DNA, which evolves slowly, may be traversed by flashes of lightning within blue skies: the interruption of the regimes of duration and of the memory of the modes of interrelation of individual forms of consciousness (economic Subjects) constitutes one of the sources of explanation for what is called an economic and/or financial crisis.

§ 72.   An economic Subject only exists in the midst of other economic Subjects and the economic Subject of the economic and financial theory presents a structure which is "for-others". This indicates first, that as a consciousness which is fundamentally open to that which is to pass and to be done, the economic Subject is at all times and in all places in projection beyond itself, towards that which is not yet, towards that which will perhaps never be, towards that which has been conceived of or imagined (image-object) with regard to a project and anticipation which constitute the essential supports for the economic action process: as such, the economic Subject is in its essence open to something other, towards the Other, and the otherness constitutes its innermost structure. It is this structure of otherness of the Subject-consciousness which irrigates all the economic and financial phenomena, concepts and institutions. The economic Subject's structure of otherness is sustained by negativity (i.e. the capacity of the economic Subject-consciousness to obliterate), (i.e. to project, conceive and imagine in a state of non-being (not-yet-being), of that which is to pass). The image-objects, which are the primary productions of the Subject-consciousness, which are found in an organised form and on the financial markets, are completely filled by this emptiness which is essential for the economic action for which it constitutes the main support. More generally, all the economic and financial concepts are haunted by this negativity, this depression of being and precisely when they seem not to be (like the concept of equilibrium which displays a completeness of being), they are pointing towards that which can literally be called their "negative" (the imbalance, the observation of which shows that it is the rule and that equilibrium is the exception). In the same way, the concept of value, which intuitively and rationally points towards the completeness of being with its attributes of equilibrium and stability, is haunted by negativity which causes the economic value to occur, i.e. the economic action of the Subject-consciousness.

The structure of otherness of the economic Subject maintains a close link with time. The projection (anticipation) of the economic Subject outside itself as consciousness is based on a time-matter which sustains it: duration. The economic action process, the formation of image-objects and anticipation take root in the Subject's structure of otherness which is based on a raw material of duration (blocks of duration) which, having a certain density of memory and a certain factor of forgetfulness, is obliterated by the economic Subject during the act of imaging and acting consciousness which initiates the economic action process. This obliteration which leads to the formation of the image-object at the starting point of any economic action is the application of a certain factor of distortion (negativity) to the time-matter of duration (with a certain pairing of memory/forgetfulness once again). This obliteration cannot therefore produce mental objects which are completely empty, since the mental object, the image-object, which will be encountered later as the fundamental support for anticipations, in particular on the financial markets and within the economic acts and facts, always retain a trace of memory, of long-time, a duration matter which is more or less obscured by forgetfulness. It is this trace carried onto the financial markets and within the economic acts which, like DNA, contains the value and must be subjected to truly relevant analysis and research.

The opening up to that which is other, to the Other, is therefore a component of the economic Subject. The economic action process, the anticipation, the formation of image-objects are structures "for-the other". The Other is at once the *other* individual consciousness which inspects the multiple roles (a conflict certainly but, above all, an inspection which states the value, the judgement) of the other individual forms of consciousness; and the Other is also a participant in the formation and production of each individual consciousness, since the innermost matter (duration in its most ultimate temporal form) of each consciousness, its DNA, incorporates and intermingles the bits of DNA from other forms of consciousness. As such, the Other is involved in a formative manner in the developing definition of each economic Subject. Finally, the interrelations which link the forms of cons-ciousness-economic Subjects are themselves the subject, in their capacity as such, of a memory and therefore of a duration (with, once again, a degree of forgetfulness). The memorisation of the interrelations of the economic Subjects, therefore their specific duration, allows an explanation to be furnished regarding the economic attitudes, behaviours and actions which seem to defy immediate rationality or the most conventional logic: the opening up of the economic Subject to the Other is marked by duration, memory and forgetfulness and the traces which last and which structure the action of economic Subjects may produce surprising examples of behaviour.

§ 73.   When an economic Subject does not behave as one might expect (the literature of economic observation contains many examples) – i.e. according to the interpretation of an economic "law" or of some or other theory –, it is not necessarily a question of an infringement of some rationality of the Subject, together with all the ambiguity which may be contained within the concept of economic rationality but, rather, the fact that the Subject's mode of operating is inadequately understood and described, that its specific space-time reference frame which operates subject to the Other's inspection *is* the framework within which the economic Subject's rational approach proceeds logically and coherently, that within this specific reference frame of a mental nature (the structure of the consciousness), duration and memory constitute the innermost, determining matter within the action process (conception of the image, decision); consequently, the fact that the economic Subject does not behave as one might expect is due to the presence, within such reference frame, of structures of duration and memory which dictate a form of logic or reason, which the economic Subject adopts at the time of the action process. These structures represent the raw blocks of duration which we have described, sections of time imprinting economic facts, events and objects, of an individual and also interactive dimension (relations with the other). Such structures are given form/distorted by memory recalls and/or lapses. Such structures evolve, by shifts which are in general very slow due to the considerable inertia resulting from the very nature of duration, but occasionally by interruptions and discontinuities which may prove to be very sudden. In fact, the significant inertia which is present within all the phenomena determined by duration and memory may lead to a form of discrepancy between that which occurs in the immediate instant (and the reaction which the economic Subject "should" have, given only the *immediate* determining elements of the economic fact, event or object, or of the "law" which is supposed to apply in some or other situation) and, second, a specific, relevant reference frame of the economic Subject which imposes links with a memorised matter which may appear to be "out of sync", without a link of apparent *reason* to that which is revealed and is at stake in the immediate moment but which will prove to be determining in the economic Subject's effective action process.

There is a sort of reaction function on the part of the economic Subject and this reaction function to that which occurs *in the immediate moment* will draw from a dense time of duration and memory in order to determine a response. The incomprehension which results from this discrepancy is due, first, to the poor knowledge of this dense time-space and the mechanisms which govern the reference frame, and second the unconditional acceptance, as it were, of economic "laws" which do not incorporate this temporal dimension or, and this amounts to the same, which do not appreciate that that which is called economic law is a living organism: the law describes and contains a regime/reference frame which is given form and distorted, as we have shown, and this is what is unique and specific within economics and finance. It involves the creation and establishment of laws whose very content espouses the nature and contours of the specific space-time reference frame of the Subject and of economics in general. Accordingly it may be difficult for an economic law to isolate itself from the regimes and reference frames of memory at the time of its definition and implementation, especially since it cannot fail to take account of the distortions to the reference frame (memory recalls and lapses).

The economic laws remain as living organisms for so long as duration and memory irrigate their DNA. When this is not or no longer the case, the compulsory laws which dominate are filled with immediacy, which represents a very high factor of forgetfulness. An economic law can only claim to apply everywhere, to everyone and to every situation, if one assumes a maximum factor of forgetfulness and an economic Subject without a specific space-time reference frame which is structured by duration and memory.

§ 74.   The economic Subject's structure of otherness is therefore a structure of duration and memory and the reaction function (the action process) on the part of the Subject includes the characteristics which are specific to such situations, effects of delay (inertia), temporal discontinuities (acceleration, dilation) and interruptions. The economic fact, act, event or object consequently contain such structures and the laws which govern them (the notions of regime or reference frame are preferable to that of a law, since there is always a body of elements which form a system at any given time, accompanied by a relative stability which is characterised by a non-linear dynamic and movement).

The Other, which is *another* consciousness-Subject, intervenes in the field of interrelation with other forms of consciousness-Subjects, irrespective of the modes and description of such modes (conflictual, emotional, respectful…), by introducing as it were its regime/reference frame, intercellular encounters which we have described. Moreover, the interrelation is itself the subject of a regime/reference frame, i.e. of a form of history, which is more or less long, which self-references the interrelation and refers what may occur in the relations with economic Subjects to a reference frame which determines and therefore surpasses reality and the meaning of that which may be immediately observed or deduced. This interrelation reference frame, like all the matrix forms which structure economics and finance, possesses the characteristics described above, in particular those of the dynamic regime.

The economic action process therefore proceeds within a field which is structured by the interrelation reference frames. Such interrelation reference frames present a form which can be compared to that of the piece of wax described in *Théorie*, a raw block of duration, "imprinted"/given form by a set of economic facts, events and objects (here by a set of interrelations in their various modes of expression), a raw block of duration and therefore of traces (DNA) left by the work of time and which is driven by memory and forgetfulness. It is these interrelation reference frames which come into play in certain situations of economic life and impose their reasoning, since the rationality of such weighty space-time systems indeed exists in the sense of an internal logic and coherence, a rationality which we classify as being shared to the extent that the reference frame is indeed constructed and driven largely by the economic Subject as we have seen (conception-production of image-objects...), but develops an energy of its own resulting from an innermost matter (the duration) which surpasses and over-determines the economic Subject in its capacity as such (this over-determination may possibly house that share of the unconscious which represents a zone and force which are distinct from the direct design of the economic Subject as consciousness).

§ 75.   The interrelation reference frames form and regroup *habitus* which are in motion, which will, for example, include the behaviours of economic action or fairness and the Other's concern or its rejection will dominate that which might be implied by pure deductive reasoning. Consequently, it is not a question of distinguishing that which would, on the one hand, be economic law (failed) and on the other a (non-economic) reality. On the contrary, it is indeed economics and the law thereof which should be defined on the basis of such reality. Such situations show, as we emphasised in *Théorie*, that, within economics, all that which comes from the immediate present (fact, act, event or object) and seems to require an interpretation adorned with all the attributes of immediate logic and rationality, in fact forms part of the specific and more serious referential forces, since that which is immediate in economic and financial terms is only so in appearance; it is always a matter of intending to move some old "rubble". Consequently we distinguish between immediate rationality (there are only immediate facts, events and objects and the whole of the economic logic and rationality lies in the link established between them; in the same way, the only action by the economic Subject is with regard to such immediate events – i.e. that which appears to) and, on the other hand, shared rationality (economics and economic law only take on meaning with regard to a field of specific reference frames structured by duration, memory and forgetfulness; all that appears within the present economic moment is present strictly in appearance only and always refers back to the more serious tectonic movements of reference frames; all economic action by the Subject stems (from) and applies to such reference frames and not to elements of the present moment; one only appears to act in the present moment, once again it is a question of moving, remembering or forgetting some old "rubble").

The relationship maintained by the economic Subject with the Other is therefore marked by duration, memory and forgetfulness. The Other is (another) block of raw duration, which intersects that of any economic Subject on association, merger-amendment, conflict; it is the person/the thing one remembers (and as such the Other is a factor in the activation of memory recalls). In any event, the field of economics and finance cannot be described without incorporating the Other, since the very structure of each individual consciousness is otherness (and therefore the structure of each economic Subject); since the economic action, which is fundamentally conception-imagination of that which is in a state of non-being (negativity), is consequently based upon anticipation as an essential support of the economic action process (to anticipate is to conceive what is in a state of non-being, what is to come to pass, it is to imagine a mental object, an image-object, which is filled with that which is not or is not yet or, in the case of an illusion, will never be). Accordingly, the Other - even before adopting the human form and face of the individual, of the other individual consciousness which intersects other individual forms of consciousness - is the very *opening up* of each individual consciousness, an opening up which is the very definition of each economic Subject.

§ 76.   There is no economic Subject without an opening up to the Other (and by Other we mean *what is different*, i.e. that which is in a state of non-being). As such, no mention can be made of a unique economic Subject, of purely referential magnitude, or of a fixed economic Subject, which is fully and completely defined. There is only a multiplicity of forms which can be called (individual, collective) economic Subjects, which evolve within a reference frame of forms of consciousness. Furthermore, each economic Subject is an elusive form in the sense that the economic Subject is a projection outside itself, towards that which is *other*, towards the Other, and the economic Subject cannot be defined once and for all by a fixed form and a complete set of contents. On the contrary, the structure of the economic Subject is made up of a reference frame of innermost time-matter (duration) which is obliterated by the consciousness's design of anticipation and projection: the economic Subject is at all times and in all places *other*, elsewhere and beyond both itself and all the reference points which may appear to belong to it. During this projection, the economic Subject encounters other projections which come from other individual forms of consciousness and, especially, a vision which adds or subtracts value, since any economic project is "for-someone else" and part of its value depends upon the view ascribed to it by other individual forms of consciousness. The interrelation of the economic Subjects cannot be reduced solely to a conflict of forms of consciousness. What is called "conflict", i.e. the not completely compatible coexistence of at least two designs of projection must not cause one to forget that one is dealing first of all with a formative relationship within the collective reference frame of the forms of consciousness: the interrelation of projects, forms of consciousness and therefore of the economic Subjects is a constitutive part of the very structure of each economic Subject once the latter is defined on the basis of the design of anticipation and action.

The Other, for the economic Subject, is both design of action (projection-anticipation) which, as such, is formative for any *other* design of economic action, since each design of economic action by an individual economic Subject is defined by comparison, with, as against, within the time of another design, and, second, it is a viewpoint which allocates meaning and value. Within the general reference frame of the individual forms of consciousness which we have described, the dynamic intermingles action processes which are in "conflictual" (or we would say "formative") mode and a production of meaning and value which results from the progress of the individual action process subject to the Other's inspection. These two dimensions concur, to a certain extent, in the fact that the economic action and the process of creation-allocation of meaning are without doubt one and the same thing in the manner in which economics has developed in the modern era.

The Other's action process forms part of the definition of the action process of each individual economic Subject. This formative inter-relation of individual forms of consciousness means that there is no universe of free electrons within the reference frame but rather a dynamic which results from the continuous, formative interrelations. The reference frame is a field of tensions and dynamics. This can be seen in the financial market where, despite appearances, there is no simple juxtaposition or coexistence of pure projects or unitary action process but, on the contrary, a continuous dynamic of interrelations which means, *inter alia*, that only relative value can be found within this reference frame (i.e. relative to the Other).

Relativity reigns within the economic and financial reference frames because everything proceeds in relation to the Other, to that which is other. The economic Subject's structure of otherness means that numerous concepts of economics are relative concepts (i.e. relative to that which is other).

4. THE CONFLICT

§ 77.   The Other is what is different, what is conflict or violence. Otherness, as difference, lies at the heart of the very definition of economics and its dynamic. Difference can be deduced from otherness, first within the structure of the economic Subject which, as we have seen, is always in a state of non-being (i.e. outside, ahead of itself), within the conception of image-objects, imagination, anticipation and projection, elements which form the economic action process whose financial timing constitutes a stage of gestation-selection, particularly through the financial market as we know it in the contemporary age. Difference is first the depression of being which is innermost to the consciousness-economic Subject, which makes it possible for there to be an economic action rather than nothing. Difference is a constitutive element of the innermost structure of the economic Subject and, consequently, of the action process. The most original part of time-matter lodges, is lodged within this depression of being which is innermost to the economic Subject's consciousness (being inadequate for itself). The economic Subject-consciousness' distance from itself to itself, which can be seen within the projection towards that which is in a state of not-yet-being and within anticipation, two essential structures of the economic action, is not an empty space and the idea of nothingness which can sometimes characterise it is in fact a temporal matter which is burnt and transformed in the same way one consumes fuel. There lies the origin or source of the economic action process. Weighty time, duration, this matter made of cold wax which is driven by a slow, innermost movement enters the combustion chamber of the consciousness (when the latter initiates an action process; duration is always present as an essential, constitutive element) and the pistons of the distance between itself and itself, by means of the projection, anticipation and the image-object, distort, inform, transform and consume duration within a design of memory recall and lapse.

The Other is difference and the otherness, in its capacity as difference, mobilises time as an essential matter (that which is, within economics, is time understood as duration – i.e. the densest temporal form) within the economic action process. By defining the economic Subject on the basis of difference and otherness, the economic Subject is positioned within the conflict and uncertainty.

Conflict and therefore violence are participants in the economic dynamics because, first of all, the structure of the Other (otherness, difference) inhabits the innermost recesses of the economic Subject as consciousness, which results in projection and action. It is by going out of itself (which is a question of its very definition) that the economic Subject encounters (must encounter, there is a necessary force here) other economic Subjects. The conflict of the forms of consciousness, which forms part of a much wider set of formative means of the act of projection and anticipation and therefore of the action (the interaction of the forms of consciousness constitutes an important element of the project formation for each of them), includes violence, a necessary element, therefore, of the economic action process. By definition, there cannot be an economic action and, consequently, an economic Subject, without a conflictual form linked to the Other (the Other as otherness of the innermost action process, of the structure of the consciousness; the Other as another consciousness, another economic Subject). From the outset (i.e. the conception of image-objects up until what we have called the "impact" with the real world), the conflict contains the violence within it. Symbolically at first since, within the economic action process, it is first a question of image-objects (the forms of anticipation and imagination), which can be seen confronting each other on the financial market (the symbolic place of confrontation of projects, i.e. of image-objects, the place of centralisation and therefore of the channelling of conflict and violence in the contemporary era). Numerous economic *forms* of a strong, symbolic nature consequently fulfil, within economics and finance, the function of expression and disclosure of a conflict, occasionally of violence, *and*, at the same time, of distancing or managing this violence: the price, the listing on the financial market, the money (...). Economic violence is first a symbolic violence because at the origin of the economic action lie image-objects and because the whole economic and financial existence continues to be inhabited by such image-objects. Accordingly, the channelling and control of this latent violence pass through forms and structures of the organisation of the image-objects, at least prior to and certainly part of the economic action process, ideally throughout the whole of its progression, i.e. up until the actual point of impact since, at this stage, there are various expressions of violence which have to be organised, channelled and controlled, but the violence has taken on a practical form and it represents work of no lesser importance but of a different degree (even if it is a question of similar type to that of violence in its symbolic form). In this regard, one notes that the actual impact which, first, has feedback effect upon or interacts with the conception-formation of image-objects by the economic Subject-consciousness and, second, the actual facts and events (impacts) which continue at any given time to be immersed within a reference frame of image-objects or symbols, the task of curbing the violence and conflict, which are specific to the economic object, continues throughout the whole economic action process, which we have described. Economics is a process of the liberation *and* domestication of violence, which sustains a permanent tension between freedom and the norm.

§ 78.　Prior to the economic action process, within the referential universe which is principally dominated by the image-objects, the form of the financial market organises the assembly, the ordered confrontation (although bubbles and crashes still exist) of image-objects (i.e. of anticipations and projects), for gestation and selection. This function of market finance is underestimated: the financial market compresses and orders the innermost and latent violence, the capacity for conflict contained within the image-objects which result from the economic-subjects within the action process. Such a role also falls, more generally and more profoundly to money, since money translates, expresses, symbolises and projects the image-objects within the economic action process, which is the process for the determination of value. Unsurprisingly, economic crises are often also financial crises (since the reference frame of image-objects – i.e. of anticipations and projects – enters a state of crisis) and, especially, monetary crises at the outset (the corruption of money, in particular through the use of credit and debt, is at the root of the crisis mechanism since credit *may* corrupt, mask, magnify unduly and in an exaggerated fashion, distort and also invent image-objects). In the so-called "Austrian" business theory of the cycle and crises, credit and debt are potentially dangerous agents in proportion to their capacity to distort image-objects (excessive anticipations, for example) or to create image-objects which should not have existed: the financial (monetary) crisis results therefrom (with the bursting of bubbles on an ever increasing basis in the contemporary era, since the financial market is a participant in the action process and in the organisation of the image-objects, as we have shown), and later the economic crisis as well.

5. UNCERTAINTY

§ 79.　Otherness (the Other), as difference within the innermost structure of the consciousness-Subject and as a dynamic of the economic action process, is the source of the close link between the economic Subject and uncertainty. Economics and finance are inhabited by uncertainty because the economic Subject is consciousness, a tearing away from oneself, out of oneself, a projection and anticipation towards that which is in a state of not-yet-being and which, occasionally, will not be. Uncertainty, even before (instead of) being that which disturbs and being therefore described and understood as abnormality (or indeed even irrationality) within the economic and financial existence, is the underlying motivation for the action process and the structure of the economic Subject. Consequently, uncertainty lies within normality, is economic normality and a failure to understand this leads to the risk of misunderstandings and disillusions. The incapacity of numerous models to encompass the economic and financial facts, objects and phenomena within the modelled forms which presuppose, in one way or another, a "normality" within the action process and a normal distribution in turn of its components, reminds us that it is in the nature of economic normality to include abnormalities of a too pure form of reasoning. Uncertainty cannot be reduced within the heart of economics and finance, since it constitutes the very nature of the economic Subject.

This does not mean that it cannot be reduced, i.e. standardised, which, for us, means that uncertainty is not as absolute as one would like to think, that uncertainty is not so uncertain, as it were. This is an important point, since economic and especially financial uncertainty is, in the common perception, accused of being irrational (consequently dangerous) to a greater extent, if it is presumed to be literally without limits, which also consequently means that one does not admit that uncertainty forms part of economic and financial normality and further that such uncertainty may also be known (since it forms part of a specific space-time reference frame as we have shown), and may therefore be understood and standardised.

Uncertainty may be understood and this is an essential point of our work. Uncertainty is known by a specific economic and financial reference frame of which it forms the logical attribute and product.

Uncertainty, in the formation of the economic matter, is both a fundamental structure which strictly speaking corresponds to the opening up of a field of the Subject's consciousness – without which the action cannot be envisaged – and a field of understandable temporal matter which can therefore be standardised. Economic uncertainty is not an empty place; it is the product of a design of negativity by the economic Subject (which projects and anticipates) and a spatio-temporal matter made of duration. It is "nothingness" for a "being" represented by duration, it is "nothingness" in the sense that it occupies the space-time where the consciousness, at any given moment, and in particular during the economic action process, tears away from itself; but this space-time is not empty since it is made up of a time-matter of duration which is consumed by negativity in the formation of the project and of an anti-matter which results from the action of the Subject's design on that which lasts and approaches or comes from memory. This anti-matter constitutes the structure of the image-object in the manner we have described.

The amount of uncertainty is proportionate to this anti-matter, a photographic negative of reality, which forms the basis of the action, but this anti-matter retains a link of meaning and structure at all times with the matter of duration, which means that ultimately there is something which is comprehensible, there are points of reference. As we have shown, any image-object, any project, any action, of an economic and financial nature, comes from and is secured within duration and, therefore, within a specific space-time and is characterised by a form of DNA. Consequently, by excluding the accusation of irrationality (in its severe form – i.e. introducing chance at the heart of the economic and financial phenomena, events and objects), a path opens through which patient research may hope to find the *trace* of this DNA (essential temporal matter and duration can be traced, in all the immediate economic and financial appearances) since there is a genetic heritage of economic and financial facts and objects (within what has been called a reference frame).

Such a path which presupposes the trace (and traceability) of duration (with a greater or lesser degree of forgetfulness) in all that is economic or financial (which means that time is the primary and final matter of such universe), creates the conditions for a possible meaning (comprehension) and a norm. Such a path therefore seeks the existence of a bundle of determinations at the heart of this economic and financial universe (time-matter, essentially understood as duration, is a deter-mining force for the economic action process and, consequently, for the facts, events and objects which form part thereof). Economics and finance are less unpredictable than they might appear.

There is therefore economic and financial uncertainty because there is otherness, the Other, at the heart of the very structure of the economic Subject and the action process which it drives; such uncertainty is neither pure chance or irrationality: it is on the contrary the setting in motion (negativity of the action design which commences with the conception of the image-object) of a genetic heritage of duration within a psychological or mental space-time reference frame (where memory and forgetfulness are at work). Uncertainty is therefore comprehensible. It cannot be eliminated, since it constitutes that which is understood to be economic and financial, in particular by the economic Subject, but it may be standardised, or indeed reduced, on the basis of a determination of the economic and financial norm which results from the analysis of the genetic heritage of the elements at play.

§ 80.   The Other, without which economics and finance cannot be imagined, also adopts at least two forms, that of conflict and that of uncertainty. These two forms constitute the economic action process and have an accessible meaning, that of the genetic heritage of duration and memory, over and above the sense, i.e. the direction of the project, which is adopted by the creative design of the image-object (source of the project and the economic action). Any economic action, and consequently any fact, object or event relating thereto, contains an intangible dimension of duration, a stock which is not inert but an angular stone of the economic project and a more volatile dimension, the product of the design of consciousness on this stock of duration, as we have described. This second dimension can be found in a sort of gas or liquid state, at the time when the image-object is formed (this is also the case during the selection and gestation phase of the image-object within the location of the financial market), or a more solid state, when the action process pursues its path up until impact with the world: in the same way that a meteorite collides with the earth, there is a progressive solidification and that which was "negativity", the "new" component in the stock of duration, an element of projection which was in a state of non-being (not-yet-being), becomes in turn a form of duration, which has a feedback effect on the new future economic actions (the stock of duration is increased), and so on and so forth.

Chapitre 4

THE NORM
AND THE RULE

1. THE POSSIBILITY OF A NORM AND REGULATION

§ 81.   The question here is whether it is possible to have a norm. As we have shown, once the corrosive and apparently fatal forces of the evolution of economics as an economic policy action have completed their work and actually detached or torn the world away from the facts and events of any reference frame, a simple description of the chain of events alone cannot suffice, even if very convincing. The elimination of that which is within this chain of events which structures the being and the Subject's role within it constitutes, as we have seen, the first reason for this objective of modern economics, which becomes the very name itself for the relationship created by the Subject with the world and with things. The elimination of this being leads unsurprisingly to a considerable degree of confusion ("God alone could save us") and, within the issue of economics which we are interested in, to the essential question, whether it is possible to radically reform an excess based on a norm.

It should be noted that the appropriation of the being by an acting Subject in order to project and transform produces powerful, dissolvent effects, in modern circumstances, on the normative, reference block of action and reflection in economic matters. By instilling negativity (to be in a state of non-being, the mode of being of the Subject's project and action, starting from the economic policy action which in fact replaces traditional economics) at the heart of economic concepts and the processes of reflection and action vis-à-vis the world, by instilling what is to be done and what is to come as modes of being, in the same way as venom, by means of the Subject which is the primary instrument of this instillation, the modern era slowly explodes what might remain from the anchorage of the main conceptual categories to a reflection of being and the modes thereof, and also of time. The concepts of value and time not surprisingly enter into crisis at the same time. The concept of equilibrium also enters into crisis, even so far as to yield place to an invasion of the real and mental spaces of economics through imbalance, a necessary concept of a landscape structured by negativity and transforming action. This crisis removes one by one the main bodies of economic regulation (including, for example, monetary policy) from the firm bases which might support a norm or a reference to an equilibrium. This conceptual, intellectual crisis precipitates the economic and financial crises of the modern and contemporary era.

§ 82.   It is not possible to re-establish the drifting raft of modern economics on a basis or norm which are absolute. Moreover, such an angular, absolute stone, i.e. which stems directly from a mode of being, has never seen the light of day or endured. However, the moment which we have called "traditional" came close, criticised, mistakenly, in proportion to its increased unreality. The undertaking is more modest, to show that using the very pillars of modern economics as we know them (the Subject, the consciousness which faces the world during the action process), it is possible to found the norm which, even from a distance, beckons towards that which is and may found, even in relative and non-absolute fashion, a certain number of categories and modes of being (equilibrium, value) and, consequently, secure once again the main bodies of regulation on firm ground. We are talking about a relative foundation, a relative norm, like a first stop towards firm ground.

Since one must start with that which has been installed, with the framework provided by the Subject's consciousness. This therefore means starting with what we have named the mental or psychological "reference frame" within the specific dynamic of the determination of the action towards and in respect of the world. This therefore means finding, within the economic action itself, that which anchors the projection to firmer ground and may validly provide a reference for a normative approach. We have shown that the very structure of the psychological reference frame, made up of memory and duration, would offer a point of anchorage, together with that which, over and beyond the action, survived and also to some extent preceded the action. It becomes possible once again to standardise (the action of the Subject), once one has managed to extract from the action process and the mental framework of consciousness which directs it (for example, the production of image-objects) a few conceptual elements which view the matter from the standpoint of that which is (since the norm always originates from that which is) and a few simple tools in order to construct the norm. Such conceptual elements, as we have seen, allow one to secure the value, equilibrium and time to forms which are semi-stable and semi-regular, invariables which can be called "relative" and which we have united around memory and duration. Although they are not absolute forms (they are relative to a regime, to time itself, to action itself which has a feedback effect), the latter provide acceptable refuges within the slots of time and action, within sequences, which are in fact the macro-financial "regimes", better known by their ideological name (capitalist regime, etc.). It is also a question of tools, which are constructed on the basis of such conceptual elements, like the image-objects which inhabit the reference frame of financial imagination. The norm will often be a construction or more simply a packaging of image-objects. For example, the norms of inflation within the objectives of monetary policy will often correspond to image-objects of the universe of prices, i.e. sections of memorised/forgotten sequences cut out of the blocks of long duration.

§ 83.   The economic norm therefore maintains a strong link with memory and duration. As we have shown, the innermost structure of the image-objects, which constitute the reference frame of economics and finance, is the essential time-matter of duration, which is more or less distorted by forgetfulness and memory recalls, which are themselves linked to the facts and events of real life and action. It is these image-objects which in turn form the structure of the norms, i.e. the values and variables which determine a reference point and point of equilibrium. The norm, in economic and financial matters, is that which is remembered in order not to forget. The normative reference point is naturally made up of memory and duration since it is there to confront forgetfulness. It is of course itself exposed to the erosion of forgetfulness or to wear and tear.

The norm is constantly attacked by the distortions introduced by facts and events which themselves trigger the corrosive phenomena of distortion – dilation, contraction – through the channels of memory and forgetfulness. This provides us with two lessons. The norm is a living thing, which is distorted and which follows the contours because it is like an imprint of what is to come. This living character of the norm should not be confused with the absence of a norm. The economic policy action whose task is to identify, format and make best use of the norm will constantly have to bear in mind this distortion of the norm in order to avoid using a defunct norm which is therefore useless. We are accordingly discussing a relative norm, which itself refers to a universe of relative equilibria, a notion introduced in *Théorie*. Relative is understood to mean a relationship to a reference frame structured by the Subject and the World (its facts and events). For all that, such a relative norm can only acquire solid substance in connection with the conceptual pillars which result from that which is and therefore from the absolute modes of being. A large part of the effort lies there as well, within the weave of this connection. The resulting norm will be no less relative. This means that the absolute norm, like the absolute equilibrium is not of this world (both literally and by construction) and that only the absolute foundations (the modes of being and time) of the relative norm are essential. This is what forms the basis of the economic norm's practical dimension.

§ 84.   The temptation of an absolute norm or that of a lack of norms are the worst of errors. The steering of relative norms, i.e. of only those which offer a truly practical dimension, will require a good deal of careful handling and one should undoubtedly also be aware of the need to anticipate the distortions of the norm. The whole issue of the economic policy action turns upon this. An economic policy action often runs aground as a result of this. The existence of relevant relative norms and the suitable direction thereof is a precondition for the success of an economic policy action.

The norm must know how to move and adapt, like a living organism, a living organism which is the space-time reference frame where it has its source, in the same way that the zones of facts, events and innovations travel and are distorted, virgin zones which require stan-dardisation or adaptation (there is always a trail of memory or history which makes a connection) to that which comes to pass and, coming to pass, either radically modifies the situation or, more certainly, moves the "rubble" of the past and revives memories, which can also lead to pronounced interruptions, since everything is ruled by discontinuity and non-linearity.

§ 85.   The contemporary economic confusion is largely due to the elimination of the norm and, more seriously, to the exclusion of the possibility of a norm. If the norm is deleted, observation constantly evokes it. Whether it concerns the financial sphere – the explosion of the crisis has literally revealed normative holes and triggered a political, normative intention – or, with less media coverage and yet more profoundly, monetary policy (vagueness of objectives and of the very philosophy of action when the central banks are described as pyromaniac-fire-fighters, when, in any event, they play a central role in the cycle of indebtedness, of financial bubbles and of consequently artificial growth, for which the same central banks bear a share of responsibility), or budgetary policy (the latest normative attempts of the Pact of Stability having also been washed away by the crisis), accordingly whether it concerns the traditional levers, objectives and tools of the macro-economic, economic policy action or of the financial sphere and its non-regulated zones, its unmanaged market segments, the norm is deleted, withdraws, while voluntarist understandings unmistakably arise, seeking to standardise once again. The traditional zones (monetary and budgetary policies) and the financial sphere are deeply connected in their confusion, since the ab-normal financial expansion is based on accommodating monetary policies, which are so accommodating that, in the crisis, they had to become ab-normal (unconventional actions).

The crisis of the economic and financial norm is the generalisation of the ab-normal. Once again, observation is faced with a wide choice. The fact of getting used to abnormally low interest rates, which are artificially low, no doubt sums up the multiple slides towards references which are not in fact references. The same is true for budgetary issues. Within the financial sphere, the abnormal norms of profitability provided over the last twenty or so years (the famous 15% of ROE – return on equity) form part of the same logic, since all abnormalities maintain a bond of necessity as between themselves (for example, between monetary strategies and standardised profitabilities for the price of assets and, consequently, of companies).

Consequently one passes, by means of shifts, from the elimination of the norm to the impossibility of a norm. What is at stake today is the very possibility of a norm. The forward flight, which is cyclical to some extent, of the traditional gearing and of the financial sphere, goes fundamentally hand in hand with forgetfulness and the exclusion of a reflection of the foundations of economics which, as we have seen, are transformed into a pure economic policy action. Firm ground is lacking, circulation replaces value, time replaces duration, reflection is introduced within imbalance and abnormality as for normalities. We have demonstrated all this and now is not the place to consider it further.

The abnormalities which increase in number certainly show the necessary consequences of economic mechanisms, if one ignores the norms, which although far from perfect, existed or were able to exist ("that which must be, must be"; the abnormal increase of credit, in various forms, could be understood within a normative framework justifying a standardised response), such abnormalities reveal above all the confusion when faced with the challenge of creating new ones. And yet, there are many subjects. Accordingly, there is an established consciousness, within the central banks themselves, that the objectives and tools of monetary policy can no longer ignore, within the contemporary, macro-financial regime as it is, the links between the price of assets, money and activity, within a more unitary vision which goes beyond the sole, current objective of the price of goods and services (inflation in the traditional sense). This consciousness may fail and the monetary policy will then be trapped within successive (non-conventional) abnormalities, slowly emptying the substance of the monetary policy action; or the effort will result in the radical reform of a new norm which will take account of this reality.

§ 86.   The multiple crises which mark the macro-financial regime essentially state the elimination of the norm and time does not help matters since the successive developments of this unitary crisis, by accentuating the intensities and therefore the degrees of accommodating response required, at each stage, make the possibility of a norm an increasingly moot case. And future crises are themselves a gradual result of the elimination of the norm.

We have shown in our first works that the modern fate of economics is closely linked to the elimination of the progressive norm and an overthrow of the original pillars which we have stressed were the modes of being (equilibrium, for example; the elimination of time conceived of as duration...). Such a reversal makes the possibility of a norm more remote.

However, it is not inevitable. What we have called a radical reform, which is a further reversal involving an excavation of the modes of being whose light no longer penetrates, within a practical system based on reality and which provides an explanation (for the space-time reference frames, for example), this work specifically aims to break the inevitable advance. In order for the norm to be or become possible, the essential concepts (time, equilibrium...) have to be cleaned-up. In order for the norm to be practical, it must be possible for it to be based within reality as the same is observed, i.e. *together with* the Subject and the action, as the latter have structured the modern evolution of economics. The objective may be attained if this double condition is satisfied (radically to reform *that which is observed* within the modes of being and time). Hence, for example, the reflection of time as duration (a mode of being, of substance) within the space-time reference frame distorted by the phenomena of memory and forgetfulness (Subject), all within the action process which is directed towards and at the world. Such a description seems to us to be closer to that which is observed in the operation of the markets and economics. And the norm can be derived from this interpretation of reality and of observation. Many norms are literally ineffective since they are not or no longer rooted in the modes of being discussed above and/or because they are constructed in the ignorance, which is sometimes assumed, of what is observed in reality and which sometimes results in the denial of the most beautiful constructions of modelled visions. The non-linearities, dilations and contractions of economic and financial space-time are an example thereof.

The achievement of the modern fate of economics as a pure economic policy action of the Subject (and by Subject we mean both the individual unit and collective entities and therefore institutions) represents a powerful dynamic of dissolution and erosion of the economic norm as a possible means of conferring meaning and limits to the action's objectives. The feeling that an action is literally "without limits", i.e. ultimately has contingent objectives, and also the feeling of a weakening efficiency (which is practical and contains meaning), all of this forms the modern substratum. It therefore seems necessary to be able to reassign objectives and therefore norms to economic policy actions. This means the most traditional and best known axes of economic policy – monetary, budgetary, fiscal, financial, market and industrial… – but also the possible new levers of a regulation. Since regulation – the lack and necessity of which is evoked by each movement of the macro-financial regime and each crisis – only becomes possible if the conditions for a possible norm are restored.

§ 87.   We have seen that it is still possible to redefine the extremely close pairing of the objective (action) and the norm (reference frame). This possibility involves considerable work on the concept of the *reference frame* in the sense that we have given such term in *Théorie* and later in *La dynamique boursière*. The practical conditions for determining the norm lie within the concepts of the reference frame (in particular the space-time reference frame) and of the (macro-financial) regime. The very necessary connection between a macroscopic dimension (the regime) and a micromental dimension which controls the decision-making terms of the Subject's action (the reference frame) make the notions of an objective and a norm possible.

This connection between the reference frame and the regime is made within a framework of relativity. This means that all the conceptual pillars which secure the reference frame-regime axis and whose foundations sink further and deeper into the modes of being (value, equilibrium and duration…) and of substance, are imagined and defined within a relative, limited and non-absolute dimension. This is the inevitable compromise if one is to keep reality on board, as restored by observation, in order to conserve a form of praxis within the credible definition of the objective and the norm. We will accordingly talk of relative equilibria and of relative, limited concepts.

This strong or limited relativity depends largely upon the Subject's status within the approach. The examination of modern economics by the dynamic of the conscious, acting Subject leaves us with little choice but to start from this basis, from the Subject, within the reference frame which it has in a certain manner imposed and which accordingly offers the most satisfactory prospect of understanding economic and financial phenomena, facts and events from a practical viewpoint. This is how the concept of the mental or psychological space-time reference frame which we have put forward corresponds to this concern that one starts from an understanding of what is actually happening. And what is actually happening takes place within a relative reference frame. On this basis, the work can be advanced on two fronts. The first approach from a conceptual viewpoint secures the elements of the practical reference frame which we have just defined to the most fundamental pillars (duration, equilibrium and value...), while attempting to found the reference frame which determines the Subject's economic and financial action within the modes of being, thus attempting to tear this reference frame away from a lack of foundation, limits, norms and purposes. This represents, for the main part, the contents of *Théorie, Dynamique boursière* and also the first section of this work.

A second approach is waiting to be introduced and used. This second approach takes economics beyond the Subject but does not eliminate the latter from a theoretical viewpoint. By determining the conditions for a possible economic and financial norm based on the reference frame, one introduces the possibility of an objective for the action (in particular the economic policy action) as well as a regulation of the said action. The Subject remains central as the place (space-time reference frame) of impetus for the economic and financial action process, but the Subject is to some extent surrounded by a set of norms resulting from the Subject's own operation (realistic and practical construction of the space-time reference frame). Such norms have the lasting characteristic of emerging from a realistic observation of the workings of economics and finance within the action process (for example, the consideration of the asymmetries of discontinuities, of leaps and non-linearities in general) and of being connected to a conceptual territory of a different type (the term transcendental might be used) on which the norms are based, rely. This territory of the substance (duration constitutes a good example thereof, which anchors the concept of time within the operation of the Subject's space-time reference frame, to the transcendental pillar of duration) provides the essential matter of reference frames, that which represents its innermost structure (it has accordingly been possible to state that duration constituted the raw material of the space-time reference frame).

§ 88.   What we have called the "first approach" allows one to reintroduce the conditions for a possible norm and regulation by bringing back towards the Subject and its action impetus a territory which transcends it (concepts of substance such as duration) while continuing to be immersed in the referential universe of the Subject itself (and of the structure of the consciousness in particular), as witnessed by the role played by the phenomena of memory and forgetfulness. A norm is possible within a system (approach) where the directionality constantly moves and continues to move from the Subject (consciousness) towards the world within the economic act and through the financial forms. However, the mooring of the universe of the Subject's consciousness to the territory of a transcendental nature where concepts which are modes of being develop, imperceptibly triggers a dynamic for restoring the balance of the causal forces and reasonings. The initial logic, at the heart of modern economics, sees the conscious Subject projecting itself towards the world where it introduces and creates forms of being through the action (foundation of modern value) within a movement which is constantly recommenced towards an objective which in turn constantly withdraws (the examination is a perpetual flight forwards). The action does not manage to fix being to the objective and the perpetual pursuit of the objective ends up deleting the meaning of the objective and the possibility of a norm and a regulation. The first approach therefore starts by constructing the mooring, i.e. the bringing together of the universe of the conscious Subject as it operates and a separate territory, which is independent from the modes of being which transcend the operating modes of the territory, which we have called the reference frame. By so doing, an attempt is made to detach the Subject's reference frame from the world and from the impacts of the action, i.e. simply to deal with it (we are still in the general process of the advancement of the action but the pure separation of the reference frame is intended to base the meaning of the impulses of action elsewhere and other than within the sole impacts which are measured and calculated in the world). At the same time, the meaning and the operation of the reference frame is attached to a conceptual territory which transcends it (*inter alia* duration, modes of being in general) by deriving the meaning from the reference frame and therefore from the general process of the economic and financial action towards this territory. A balancing movement, to restore the balance, is progressively commenced.

§ 89.   At the end of this movement, a second approach still has to be constructed, which witnesses the reversal but does not deny the Subject. The modes of being move towards the Subject, literally come towards it within the reference frame, within an economic and financial action process which travels towards the world. The impact of the action on the world changes its nature, the objective remains the same but the foundations for its legitimacy and meaning are altered, the norm naturally finds its source prior to the action process. This reversal is that of economics and finance imagined beyond the Subject, but without denying the Subject.

Within this layer (much in the same way one discusses the ozone layer, the different layers of the atmosphere) of modes of being (and consequently just being itself) lies the possibility of equilibria, values and absolute norms. This relates to what cannot be observed, which therefore escapes the regime of the other layers described within the economic and financial action process (the reference frame of production of image-objects; finance, the market, the actual impact). The relative, limited values belong to this group. What cannot be observed possesses an ambiguous status, is a participant in the action process within a regime of relativity which is more or less limited and, at the same time, escaping "being seen" and the consciousness and, therefore, referring back to that which cannot be "seen", i.e. also that which the conscious Subject cannot have a pure, clear awareness of. That which cannot be observed, but whose usefulness and necessity are established in the reference frame and action process, refers back to something which is but is not revealed, while simultaneously structuring the action. This is true of the real interest rate or anticipations of inflation, essential notions for the understanding of the world, the action, economics and finance, and yet which cannot be "seen", when to see also means to understand or to be conscious of. Such unobservable notions mobilise the mental space-time reference frame through which they pass in transit (the anticipations of inflation involve a concept of time, duration, memory and forgetfulness, a temporal substance). Such unobservable notions all incorporate one or more modes of being which refer back to a dimension which transcends the strict reference frame of the Subject. The same is true of duration.

Economics is based on unobservable notions in order to allow to be seen that which can be observed. Such notions often open up, in the manner of a door, towards this layer of modes of being which we have discussed.

Let us return to this second approach which henceforth connects four sub-approaches. The modes of being (1), sustain the mental space-time reference frame of a Subject which accommodates them as events which come towards it and whose product is the image-object, the innermost structure of the Subject's reference frame (2), image-objects which are organised, valued and selected by finance and the market, literally for the purpose of impact with reality (the acting consciousness takes over from the imaging consciousness) (3), for a final gesture for the completion of the action which includes the contact and impact (4), with a feedback loop (1). This segmentation has a static value; it also contains a dynamic which can be compared to that of a cycle.

The completed turnaround simply involves detaching this layer of absolute territories (modes of being), i.e. identifying this origin as such, which was present within the genealogy of the main notions which structure the reference frame, but the latter were not allocated to any particular region. By showing that the fundamental structure of the reference frame itself originated from a substantial reference frame (in the sense of substance, being), the turnaround has been commenced, since the foundation, the value, that which is, is no longer strictly identified with the result of the Subject's action, that which settles upon impact but, on the contrary, looks towards that which approaches the Subject and is housed deep within it, within the structure of its consciousness (the reference frame, duration…) and therefore permeates the space-time reference frame which is the place where the economic and financial action process is determined and driven.

§ 90.   There is a turning point in the theory of the Subject once one passes from a movement directed towards the world of an action of transformation which alone defines the economic Subject, to the collection of what is, of that which comes through the Subject, for the action. This reversal authorises the surpassment of the theory of the Subject in the modern age. The economic Subject is, fundamentally, the person through which that which is happens (comes). This means that the Subject is the place where the event is formed, in the double meaning of, first, that which comes towards the Subject, comes to inhabit it and to constitute or structure all the reference frames in the sense in which we have used this term and, second, that which happens as a result of the contact with the world through what we have called the "impact". The two dimensions are fundamentally connected since the action, strictly speaking, of the Subject directed towards the world – that which specifically forms economics at least in modern understanding – stems from that which comes towards the Subject and constructs the reference frame within which the action process and its development are in fact created and constructed, as we have described, up until the impact.

Adopting our approach, therefore, the Subject is an active receptacle for that which occurs. By "that which occurs" we mean "that which is" and, in particular, that which comes to the Subject within and through the time-matter of duration. That which comes to the Subject, that which is and duration are one and the same thing. By having shown that the essential matter of the space-time reference frame which defines the economic Subject was duration (itself given form by memory and forgetfulness), one has implicitly stated that the economic Subject could only be constructed within the flow of openness to that which comes (happens) and that this manner of constructing the Subject through the openness to that which happens (comes) definitively prevailed over the definition of the modern economic Subject (i.e. the transforming action of projection (pure negativity)) and over the world. Here lies the surpassment. The Subject is above all an openness to that which happens (comes) and by stating this, one incorporates both the body of temporal *continuum* which forms time-matter within duration and which structures the Subject's *psyche* (reference frame, perception, consciousness, means of knowledge) and all the impacts of the Subject's action in its projection towards the world in the sense that we have described this action process (which does not disappear from the theory of the Subject – quite the contrary), impacts which have a continuous feedback effect on the Subject and the time-matter of duration. The essential structure of duration is, as we have seen, given form and distorted by memory and forgetfulness but also, at the same time, by that which, literally, occurs within the world at any time, a series of events including the impacts of the individual or collective acts of the Subject itself.

The economic Subject continues to be defined by the action process undertaken with regard to the world but this same process is itself described as an opening towards that which is and the very structure of the Subject (the consciousness, the reference frame), which is the true centre of stimulation of the action process, is described as specific space-time matter of duration. The economic action becomes the dynamic of that which is. This means that any economic action fundamentally consists of burning time-matter, duration in this instance, in the same way one burns wood in a stove or coal in an engine, in order to produce the Subject's movement of projection (negativity) outward, towards the world. The economic dynamic, that of the economic action is completely encompassed within this vast block of wax (the raw material of duration, of that which is, which happens (comes)), which is consumed to a greater or lesser degree, more or less quickly, which is consumed in proportion to or in connection with its consumption by the

Subject in order to sustain the action and projection process towards that which is not yet in being (the project). That which is sustains that which is in a state of non-being. Consequently, it will no longer be a question of defining the economic Subject and, consequently, the economic action itself, by the mere obliteration of that which is (negativity at the very heart of the projection towards that which is in a state of non-being), a definition which is terribly effective and which lies at the heart of modern economics and therefore of the modern age, period, given the extent to which the word "economic" expresses the essence of the purpose of this special age. Or, rather, not solely, not in this way. By showing that this wrenching movement is only possible if one consumes raw material which forms the very structure of the Subject, of its consciousness and its reference frames, the action process is secured to firm ground which transcends the Subject, since such raw material, a dense and basic structure is, precisely, that which happens (comes) from any moment in time to the Subject. The economic action can only obtain a dynamic from this launch base which is at the same time basic energy. Consequently the determining factors and sources of the action and the economic and financial or market facts can be better understood, as we tried *inter alia* in *Dynamique*, in particular by taking into account the dynamics of the specific space-time reference frames connected to duration, memory and forgetfulness. Once again, *Théorie* and, especially *Dynamique*, opened up these exploratory paths.

§ 91.   The issue of economics, in the modern age, is that of the Subject *and* the norm. There is also a separate issue of the Subject. What we call "economics" in the modern age, as we have shown in *Tractatus* and in *Généalogie*, is a movement, a purpose which can be closely linked to the emancipation of the Subject-consciousness and its appropriate and transforming projection towards, on, in the world. Economics are the Subject's action, whether the Subject is an individual or a collective body. This is the issue which can be raised separately, that of the Subject, and initial research involves, as we have tried to do, reporting this movement by the Subject within the action process, its dynamic, its sources, its reference frames, from the universe of the consciousness, of the economic Subject's own imagination which perceives and acts, up until the real world where the action process produces an impact, through the modern forms of production and organisation of the representations and anticipations which are specific and essential to the mode of projection of the Subject whose action is directed towards that which is not yet in being or, more accurately, which is in a state of non-being, representations and anticipations which we have grouped together under the generic term of image-objects. Such modern forms include, first, the financial market or, in other words, market finance plays a formative role in the modern action process involving the Subject, the world whose manner of relations constitutes, literally, economics in the modern sense.

§ 92.   Accordingly such a separate issue of the Subject exists and a first research approach directed towards archaeology and the Subject's dynamic in its relationship with the world, a relationship which produces realities and representations, facts, events and imaginary worlds or anticipations, all of which we group together under the name "economics". While exploring this approach of the Subject one can only realise, an inevitable and possibly tragic purpose of modern economics, that the economic Subject as the same may be described in its relationship with the world, moves away from the idea of a norm in proportion to the apparently limitless extension of the domains of its transforming projections. In fact, the very idea of standardising is dissolved within the action process given the extent to which the impacts themselves on the world, in the world, support the norm and the value. The norm, in an action process which transforms the world and which establishes the value afterwards, i.e. after the occurrence of the impact which modifies or transforms reality or the world, therefore disappears and only survives, in reduced and damaged form, at the end of the action process, in the "result", the identity or even the tautology where that which is made is the norm of that which was targeted. At the end of the chain, an after the event concept which in fact reduces the action process to its result, *whatever happens* (the only meaning of the action process, therefore its norm, lies in the impact on reality).

§ 93.   The second research approach involves revisiting and taking over the second, separate issue of the norm of the economic action process and, at the same time, connecting once again the two separate issues of the Subject and the norm by founding the norm as closely as possible on the Subject and not on the impact (the result) of its action process directed towards the world. This undertaking itself includes two periods of time or sequences. At first, it is a question of showing that the economic Subject constitutes a structure which stimulates a dynamic which is the economic action process, a specific structure endowed with a particular space-time reference frame and an innermost structure of time-matter (duration). This first stage shows that the economic Subject may and must be anchored within the specific methods of references and operation. It is thus shown that the methods of determination and stimulation of the action process refer back to (i.e. originate from), modes of being and time which overhang, determine and transcend the strict forms of the action, forms which are filled and structured by pure negativity (transforming projection towards that which is not yet in being). It is shown that the forms of the Subject's action in the process which leads to the final real impact on the world are forms inhabited by negativity but which possess an innermost raw matter, an essential, dense structure made up of time-duration and modes of being, a structure which is continuously obliterated by the Subject in its action process.

§ 94.   It is therefore possible to found the forms of action on firmer ground where the possibility of a norm exists again, far from the actual impact of the action. This is the objective of the second stage. A practical approach for the determination of norms becomes possible. Once the economic action process is described as the obliteration of matter, it becomes possible for the Subject to be supervised but not denied and for the process or development which moves from the Subject to the actual impact (and back) – this is the only modern understanding – to be connected to a much wider process where that which constitutes such matter comes to the Subject and lines, inhabits the depths of its reference frames within which, in the same way that a spark creates an explosion, the interplay of the obliterating consciousness produces forms inhabited by negativity (the image-objects), i.e. through the project, through the transforming action. This negativity produced by the consciousness of the acting Subject (which at first perceives) provides the key to the fundamental temporality of the economic project – and which is very generally found on the financial markets, which organise their exchange and movement: anticipation and projection which refer back to a being which is in a state of non-being. However, this temporality provided by the Subject's obliterating consciousness cannot be what it is and cannot endure without the dense, raw matter which provides it with energy as it were and this is essential: the weightier the temporality, which looks on from the viewpoint of being, which is on this occasion the temporality of duration. These two dimensions of time form one and the same within the economic and financial Subject, since the Subject's space-time reference frames are explosion chambers which combine the two. The Subject is in a state of being (temporality of duration) and is also in a state of non-being (temporality of the obliterating consciousness).

This has considerable consequences. Negativity, this vapour which inhabits the image-objects, these forms of projection and anticipation which structure the action process on the world through the financial markets in the modern age, this negativity finds its meaning, connection and mooring in a matter which founds it and surpasses it, explains it and transcends it, i.e. these blocks of duration, a section of time which is itself in slow motion and driven by memory recall and lapse. There resides the innermost matter of the Subject, a matter which surpasses it, a matter sustained by time, by facts, events, the world, the duration of the Subject, its life and its action. Confronting this reality of being, there are two main driving forces which create the movement: the obliterating consciousness, memory and forgetfulness.

Consequently, the economic and financial facts and objects which, as we have seen, can all be reduced to one or more forms of image-objects produced within the Subject's specific space-time reference frame and which inhabit the financial markets like active ghosts float within Scottish castles, originate from the fundamental matter of duration. This matter commands the principal modes of being which structure economics and finance (including value or equilibrium). Consequently, economic and financial facts and objects may not only be explained but standardised on the basis of this transcendental field of time-matter, relative references since this matter remains alive, in slow motion, driven by the impulses of memory and forgetfulness in relation to all the facts and events which, at each instant, come from the world.

§ 95.   The field of the economic and financial norm proceeds from that which makes the fundamental modes of being conceivable (value, equilibrium...) and which, unsurprisingly as shown in *Tractatus* and *Généalogie*, the modern age has overturned (thus economics become the "reflection" of imbalance and equilibrium sinks into oblivion like a curiosity from another age) or contorted its contents, as it were. Accordingly, value in the modern sense is conceived on the basis of the negativity of the obliterating consciousness which projects the action, and also on the basis of the result on impact, whilst the value continues to be defined for us, in the final analysis, as a process reminding us of a deeper time-matter in order to create an energy (that of the acting Subject); that which has value is at all times and in all places that which includes a high index of density of time-matter thus defined, of which duration is one of the principal elements. In the same way a diamond contains more or less carats, any economic and financial fact or object contains a certain presence of this fundamental DNA, which will produce the energy of the action and the quality of the action when set in motion.

Accordingly, even if the image-objects which have been sorted, exchanged or destroyed on the Stock Market may seem to be pure bubbles, sometimes empty of projection – and certain prove to be true illusions – there is always a DNA of time-matter attached to any project, any action, which can be defined, estimated and which contains what we call the value of an economic or financial image-object, fact or object. At any given time, the latter may be brought back to this reference point which normally proceeds with a sufficient degree of inertia to afford an opportunity for it to be observed. In the same way, at any given time, a norm may be defined for a set of economic and financial facts, events or objects, since the latter may be reduced to one or more series of DNA of the same type.

The determination of the economic and financial norm consequently involves, for a series of facts, events or objects which can be described as economic or financial (growth, inflation, the real interest rate, a company's results are the best known examples but there are many others), defining the relevant transcendental field (we have seen that it is largely defined on the basis of a time-matter made up of duration) and, consequently, the space-time reference frame which is itself relevant, within which reference points are identified as points of the framework and therefore the structure of the norm. It is a *series* of economic and financial facts, events or objects which is connected, in its capacity as a phenomenon which is specifically economic or financial (inflation is a series, a complete phenomenon which encompasses facts, events and objects), to a specific spatio-temporal field which possesses a space-time signature. We know that this space-time signature is not itself fixed or moored to the impulses of memory or forgetfulness. By securing itself to this field which transcends it (because it is made up of it), the economic or financial series acquires consistency and meaning as a series, i.e. a total phenomenon, a complete economic or financial structure. By securing itself to this field, the economic series acquires access to the key, i.e. the possibility, of the modes of being which provide meaning to the norm, i.e. acquires access for example to value or equilibrium. Since such modes of being of value or equilibrium only acquire meaning insofar as a matter or element can be identified and defined, which one can presume is in a state of being, without having to ask whether it is the ultimate essence for all that. It is because a field of time-matter may be confined (i.e. in simple terms, a set of sequences of time which form duration like geological layers or rings of age in a tree), a field of time-matter which will enable the specific space-time reference frame of economics and finance, that a link can be established between that which has value and a certain degree of intensity or density of this raw material. First, that which, like DNA, contains an intensity of matter (we could say of duration, in the sense of being, in which we use the term duration) has value. The existing facts, events and objects which have value are certainly often the results (we have used the term impact) within the reality of projects which developed from a zone of inexistence since they were to occur, to become; anticipations which were more or less imagined, imaginary or illusory. This may mean that the value within the project is at the stage of the image-object (and, therefore, that such value remains somewhat ghostlike). That is not correct: the value lies in the intensity of time-matter which founds the image-object which is projected onto the white screen of the financial markets after having been projected onto that of the consciousness and before progressively loading itself with reality up until impact. Accordingly, the image-objects, since they originate from a time-matter which transcends them, found their values there and nowhere else and it is this value that can be found at the end of the process within the real object, after impact.

§ 96.   Value is, first of all, as we have said, an intensity (of being) of time-matter. However, that is not enough. The intensity of time-matter is certainly provided in the same way as the fraction of real gold within a gold coin but not once and for all, since the coin may change. We have seen that time-matter, provided in unrefined fashion like a section of time and being, evolves, is distorted, contracts or dilates according to the stimulations of the imaging/acting consciousness (which obliterates such matter in order to project it into the action by transforming it into energy), and to the recalls or lapses of memory as well. This means that there are series, objects, projects and economic and financial "things" which exist in order to encompass everything which may fall within this sort of designation, including the initial intensity of time-matter, which may be higher or lower, more or less concentrated, and will diminish and others whose intensity will increase or, more simply, be more present, more in demand because the imaging capacity of the Subject will be more stimulating and active or because the memory will maintain a dynamic of intense energy.

Accordingly, value is a function of an initial intensity of time-matter (a static dimension); a relatively stable and to some extent absolute element of reference. However, since this initial intensity may be more or less intensely in demand, used or stimulated within the action by the consciousness, the memory or value may itself be modified, become less stable, in the same way that, in ancient Greece, there were special periods of time when the presence of gold or silver in the reference gold or silver currencies diminished, even though the object (which we will refer to as the image-object) remained unchanged in appearance. There lies the issue of value.

§ 97.   The value may accordingly be both a yardstick within the field of the norm, may experience fluctuations as a yardstick and, finally, be more or less "demonstrated", "realised" or mobilised in its capacity as energy. The first dimension is immediate: the delimitation of a field of time-matter which creates consistency for one or more economic and financial series, provides the place of reference and the reference point, and therefore the value; this time-matter transcends and determines the series; this time-matter experiences a dynamic when it comes into contact with the impulses of the consciousness and the memory of a economic Subject. The second dimension (experiencing the fluctuations as a yardstick) expresses to a large extent this final point. The time-matter of reference, which we have said is in a state of being (duration constitutes the major strength), is not absolutely static. The time-matter which we are discussing is relative transcendental reality, i.e. cannot claim to be absolute time but is, instead, a relative form (i.e. a certain section cut out of the practical time of economic and financial facts, event and objects, with regard to a consciousness of the economic Subject) of absolute time (one always reasons on the basis of a section of time which is sufficiently large and complex in order to form duration and a relative but not total reference for an absolute equilibrium or value). Consequently, the only accessible time-matter within a practical approach (a temporal section of duration which forms the average, to simplify matters to the extreme) constitutes an organism which is in natural motion (in the sense that such motion results from the mere lapse of clock time, all else being equal), a slow motion which contains a linearity which is that of clock time. Next to this movement which we have described as natural there exists a second dynamic of another type, marked by discontinuities and interruptions. This dynamic is provided by the imaging consciousness (production of image-objects by and within the financial imagination) and by the forces of memory/forgetfulness. This involves, as we have seen, powerful distorting and transforming vectors of time-matter, which will therefore experience fluctuations as a yardstick. The point is an important one: we manage to establish, from a practical viewpoint, fields of time-matter as a refuge for the references for value and equilibrium and, consequently, normative points of reference (the possibility of a norm); such fields form relative universes, however, in the sense that they are not purely sufficient of themselves: the very existence of a Subject which stimulates the processes of the consciousness (imaging, memorising and forgetting…) and therefore of action, is enough to maintain the movement. The value thus manages to exist on the basis of the fields of time-matter which define themselves because it provides their innermost structure, which we have named the space-time reference frames. Such fields, even relative ones, therefore provide the possibility of equilibria (themselves relative) and therefore of norms. To think of defining, for the economic series called "inflation", a field of time-matter thus involves identifying the most relevant temporal "section" in order to explain the behaviour of the series within a given macro-financial regime, a block of duration and memory (and also of gaps of forgetfulness). This section forms an initial field of time-matter (duration) which, driven by the impulses of the imaging consciousness, of memory and forgetfulness, forms a space-time reference frame, an explosion chamber within which the action logic is incubated and then propelled. The field of time-matter for inflation will certainly include series of prices, settled by memory, but also all forms of elements which, with regard to a price, existed when the said price was formed and provide it with its meaning as well to some extent.

The value therefore experiences fluctuations in its capacity as a yardstick, on a base of equilibrium which is itself in motion and on a base of time-matter which is itself slowly drifting, a sort of inert motion in a normal regime, which does not prevent, – in fact quite the contrary – the sudden discontinuities or even more violent interruptions when the flashes of the imaging consciousness, of memory and forgetfulness, whether or not at the time of a mere fact or event which, as such, would not have held any energy, set the surprisingly powerful processes and flights of enthusiasm in motion. The benchmarks, the references and therefore the norms are always elusive, moving targets and the normative task can be compared to the labour of Sisyphus. In the same way, it can be more easily understood that fraud and all the phenomena which seem to deny the form or note the lack thereof, stem from grey areas where some economic and financial fact, event, object or innovation has caused a field of time-matter to lapse and, with it, a set of points of equilibrium, value and benchmark. This process of the sudden aging of the norm, which causes its circumvention or obsolescence, is the expiry process of a field of time-matter, which comes from memory or the (imaging and acting) consciousness. An intervening period opens up when, for some time, a new (in the sense of different) field of time-matter is progressively outlined, which provides sense and coherence for the new data (facts, events, objects) relating to an environment, which we have called the macro-financial regime. The strictly legal work of determining the new form will accompany this carving out of another field of duration and therefore of being.

Finally, we have emphasised a third dimension, which requires that the value is more or less evident, realised or mobilised in its capacity as energy. This dimension is different from the previous one, which characterises the dynamic which is to some extent specific to the time-matter (i.e. that which arrives when all else is equal, i.e. without any special stimulation or intervention from the conscious Subject which conceives the images, anticipates in order to act, remembers and/or forgets). We have however introduced the Subject's impulses in order to indicate the discontinuous dynamics which could result therefrom within the field of time-matter and within the specific space-time reference frames, discontinuities which can be found at work with great constancy in all the economic and financial series. Within this third dimension, there is the idea that the primary time-matter may be dilated or contracted significantly by such dynamics, i.e. that the energy (in the sense in which we defined it in *Dynamique*) derived from the shock between, first, the impulses of the forms of consciousness, of memory and forgetfulness, and, second, time-matter, may vary considerably *for a given unit of time-matter.*

§ 98.   The value is therefore both a stock (i.e. of time-matter, of duration) and a flow (the energy liberated by the shock between the designs of the imaging and acting consciousness, or the impulses of memory and forgetfulness on the one hand and time-matter on the other). This means that any economic and financial series (the results of a company, market prices, real or financial variables) has a fundamental value, as it were, which is attached to one or, more rarely, several fields of time-matter and a value, which is more fluctuating, which is linked to the intensity of the mobilisation of the time-matter, for any form of project. This relates to a value provided by the degree of energy released by the mobilisation of this duration, of this block of time-matter by the imaging and acting forms of consciousness and also by memory and forgetfulness. This can be shown as:

$$V = f(Vf, Ve)$$

where Vf = fundamental value and Ve = value – energy.

The value which is said here to be fundamental is the gross value of the relevant field of time-matter for the series. We have seen that this gross value provides the platform for what we have called a (macro-financial) regime and a *relative* general equilibrium which itself encompasses an infinite number of relative equilibria. This gross value is characterised by a certain inertia (since its innermost structure is duration and compression of the past) and a certain stability (general resilience to economic and financial events, facts and objects which make up the daily life of linear clock time – unless the latter highlight a major flaw and require a reversal) up until the development, the breach or reversal of the regime (from the development, a central scenario, to the crack in the regime, which is called a crisis). This gross value therefore retains a relative nature, which is doubly relative since it takes root in an initial field of time-matter which is a section of duration *among other* possibilities (which makes this gross, fundamental value necessary and also reveals the uncertainties) and, moreover, since it experiences the shocks originating from the contact with the Subject (the imaging and acting consciousness, memory recall and lapse) and the world (the facts, events and objects).

§ 99.   In the practical world of economics and finance, it is (Ve) which appears and which remains visible, with a certain volatility, while drawing all its meaning from (Vf) which underpins it by means of a field of time-matter. It is this link of necessity and also of uncertainty between (Ve) and (Vf) which means that (Ve), contrary to the strong temptation to consider it as only an unpredictable variable, which is ultimately devoid of meaning (random walk, critical representation of economics and finance as contingencies within an absurd universe), is finally based on a fairly firm platform. In the practical world, (Ve) should be at least equal to (Vf), provided that the impulses of the consciousness, of memory recall and lapse are non-existent (no impulse, i.e. C, $M/F) = 0$). $(Vf) = (Ve)$ for $(C, M/F = 0)$. However the situation where $(C, M/F = 0)$ corresponds in fact to a lack of impulse from the consciousness, from memory and forgetfulness, and therefore to a lack of bombardment of electrons on the time-matter. Once there is a bombardment or a shock with time-matter, the latter may dilate and grow but it may also contract. In this case, i.e. when $(C, M/F \neq 0)$, (Ve) may be greater than (Vf) but may also be *less* than (Vf) . When $(Ve) <$ (Vf) for $(C, M/F \neq 0)$, one is in the so-called zones of undervaluation, which one can expect to produce a standardisation, but without complete assurance since, as we have seen, (Vf) may also experience a variation which may be more or less slow or more or less marked. This means that what may appear to be an undervaluation may occasionally not be, since the underlying value (Vf) is itself undergoing a revision of regime. Conversely, when $(Ve) > (Vf)$, practices and territories of overvaluation become possible, subject to the same limit stated in the previous situation, since once again (Vf) may have moved (less than one might wish to say however; there lies the traditional argument of the periods of bubbles; however, the regimes, as we have seen, are slower and more inert than one would like to believe).

The instantaneous economic and/or financial value is therefore, at any given time, the product of a so-called fundamental value provided by a predefined field of time-matter and of a so-called energy value provided by a certain activation or, on the contrary, a deactivation of such time-matter within at least a triple dimension of production capacity for image-objects (imaging consciousness), of intensity of memory recalls and also of intensity of lapses of memory. The so-called energy value is the variable which appears on observation, which is "visible" in the same way as a nominal and visible interest rate and a real interest rate is not. This is because the fundamental value is not immediately visible but is nonetheless accessible through the reiterations around the notion of a referential field of time-matter. Although the instantaneous value (so-called energy value) may seem extraneous to any form and, as it were, left to its own devices; it is, in fact, always possible to attach it to a field which contains within it the possibility of a norm.

All these arguments are intended to show the possibility of a norm even though the majority of economic and financial variables, i.e. the series (facts, events and objects), seem in modern times increasingly beyond reach in the sense of the capacity of comprehension and the capacity of normative control. This feeling is not unjustified given the extent to which the modern use of economics has progressively dissolved and eliminated (*Vf*) and improperly left (*Ve*) alone. The modern use has however managed to effect a separation between (*Vf*) and (*Ve*) and emancipation of the Subject (*Ve*) in a form of self-referenced isolation. However, the elimination of (*Vf*) for the modern man does not mean a definitive disappearance or destruction. (*Vf*) is there for anyone who takes the same road of a referential field which contains a certain coherence in respect of the modes of being (time-matter and duration are in a state of being) when faced with the imbalance and inexistence logics borne unsurprisingly and *legitimately* by the Subject within the action (the project remains as that which is in a state of non-being). By showing that the Subject cannot be left to its own devices but, on the contrary, operates on the basis of fields of reference containing equilibrium, even if only relative, one is afforded another chance to overcome in positive fashion the sole criticism, which is moreover justified, of the modern purpose of economics and finance being under the yoke of the conscious Subject, conqueror of a world to be transformed.

§ 100. Thousands of possibilities unfurl, on an almost unlimited basis, once it is shown that the economic and financial fact, event, object or act are the result of a shock between a design (imaging and acting consciousness, memory recall and lapse; other forms of design can be identified and this forms part of a future research topic) and a block of duration which forms a field of time-matter, such a shock occurring within a specific space-time reference frame whose structure we have provided; once it is established that everything which, in economic and financial matters, appears (the fact of observation), not only does not form part of a pure and complete chance or contingency, but can be linked to firm ground from two points of view: any economic and financial *series* (set of facts, events, objects or acts) only acquires a necessity and therefore a meaning if it is in close relation to a coherent field of duration (time-matter); and, moreover, the innermost structure of the unitary elements which form the series (some or other price for the "inflation" series), and the structure of the series themselves are made up of such time-matter; once it is understood that the shock between the Subject's designs and the duration/time-matter releases or destroys an energy within a space-time reference frame which is not that of clock time nor of the space of playing fields; this means that the norm, far from being an inaccurate representation of inertia, stability and homogeneity, which are to some extent perpetual or eternal, is created, lives, develops and dies within a milieu which is traversed by discontinuities and violence, interruptions, contractions and dilations. This last point is important since it runs counter to a good part of the traditional *normative* work. Once one accepts, as we have, that there can be no satisfactory understanding of economic and financial phenomena (or market phenomena in our work on market dynamics) without taking unconditional account of such a specific space-time reference frame, it may be tempting – it is a continuous and dominant temptation – to declare or even consider that it is impossible to determine a norm, seeing a sort of contradiction in the terms. Such an attitude is an abdication. On the contrary, it is by starting from the special features of the space-time reference frame of economics and finance, which are certainly disconcerting, and its modes of operation that one must and may establish the norm within this living organism. The norm, in its innermost conceptual structure resembles the milieu within which it finds its source and develops. To take this referential requirement of the norm truly into account is undoubtedly one of the main theoretical priorities when considering modern economics and finance as being *beyond the Subject but also with the Subject*. A large part of the difficulties and rejections regarding the requirements of economic and financial normative work is due to what can be described as an incomprehension and misunderstanding of the very idea of a norm.

The modern impression of the increasing impossibility of a norm leads one, in fact, to look more closely at the very idea of a norm. The idea of a norm is often discussed within a field of theoretical comprehension of phenomena which the said norm was supposed to control and regulate, which is at least inadequate and occasionally quite simply incorrect, in the light of the observations made. In particular, the idea of an economic norm was developed with and within a certain economic and financial reference frame, requiring linearity, for example, and not adopting duration, memory and forgetfulness; in short falling outside the idea of a specific space-time reference frame which we have advanced. Not only was the description of economics, which the construction of the norm was supposed to apply to, incorrect but, in addition, the true operation of economics and finance proved to resemble only remotely what was understood to be "normal". The crisis surrounding the idea of an economic and financial norm, and consequently the idea of regulation, is an intellectual crisis where a certain number of themes (linearity, symmetrical rationality, a homogenous three-way-split of past-present-future...) are seriously called into question. This will not result in the disappearance of the need for a norm nor of the possibility of constructing such a norm.

For that, we consider that it is essential to (re)commence with the economic and financial Subject (*homo economicus*) since that is the focal point for the economic and financial action process, a process which constitutes the dominant structure of economics and finance in the modern era. There is accordingly an economic Subject, and its mode of operation and its reference frames; we establish from the outset the strong proximity/identity between the Subject's mind (and all that may be connected thereto) and the structure of the consciousness. In our view, the dominant structure, by far, of the economic Subject's approach is the consciousness. This consciousness is targeted: as such it is an imaging and acting consciousness (it is acting because it is imaging), an obliterating force of projection and anticipation. This consciousness is not only force of negativity; its innermost structure is temporal, made up of duration. All things considered, the time-matter (duration) is distorted/given form by the designs of the consciousness, which may take many forms and are often described as psychological (remorse, feeling of fairness...) but which, if one wishes to cut to the essential, are based on the fundamental forms and structures of the image (imaging consciousness), of the memory (remembering cons-ciousness) and of forgetfulness (forgetting consciousness). These are the three pillars of the acting consciousness. It is always and throughout by means of these axes that the design of the economic and financial action travels down its path towards the world and actual impact, through *inter alia* the financial markets, which are forms which gather the image-objects. Since the economic act is always an image which follows the path of reality and the impact.

§ 101.   The *animal spirits* which are rightly discussed by Keynes and later by others have the virtue of drawing attention to the principal topic which is that of the modes of operation and reference frames of the economic Subject (*homo economicus*), and more specifically to their particular nature. That said, the term "animal spirits" creates a certain degree of confusion, since it deludes one into believing that the mechanisms, reference frames and manners of acting within economics and finance elude any rational, and consequently normative, approach, such "spirits" developing *besides* the conscious structures of the Subject's reasoning. We do not agree with this: the work on the *animal spirits* must be careful to show the existence of a specific, comprehensible space-time reference frame which may accordingly produce norms. Secondly, we greatly prefer the term *consciousness of the Subject* to that of *animal spirits*: it is indeed the consciousness and its various terms of design and reliance on time which constitute the heart of the system. *Consciousness, time, design.* Thirdly, and this is linked to the previous point, one should not disperse ones ideas in order to point out every possible psychological form; there are plenty, and we will show, with interest, that they assist the understanding of certain economic and financial phenomena. It is more important, at least at this first stage, to look for and put in place the framework, the specific space-time reference frame of the conscious economic Subject, a framework within which all occasional psychological forms (remorse, fairness…) may be described.

There are accordingly no particularly "animal" spirits but only a spirit, the spirit in the sense that it forms one, together with the conscious Subject, in its targeting of the world. This defines the said spirit's need to understand and the mode of being and operating of its own reference frames. Together with this requirement, one has the requirement of what should be called a *theory of knowledge*, since the central issue of modern economics is the relationship between the economic Subject (*homo economicus*) and the world, a relationship of design, perception, apprehension, inspection and transformation within an action process which passes in transit in various psychic (images, anticipations…) and practical (financial markets…) forms, a relationship which is progressively invaded by this Subject which the modern era emancipates and projects without limits. This economic and financial Subject is consciousness (of); this fundamental point introduces the economic and financial Subject (*homo economicus*) as the pivotal point of a theory of knowledge on which a theory and later a praxis of the economic and financial action can be based. Modern economics, as it is structured and as it develops, summons to its core a theory of the Subject/consciousness (of) which is a theory of knowledge and an ontology.

This means that the various purely, or specifically, psychological angles, which have to a certain extent been successfully included within the expression of "animal spirits", angles which are all interesting, fruitful and legitimate, nonetheless lack an issue and ambition: modern economics and finance require a theoretical thinking of the economic and financial Subject which cannot be limited to a psychology of attitudes, behaviours and phenomena, even if the relevance of such an approach can be established, which is the case; particularly, if it means implying an irrationality in the sense of an incomprehensibility of the matter at issue ("animals"). It is preferable to remember what is essential in this incomplete psychological approach: the economic Subject lies at the heart of the modern economic and financial system; this Subject responds to pronounced special features of nature and operation, which permeate the economic and financial phenomena and acts to a profound extent and which have to be understood. This is essential but, as we have shown, this double effort must be effected from the starting point of a theory of the Subject which is a theory of knowledge and ontology. In particular, if one starts from the definition of the Subject with consciousness (of) and design, there proceeds a possible understanding of the economic action process. To place oneself within such a framework is all the more important, if the said theoretical framework of knowledge (imaging consciousness, acting consciousness, remembering consciousness, forgetting...; modes of being of duration understood as time-matter and essence – that which is – and structures the conscious Subject as well as the action process within which the Subject projects itself), therefore provides the means and the tools for reflecting upon the norm (i.e. the possibility of a economic and financial norm and regulation), reflecting therefore on the limits for the Subject and its action process in respect of the appropriation and transformation of the world, which seems, in effect, to be "without limits", without norms and therefore devoid of meaning; therefore reflecting on the limits for the Subject, beyond the Subject but *with* the Subject, i.e. starting from the innermost structure which defines it and permeates the economic and financial facts, events, acts and objects, as we have shown.

This theory of the economic (and financial) Subject, *homo economicus*, is economic (and financial) ontology and theory of knowledge first, in order to provide the framework of reflection within which the facets of pure psychology, sociology, ethnology… of all the prisms of human sciences may place themselves like so many coloured pieces of a stained glass window. Since all such prisms of human sciences have in common an economic Subject which contains the requirement of being considered as an economic Subject which knows and acts (the structure whose framework we are proposing) while being described, by the menu as it were, in its attitudes through human sciences. There is, through such prisms, only one sole economic Subject which carries within it the nature and conditions of the relationship with the world in the modern era, a relationship which specifically takes the name of economics (accordingly everything becomes "economics" within reality and within language); this unique economic Subject requires a unitary theory which may federate and give meaning to each of the individual approaches adopted by the various human sciences.

§ 102.   Such an approach leads one to search for the essential principles which support the structure of the system [economic Subject/world], the relationship being effected by what is commonly called "economic action". The same applies to the duration, memory recall and lapse within the theory which we have advanced. These pillars must be such that all the other aspects advanced by human sciences (often in the manner of observed behaviours which contradict the traditional assertions of economic science) may find their place and an explanation underneath the framework thus constructed. This is in particular true of the themes of the "Behavioural School", an approach which makes an observational link between the behaviours of the Subject and the economic act, which often run counter to the assertions which the theory could advance up until then. Such an approach, which is fruitful, is very largely based on the observation of behaviours which are sufficiently recurrent for them to be presented as forms of psychological "laws" (this is true of monetary illusion and therefore of the inflexible reduction of nominal variables, including wages in particular). Observations of fact resulting from the Subject's action are described in this way but nothing is said of the Subject itself in more general terms, i.e. from the point of view of the relationship between the economic Subject and the world, structures therefore of perception, imagination, of space-time reference frame, anticipation… all structures which determine in a crucial manner the economic action process strictly speaking and which in fact define a theoretical field of economic knowledge and ontology.

Thus, by way of example, a certain number of particular themes discovered by the Subject's observation in its acts (monetary illusion is an example thereof) owe, in addition to the special topic contained in each, their recurrence, i.e. the repeatability or reproducibility of the observations relating to them, to powerful effects of memory, memory which constitutes what we call a structure in similar fashion to forgetfulness which is linked to memory. We have furthermore proposed in *Théorie* an interpretation of the economic cycle in which the dynamic is largely provided by this fundamental structure [memory/forgetfulness]. And numerous themes advanced by the "Behavioural School"'s research are not relevant (solely) because of the theme at play but also due to the fact that "weightier" structures of memory are at play above such themes, structures which refer back to a theory of the economic Subject. To put it plainly, even if the notion of "animal spirits" states clearly that economics depend inevitably on a certain number of functions and structures of the economic Subject, it remains unfortunately very vague in its purely theoretical approach.

The said vagueness can be seen more clearly within the heterogeneous and slightly disorganized inventory of themes identified by observation which have a sufficient recurrence and are presented as "animal spirits". Here one finds, all mixed up, themes which are, strictly speaking, economic (monetary illusion) presented as characteristics of the animal spirit, indeed as an animal spirit, without asking which fundamental structure of the knowing and acting economic Subject this behaviour can be associated with (since here monetary illusion is not a structure of the Subject, an "animal spirit", but rather a consequence within the sphere of action and behaviours); without assessing, as we stated, the effects of memory which may influence the inertia of behaviours and the recurrence thereof. One can also find themes which are not strictly economic but rather moral (fairness, equity) but which are not connected to an analysis and a theory of the economic Subject in its dimensions of values and ethics. The fact that numerous economic and financial behaviours are observed which, counter to the economic rationality which is traditionally accepted, incorporate a dominant, moral determination is not, strictly speaking, an economic question (unlike monetary illusion, at least on first analysis) but refers back to the nature of the economic Subject: does the economic Subject – which, as we have seen, is able to produce norms and limits within the strict field of economics and finance – proceed in its action directed at the world from moral references? In other words, if the behaviours observed in acts within economic life bear witness – which is the case – to determining factors of a moral nature by the economic Subject, then a theory of the economic Subject exists, which, after setting the framework for the Subject's action, has to examine the ethical sources thereof.

§ 103. This therefore means, in all the work which we have conducted, a theoretical approach proceeding from the conscious/unconscious Subject (imaging, acting, remembering, forgetting) to the norm, that we must question the place which ethics may hold therein, given that observation tells us that, at the point of impact with the real world, numerous economic acts, facts and objects are masked by an ethical design such as fairness.

1.1. *THE NORM AND THE FIELD OF REFERENCE*

§ 104. The norm, in terms of its very definition and structure, cannot be different from the definition and structure of the field or reference frame, where its role is to order the economic and financial series. Since the order of economics and finance is so specific that the established categories of order and disorder have to be overturned, practical norms must be the result of rigorous work to render coherent the structures of the norm and that which is normalised. Accordingly, any objective (norm) whatsoever, must form, be formed according to the method of formation of the controlled variable or series itself. If it is established that, within the operation of some or other economic or financial field, the designs of an imaging consciousness, of memory or forgetfulness are the pillars of a particular or specific order (this concerns in fact the normality of economics and finance), then the objective (norm) will be constructed on the basis of such pillars and, second, one will ensure that the norm which is constructed in this way does indeed have its effects within the specific operation of the field or reference frame. It makes sense to incorporate the effects of memory or forgetfulness, image-objects within an inflation objective because the "inflation" series, within its field, within the specific space-time reference frame where it is located, lives within such a reality, such an order. The norm, as we have said, is alive and reacts to facts, events and objects of this environment, whose discontinuities may be surprising. Finally, the resonance of the norm within its referential field – which defines a specific "order" of economics and finance –, the elasticity and reactivity of the norm within this environment, must be accompanied by the norm's capacity to bring an environment which distances itself too much from its DNA (field of time-matter in particular) back towards its base. There lies a great difficulty, since a change of regime within the field, the reference frame – even though the fundamental calibration of the norm was initially correct, in tune with the special features discussed – may make the norm obsolete. A good deal of attention should therefore be devoted, in normative work, to the evolutions and especially to the interruptions of regime (the "normal" evolutions of regimes are fairy slow and marked by a certain degree of inertia but experience shows how linear "false calms" may be misleading, hiding sudden discontinuities). Moreover, from the point of view of normative efficiency, the discrepancy which appears between the objectives (or certain objectives) of the norm and the referential field may turn out to be desirable, since the norm in fact then plays its role as a force of recall (this objective of recall may be expressly desired by the economic policy, which then seeks to base itself on the reference frames of memorised series, for example, in order to direct the action and the activity, as we have shown in *Théorie*). The objective, in such cases, having been maintained, will seek to bring back to a field of time-matter, which defines a relative or limited equilibrium, the series which break away from it fairly sharply (the norm then often contains the memory of the series or facts and events which are related to it); by being introduced in a more voluntarist manner, the objective (norm) may also seek to play with the memory and/or forgetfulness in order to move some old "rubble" within the DNA of the economic and financial series or, on the contrary, aim for a cleaner break. The economic policy action only appears to act upon the immediate moment (see *Théorie*).

§ 105.   The possibility and effectiveness of the economic and financial norm are complete within the nature of the relationship between the norm and what we have called the field of reference, the specific reference frame, which are governed by a sufficiently stable regime to merit the term of regime but sufficiently unstable to establish the existence of evolutions and interruptions, dynamics which may or may not cause disturbance, or even destroy the relationship between the name and the field of time-matter depending upon whether the norm manages to obtain, through the movement of evolution or interruption, a refuge which remains relevant or, on the contrary, will lapse because of the dynamic (the question whether a norm remains relevant, although the evolution of the field seems to state otherwise, is an essential one; it is a question of analysing real evolutions within the field and decisions of economic policy as well, in order to assert this or, rather, to impose the norm in order to force a targeted evolution of the field).

The relationship between the norm and the field of reference is therefore central. The norm emerges, must emerge from the specific space-time reference frame which structures the field. This first coherence of innermost structure (same fundamental characteristics of space-time, of the reference to duration, memory and forgetfulness in the construction of the field of the economic and financial series and its operating mode: the series' norm and field must speak the same language, that is the initial condition for a possible norm). Second, there is the question of correlation, alignment between the regime which governs the field of the series (for example, a block of duration, of time-matter with the reference x) and the regime which governs the norm. Several cases may arise which indicate that the relationship is multiple and, especially, that it may be the object of a design of economic policy action. The two regimes may be aligned as follows:

$$(\text{refl}(x) = \text{ref2}(y) \text{ where } x = y).$$

This corresponds to the periods of "normal" conditions, when the determining factors of the field's regime are stable and even provide the feeling of linearity of the reference frame's operating modes. The norm merely traces this regularity and stability and this suffices to render it credible and effective. Another general scenario shows that the two regimes may not be connected:

$$(\text{refl}(x) \neq \text{ref2}(y) \text{ where } x \neq y).$$

In a scenario $(x > y)$, there is a more or less sudden mutation of the regime of the series' field (disinflation, deflation with regard to the "inflation" series), as compared to a regime of the norm which does not change (for example, by means of exaggeration, an inflation norm-objective in a regime of disinflation or indeed, in principle, of deflation, a norm of 15% profitability of companies' return on equity as an objective within a context of 2% growth and not much higher price increases). The (established) norm must resist, oppose or resign (change). It can be seen that the field of possibilities is fairly wide, as is that of action. If it resists: analysis shows that the evolution of the field's regime is not serious enough to justify the relinquishment of the anchorage. If it opposes: this involves a variant, where the norm will be modified, *in the direction which it used to be*, accentuated in order to counter and resecure a field which is prey to a drifting. If it resigns: the change of norm (of the norm's referential regime to be more precise) results from a breach of the series' regime, which is longstanding and established, or from an innovation or novation which modifies the field (grey, non-standardised, non-regulated zones which are typically revealed by the movements of economic and financial innovations, the triggering of a crisis within the grey zone which precipitates the creation or change of norm). In this last situation, it can often be seen that the economic and/or financial crisis is the element which triggers the norm which either did not exist or existed but was not relevant (a circumvention in certain cases). It can thus be seen that, in such occurrences, the norm is running behind the field and the evolutions/mutations of its regime; this opens up another possibility, that of the pre-emptive determination of the norm, which is in fact very rare but which remains a possibility for the economic policy action, provided the latter allocates itself adequate resources for an upfront analysis of the changes. Finally, if $y > x$, there is a situation where the series' regime is reasonably stable but the regime of the norm is mute. These are the situations in which the economic policy action decides to modify the norm or establish it with the intended modification of the regime of the field of the series. Since, and this should not be forgotten, although the regime of the field of the economic and financial series is as it were information of that which is (and by that we mean that which has been, which lasts, even if accompanied by discontinuities of memory recalls and lapses) the norm, for its part, is always and throughout the act of the Subject's design (collective in this instance in the majority of situations) as an economic policy action.

§ **106.**   One of the main problems posed by the norm, once the question of whether it is possible has been overcome, is that of its capacity to forewarn, which means to see far into the distance in order to forewarn. The norm often appears, in fact, to lag behind evolutions within the field of the series which it is supposed to regulate. This reflects a fact: the norms are not sufficiently considered as living organisms, which are continuously adapting (or being breached), just like the fields of economic and financial series, which are the subject of regulation. It is less a question of constantly changing the norms – nothing would be worse for their credibility, since the time-matter of duration is ultimately the guarantee of such credibility – than of constructing and organising the norm so that it incorporates an adaptive dynamic within its life. A major effort still needs to be made with regard to the determination of new generations of norms considered as (self-)adaptive organisms which react to or even forewarn of that which may occur within the field which governs the series.

Furthermore, we have seen that the economic and financial dynamic largely depended upon the shocks which occur between a time-matter of duration and the impulses of the Subject, whose imaging consciousness, memory recall and lapse constitute significant dimensions. Such shocks between time-matter and the designs of the Subject determine the field of dynamic or active time-matter within which most of the economic and financial series evolve, and whose regime they define. The norm, for its part, only exists through the Subject's design based on the time-matter which forms the structure of the field of the series and by separation from the said field (extraction). It is accordingly a *different* design of the Subject from that which, through its impulses, forms, determines and drives the field of the series and its regime and which has a different nature. This suggests that there is a form of normative consciousness, which establishes the norm beyond, set back from, outside the field of the series. What is the true nature of this design, of this consciousness which we call the normative consciousness?

This normative consciousness borrows largely from the imaging and acting consciousness which we have described in *La dynamique*. It sets before it objects which are in a state of non-being but which we know are, in their innermost structure, constituted from a time-matter of being and duration (in many respects this comes to the same thing) in which the Subject-consciousness's design of negativity will pierce a hole which is the (normative) project. As such, the norm may be described as the outcome of a process which involves the production of an image-object. However, the projects found at the heart of the Subject's action process – from the image-object up until the actual impact, passing through the financial market phase – and the process of determination of the norm are not necessarily of the same type. Intuition would suggest that the possibility of a norm and therefore its capacity to transcend in order to regulate, involves an essential differentiation with regard to the field; moreover, if the same economic and financial Subject informs the time-matter within the field of the series by means of its designs *and* produces the impulse of the design which produces the norm, is it not, in fact, impossible to be both there (the field) and elsewhere (the norm)? We consider this risk to be exaggerated. The norm, while originating in terms of its structure from the being of duration and time-matter which transcends the whole action process, beyond and with the Subject, is the very assertion of the act of the economic and financial Subject.

This is what has been lost in the modern era, due to the fact that the Subject is the means by which the norm is determined, that by this very act, the Subject limits, transcends and surpasses itself, far from any intention of absolute assertion regarding things and the world. To say that there is a possibility of a norm, that the economic and financial Subject can be transcended and limited in its relationship with the world and that the most important act of the economic and financial Subject is to establish the norm before it, all amounts to saying the same thing.

1.2. THE NORM AND NORMALITY

§ 107.   Consequently, the possibility of *normality* arises for modern economics considered within the implacable logic of a projection which appropriates and transforms the world, which is that of the economic Subject as such Subject is constituted in the modern times. Within this system of logic, there is strictly speaking no economic norm (and, consequently no moral or political norm), since the pure action project (which is in a state of non-being) occupies all the space and is, above all, reduced, in its very meaning, to the impact which it has on the world: the norm arises after the event, is subject to the impact and is therefore largely dismantled. Within this system of logic, as we have largely shown (*Tractatus*, *Généalogie*, *Valeur et temps*), there is a reversal of concepts and values (equilibrium *versus* imbalance, for example) and the effacement of concepts of being which may found the norm (accordingly equilibrium is given increasingly less consideration and economics becomes a form of reflection of imbalance).

We have shown the conditions in which it remained possible to overcome the deadlock ("Only a god may save us" – in short) as indicated by a diagnosis, which was moreover justified. The possibility of constructing a norm for economics and finance *with* the economic Subject, a norm which comes within the economic action process, involves consideration of the completely specific nature of the space-time reference frames of economics and finance. This specific nature, which can be seen as an abnormality of economic and financial behaviours and phenomena and a reason not to try to standardise or regulate, constitutes the platform of normality for the economic and financial modes of operation. This is a fundamental point. It is only on this basis that we can construct a norm, within this normality. Much time has been lost by refusing to accept the completely specific nature of the reference frames and fields of economics and finance, in particular the special mental nature of space-time. This represents normality for these universes, which are born and are sustained, as we have seen, by the dynamics of interaction and choice between the obliterating consciousness of the economic Subject which imagines or projects by obliterating (to imagine or anticipate is first to establish that x is in a state of not-yet-being; the role of negativity is essential) and a serious and dense time-matter, which is filled with duration. The Subject's consciousness behaves like a gene gun bombarding dense matter in order to create energy. And the economic Subject, the whole of whose action lies within this bombardment, finds its limit at all times and in all places, and this limit is confused with ours, within this time-matter made up of duration. Consequently, the use of the term animal spirits may be misunderstood and may be misleading if one means some form of incomprehensible abnormality, irrationality, contingency or chance which might consequently lead to a conclusion that it is impossible to standardise or regulate, or ultimately to a profound incapacity. The term *animal spirits* is an appeal for the economic and financial Subject, and at a deeper level for the imaging and acting consciousness, to be understood, together with its operation within the action process which leads to the impact with the world. This effort to understand shows that the economic Subject is not pure obliterating consciousness, pure negativity or limitless freedom; that the economic action, similarly, is not pure negativity. The economic Subject and the economic act or action are based on a platform of time-matter on which the designs of negativity also operate (release of energy, the energy which lies at the heart of economics and finance; but the economic Subject is nothing without this platform and in any event cannot be reduced to its sole capacity to obliterate in order to create or destroy), a platform which also constitutes the horizon of the economic Subject, the project and the economic action. This horizon represents a limit, a norm. At any moment, the imaging and acting consciousness of the Subject may bump into and bounce off duration (the fundamental time-matter), producing energy, dilations and contractions within the space-time reference frame. At any given moment, it is the horizon of duration which, like a force of recall which is itself in motion (the regimes evolve, change and are sometimes broken) provides the limit, norm or meaning. There is a comprehensible whole, including an imaging and acting consciousness which produces designs, a time-matter of duration, an explosion chamber where shocks occur and which is a specific space-time reference frame of a mental nature. This comprehensible whole which contains such fundamental elements forms a normality. By establishing the possibility of a comprehensible whole which forms a normality for the economic and financial facts, events and objects, one is refusing the rejection or dimension which are sometimes implied by the negatively fatalistic interpretations (animal spirits, incomprehensible elements, financial markets given over to irrationality, abnormality leading to a rejection of regulation).

§ 108. What makes regulation possible is therefore the fact that there are not only pure, obliterating designs of the consciousness *and then nothing else* and that there is, also, a fundamental time-matter filled with duration. It is the latter which, like a force of recall, designs and provides both the horizon and limits for the projection of the conscious Subject's design and the platform of time-matter which will determine and constitute the structure and contents of the norm on which will be based the rule creating regulation. An economic Subject which is pure consciousness, a designer of projects in support of the action, pure negativity which is always outside itself and directed at an object which is in a state of non-being, is literally limitless. It is above all *without substance, without matter* since the obliterating design which determines the economic and financial action, in the same way that one lights a fuse, cannot be conceived of practically without this fuel made up of matter, without this innermost framework of the structure of the imaging and acting consciousness of the economic Subject. Such a Subject is undoubtedly so pure that it does not exist. We must on the contrary try to show that, always and everywhere, the dynamic of the economic and financial action implies a Subject which produces designs based on time-matter (duration) which sustains this process. It is this time-matter which constitutes the platform which both sustains the action and assigns its limits (which are those of duration and of memory). Conversely this enables one to state that forgetfulness constitutes undoubtedly the most corrosive element for the structure of time-matter (there are certainly forms of forgetfulness which are necessary or even favourable for the dynamic of economic action but here we are in a deliberately extreme situation). The work of corrosion and destruction of raw time-matter by forgetfulness renders the imaging and acting design of the economic Subject not redundant but without matter, blindly turning in neutral, as it were, limitless and therefore without reason (meaning), the explosion chamber (specific space-time reference frame) where up until then designs and time-matter met which were no longer functioning or, instead, were producing image-objects without matter or framework, more or less harmless illusions.

1.3. *NORMS AND TIME*

§ 109. The norm is founded within time-matter and duration, since the norm defines a rule which did not exist on the basis of an event which is perceived to be new and which reveals the unacceptable nature of the non-existence of a rule or the obsolescence of existing rules, but which cannot, however, ignore that which has occurred in duration and which therefore defines by memory that which is acceptable, at any given moment: the rule is anchored within time-matter, as we have defined the same.

The economic and financial norm responds to what is new (and may even seem to arise from nowhere) but must, in order to be effective, also respond to the incorporation of that which constitutes, within duration, the field which it intends to invest and regulate. The novelty is only superficial. Quite often, it is instead a series of events which throw fresh light on economic and financial facts and objects which are already present, i.e. have been registered within a field (a block of space-time) for a certain period of time. This "fresh light" is literally a new, alternative way of looking at, perceiving or projecting oneself within a given field of economics and finance. The relationship between the economic Subject and this economic and financial field then changes, the appearance of economic and financial "innovations" often indicating this change in the relationship which is another way for the economic Subject to continue the economic action process as we have described it. Such "innovations" indicate a new stage in the economic action process and new resources (the "innovations") for the performance of this action by the economic Subject.

However this "novelty", the "innovations", which shift the vision and the point of view of the economic action process (and not the process itself) affect the constituted time-matter, whose density of duration must be taken into account within the norm, containing precious information. As such, the norm is still continuous since made up of duration, a means of transit for the same economic and financial field (set of facts, events and objects) from one phase (one moment) of the economic action process to another (from one regime to another, in more general terms).

This continuity of duration and time-matter on which the economic and financial norm is based and constructed contains the memory and the trace – which forgetfulness effaces to a greater or lesser degree, which explains the dynamic of this matter – of that which is deemed to be acceptable at any given time within the economic and financial field and within the economic action process. This is an essential point. The norm will always shift the cursor within the field of that which was acceptable and which no longer is, of that which was not acceptable but becomes so. Unless it is rooted in the time-matter of duration and memory, this fundamental role of the norm is impossible, the norm itself is impossible.

The structures which govern that which was acceptable or accepted can be found, stored, within the time-matter of duration and memory, within this block cut out of time. Like time-matter itself, such structures of the acceptable and unacceptable undergo distortions, moving in non-linear form as we have described. It is not a question here of moral structures, strictly speaking, even if the link exists, but rather of that which certain authors (Schiller) have called "animal spirits", like, for example, the feeling of "fairness" (equity, acceptability). Once again, it can be seen that all these forms which are called rather hastily, and rather vaguely, "animal spirits", form part of the modes of the economic Subject's consciousness and, more profoundly, of duration and memory which constitute its innermost structure. Accordingly, the fact of observation – which can be added to the file on "animal spirits" – that "fairness", from among other (moral or behavioural, or both) structures may play an established role in economic and financial phenomena, as a significant structure of the conscious economic Subject, can only be explained and understood by incorporating a time-matter of duration, memory recall and lapse, in non-linear motion, given form by the Subject's designs and by that which chooses, from within the world, the economic and financial facts and events, and by sustaining, as we have shown, the economic action process.

The link between time-matter (duration, memory) and the different structures of the Subject's consciousness (whether they, or the manifestations thereof, are said to be behavioural or psychological) which are sometimes called "animal spirits", provides a key to the interpretation of numerous economic and financial phenomena. The explanation provided solely by means of the "animal spirits", without establishing a principle of the Subject's consciousness and exploring the aspects thereof, will not suffice. However, a careful exploration may help clarify a few contours of key concepts, such as *propensities* (to consume, to save…) or equally important relationships, such as that of unemployment and inflation.

2. THE RELATIONSHIP BETWEEN UNEMPLOYMENT AND INFLATION

§ 110.   The inflexible reduction in wages (attributed to an animal spirit of "fairness", i.e. of equity and acceptability more generally) at a time when deflationist pressures roam, may lead to an actual rise in wages when, effectively, prices drop, and a rise in unemployment which restores equilibrium. This means that the anticipation of inflation (the reduction in this instance) is not correct: the economic Subject commits an error of anticipation. As such, the phenomena of nominal inflexibility in the reduction (here of wages) would be linked to what is indeed the mediocre quality of anticipation of inflation but also, perhaps, to a greater difficulty in anticipating a reduction than a rise in inflation, all the more so when in zones of low inflation (asymmetry of anticipation). Conversely, the anticipations (of a rise) in inflation when inflation is rising would be of better and increasing quality, restoring the relevance of an unemployment/inflation trade-off in a zone of high inflation in the absolute *and* of anticipation on a rising trend.

Such a structure of phenomena resulting from observation may be understood by introducing time-matter (duration, memory) to an explanation of its structure and operation. That which is described as an error in the anticipation of inflation and which, in fact, may be compared to a quasi-lack of anticipation of inflation, especially in times of low inflation, may simply be explained (using a somewhat self-validating argument) by the very low traces within memory and duration of situations of low inflation with deflationary warnings, nominal inflexibilities in wages and a rise in unemployment. There would quite simply not be enough time-matter within which an anticipation of inflation (a drop in inflation in this instance) could take root and develop. What certain people may describe as "fairness" in order to explain the nominal inflexibility of reduction, i.e. that which in general forms part of what is *acceptable* – which can be distinguished here from that which is moral – is in our view that which, within duration, together with a certain factor of forgetfulness, has been accumulated and stored within memory and which, in fact, results in our non-acceptance or acceptance of a certain economic phenomenon within a given situation. What is *acceptable* ("fairness") is that which one remembers, together with a certain factor of forgetfulness. What is acceptable is that which has lasted, that which has sufficiently endured so as to have left a trace. Consequently, it can be understood that a time of crisis is when, quite literally, forgetfulness accomplishes its task and there remains only that which is unacceptable. The phenomena of inflexibility are the phenomena of duration and memory and form part of the "normal" operating mode of the economic Subject's consciousness and of its reference frames as we have described the same, and which is poorly translated by the sole term "animal spirits", which introduces a music of irrationality and absurd contingency when, on the contrary, there is a structure at work which is strictly based on a time-matter and, more generally, a specific space-time reference frame of duration, memory recall and lapse.

§ 111.   Let us return for a moment to the well-known trade-off between unemployment and inflation. We have seen that we can, with some degree of assurance, state first that within zones of low inflation (and we should add, essentially of low volatility), there seems to exist a form of monetary illusion, which we have defined on the basis of "mistaken" (adaptative) anticipations of inflation which explain the nominal inflexibility of certain variables, including wages, such an "error" of anticipation perhaps being due itself to phenomena of low memory (such a phenomenon can readily be called a "low frequency effect of memory" or a "low frequency memory"); second, that within the areas of high (and very volatile) inflation, there seems once again to exist an inflation/unemployment trade-off based on a mechanism of (adaptative) anticipations of inflation which operate better, in the sense that the cumulative projection of additional increase prefers to base itself on a stock of memory; it can be stated, in such a case, that there is a "high frequency effect of memory", or a "high frequency memory". It can be added that in addition to the distinction between areas of low (and not very volatile) inflation and areas of fairly high (and generally very volatile) inflation, there is a relevant distinction between the short- and long-term in the determination of the trade-off between unemployment and inflation. In this instance, the monetary illusion (and, therefore, since we have defined it accordingly, the "mistaken" anticipation of inflation) would be all the more pronounced, since the space-time reference frame, as we have described the same for the economic Subject, would be located within a "short-term" horizon. Such a phenomenon would mean in return that the "low frequency" effects of memory (i.e. brittle effect of discontinuity, volatility, interruption and low density of time-matter) would be all the more numerous and pronounced given one's location within a short-term mental space-time, therefore explaining the "mediocre" quality of the anticipations of infla-tion (mediocrity is understood to mean a difficulty in incrementation or the "notching up" of anticipations layer by layer which will enable a dynamic to be set in motion, a moment which is not self-cumulative and self-validating; it is also understood to mean a problem in basing oneself on a "block" of duration, of time-matter stored within memory, simply because, in fact, not many events which have actually occurred may form a semblance of firm ground on which the anticipations might be based); the *low density* of memory (and of duration), and therefore of time-matter where the anticipations, and more fundamentally the economic Subject's action process and projection are secured, based on and within the space-time reference frame of a mental nature, this low density of what is observed and experienced explains in large part the phenomena of (nominal) inflexibility of the economic and financial variables.

§ 112.   Such a density may be stimulated in a more artificial manner. The economic policy action may acquire such an objective. The territories of low frequency memory (low intensity of time-matter, duration), which generally correspond to modest levels of accumulation of facts or phenomena on which, once stocked in memory, the economic Subject's consciousness might be based (this applies to the drop in nominal wages in times of quasi-deflation), only offer overall a very small number of supports for the imaging and acting consciousness, i.e. very few blocks of duration or memory on which to found the image-objects of the economic action process as we have defined the same.

The economic policy action may consequently take place in a contrary manner i.e. counter to that which is indicated by the sole direction of time-matter constituted by the accumulation of memorised facts (we know that this stock is fairly low and fragile). "Counter to" means that the economic policy action will try to correct the low level and fragility of the "actual" memorised foundation (facts, events and objects which are actually real, which have been observed, experienced and memorised), which can only create image-objects which are themselves weak and fragile, by stimulating the production of image-objects of pure negativity, as it were (any image-object is obliteration but certain image-objects are designs of negativity based on real memorised consolidations, others are pure designs of negativity, going so far as the extremes of so-called illusory projections). This task of diverting the course of rivers, as we described it in *Théorie globale*, involves introducing a formative image-object in order to affirm a direction which is inadequately affirmed, or indeed not affirmed, by the traditional image-objects stemming from the memory of that which has occurred. Such a formative image-object is in fact implanted within the reference frame of existing image-objects and this corrective implant (which presents a somewhat artificial aspect, in the sense that it is a pure image without any referent of that which occurred, has been recorded in time and more or less memorised) acts within the specific space-time reference frame by introducing a mutation, when there is no pre-existing image-object, or an accelerated development of such a pre-existing image-object, when one is actually present. Such an intra-cellular task may allow changes of regime to be considered. This is true of monetary illusions in a low area of inflation with low volatility which produce minimal inflexibilities (wages) and cause the trade-offs between inflation and unemployment to become blurred: we have shown that the low level and fragility of time-matter (memory), which may form the platform for flexibility in the reduction of certain variables in nominal terms (including therefore low level and fragility of the anticipations of inflation), were undoubtedly largely responsible for this fact; that, consequently, the space-time reference frame which receives the image-objects, unless it undergoes a mutation, would continue to reproduce – in a self-referential and cumulative manner – the barriers and blocks which are attributed by some to "animal spirits". The modification of the space-time reference frames (and therefore of the image-objects which form the innermost structure thereof) forms part of the tasks of the economic policy action.

§ 113.   By returning now to the issue of a trade-off between inflation and unemployment, we wish to note (see *Théorie*), in addition to that which has just been stated regarding the effects of memory (low and high frequencies correspond to different regimes in the density of time-matter) that the trade-off must be considered, as an issue, on the basis of a *global* theory of inflation, which means inflation as a complete phenomenon of information/distortion of money (speed) within the real sphere *and* within the financial sphere. Consequently, the anticipation of inflation must be broken down into an anticipation of inflation in the price of goods and services *and* an anticipation of inflation of financial asset prices, consistent with the point which we made in *Théorie*, i.e. that the velocity of money can itself be broken down into a velocity within the real sphere and a velocity of money within the financial sphere, the two channels communicating and complimenting each other to a fairly large extent. The eclipses or even the lack of trade-off between inflation and unemployment might therefore simply be due to the failure to take account of the anticipations of inflation in their two component parts, the real and the financial, which nonetheless form one, profoundly unitary character.

Accordingly, that which may be described rather hastily as a "mistaken" anticipation of inflation merits further reflection. More specifically, the addition of anticipations of inflation to the analysis of a trade-off between inflation and unemployment did not suffice to explain the *majority* of situations (the "increased" version of anticipations already constitutes a significant step). It might well be the case that even if classic or traditional inflation in the price of goods and services remains moderate, and the anticipations likewise, the inflation of the financial asset price (and the related anticipations) rises, in terms of level and volatility. Such anticipations in the progression of the financial asset price (which are themselves linked to the cumulative effects of forgetfulness – of periods of down-trends, if one cuts to the essential – and of selective, summarised memory – only the series of increases in the price of assets remains, for example, in the memory) do not maintain the same relations with the unemployment variable as the anticipations of inflation in the price of goods and services are supposed to maintain with the same unemployment variable. In particular, the passage through wages (an anticipated rise in the price of goods and services may logically lead to wage claims which, if granted, may themselves lead to a drop in the companies' level of profits and then to unemployment, which will progressively discourage wage claims and which will lead to moderation in prices and in the anticipations of prices – and their volatility) is not effected in the same way when considering the financial asset price. The rise in the price of assets and the anticipated rise tend – or at least observation would so suggest – to replace as it were the pure wage claim (the revenue can be entered as a function of the *anticipated* rise in wages and of the *anticipated* rise in the financial asset price and the two anticipated variables are governed by memory and forgetfulness as we have established and show a negative correlation): the *anticipated* rise in the prices of assets produces an effect of comfort and assurance which is purely psychological (when the person does not itself directly own the financial asset but instead benefits from a positive environment which influences and steers it) or real (when, effectively, the person does own the financial asset and the actual or latent capital gains sustain a positive logic of anticipations); the psychological or real effect of comfort leads to one not expecting too much from the wage component of the revenue.

$$Y = f(\text{Inf}(gs)\ \text{M/F}, \text{Inf}(ap)\ \text{M/F}$$

$$\begin{aligned}
\text{Inf}(gs) &= \text{\textit{Inflation of prices of goods and services}} \\
\text{Inf}(ap) &= \text{\textit{Asset price inflation}} \\
\text{M/F} &= \text{\textit{Memory and forgetfulness}}
\end{aligned}$$

where $Y = \alpha\ \text{Inf}(gs)\ \text{M/F} + \beta\ \text{Inf}(ap)\ \text{M/F}$

and $\alpha = -(y)\ \beta$

§ 114. Consequently, the mechanism concerning the trade-off between unemployment and inflation operates somewhat differently. The anticipated rise in asset price inflation *at first* stimulates activity (financial valuations and activity, if one advances a positive psychological effect on demand, as we do). This is true at first and while such inflation remains within "reasonable" territories of level and volatility, although it is of course difficult to establish such territories. Threshold effects exist, however, above which one enters a negative logic inferred by the asset price inflation (excessive debt, over-investment and/or over-consumption which are encouraged and masked by the rise in the financial asset price), which finally results in a drop in the rate of profits and unemployment, linked to a drop in prices (deflation logic). Here one recognises the traditional area of trade-off between (traditional) inflation and unemployment.

Our idea here is, first, that the anticipated inflation is twofold (real, financial); second, that the nature of the trade-off between inflation (real, financial) – understood as a global, unitary phenomenon – and unemployment itself depends upon the trade-off or relation between the two main components of *anticipated* inflation (price of goods and services, financial asset price); finally that there is indeed a trade-off between inflation and unemployment but that it is less simplistic than the relationship between inflation in the price of goods and services and unemployment may imply, even if one increases the said inflation of anticipations, since the trade-off exists between global inflation and unemployment.

Accordingly, when, in the 1990's there was a low level of real inflation, a drop in American unemployment in a climate of financial asset price inflation, there was a triptych whose logic we described in *Carnets monétaires*, the rate of interest (reduction permitted by the extreme good sense of traditional inflation) playing a role of transfer to the asset price (rise) and the wage wisdom being as if offset by the rise in asset price (and, especially, the rise in credit which is stimulated by a positive perception of the economic climate and the future). The financial asset/credit pairing will later be the source of the deflationist correction.

There is therefore a reduction in unemployment which does not lead to a rise in inflation in the traditional sense because, in particular, there is a progression of inflation in the financial sense. There are therefore situations where the trade-off between traditional inflation and unemployment is not verified because financial inflation is not taken into account. The taking into account of financial inflation may explain the concurrence of very low unemployment and the lack of inflation in the price of goods and services. Two remarks become immediately pertinent. First, if one wants to consider global and unitary inflation (real and financial), there is, in the formative phase of the bubble (the USA in the second half of the 1990's), a rise in global inflation (through the financial component which maintains a negative, and causal, correlation with traditional inflation) and, simultaneously, a reduction in unemployment, although the explanation of the relation is of a different, novel nature when compared to the traditional explanation of the relation between traditional inflation and unemployment. Second, the trade-off between real inflation and unemployment is only suspended in the *short-term*: the financial asset price inflation disturbs the trade-off between real inflation and unemployment in the *short-term*. In the medium-term, when the financial inflation (in particular when associated with credit excesses) has led (when it does lead) to the bursting of the bubble, the drop in the financial asset price is accompanied by a simultaneous fall in the price of goods and services; there is a positive correlation between the two components of inflation and there is indeed a reduction in global inflation *and* a rise in unemployment.

§ 115. A global, rising inflation (rise of financial inflation; moderate level of real inflation) and low unemployment may accordingly coexist. A drop in global inflation (drop in the two price components, real and financial) and high unemployment may also coexist. The inflation and unemployment trade-off is restored within a global dimension. These two sequences require clarification.

We have seen that real inflation (this means the inflation in the price of goods and services) and financial inflation were negatively correlated *in the short-term* and in the situation which can be described as a normal regime (i.e. without extreme, real and especially financial, movements). The reduction in real inflation stimulates the financial inflation and the rise in the same real inflation hinders an increase in the financial asset price. In both cases, the interest rate adjusts the preference between shares and bonds which, as we have seen in *Carnets monétaires*, plays a significant role in short-/medium-term fluctuations (around two years) of the stock markets in periods of normal conditions. Consequently, a reduction in unemployment and a lack of real inflation may coexist (effect of "comfort" or wealth stimulated by the presence of rising financial inflation), which has a net effect (real and financial global inflation) depending upon the extent of the rise in financial inflation, which may start to differentiate the so-called "normal" regime of the bubble regime. The more one advances towards the bubble, the greater the reduction in unemployment *and* the rise in global inflation with a reduction in real, traditional inflation.

In normal times, i.e. without any interruptions or excesses, the rise in financial inflation may end up stimulating real inflation, in a context of low unemployment, and one then experiences an expected unemployment/inflation trade-off between unemployment and real inflation in the medium-term. However, since the phenomena of the bubble and the bursting of the bubble are natural within a macro-financial regime where asset prices play an essential role, one is more probably in a situation where financial inflation (bursting of the bubble) and real inflation (reduction in activity, rise in unemployment) drop as a result of the rise in unemployment.

Finally, the inflation/unemployment trade-off remains relevant in the medium-term even if, in the short-term, the inflation component linked to the prices of financial assets disturbs the traditional relationship between real inflation and unemployment. In the medium-term, the rise in unemployment and the reduction in global inflation (made up of real inflation and financial inflation) go hand in hand within the macro-financial regime incorporating the financial asset price and, accordingly, running the final risk of deflation, as we have shown. Accordingly, in this sense (that of the final risk of deflation), the global inflation/unemployment trade-off is verified, especially, it might be said, since the dimension of financial inflation is taken into account. In the other sense, as it were, financial inflation prevents real inflation and unemployment coexisting in the short-term. One cannot exclude the possibility that this coexistence may be established later in a normal regime. In the "patrimonial" macro-financial regime (i.e. incorporating the financial asset price) there is instead a sharp rise in the financial asset price (transfer to a bubble regime with an increase in global inflation in a context of low unemployment) in the first sequence and then a switch after the interruption to a deflationist-style regime (bursting of the bubble, generalised reduction in the level of prices and therefore of global inflation).

§ 116.   We have attributed the numerous special features of the financial universe and specifically the market universe to what we have called the "specific space-time reference frame", which we have described on the basis in particular of the structures of the conscious economic Subject. By so doing, we have, in a certain manner, isolated a specific operating mode of the Stock Market (by which we mean all that which relates to the financial markets and to finance), for example all the non-linearities and discontinuities within the space-time which is neither that of clock time nor that of playing fields, and this specific world has been described as the "normality" of the Stock Market.

Such a special nature-normality contains an insurmountable dimension which is specific to the very structure of financial phenomena. It may, as Allais suggests, also incorporate the disturbances which are specific to credit. The abnormality of the Stock Market would not then be as "normal" as one might have described. Let us return to this point.

The characteristics of credit and its cycle – its excesses – would therefore be at the origin of at least one part of what appear to be special features of the Stock Market and which are insurmountable in structural terms (i.e. those attached to the very structure of the operation of the markets and of finance). In particular, the irrational nature, the abnormal nature in the full sense of the term, of the Stock Market phenomena would depend less upon the special nature *as such* of the Stock Market but rather upon the disturbances imposed by the credit cycle on a market reality which, without such disturbances, would show less surprising and more conventional forms of normality. If one pursues this line of thought, the special features and mystery of the Stock Market would above all be the external sign of the disturbing dynamics of the economic cycle and its determining factors.

In fact, the Stock Market itself forms part of the global economic and financial cycle and it is therefore a somewhat delicate matter to isolate absolutely that which, of itself, stems from the market nature of the determining elements of the more general cycle of which the Stock Market is in fact one element, in interaction with all the other elements.

We have shown that in the progression of the cycle and the Subject's action process more generally, the Stock Market (the market) plays a precise and particular role, the organisation of the exchange, valuation and transformation into action or destruction of image-objects, an organisation which forms part of a specific space-time reference frame. The specific nature of this structure does not stem from the disturbance of the cycle (and in particular the disturbance of money through the excesses of the credit cycle) but probably accentuates the disturbance itself by offering it room for expansion. Financial bubbles and credit excesses often go hand in hand and the Stock Market, in the various developments of the bubble from inflation to the moment when it bursts, then presents abnormal features which are particularly marked, but which however only accentuate the fundamental features of the market structure (dilation and contractions, concentrations and accelerations).

In fact, rather than finding within the credit cycle and its disturbances the factor of financial abnormalities and special features of the Stock Market (the permanent nature of such special features cannot be reconciled with the disturbances of credit, which are by definition more sporadic, which implies that there remains a part of the market phenomenon which cannot be explained by this element, which is insurmountable and forms part of its very structure), and therefore rather than seeing a causality of the credit cycle directed at the structure of market phenomena and the Stock Market itself, we think that the proposition should be reversed in part and that one should see within the structure of the Stock Market as we have described the same (based on a specific space-time reference frame of a mental or psychological nature, structured by duration, memory recall and lapse from the act of projection-imagination of a conscious economic Subject), and therefore see within this specific structure which can be found *inter alia* within the Stock Market, the informing and distorting matrix of the credit cycle, and more generally of the global economic and financial cycle. This is the theory which is developed in *Théorie*.

3. NOMINAL INFLEXIBILITIES
MONETARY ILLUSION

§ 117.　Monetary illusion, which means in particular that there is a form of resistance to the reduction in nominal values (including wages), is both an observed fact which is sufficiently documented and recurrent in order for one to be tempted to see it as a form of law or character trait (depending whether the matter is approached by the economic mechanism or from the strict point of view of the Subject), and an aspect of the "animal spirits" or the manifestation thereof. Accordingly, the principal means of understanding this resistance to the reduction in nominal values would lie within the very structure and operation of the economic Subject. Consequently the rational mechanism which, all things being equal, would desire the necessary adjustment, for example in a period of deflation, to be effected by means of nominal values, breaks down and fails to operate.

This finding does not, however, go so far as to state – if indeed such is the case – why and how the specific structure of the conscious economic Subject (its space-time reference frame, where the different forms of the consciousness operate, whether imaging or acting, forgetting or remembering in particular) in fact procures that such an inflexibility can be observed. Furthermore, it is not stated that this is not a matter of a certain configuration of the conscious structure of the Subject and not a definitive and stable element; consequently, what one tends to consider as a stable fact, or almost a truth or law, might include a greater element of instability and therefore, possibly, change, evolve or indeed even disappear. This depends in exchange on one's interpretation of such inflexibility.

§ 118.   The phenomena of inflexibility and resistance, once one looks at the structure of perception, imagination and action of the conscious Subject, place adhesions and delays in the path of that which retains, attaches or produces: duration and memory. The process therefore involves, more generally, establishing, for a certain number of economic and financial phenomena, that the mechanism of the sequences is that of the relationship of the conscious Subject with the world, that the truth of this mechanism does not exist outside the conscious Subject, within the real world of facts and events, but is on the contrary only accessible from the referential structure of the conscious Subject itself. In the case of nominal inflexibilities, it is probable that powerful effects of memory are at play as a result, first, of the fact that in normal times (and times are, more often than not, normal) the rational need to see certain nominal values adjusted downwards does not apply, and consequently very few memorised occurrences, even if exceptional, remain within the time-matter which constitutes the referential structure of the economic Subject; second, another possibility, that only a few *real* values can be found within the blocks of duration which line the space-time of the Subject's imaging and acting consciousness, and that the Subject's designs inform, mobilise and drive: numerous real values cannot be observed and the economic Subject's memory has above all the ability to imprint and store vision and action. This means several things. Since memory is linked to *vision* (i.e. to that which has been experienced and observed), the nominal inflexibilities could thus be explained; in the same way, such inflexibilities could, in theory, flow back or evolve once the experiences of reductions in nominal values, within a process which can be described as an apprenticeship, are remembered. The nominal inflexibilities would therefore be due to the low presence within memory of downward adjustment options and, moreover, by definition, the lack of experiences (facts, events) of real values. Consequently, the phenomenon would be potentially reversible over time within a process of apprenticeship (and therefore of memorisation). The nominal inflexibilities would only exist for an economic Subject which does not have enough experience of downward adjustments and therefore of apprenticeship.

This apprenticeship may also, possibly, be that of real values, by associating real reasoning to the experience of downward adjustments of nominal values. This could only stem from an educative voluntarism and apprenticeship whose feasibility and chances of success are hard to evaluate. This is because the real values and nominal values are different in nature from the point of view of the economic Subject, of its space-time reference frame and its operation. The nominal values are involved in the raw material of duration and memory, this dense time-matter which we have described and on which, like an artillery bombardment of electrons, the various forms of design of the Subject's consciousness operate. Real value, in turn, is an image-object in the sense in which we have defined it, a product of the imaging consciousness. Since real value cannot be observed and since moreover the deflator of nominal values, of *anticipations* of prices cannot itself be observed but *can be imagined*, there is a process of the imaging consciousness which may vary ranging from a realistic projection (in the sense that the real value will effectively enter the economic action process up until the actual impact with the world) to an illusion.

§ 119.   The real values are image-objects produced by the economic Subject. As such, they too are products of the financial imagination. This does not mean that they are necessarily illusions in a disparaging sense. On the contrary, that which is "real", in the sense of the "reality" which characterises numerous concepts and expressions of economics and finance (real interest rate, real revenue…), is that which evidences that which is, that which approaches the Subject in its action, that which provides a platform, stability. We have shown that this platform is closely linked to duration, this accumulated, reduced, compressed time from which the blocks which are cut out and transported to memory constitute the fundamental level on the basis of which the economic and financial processes take root and develop. That which is "real" and which, on first analysis, stems from a projection of the consciousness which is in a state of non-being (anticipation of inflation for example, which refers back to a function of the imagination and the obliterating consciousness), in fact constantly preserves an essential anchorage within that which lasts (time) and approaches the Subject's consciousness together with memory and forgetfulness. The real value therefore stems from an obliterating design (in the sense of anticipation, imagination and projection towards that which is not, or is not yet) which operates on an extremely dense platform of compressed time, a compression which lasts, a block of duration which memory has brought to/towards the Subject and which is set in motion by the dynamic of memory recalls and lapses.

It is not certain that words actually say what they seem to state. Accordingly the economic *reality* (i.e. the world of economic facts, events and objects) seems to refer back to something which is other than the *reality* contained within *real values* (rate, reality...). In the latter case, as we have just seen, what cannot be observed (no one has ever seen a real interest rate) refers back to both what is hidden and what is imagined in the sense of a project as an object of the consciousness which is not present, not constituted and which is targeted to be in a state of non-being/a state of future being. This projection stems to a large extent from that which, in fact, is hidden and which approaches the consciousness to the same extent as the consciousness moves towards that which is hidden. That which appears to be hidden is that which lasts, which, on a more profound level, is and approaches the Subject in order to clarify the latter's conscious designs. Economic *reality*, in turn, in the sense in which we have defined it above, forms part of that which can be observed and therefore of that which is perceived (i.e. targeted in the act of perception by the consciousness), the point of impact of the Subject's economic and financial action process (which we have named *impact* with the real world), a set of economic impacts, facts, events and objects which constitutes *the world* and which in turn has a feedback effect on the Subject-consciousness in the determination of the economic action process.

Accordingly it is real values which are adjusted rather than nominal values. The slow and silent transformation of anticipations, and more generally of projections – which directly involves the conscious Subject ends by distorting the real value in places where the nominal value does not seem to want to move. As such, it is inaccurate to state that the nominal values are the only ones on which the conscious Subject's action has an effect (which in this instance would be consciously opposing their downward adjustment): the real values, which are broader, reflect in their movement the structure of the Subject's consciousness and its dynamic. The real values are constantly distorting like a subterranean continent, a hidden world which is and lasts and continuously approaches the Subject's consciousness, together with memory and forgetfulness, in the manner of a wave, whilst the nominal values often do not move or do not seem to move (the insurmountably unobservable nature of the real values moves aside to allow this interplay of subterranean drifts).

§ 120.   The nominal value can be written as a real value increased by an obliterating design of the consciousness, i.e. a projection or anticipation (of inflation, for example). It is this last, essential component of the nominal value which holds the key. The full force of the economic Subject's consciousness is exerted on this component, which sets memory and forgetfulness in motion. Once again, it can be seen that it is still a question of moving some old "rubble" of the past, remembering or forgetting it, since one only appears to act on the present moment and, here, on what is most immediately observable. This means that in order to procure that the nominal values move and adjust, as one might expect in advance that they would, it is necessary for that which, within them, determines their innermost dynamic – i.e. that which we have called the act of design of the economic Subject's consciousness, i.e. the anticipation, if we wish to use the term most commonly employed, although it does not cover, far from it, all the occurrences and situations – it is therefore necessary that this determining factor of the dynamic of the nominal values sets itself in motion or is set in motion, a block of duration, memory recall and lapse.

§ 121.   It can accordingly be seen that inflexibility in the reduction of nominal values, or at least certain of them, is due to the very inertia of the targeted (anticipated) components and, ultimately, to the time-matter (duration) which constitutes the basis or platform thereof: this time-matter may, as we know, advance a certain inertia before suddenly experiencing accelerations, contractions or dilations. The inflexibility, at least initially, of certain nominal values, stems from this form of (initial) slowness, from this factor of inertia advanced by duration and memory in contrast to the immediate event which arises. This may be the object of an economic policy action intended to stimulate or, on the contrary, efface some or other element of time-matter which defines the target of anticipation since, as we will remember, the situation is as follows:

$$Vn = Vr + CF/M \qquad where \quad Vn = nominal\ value$$
$$Vr = real\ value$$

and

CF/M	$=$	$f(t, F, M)d$
CF/M	$=$	*design of the economic Subject's consciousness within the specific space-time reference frame (time-matter made up of memory and forgetfulness)*
t	$=$	*time (substance)*
F	$=$	*forgetfulness*
M	$=$	*memory*
d	$=$	*duration*

In the absence of such an initiative of economic policy action, the more or less linear passing of the course of events ends up modifying CF/M and therefore Vr, and ultimately Vn. The reality within this interplay is what cannot be directly observed (Vn); however, Vn is determined by Vr (CF/M). Such a concept of reality is close to that of truth, and in any event distinct from that which is understood, moreover, by reality, namely all the events, facts and objects, whether or not they result from the impacts of the conscious Subject's economic action process aimed at the world.

Furthermore, an experience of the downward adjustment of certain nominal values might involve the memorising and later the recall of such occurrences or events (or even, in their absence, a conceptual simulation): in this case, the adjustment of CF/M is such that the movement of the real value is accompanied by a no less significant movement of the nominal value. The nominal adjustment and the real adjustment converge since the design/anticipation component of the real value is henceforth made up of a living memory of downward adjustments of the nominal value. Such a configuration remains rather difficult to obtain since such occurrences are too rare in reality (observable facts or events) in order for them to be imprinted upon/inform a time-matter of memory and duration. This amounts to saying that CF/M is led to produce image-objects which go so far as to modify Vr, and therefore Vn, which brings us back to the earlier situation where causality proceeds from Vr towards Vn.

Chapitre 5

ECONOMICS AND MORALITY

(The possibility of a moral code within economic and financial action)

1. VALUE AND MORALITY. PRACTICAL-MORALITY

§ 122. The economic Subject is accordingly not a completely free entity which can do whatever it wants and whose acts are completely integrated with the original design which sets the action process in motion. As we have seen, this design, which sets in motion the memory recalls and lapses in particular, operates at any one time on its genetic heritage of duration within a specific spatio-temporal reference frame. This heritage determines what will become of the action process and, ultimately, what will happen to the impact within and on the real world. It is also imposed upon the Subject precisely because it constitutes the innermost structure and matter thereof. The economic Subject only exercises its freedom insofar as, first, it assents to some extent or takes on board (to a certain manner, it has little choice, given that it is a fact) a situation and the possibility of a refusal creates the conditions for a crisis and a paralysis of the action process; second, it exerts a design of negativity – pure autonomous freedom in this instance – over a "stock" of duration, of time-matter, which provides the essential fuel to be consumed in the creation of the image-object and which, thereafter, will accompany the dynamic of the economic act.

The economic Subject therefore acts subject to a certain degree of necessity and the action process, irrespective of the stage (image-object, financial market or action of impact) which is reached due to the force of the imaging and later acting consciousness, cannot be described as unpredictable or contingent.

It is within this necessity that the possibility of a norm, as we have discussed, takes root. The possibility of such a norm and more generally the possibility of meaning, of understanding, of limits and regulation do not however state – and cannot state – whether that which occurs during the act, during the economic and financial action is something which has to be or should be, i.e. whether the action which thus takes place is moral.

§ 123. A distinction should be drawn between that which forms part of the economic value and that which forms part of the moral value, since the two dimensions do not overlap, even if the use of the term value within economics and finance without any particular qualification, maintains a considerable degree of ambiguity regarding the presence of morality within economics and, especially, within the economic action process. The economic value may, on an initial, far too rapid, analysis be thought to be similar to the sole tangible *impact* within and on the real world, the immediate manifestation of that which has resulted, of that which, in the order of impact, has replaced the image-object, the project, the anticipation and all this "positive negativity" (that which is in a state of not-yet-being) which is arranged, sorted and organised on the financial market; the sole, tangible impact, a product of a Subject defined as pure freedom, an absolute creation from nothingness, this creative vision of the Subject which does not allow one to determine how the said Subject incorporates morality within an action process which can consequently be deemed to be random, contingent or arbitrary (the economic Subject does what it wishes and economics are driven by a pure will of chance, which is without limit and to a large extent incomprehensible or irrational). This vision concentrates the strongest concerns and fears with regard to a voracious, absurd, immoral and limitless appropriation of the world and of men, by means of an economic process which is steered by an economic Subject without any master or form of control.

As we have shown, this vision is neither complete nor satisfactory. In particular, the economic value cannot, at any one time, be reduced to the sum of the manifestations of a project's or anticipation's impact. The economic value, within an action process and the outcome thereof, is always defined by means of a stock, a DNA, a genetic heritage of duration (accompanied by memory and forgetfulness) – which cons-titutes the essential innermost matter, the indelible trace which marks any economic and/or financial event, act, object and fact; and by means of a pure design which sets such stock in motion, informs and drives it, prior to the commencement of a process, in the same way one warms a piece of wax. This genetic heritage of duration, memory recall and lapse *determines* the action (image-object, project, anticipation), the product of the impact of an action process, the economic value of the action and its outcome and the economic Subject itself, since this form of superstructure which constitutes the innermost matter of the Subject is also essential to the Subject, which must appropriate, assent (to) and assume that without which it is not only nothing but without which the action itself would remain impossible.

§ 124.   If the economic value is determined by (depends upon) a genetic heritage of duration, memory recall and lapse, it is not stated whether such economic value is moral. At this stage, the distinction between economic value and moral value must be restated. Moral value, for its part, resides ultimately in *that which is*, which therefore controls economics over (or under, if one agrees to consider this as the foundation), and therefore beyond the economic Subject. This ontological territory *of that which is*, which we described in *Généalogie de l'économique* and in *Valeur et temps*, houses all the means or modes of being, including equilibrium and value. Value, whether economic or moral, stems from *that which is*; in this way, the bridging may be effected: provided that the genetic heritage (which we have called the DNA) of duration, memory recall and lapse which forms the basis of the economic value (and, therefore, the economic and financial action process, within the same movement, since it is strictly speaking equivalent) may itself be based ultimately on the ontological territory of modes of being – which we believe to be the case, as we have submitted –, then economics, the economic action process, the economic value and the economic Subject may in theory obtain access to a moral content.

§ 125.   We therefore distinguish between the sole "stock" of time and of duration which enters and leaves the memory (the dense piece of wax which we have said forms the innermost matter of the whole of economics and finance) and, second, the ontological territory of being and of time. The first dimension, which is directly accessible to knowledge, is duration in the sense of the accumulation of that which has been/is, which is indeed a relatively dense and inert form but nevertheless in internal movement, whilst *that which is* is and overhangs economics from another ontological region. The duration which constitutes the genetic heritage is therefore based on the time housed within the region of being which we are discussing and this link provides the coherence for the whole of economics and morality. Unless one accepts a moral relativism (i.e. morality is based on the region of duration and memory, where the value and point of reference depend upon that which lasts/has lasted and may therefore progressively *change* subject to the very act of the economic Subject in its relations with the world) – which we do not – morality is unattainable and cannot be observed.

We will call the location of the genetic heritage of duration and memory, which we have described as the innermost matter of the specific spatio-temporal reference frame where the whole economic action process unfurls, *practical morality*. This is a practical moral dimension since it houses the *habitus*, the practices and modes of thinking which assert themselves more strongly (and may even occasionally appear to be eternal or timeless), if they contain a significant amount of duration and memory. Accordingly, *"fairness"*, which is a formative feature of the conduct of an economic Subject's act advanced by Schiller may either refer back to an intangible mode of being or be based in this stock of duration-memory, a dense lava which is in slow movement. In this second instance, meaning and perception will change sooner or later. Numerous concepts and notions which are present in economics and finance, which have a timeless appearance, nonetheless possess a life and limits, which allows one to understand that what is accepted at certain times or periods may no longer be, that accordingly what has been authorised pursuant to one norm may, pursuant to a new norm, become fraud. This existence of *habitus*, which creates the existence of norms and regulations, forms part of the relatively stable framework of duration and memory, which we have described. This framework is ultimately based on a region of being, which it is hard to say anything about but whose conceptual premise allows one to base the economic act on a more solid basis from a moral point of view. The genetic heritage of duration, memory recall and lapse remains within this region of being which is the subject of our premise. It is sufficiently dense and solid to impose itself upon the Subject and determine the action but can only offer, first, a limited transcendence (to that which, of that which has taken place, which still lasts), and, second, does not house the moral content or assertion (that which remains of that which has taken place, i.e. *habitus* is still not moral).

§ 126. Economics are inevitably separate from morality to the extent that economics, in the form in which we understand it, especially in the modern age, only exists in a historical dimension of temporality linked to that which has been experienced. This dimension is indeed ultimately linked to a region of being on which a code of morals can be based, to the One in short, whether in relation to value, equilibrium or time, but this dimension, which constitutes economics as it appears to us and as we practise it, has limits (the equilibrium or value is relative and not absolute, the reference points of duration experience distortion and relative instability). This dimension is together with, within or for the economic Subject, as we have shown, and the presence of the Subject at the heart of the economic and financial action process implies an incompleteness and a certain dose of non-being, which insinuates itself everywhere, into all the machinery and without which the action itself could not even be contemplated. Within this dimension, the multiple dominates the One and the Other makes a formative *pas de deux*, together with and within the Subject.

And yet, all that is at work within this *practical* dimension bears the trace, in a relative form, branded by the limits of incompleteness, value or equilibrium in particular, of that which is and which bears the very bedrocks of morality from an ontological region. Accordingly, the economic value takes root in this practical dimension and the moral value in the region of being and, on first analysis, economics and morality cannot be confused (this is the source of numerous misunderstandings, in particular in the contemporary age). However, at the same time, the economic value is traversed (by), its concepts, even those which are fundamental (duration in particular) are secured to a transcendental field (value, equilibrium, time) which contains the possibility of a moral code, although the dimension of economics, which is mainly practical since it is inhabited by the economic Subject, and therefore the action, cannot carry more than the possibility of the norm (and therefore of regulation), which is already considerable. We have therefore described the dimension of economics as one of practical morality.

This means that while confirming the radically separate nature of economics and morality, we are establishing conditions for the possibility of moral roots within the practical field of economics, which may *accompany* the economic action process conducted by the Subject, starting with the imaging and acting consciousness and ending with the actual impact with the world. These roots which may therefore irrigate economic practice (and economics is reduced to the practice of its action process for the economic Subject) should be clearly distinguished from the norm within economics and finance. We have seen that the conditions for a possible economic norm are based on the time-matter of duration, memory recall and lapse (and as such ultimately refer back to a trace of that which is, i.e. to the One) but the norm is rooted in a damaged field of being, where duration is indeed present but full of the Subject's past action, distorted by the consciousness' intended action, by the memory recalls and lapses. This field of being is sufficiently solid for there to be an attempt at a definition of a norm on which a regulation can be established, but still sufficiently fluid so as not to offer the strongest assurances of a unit, of the One without which a moral code cannot be founded.

§ 127. This ultimately fluid nature of the practical-moral dimension where economics as we perceive it takes place, has largely to do with the presence of the economic Subject within the dimension, a Subject principally defined as an obliterating consciousness and whose projection through the negativity which sustains anticipation, makes the action possible. We have shown that this dimension, once it was described on the basis of the categories of duration, memory recall and lapse, as a formative link with those of value or equilibrium (relative and not absolute concepts), exposed itself not only to knowledge, to the possibility of being analysed and understood (dismissing the prejudice of irrationality, the random walk and also of immorality) but also to the possible construction of norms and regulations. However, such norms cannot say what must be, what is right or wrong, when such norms are taken from within a dimension of the multiple, of a time which is ultimately that of the duration accumulated by history (the facts, events and objects) of the Subject in action. At the same time, because historical duration carries within it the trace of a unitary time, connecting all the relative concepts of the practical dimension (value, equilibrium) to a more solid region of being, an attempt may be made to create a moral foundation for economics and finance.

This also means that, if economics and finance may or must be understood within the immediate, practical dimension where the economic Subject rules, they may and must also be considered over and beyond the Subject, where its ultimate foundations and the possibility of a moral code are located. This task may be accomplished since the practical dimension of economics, insofar as it is correctly defined and described, proves to be a practical-moral dimension where everything which is in play at any one time looks constantly towards that which is and which creates.

There are no practical economics without the economic Subject and, consequently, economics must be considered over and beyond the Subject. We have shown that the economic (and financial, since finance is a stage of the process in the form of the financial market) action process, with which economics is identified in the modern age, is initiated by the act of design of a Subject defined as consciousness, starting from a specific space-time reference frame structured by duration, memory recall and lapse – more generally by time. This act of the conscious Subject is not that of a pure and total freedom nor that of a pure and absolutely optimising reason. There is, within the act of the economic Subject, a space-time reference frame whose innermost matter is duration which, to some extent, is imposed upon the Subject, which must assent to it, which must accept it. This essential dimension, which gives meaning to the concepts of value or equilibrium (in relative mode), ultimately refers back to something which transcends the Subject, which comes from somewhere beyond the Subject. This transcendental region which comes to the Subject, even though the Subject has not chosen it, may certainly be the subject of psychological/historical analyses (the layer of the past, or of experience, whether individual or collective, which fashions *a situation* of the Subject) or even with regard to the unconscious (this layer which determines the Subject, this block of accumulated time-matter is more or less anchored within the consciousness and the mechanisms of forgetfulness which we have described may refer back to the said unconscious). Without denying these possible interpretations, which accord importance to the Subject, we locate the region which, ultimately, founds and irrigates the specific space-time reference frame where the Subject acts *over and beyond* the Subject, a region where one can find that which is and lasts (time and duration); the duration described within the practical dimension of economics only exists and takes place in relation to a concept of time which overhangs it and which approaches the Subject, rather than being chosen or constructed by the Subject.

§ 128.   This is why we state, first, that economics can only be approached, in the modern era, in order to understand and identify the issues at stake, on the basis of a formative interaction initiated by the Subject and, in general, of a pairing between the Subject-consciousness and the object since modern economic thinking progresses generally from the Subject's design and moves towards the object which the capture establishes and constitutes (as such, modern thinking is as much that of economic *objects* as of the economic Subject; the omnipresent reference to *homo economicus*, i.e. to the Subject, masks to a large extent the latent omnipresence of the economic *objects* of the design); second, that the modern conception of economics, which is smothered by the economic Subject (within its economic and financial action process), and, even more by the proliferation of *objects* – since the Subject's design is only capable of giving birth to that which is in object mode – has lost sight of that which continues to try to point towards being and time, beyond the Subject but with it, within the space-time reference frame of the Subject itself, in the form of traces to be rediscovered since they can be known (duration). The Subject is neither absolute freedom nor total reason precisely because a body of decisions approaches it, moves beyond it, and this body may to certain persons appear to be non-elucidated regions of the Subject itself (which explains the attempts at psychological or psychoanalytical analysis) which point towards a different ontological territory.

Consequently, it can be understood that the economic Subject can only be understood as an optimiser subject to certain conditions and constraints. The diagrams of absolute, rational optimisation are only valid for a representation of the economic Subject as a form of complete (and total) rationality and absolute freedom which is erroneous. The economic Subject only acts within the context of a reference frame which contains decisions, which are so many points of reference for its knowledge and its regulation through norms and decisions which themselves refer back to an ontological region located beyond the Subject. This does not mean that the Subject does not represent rationality or optimisation but that such optimisation operates within a reference frame of space and time where a certain number of elements come to the Subject as a situation whose action must literally take the parameters on board, and we have moreover defined the economic action as a product of a design of a Subject-consciousness (negativity, projection, anticipation) and of a stock of time-matter (more generally space time), the innermost matter of which is duration).

This is how one can, for example, understand that the diagrams of total/pure optimisation come up against the existence of nominal inflexibilities (wages are one of the best known examples), although this does not mean that the Subject is neither rational nor an optimiser. We have analysed such phenomena of inflexibility above and showed to what extent they *can be understood* provided that they are replaced in the relevant context of a space-time reference frame of the Subject. By doing so, and by continuing along this path, one can show that it is not so much the lack of actual demand (Keynes) which constitutes the blocking element of the macroeconomic cycle but, more immediately and more simply, the existence of phenomena of (nominal) inflexibilities which are neither economic observations (they can be learnt and understood) nor more or less stable features of individual psychology, but rather *a fact* of presence within the space-time reference frame where the process of action, duration and memory is formed, which also means that such inflexibilities may eventually disappear, as we have stated.

§ 129.   The economic Subject is optimised to the same extent that it is an optimiser. There is a whole mental world of space and time which comes to it, even before its design of comprehension and consciousness sets in motion, such world being dense matter pierced with forgetfulness and incomplete memories, which comes to it in order to constitute it (and the economic Subject is only *constituted* in order to accept that which comes to the Subject, borne by duration). "It" comes, talks and structures the specific space-time of the Subject, the imaging, acting consciousness and, in general, the economic action process. This "It" may be described as unconscious matter, which may possibly be recalled by memory (we have described the possible relationship between the structures of forgetfulness and the unconscious in the formation of economic phenomena), and the memory recall will then literally act as awareness. However, we prefer not to have recourse to the unconscious and rather to talk of matter which *constitutes* the space-time reference frame and the consciousness (therefore the act of consciousness), i.e. a temporal matter which is both *different* as compared to the consciousness but without which the consciousness could not be consciousness nor could the economic Subject be completely the Subject. This matter is both the essence of the economic act of a Subject which creates objects and economic phenomena and the structure of the economic Subject's freedom, such Subject only being free subject to the dual condition of consent to such matter which is different in numerous aspects and of transcendence within the image which announces the economic and financial action and object. This matter inhabits, constitutes and structures all the objects, phenomena, acts or authentically economic phenomena. The economic object is the product of an action process which merges a design and a time-matter which exists and develops over and beyond the Subject.

Within this context, the economic Subject is not an optimiser on the basis of or starting from structures which are *a priori* of understanding (even if the same can exist *in other respects*) and structures of moral value, but rather with the weightier structures of space-time matter which are imposed upon it as it appropriates them in order to exist as an economic Subject. The necessity (that which must be) emerges from such matter through the decision which results from duration/memory. This necessity of what must be, in the sense of what is to come, of what is coming, identifies with the dynamics of the time-matter which is at work within economics and finance, and such a necessity of what is coming since it lasts (there is an analogy between that which comes and that which lasts, between the future and that which remains, from the past). This necessity of that which must be binds the Subject while also liberating it (it frees itself by accepting and transcending that which is borne by this matter). The Subject is a machine which transforms this type of decision into freedom within the space-time of the consciousness and into an economic object within the real world.

The necessity of that which must be does not state that which must be right or wrong. We have said that the economic Subject accepts what must be and which comes to it. The launch of the action process such as a transcendence or transformation of that which comes to the Subject (which in fact inhabits and constitutes it) as time-matter of duration, relies upon such an act. The Subject exercises its consciousness on such matter which forms a structure which is *a priori* not purely, but sufficiently, dense and inert, sufficiently borne by duration and memory to be seen perhaps as an apriorism with regard to the Subject. However, this is not the case: this matter moves with an internal energy (in particular memory/forgetfulness) and interacts with the designs of the consciousness, since the consciousness and this matter form one whole.

§ 130. In our analysis, *that which lasts* constitutes the principal determining structure of the action and, in general, of economics and finance. That which lasts (which we have named matter in its form which may be more or less damaged in the simple past, accumulated past or, on the contrary, presented as something which is (being)), brings its own reference frame to the structures which are specific to understanding and perception and to the Subject's judgement. We consider that the structures of duration are weightier and have a deeper significance within the understanding of the economic Subject and the action process, than the *a priori* structures of a Subject which is completely free and which, moreover, does not exist (insofar as such liberty is not defined *together with* duration).

2. THE THREE REGIMES: ACTION (THE SUBJECT), PRACTICAL MORALITY, BEING-DURATION

§ 131. Accordingly, there are three cardinal points in our representation. That which lasts determines the structure of the specific space-time reference frame within which the economic Subject unfurls its action process. This first cardinal point or axis is, in its most damaged form, a mere section of an accumulated past, a slice of history, a stock of that which has occurred. This stock of time-matter, which is also a flow which disperses, is *for* a conscious economic Subject to which it grants an innermost matter and its structure. We will call this cardinal point "practical-temporality" in order to signify that the time-matter of duration (a mere accumulation of history which one remembers to a greater or lesser extent in its simplest version) constitutes its essential dimension, and that the reference frame where one is located is that of the progression of an economic action process by/on behalf of the economic Subject: we are in a practical dimension, of finitude and action.

Practical temporality constitutes a structure of determinations which leads to a certain necessity in the development of the economic action process, from the formation of the images by the imaging consciousness up until the actual impact with the world. All the economic and financial objects, facts and events are steeped in practical temporality (in the sense of the raw matter which constitutes them), and the economic Subject itself only takes shape in relation to such necessity (for example, the only consciousness, which founds the economic Subject, is of an *object* and the act of consciousness itself can only take place by means of a design of negativity over a constitutive time-matter: the object and the *time-matter* are practical temporality as we have defined the same).

As a structure of determinations, *practical temporality* is located at the origin of that which must be, including with regard to the economic Subject. The latter only exists and experiences as a Subject within the transcendence of this practical temporality, within that which we call (economic) action, a transcendence which is, by construction, an acceptance of the structure of the determinations of *practical temporality*. The *a priori* possible structures of the economic Subject's understanding, perception and judgement (including moral judgement) only develop within the prism of the determinations of practical temporality, and such determinations may be so strong that the very idea of structures, which are *a priori* distinct from that which has been forged by time-matter, may weaken so as to leave room for the sole structure of practical temporality.

Practical temporality is a structure of determinations which runs through the economic act and its impacts, and therefore forges that which must be. This form of principle of reason, which enables one to assert that elements exist within the economic and financial process which can be understood and known (even though certain phenomena are accused of being irrational or random walks) is still not, as such, the foundation for a code of morality or a principle of moral reasoning. *Practical temporality*, which comes to the economic Subject as a determination and a principle of reason, is not the place which houses the principle of moral reason but rather the place which houses the accumulation of *practices*, facts and events, which are remembered to a greater or lesser extent or, on the contrary, forgotten, and which bear the trace of that which must be (right or wrong). Such traces of moral practice, like sections of history, constitute what we have called *practical morality*. Practical temporality is a form of practical morality. Such *practical morality* constitutes a structure of determinations, within that which must be right or wrong, which can be described as past experiences which exercise their influence on the economic Subject in the development of the economic action process. When the economic Subject acts and when its action bears the mark of that which must be (right or wrong), the determinations which result from the practical-temporal structure are exerting and expressing themselves, traces of memory and forgetfulness which have to be distinguished from original, living, moral principles. Practical morality only bears a trace of that which has been and which lasts in a more or less pronounced manner, a light travelling from distant stars, which are sometimes alive and sometimes dead. Practical temporality is not therefore the guarantee of a moral basis or a structure which contains an ethical code within an economic action process, i.e. at the heart of the development of the Subject's action and the manifestations of the imaging and acting consciousness (economics as the same appears, i.e. the sum of its manifestations).

§ 132.   The second cardinal point or second axis is the economic and financial Subject. In essence, the economic Subject can be said to be the means by which that which is described as economic and financial comes to pass (the fact, event or object…), within the context of a process which we have described as economic action where the conception of image-objects by obliteration (projection, anticipation) of the time-matter of duration (practical temporality in the sense in which we have used such term) sets in motion a process, a dynamic path which leads to reality after the gestation of images, in particular within the selection, incubation and gestation chamber represented by the financial market.

The economic Subject is thus structured, i.e. defined or constituted, by the time-matter of duration (practical inertia) to the precise extent that the Subject is the negativity of the design of consciousness with which it is identified and without which the economic action and economics in short are inconceivable. This time-matter is the object of the Subject's conscious design, which implies that the economic Subject is endowed with a distinct structure which to some extent produces the capture or design and, at the same time, the design "increases" the time-matter, which may itself also, in turn, modify the design.

Accordingly, in the original distinction, there is a capture, the Subject's act of design in its capacity as consciousness and reason and, second, a matter which forms the *object* of obliteration in order to set in motion the economic action process through the conception and production of image-objects. The whole [design-matter] forms the specific space-time reference frame which we have described, an explosion chamber where the dynamic energy of economics and finance is produced. The design/matter distinction allows for the possibility of an *a priori* structure of the design (of the capture); a pure, prior form. This pure form which "informs", distorts and drives the time-matter and which does not necessarily contain moral values (it is less a reference frame than a set of equipment for the transformation of time-matter), the economic Subject in its moral dimension, is structured by what we have called practical morality, which is a trace of morality, a moral practice which lasts (to a greater or lesser extent). Practical temporality, which is also practical morality, is therefore binding on the Subject, with the serious limitations which we have stated: this matter only bears traces of a moral code and states what must be rather than what must be (is) right or wrong.

The economic Subject is therefore in action, the action of capture and design. We will call this act of projection of the consciousness the *design-capture*. The *design-capture* acts upon what we have called *practical temporality*, i.e. the matter of duration. The act of design and capture is the obliteration of the temporal matter constituted by practical temporality. The result of this act of design and capture is the *design-capture*, the product of negativity and matter and the contents of the image-object produced by the imaging consciousness, the contents in general of the specific space-time reference frame (the combustion chamber of time-matter where the internal combustion engine combines a spark, which is the design/capture of the consciousness and the fuel, which is duration).

The *design-capture* is the product of the capture and the design and is also the very act itself of capture and design. The fundamental structure of the *design-capture* is twofold. An initial structure contains the raw material of practical temporality resulting from the act of projection of the consciousness by means of which the Subject is defined; the economic and financial Subject is made up of time-matter, i.e. of duration, memory recall and lapse, time matter which is continuously set in motion by the consciousness which targets and captures: this is the origin of the economic and financial dynamic. A second structure, the framework of the design, is made up of the inferred structure of the design, which the Subject crosses with practical temporality. We have stated that this inferred structure is, to a certain extent, difficult to distinguish from the structure of time-matter (i.e. the inferences can be interpreted as practical forms of duration, which have emerged from facts and *habitus*). Without dismissing this interpretation, we preserve the distinction here.

The *design-capture* therefore presents a force which is dominated by *practical morality* as we have defined the same: the economic and financial Subject is *inhabited* (within the same meaning as the word *habitus*, i.e. all the practices and all that is borne by duration) by the *habitus* of a moral nature, conveyed by duration and driven or distorted by memory recall and lapse). A second force is structured by the apriorisms, certain of which may be moral, and which cross-refer, unless one assumes the existence of a pure, inferred structure, to an ontological region which is different from the regions of practical temporality and the *design-capture* in its initial structure which we have just described above. This ontological region where apriorisms are located is transcendental and refers back to the order of that which is. Accordingly, unless one asserts that the Subject's design is simply *habitus*, practices conveyed by duration (*practical temporality* and *practical morality*), within the progression of understanding and of moral judgement, it must be assumed that such a pure and autonomous region of the Subject exists, an *a priori* structure, and, consequently, a link with a superior, ontological region which guarantees the origin and creates such apriorisms or such pure categories.

The third dimension is located over and beyond the Subject in a superior, ontological region, which nonetheless determines the Subject on the basis of that which is and which lasts, since the two concepts are identical, if not analogical. This region of being-duration, which transcends the regions of practical morality and of the Subject (acting), holds the key to the meaning, to that part of economics and finance which is comprehensible. We will come back to this later.

3. THE TWO LEVELS OF ECONOMICS AND MORALITY

§ 133.   We have seen that there were two circles or two domains, that of acting, i.e. of pure action in the sense that the mechanisms of the economic action process, which we have described, develop irrespective of the moral characterization which may be given, independently of any ethical dimension, and that which we have called practical morality, a domain which essentially sustains action on the basis of a matter and a space-time reference frame which bear the trace of another trans-cendental, ontological region where one would find that which is, practical morality, as its name suggests, mixing the trace of that which is (for example, duration for the determination of value or equilibrium) and the finitude of that which has been experienced by the Subject (the time-matter of duration intersecting human history, a block of duration which is indeed vast but not limitless and which is itself traversed by the volatility of memory and forgetfulness).

The economic action is not, as such, moral and that which occurs within the process of acting, in its most practical terms (which we have called the *impact* in and on the real world) is not, in principle right or wrong. Furthermore, this is a concern which is sustained by the apparently limitless appropriation of the world by the acting Subject. There do not in fact appear to be any limits, starting from the imaginative world and the conception of image-objects up until the formalisation of the practical action, passing en route through the financial market's gestation/selection phase – there do not appear to be any limits.

And yet, as our work has shown, there is a tenuous thread, a trace which opens up a link, a path towards an ethical basis for economic and financial action, since the DNA of the image-objects which inhabit the space-time reference frame and finance before locating the armed wing of the actual action, and the DNA of the projects, bears the trace, in its very matter (time, duration), in a finite and incomplete form, of a different, ontological nature which is fuller, more complete. Such finite and incomplete forms can be found within *practical morality*, the universe of time-matter of duration, memory recall and lapse which gives meaning, with its limits, to a structure of concepts which looks towards that which is (value, equilibrium) from the basis of a being and time pairing which embodies and summarises *that which lasts*. This glance towards and link with a third region, of greater ontological density take place from a domain of *practical morality* where that which is manifests its presence but within the finitude and limits of the Subject (*that which lasts* is that which lasts *for* the Subject).

§ 134.   However, the workings of economics and finance in the context of the Subject's action, as we have described it, brings about the possibility of "restoring" and founding the economic action process within this ontological region, located beyond the Subject, a region of that which is and lasts, a tautology for referring to the regime of being-duration. If such an effort is not furnished in order to enable the *practical-moral* "aspects"/appearances to be secured, i.e. in a finite universe, concepts of value or equilibrium within that which seems to inspire them (that which lasts, that which is), then the *practical morality*, the intermediate world of a specific, space-time reference frame for a Subject-consciousness, threatens to swerve off course or swing towards what might be called *practical-practicality*, the final moment of the pure execution of the economic and financial action process (the impact) and, above all, to be progressively or suddenly invaded by forgetfulness, the specific space-time reference frame, where the image-objects are created, emptying itself of its time-matter (that which lasts), delivering these same image-objects up to the financial markets and then at the final moment of impact, to a lack of meaning, to a feeling which mixes the fatality of an appropriation process which destroys the world with the absurdity of an oblivious force which seems to be dominated by irrationality and incomprehension. This feeling of a sliding motion, which in our view represents an interpretation of the modern age (see *Tractatus*), finds therein a possible explanation but does not imply a fatality since the shift, which is a serious force of modern times in the confrontation between the Subject and the world which has taken on the very name of economics, may be reined in and even reversed.

The reasons behind the hope of a reversal (which does not mean the abandonment of an action but consciousness, while acting, of the involvement of that which is and lasts) can be found within that which pulls the economic Subject, in its active relationship with the world, along towards the infinite and incongruous appropriation, within this very same force. Such reasons exist together with the space-time reference frame and especially with time-matter (that which lasts), which carry meaning from a more distant region.

What one means by this is that our quite literal incomprehension of the processes of finance and the markets (and of economics in general), which we attribute to their irrationality is simply the manifestation of an intellectual and moral abdication regarding the task of understanding. This task, if properly carried out, allows one to perceive elements which are comprehensible for a Subject and to appreciate that these very comprehensible elements, which do not suffice as such to tell right from wrong for the purposes of economic and financial action, points towards that which from a superior, ontological region can tell right from wrong. It is this task which we have stated to be a matter of modern urgency.

§ 135.   That which must be (and, consequently, that which must be right), within economics and finance, often forms part of *that which lasts*, within a practical morality where the duration of a practice provides the foundation for an ethical code. If one expands this reasoning in an absolute manner, one perceives the categorical imperative represented by that which lasts absolutely, which does not stop lasting, which lasts eternally, which mixes being and duration. This categorical imperative and this *a priori* form which binds the Subject's behaviour in the economic and financial action process, undoubtedly refer directly to this third region which we are discussing, that of being-duration; there is, within the constitution of the economic conscious Subject, something which expresses, in the nature of a foundation, this duration which is so intense and so concentrated that it forms, *a priori*, a moral imperative.

However, in the vast majority of the situations of economic and financial life, the issue of what must be (right) appears within practical morality, i.e. within an intermediate structure where what must be may seem to borrow from a superior, ontological region and, at the same time, be the result of a practical process which has lasted, and the two may merge. Accordingly, the concept of "fairness" (equity), which is often referred to in the texts on the economics of animal spirits (which interestingly includes the issue of moral principles), is both an *a priori* form (imperative) and a practice over duration, and the two may theoretically be merged for ever.

That said, within practical morality, and therefore within that which is captured and set as a principle by duration, it does not stand to reason that everything which lasts is necessarily moral, if such duration has permeated practice to a sufficient degree. However, it can clearly be seen that the majority of special and original features of conduct and of economic life, which seem to run counter to what reason would expect and which are consequently described as "animal spirits", can be understood and analysed as phenomena of duration and memory, whether or not linked to practices. The time-matter which constitutes the economic Subject and irrigates the economic and financial action therefore contains within it, like an imprint or trace, the imperative of what must be (right) since what must be, in terms of economics and finance, is confused with that which lasts.

The time-matter of duration and memory which constitutes the innermost structure of economic action therefore contains the necessity of what must be. The understandable nature of economic action depends upon the access to such necessity and primarily to the presence of necessity. If such access remains impossible, then the economic action seems senseless, driven by an empty and absurd necessity. The first task is to make understandable that which is only slightly so and, by so doing, to reveal the structure of economic phenomena, which is based on that which lasts and, by so doing, link the said duration to that which continues to last, i.e. to the solid place where that which is is located, the solid place where that which must be/is (right) is also located.

§ 136. Accordingly, the possibility of a moral code within economic and financial action is located within the reference frame of time which structures it. It is only a possibility, since the force of the action process may sweep everything away with it. However, any economic action commences from a reference frame of time-matter which bears the trace of that which must be right: at the key moment, when the image-objects are conceived - which, after passing through the financial markets, will form the central core of the final form of the action - the possibility of a moral dimension to the action is determined. Any action bears within it, within its initial matrix, the possibility of its ethical dimension, which is buried within its specific heritage of duration to a greater or lesser extent. This possibility will be made more remote, if an inadequate effort is made to understand this or if there is, quite simply, an element of forgetfulness.

The economic act is design or purpose and this design, like the warhead of a rocket or missile, is made up of time-matter which is language, the language of that which still lasts and is present. This language is encrypted and deciphered within a specific space-time reference frame. This matter-language includes the elements of that which must be (right). This enables one to understand that, in certain situations, the action will incorporate a dimension which will cause the economic Subject's behaviour to divert from a path which seemed to be fatal and linear: the Subject will not behave as the majority of parameters had indicated. The Subject will accordingly take into consideration what is right or what should not be done, and it is from a reference frame of duration that memory will recall the motives for a moral code. On the other hand, it is forgetfulness, the lack of knowledge or existence of such a heritage of the root of value which will precipitate the action, in the same way as a machine running in neutral, towards a never-ending purpose.

The possibility of a moral dimension for economic and financial action is closely linked to the exercise of memory by the conscious economic Subject over a stock of time-matter (that which lasts): the meaning of the economic act's destination (purpose of the design) and in particular its meaning from the point of view of that which is right or good are the functions of memory applied to a section (stock) of duration. And memory of that which is good or right is the determining element of the ethical meaning of the design. By assuming that the rate of memory is maximal and stable, if not constant, one can then consider that it is a structure of values which is comparable to *a priori* forms. This represents an exception to reality which will always see the partial and/or diverse, instable and volatile rate of memory. And the rate of forgetfulness may be such that the action then proceeds without a reference frame, a design without meaning or *practical-moral* references, to use our terminology. Within the domain where we have placed the determination of the economic action, a domain which we have described as *practical morality*, the ethical substance of the design is memory of the ethical practice and this substance is duration of that which is right or good and, in this sense, duration of that which must be, since, ultimately, that which lasts and that which must be converge.

The ethical substance of the design which contains the economic action is memory, a recall of a reference frame of duration of that which was right or good and which lasts (it is also, therefore, forgetfulness of that which was not right or good). One accordingly means by this that the structure of the reference frame of economic action, which is made up of blocks of duration cut out of time and remembered or forgotten, includes, within the humus of initial duration, as if taken from the rest of the stone, elements of an ethical nature, linked to the practices and values, both of which are connected (and which we have called *practical morality*) within a time-matter of duration and memory.

The term *practical morality* shows that it is through the practice which is present in duration and memory that the Subject's economic act incorporates a dimension which is described in different terms by the authors ("animal spirits") but which refer back to moral elements. These elements form part of the determination of the economic act through the intermediary of the actual practices which they have influenced and which form part of a memory. This dimension of memory and duration of practical situations with a moral dimension does not eliminate the reference to values but such values move towards the action and the Subject by means of practices which structure duration and memory as a specific space-time reference frame. What is found within the domain of *practical morality* is time-matter which sustains the image-objects which will themselves drive the action process. They are not, strictly speaking, values but rather practical traces of values, such values residing in turn within a purer ontological region.

The economic action process, as we have described, therefore incorporates, among the image-objects produced by the imaging and acting consciousness, and based on the matter of duration and memory, image-objects which are the moral representations sustained by a time-matter made up of practice which have lasted to a sufficient degree so as to be present and, by their very duration and the memory attached to it, to obtain a status of value, which is not absolute but rather relative to the elements, facts, events and objects which have accompanied it. Therefore, the moral value present within the economic action process is always *relative*, relative to the practices and to the finitude of the time-matter mobilised by a Subject which is itself captured within a finitude. However, the greater the density of duration of these relative values (which are practices which last), the closer such values come to the status of absolute value, i.e. that which is and which lasts, *absolutely*, although they never quite reach it.

§ 137.   Economics and morality constitute different spaces and dimensions. Since economics proceeds above all as an action process of the Subject towards the world and since this process is sustained by projections (image-objects) and time-matter, economics cannot ignore morality in the same way that it cannot ignore all the decisions and environments of the Subject and the world which, after the sections have been cut out, constitute the temporal reference frame and the matter on the basis of which the action will proceed. As such, morality is the trace left in the material, a material itself in part, which forms the foundation for the economic act. Moreover, the conscious Subject which creates the image-objects and, in general, the imaging and acting consciousness, commences the act of economic projection at any given time by "carrying along" with it all the moral representations.

The innermost material of economics bears a trace of moral representations and decisions and the economic Subject, a consciousness which commences a process of creation-destruction of this material of duration and memory, cannot ignore it.

§ 138.   There are two levels. The level of *practical morality* is made up of all the practices where the action was placed in a situation of a moral nature. Such practices are moments or sequences of the economic Subject engaged in the action process and therefore sections within time-matter, in the same way as other facts and events. This temporal matter incorporates the space-time reference frame of the Subject which initiates the action. This matter is involved in the flow and stock of duration and memory.

This practical level bears the traces or signs of values, in two respects. We are not dealing with values as such (which belong to a superior ontological region) but values which are placed within the practices which involve the economic Subject in the economic and financial act. There is, in addition, an effect of memory (and forgetfulness) on this dimension of practices. The whole takes on the specific forms of the space-time reference frame which has been described and which acts as the framework and operating mode for the economic Subject within the general process of projection, imagination/anticipation, action/transformation.

The practical-moral level therefore bears the lights of more distant stars in the same way as the practices of a moral code within the (economic) act refer to values. The stronger the light and therefore the more firmly the moral practice is anchored within duration and memory, the more such practice will appear as the value itself and, also, as the *a priori* structure of the economic Subject's (moral) judgement (although, in our view, they will not be confused, since the different dimensions are not fungible). Without dismissing this possibility, it is rather the hesitant and unstable lights which dominate real situations. The volatility of duration, linked to the corrosion of memory by forgetfulness, constantly threatens, whether progressively or suddenly, to distance the star from the value, which will not disappear but its rays will no longer reach the world of action, or in any event not in a manner which will suffice to regenerate and maintain the memory and *practical morality* which lasts, ultimately the value itself which lasts. The Subject itself is stripped of this matter which, unless it exists *a priori*, disappears from the reference frame of the economic action.

Forgetfulness constantly threatens practical morality with an obliteration of the link between the ontological region of duration (onto-duration, being-duration) and absolute values. The eradication of value, or rather its disappearance, then leaves the reference frame of economic action literally without any memory of practical morality, which will not prevent the relevant action from continuing, but it will be cut off from its moral heritage and henceforth sustained only by practical acts which lack the same dimension.

§ 139.   The second level is that of absolute values. This is the level which supports meaning and the dynamic which we have called *practical morality* (second region) and the region of action and of the impact itself with the world (first region). The third region is that of the ontological level of (moral) values which are present within practical morality and which will, from there, incorporate the time-matter of the image-object and of the action itself.

Such values belong to a region of being-duration (onto-duration), in order to show that they are classified by the fact that they last, and last so long as their duration is identified with the fact that they are, their being is identified with the duration which is present within them. Within the second region of practical morality, in damaged form, exists the fact that energy, the first element of the economic and financial action process, is provided by the temporal matter of that which lasts. However this is a duration for a Subject-consciousness and memory; these concepts do not have the same full ontological substance as that of the absolute values of the region which we have just discussed (being-duration, onto-duration). However, at the same time, it is essential to note that these damaged (relative) concepts reflect a link and meaning back to the absolute values, and the presence of a connection between economics and morality depends, ultimately, within the region of action, on this coherence.

§ 140.   Nothing much can be said about the third region of being-duration or of onto-duration. Here one finds values which, over and beyond the Subject (although the latter is inspired, i.e. structured, by them), are complete of themselves and of which it can be said that they are in the same way that they last. Since, and this is true of economic concepts and in general of economic and financial life, there is a profound analogy (and much more than a simple analogy) between that which is and that which lasts. To the exact same extent that the fundamental concepts of economics (value, equilibrium...) are described as modes of being, it is then legitimate to try and define them on the basis of duration, memory and forgetfulness. Within human life, this truth of duration, memory and forgetfulness is developed for a Subject, *homo economicus*. However, the same truth also exists over and beyond the Subject.

EPILOGUE

§ 141.   Value – whether economic or other – may at all times and places be identified with that which is, which perseveres in its being and which lasts. The similarity which can be established between that which is and that which lasts constitutes the basis for the approach we have taken. Within the space-time of the economic Subject unfurling its action (the economic and financial action), within the human finitude of consciousness projected towards the world, that which is and that which lasts constitute finite concepts and relative dimensions, constructed with the historic depth of human experiences and practices within a certain environment (duration then adopts a relative and finite form), the memory and forgetfulness of a Subject-consciousness, indeed a space-time reference frame which mixes its elements in order to create the imaging and acting dynamic. Within the Subject's space-time, therefore, that which is and that which lasts, and also memory, are concepts which look towards their absolute source, a superior ontological zone which creates them.

Accordingly, duration, which is so important for the understanding of observable economic and financial phenomena, defined in a relative and finite manner by a certain historical section of slices of time with regard to a Subject, accompanied by memory recalls and lapses with regard to a Subject and even by that Subject, a section which provides the basis and the point of reference for a certain definition of that which is and therefore for a certain number of essential concepts such as equilibrium and value, concepts which, for the same reasons, adopt a relative dimension within this space-time of the Subject; this relative duration can only be understood as an incomplete form of a duration which is confused with that which is, in a more absolute form, to which the absolute concepts of value and equilibrium will ultimately attach themselves. Discernable duration, which we call relative, bears witness to a transcendental form which, in return, creates it by making it understandable.

Within the space-time of the economic Subject which develops the action, the moral dimension is not absent. It fits within the historical sections of slices of time and of life, within duration and memory, in their finite and relative forms, like a trace-witness of that which is absolutely and which lasts, but which cannot be observed nor described, and without which, however, the purpose of the meaning of economic action cannot be established and economics remains incomprehensible. One has to advance the premise of an ultimate region of pure being and duration in order for that which bears the trace and the meaning to become clear and discernable. This region of being and duration remains beyond the economic Subject, which in turn fully occupies the region of imaging and acting consciousnesses, which the action itself continues, like an arm of execution and impact, and is often the only facet of the action which is visible or can be seen. Within this very important region of the imaging and acting consciousnesses, this sort of region of lakes where the rivers of memory, and of that which continues to be present and which lasts, converge, the moral code in action and a practice of values reaches us, embedded within the large sections of time, scattered and mixed with the rest of the glacier of memory and duration, which ultimately always gives back, under the sun's influence, that which it acquired during the winter. Economic action and moral life are not inevitably separated.

PART II

THE ECONOMIC SUBJECT, FREEDOM AND SOCIETY

Chapitre 6

THE FUNDAMENTAL MODERN IDENTITY
(Freedom, Subject, Consciousness, Action)

1. ECONOMIC FREEDOM AS ACTION PROCESS AND RELATIONSHIP WITH THE WORLD

§ 142. Economic freedom, as a concept, is not self-evident, because economics, in the modern era, are in fact the very expansion of the (economic) Subject towards the world and the very name of the relationship which modern man has with the world. The concept of "economic freedom" may accordingly seem to contain a pleonastic dimension since, ultimately, it would only be a question, within what we call economics, at all times and in all places, of the effort and impact of one freedom, that of the Subject. The modern achievement of economics as the taking of control by and from the viewpoint of the Subject as consciousness would guarantee the development of free forms and, ultimately, of freedom. Once the pre-eminence of a Subject-consciousness, constituted of freedom in its essence, has been established, i.e. having an infinite capacity to project, anticipate and transform, and therefore to act, namely the capacity to imagine what is (will be) in the state of non-being (not-yet-being), then to some extent an identity between Subject, freedom and action will also be established, thus defining economics as the forms and modes of impact of this triptych. The action of the free Subject would suffice to define economics and, consequently, economic action and economic freedom, always from the viewpoint of the Subject (*homo economicus*), would in turn form one identity.

Economic freedom would result from the very fact that everything which is economic is impact, the movement of action of a free Subject (the free nature of the Subject-consciousness ensures, at the very impact of the action, the economic freedom of the whole). Ultimately, what we call economics would essentially be the name given to the whole of the acts of free consciousnesses throughout the world, and such acting and imaging consciousnesses, by their sole, totalising presence, would impose (economic) freedom. In fact, economic freedom then verges on a form of tautology since that which is economic can only, in its essence, be the product of a freedom from freedom.

This approach is consistent with the manner in which what we call economics in the modern era are structured, the invasion of the Subject which we have described elsewhere. The tautology which is accordingly established at the core of the concept of economic freedom (everything which is economic is at all times and in all places free, is freedom) founds in the same movement a sectarianism of freedom and, no less excessive, a fearful rejection not only of this evolution but of the very idea of economic liberalism, in general.

However, although it is difficult to refute the fact that economics should be defined on the basis of the Subject's action in the modern era, a Subject which is itself defined as a free, acting consciousness, nothing guarantees that the (economic) action process itself will produce economic freedom, economic freedoms. By using the expression "production of economic freedom(s)", the point of view is shifted, by placing economic freedom at a distance from the (economic) Subject and its action, thus breaking the identity (the tautology discussed above), and thus placing economic freedom as the *result* of the economic action process (economic freedom is assessed on the basis of the whole structure, which includes the action process and its impact). One seeks to demonstrate, in the wake of the works of *Théorie du Sujet économique*, that, left to itself, the economic Subject defined as free, acting and imaging consciousness produces no or few economic freedom(s) even if it is driven, both in theory and in its essence, by freedom. It is the paradox of economic freedom that it is continuously threatened in its very essence by the very existence of a free Subject-consciousness which controls the economic action process. Consequently, one seeks to demonstrate that, in certain circumstances, and only in certain circumstances, the economic action process may be able to produce or guarantee economic freedom. These are the circumstances which allow for the possibility of a norm and of institutions, whose essence is linked, and which we discussed in *Théorie du Sujet économique*.

As can be seen, departing from the tautological identity [Subject-free consciousness-action] = [economic freedom] constitutes a point of passage. It is by loosening the noose of this constraint (which is appealing in its obviousness: if the economic Subject is freedom in its essence, then that which is economic is freedom in its essence and only economic freedoms exist), that we can update what we have called the paradox of economic freedom. However, once having dared to discuss the concept of economic freedom as being removed from the (economic) Subject, as the object of a process, we still need to define it within this status, and to identify within the economic action process itself the conditions which make it possible, since economic freedom is contingent within the economic action process and therefore rare. Economic freedom may or may not be. The necessity of the approaches which establish the identity between a Subject and economic freedom (the existence of a *necessary* link between economic Subject and economic freedom) are, for us, an additional sign of the modern achievement of economics which we have described elsewhere (*Tractatus*, *Généalogie*, *Valeur et temps*).

By establishing the concept of economic freedom as an object (this is to a certain extent the custom of everyday language, which refers to "the economic freedoms" as being accompanied by a form of status which is external to the economic process itself), one establishes this object, in a methodological manner, as the object of a targeting process, the targeting *of* that which contains the economic freedom. Economic freedom is not therefore completely identified with the design of the free, acting and imaging consciousness which initiates the economic action process (theory of identity), even if its essence contains a common trace or origin, its being originating in the essence of the economic Subject (freedom understood as design and therefore "filled with" negativity). The core of economic freedom, as a concept, does indeed contain this DNA. Economic freedom is experienced within the very design in action, at the most preliminary phase (imaging consciousness, anticipations). However, as we have noted, the concept should not be confined within the identity of a Subject which is, as it were, condemned to be free and *all* of whose economic designs, whether they have remained as designs (image, anticipation) or have led to an impact with the world are signs, evidence of an economic freedom. Since economic freedom is also the object of a design, in both the first phase of the economic action process (the structuring and selection of images and anticipations) and the second phase of the action (impact and constitution of the actual object of the design).

Economic freedom therefore lies within the very movement of the free, imaging and acting consciousness which initiates the action. It also lies within the object which is formed on impact of the action process, like a concretion. It is *the* economic freedom insofar as its essence refers back to the Subject's freedom. It is *an* economic freedom in the sense of a particular object which is constituted during or at the end of the action process. In both cases, we have to clarify the status of such concepts.

The economic freedom, which can be identified with the freedom of the Subject itself in its essence, has to overcome the difficulty referred to, i.e. any economic action process does not necessarily reflect the economic freedom, does not necessarily produce *an* economic freedom.

By placing the Subject at the heart of the relationship with the world and by defining *homo economicus* as freedom and the freedom itself of the Subject based on negativity and as an obliterating capacity, the modern age establishes a close connection between freedom and action, and economics themselves are considered to be an action process of the free Subject. This means that, progressively, a connection is established between economic freedom and economic action to such a close extent that they merge. The consequence of this is to define economic freedom, after the event, as it were, as that which results from the economic action. Placed between, at a preliminary phase, the premise of a pure freedom of the Subject and, at a later stage, the legitimacy of the economic action, economic freedom appears to be solid and protected: its existence is "natural" insofar as it only extends the Subject's free essence; its reality within the world is in proportion to the economic action, i.e. it is the economic action which justifies, or literally "demonstrates" economic freedom. Consequently one notes policies which aim to stimulate doing, the action as such, which is laudable, but which fail to take any particular consideration of the economic freedom which appears in terms of its substance to be established (*homo economicus* is free) and the legitimacy of whose form comes through the action, the two forming a referential and validating loop.

The modern essence of economic freedom is linked to the economic action within an economic action process ruled by the Subject. Economic freedom, as a concept, increases in importance with the modern emancipation of a Subject considered as freedom. As the link established between freedom and action through the work of negativity within the project, anticipation leads to a definition of economic freedom based on the intensity of action (the more one acts, the freer one is). This enables us to clarify the identity referred to above between the structure of the economic Subject, as the same emerges in order to play a dominant role in modern times (consciousness, freedom-negativity and action are some of the key elements of this structure), and economic freedom (between freedom and economics as well). Economic freedom is the freedom of the Subject but, to a greater extent, the action of the Subject, which uses up a large part of the definition of freedom.

This leads us to look more closely at the economic action process of the Subject, which both develops freedom in its very essence and also produces economic freedoms *in certain circumstances*. In particular, economic freedom, as object of the economic action process which it stems from (in the sense of "economic freedoms") and also sustains (the process of the imaging and acting consciousness is based on a theory of the project and of freedom), is impregnated, in its very nature, by the individual Subject-consciousness (in the sense understood by individualism), by a pure, total and Promethean vision of freedom (the concept of which is almost dominated by that of desire), which projects and obliterates within the immediacy of a *sui generis* sudden appearance, therefore by a theory of the Subject which affirms the latter's freedom from an ontological point of view but does not manage to provide a solid basis for the collective processes and structures, whether with regard to the collective institution, as compared to or faced with the total individual, with regard to just the institution itself, or with regard to the Other, the otherness which means that the Subject's freedom develops among/against other freedoms, and which also fails to provide a basis for economic action within time, whether with regard to the structures and processes of memory and duration, faced with the lightning speeds of a consciousness without matter, density or history, or with regard to the possibility of a norm and therefore of regulation.

One means by this that economic freedom can only be considered together with the Other, the collective and the institutional, the norm and regulation; that a theory of the economic Subject is possible, if it incorporates these points (see our work *Théorie du Sujet économique*) and surpasses the totalising Subject which is so pure, so free and so alone in the world and so demiurgic that the (economic) freedom has difficulty existing around it when all seems to be freedom and action. This totalising Subject is indeed that which, since the modern turning point, develops within what we call economics, i.e. the action of the free Subject (the three words form one identity) within the world. However, we have shown that this Subject could be surpassed and, first of all, that the Subject, which we call totalising, pure freedom, did not exist, or at least did not correspond to the more realistic structures of the imaging and acting consciousness and the temporal matter of memory and duration which forms its innermost constitution. By reforming the theory of the Subject as a theory of the economic Subject, by genetically modifying *homo economicus*, a theory of economic freedom becomes possible, which surpasses the sole, formidable identity which imprisons economic freedom within the action of a totalising Subject. This surpassment also represents the possibility of a norm and also of a moral code.

§ 143.   We therefore return to our approach, to consider economic freedom by avoiding the tautological trap which suggests that, ontologically, everything which comes from the economic Subject, understood as a free consciousness, is branded by freedom and, therefore, stems whether closely or more remotely from a form of economic freedom; which also suggests, from a practical viewpoint, and by extension, that all that is economic action or which through its effects and impact forms part of an economic action process of the Subject, is the expression of an economic freedom or creates or produces economic freedom or economic freedoms.

The economic action process is indeed the act of a Subject (individual or collective body) defined by a consciousness. This consciousness is defined as freedom, i.e. a force of project and therefore the capacity to imagine (imaging consciousness) that which is in a state of non-being or not-yet-being, to imagine that which quite simply is not, to produce, through a financial imaginative world, whose structures we have described, images which form the basis of projects which will progressively constitute the action itself up until its actual impact. Such a force of projection within that which is not, an obliterating, imagining and creative force is, at the heart of the economic action process, the force of freedom and liberation (of that which is). Economic freedom takes its source and anchors itself in its essence to the very structure of the consciousness of the economic Subject, i.e. to this hole in being which beckons that which is in a state of non-being, and therefore the economic action. One can understand the extent to which it is profoundly necessary for the economic action to be linked to this beckoning, this need created by the decompression of being which constitutes the free consciousness. The projection of the consciousness of the economic Subject beyond itself, which constitutes its state of being, necessarily summons the economic action and the two faces of the same mirror, which are represented by the economic Subject's free consciousness (*homo economicus*) and the economic action process and which call to each other through an interaction of cross-references and cross-legitimation.

Accordingly, to say that the Subject is an obliterating force (therefore freedom), therefore a force of anticipation (here lies the basis for the key role of anticipations in economics) and to say that there is economic action within a process which moves from the crude production of image-objects by the consciousness, their sorting, selection and organisation by the form of the financial market (this physical consciousness), up until the final preparation of the action itself and its actual impact in the world and the constitution of an object from the impact which consequently has retroactive effect on the whole chain of the process, is to state the same reality, the same necessity.

Economic freedom must therefore be considered, in its essence, from the viewpoint of the economic Subject itself (*homo economicus* in short, and insofar as the concept is defined). This is the intended purpose of modern, western thinking and of economics in particular, which is the name of the new and exclusive relationship which binds the Subject to the world.

However, this force of freedom and obliteration, by extending its systematic domination over the world, a monopolisation and examination of things and people, in particular by technical means, at the most contemporaneous moment of this modern period, has literally and paradoxically ended up causing concern, the more it asserted itself. Here we are touching upon one of the most formative, paradoxical forms of the modern era, for economics in particular. The emancipation, liberation and promotion of a free Subject, which masters and possesses nature, a consciousness which obliterates and produces projects and action, will gradually instil concern regarding the lack of limits, norms, morality and regulation, from a metaphysical (ontological) viewpoint (a crisis of ideologies) or more strictly financial viewpoint (the possibility of a norm and of regulation within a context of financial crises). The totalising nature of the Subject, which is a free, pure force without limits, whether the Subject is an individual (the forces of individualism) or a collective body (dictatorial forms) can only lead one to question the paradox which, in the modern era, sees the assertion of the Subject's freedom go hand-in-hand with the ultimately fragile status of economic freedoms, to mention merely its freedoms alone. One cannot negate the emergence of a circulation of individual freedoms, both economic and political, as a necessary counterpart to the assertion of the free Subject and consciousness, which creates projects and action, as being the heart of the economic action process and, in general, a central force of modern times.

However, nothing seems able to control the individual and/or collective forces which are released by this modern turning point, these forces of a will which wills itself (freedom yields to the oblivious force of will as the central pivot of the regime). Consequently, and at the end of an ongoing process which is not yet completed, the very status of economic freedom seems weakened and threatened by the very force which gave birth to it, which supported it and helped it develop.

The question evolves, in its very formulation. Although one is not required to question the fact that economic freedom takes its source and is created in the modern era within the Subject's freedom (*homo economicus*) and its action (economic action process), first one has to demonstrate that the difficulties mentioned above have resulted in an inadequate and unrealistic consideration of the economic Subject (*homo economicus*) and that, provided that the essential structures and matters of the economic Subject are correctly defined, then, through the possibility of a norm and regulation in particular, through the taking into account of memory and duration in the very structure of the Subject-consciousness and therefore within the economic action process as well, the freedom of the economic Subject, together with its product on impact, may be considered without contradiction, however paradoxical it might seem; second, one has to demonstrate that economic freedom can and must become independent to a greater extent than it has up until now, by comparison with the sole economic Subject, placed at a distance as the *object* of the economic action process as well, a process which is governed by the adequately described structure of the economic Subject, since the economic action process produces economic freedom(s) in the same way as it produces image-objects (and economic freedom, prior to being the object on actual impact, is an image-object).

(Economic) freedom is the very name of the economic action process's movement and dynamic and is of the same essence as that of the economic Subject, in its structure, but is also an autonomous object of the economic action process and of the design, a fragile autonomy which in return protects the economic action process from its possible shifts, to some extent *from the outside*, especially when such objects (economic freedoms) are appropriated and defended by institutions which confront the Subject and, occasionally, take on the role of economic Subject (e.g. the central Bank).

§ 144.   To ask what economic freedom is requires one, first, to isolate the freedom whose source leads back to the emancipated Subject and, second, to question economics as an action process of the (economic) Subject as the same is implemented and develops in the modern era. It is not an easy matter to isolate the two terms since the question of economic freedom is not that of the development of freedom (that of the Subject in this instance) within a particular domain which would be that of economics, since economics are themselves the name of the development which, in the modern age, is specific to the freedom of a Subject presented as an acting consciousness and which has adopted, for the purpose of the so-called economic discipline, the name of *homo economicus*. This means that, originally, i.e. in the modern era, which is ultimately a fairly recent origin, the question of economic freedom includes a philosophical dimension and, in particular, the dimension of the Subject. Paradoxically, it is in the modern era that the economic discipline is splitting off and becoming independent, which makes it even more difficult to consider economic freedom in its totality.

Economic freedom becomes, in the modern age, one of the dominant forms of the relationship which man maintains with the world, through action. The term economic describes the concept of freedom in order to signify that the Subject experiences its freedom mainly (but not solely) through the action (from the production of an image-object up until the impact itself), through the project and the exchange which announces the projects (the financial markets), from the viewpoint of the transformation of the world which is, at the same time, a transformation of itself, since the definition of the freedom of the economic Subject (*homo economicus*) as a projection beyond itself *necessarily* summons the action which transforms the world (and itself). There is a profound link between the emancipation of the Subject, as freedom, and the transformation of the world, which is *a priori* limitless, provided that the Subject is presented as pure and total freedom.

Consequently, one has no other choice than to commence with the (economic) Subject in order to try and understand economic freedom, since the development dynamic of what is called economics is that of the Subject. Since freedom is largely defined by means of the Subject's action, economic freedom is itself often reduced to the question of freedom to act. The question of freedom to act, which itself includes a wide spectrum of sequences and questions (the conception and production of image-objects, the exchange and valuation of the said image-objects which represent the same number of anticipations and projects for that which is in a state of not-yet-being, up until the exercise itself of the action, filled with matter, this *praxis* of impacts within the world and the real traces which it leaves there).

It is indeed peculiar that the question of economic freedom has *ended up* (since nothing preordained it entirely for that purpose at the outset) being merged (and resolving itself) within the question of freedom to act. This shift, which then forms the essential part of the works and the commentaries (how to preserve it, how to extend it, above all extending it, how to remove anything which may prove to be an obstacle to it – and consequently everything may prove to be an obstacle), is that which forms, in the structure of modern economics, the identity between freedom and action from the Subject's viewpoint. This shift is far from self-evident and we have moreover demonstrated that it contains the essence of modern economics right up to the mutation of economics into a technical act of appropriating the world and into economic policy.

Economic freedom presented as economic action is consequently judged on the achievement of its purpose and the maximum (optimum) mobilisation of resources. Furthermore, the action which defines economic freedom in its modern use is that of the (economic) Subject understood in its form as an individual, and not, as it should, also in its form as a collective body, as an institution. The identity forged between the freedom and action of the individual-Subject constitutes a weakness in the construction of the economic Subject's role within the economic action process, since, when the economic Subject is deprived of a collective and/or institutional form, the subjugating freedom of the Subject-consciousness then develops within and through the action which is limitless, without norms, constraints or external opposing forces (institutions) and its very structure of pure force-will makes it inappropriate for it to secrete such anti-bodies within the economic action process. There results the paradox which we have discussed, after which the Subject's freedom ultimately supplants the economic freedom by emptying it of its possible conditions. This shift lies at the origin of the fundamental debate, within the discipline, regarding the extension of economic freedom in the context of constraints and obstacles (the State, the central banks...); there cannot be any limits to this will in the name of economic freedom, since it is of the same nature as the (individual) economic Subject in its modern essence. The projection within the Subject's (technical) act of appropriation of the world goes hand in hand with the issue of the extension of economic freedom, by exploiting it (it is a question, both in its trend and in its substance, of extending rather than preserving it). What is then called economic freedom is an extension of the action domain, an instrumental form of the Subject's total and totalising will-freedom. Imprisoned within this role, the concept of economic freedom cannot help but be exploited within the economic action process, in at least two ways. First, economic freedom is one part of the tangible result of the action itself, since economic freedom is only experienced and only finds its meaning within the specific act of the Subject, which means that the essence of the economic action dominates and masks that of economic freedom, which is accordingly a subservient and secondary concept within economics (even though economic freedom, when considered strictly, should be a positive and constructive opposing force with regard to the economic Subject, it is henceforth dominated within the accelerating movement of the Subject's project). Second, the concept of economic freedom adopts an identical structure to that of the economic Subject, i.e. a projection forwards and beyond, in a state of not-yet-being, a flight towards that which must be acquired (and never attained, leading to a further projection) while being continuously lost. This structure which makes economic freedom as a concept a place of negativity which is only maintained by the action of projection and the conquests of new economic freedoms, produces a certain number of worrying difficulties. The concept of economic freedom is consequently beset, in the modern version which we are describing, by a permanent instability, due to its system of negativity directed towards unceasing action; consequently the unceasing quest for new "economic freedoms" (the inverted commas indicate that these are presumed and self-proclaimed economic freedoms which, in our view, as the process which we are describing develops, represent economic freedoms to an increasingly lesser degree); it is a considerable paradox to witness the debate on "economic freedoms" in fact focus on the extensions of the domain of action and strength of the Subject (particularly but not solely as an individual), on the results of action attempting to escape, through its nature and construction, from norms and limits, rather than on that which should be, or should never have stopped being, economic freedom.

§ 145.   Once economic freedom is likened to freedom of action, the freedom to act (that to which the omnipresence of a Subject defined by the project and thus by the action condemns it), economic freedom becomes the marker for the results obtained by the (free) economic Subject in its relations with the world whose limits are constantly pushed further back. Economic freedom is defined by or on the basis of the factor of resistance to the Subject's act, a definition effected in relation to, or by default by, the object-obstacle which has to be moved or removed (that which impedes). Accordingly, numerous debates on economic freedom relate, for example, to the "necessary" reduction of the role of the State in the economy (actor), barriers of all sorts to the circulation of goods, services, capital and persons (territory). The concept of economic freedom has the particular characteristic that its essence can be found outside it, as if removed from it, within the object of an intention to reduce, since the said object is an obstacle used to define the action which is economic freedom (which is defined on the basis of the design which must remove the obstacle which prevents economic freedom from asserting itself and from expanding). The concept of economic freedom is filled with a negativity which calls it towards this object which is defined in advance by the resistance which it counters to economic freedom. Economic freedom is the project to expand economic freedom. *Ex post*, the concept of economic freedom includes all the realisations, results and concretions of the impacts of the economic action within the world, and in fact, without any limit or norm in order to indicate where such a dynamic must or may stop, any concretion of impact is able to claim the status of economic freedom. Economic freedom is the vital movement of negativity which contains the action (negativity by means of which the projection and the project are formed), *the* economic freedoms are the points of impact of such methods of action processes towards and within the world and which form objects (products of a design), as if by depositing a sediment, objects which are bearers of a status which is henceforth external or exterior to the economic action process but which exercises, from such an external position, a more or less active presence over the economic action process in return, and such active presence may or may not take the form of a norm and therefore of a regulation which is likely to modify the economic action process itself, in its development and aims. We have understood that, first, there is no form of advance guarantee that this should be so, on the contrary, since, as we have shown, the very structure of the economic Subject as established in the modern age implies, without the necessary force of recall required for a norm and therefore for a regulation, that *all* the points of impact of the action within the world are able to claim the status of economic freedom. Economic freedom is a practice, a *praxis* which experiences, when placed in such structural conditions of the economic action process, all the difficulties in asserting its independence in order to reflect and, in particular, the task of regulation of the economic action process which is the responsibility of economic freedom cannot be carried out. Second, it seems therefore that the satisfactory introduction of the concept of economic freedom has to pass, at the outset, through a theory of the economic Subject which fixes the terms for a possible production of economic freedoms, within the action process which may assume the role of a norm and a regulation and, in return, may provide the phrasing – i.e. the regulation – of the whole economic action process. Since an economic action process, governed by an economic Subject which is pure, active freedom-will, individual and without any conceivable limit to this vital force, supplants the possibility of regulation through the production of economic freedoms. Economic freedoms do not precede the just and optimal economic action process, since such freedoms are the product of the said process which asserts its independence in order to regulate it. The solution therefore lies at the heart of the economic action process and within the very structure of the economic Subject. More specifically, it is a question of locating, within an adequate structure of the economic Subject, the elements which produce a possibility of norms. This is the work which we carried out in *La*

Théorie du Sujet économique and to which we will return on a regular basis throughout this work. We should already bear in mind that *the* economic freedom(s) (the concept is the same, in its ontological dimension which refers to the ontological structure of the Subject and multiplies in the independent active forms which it may adopt) see their essence (i.e. their structure) impregnated, imprinted in the same way as DNA by the structure of the economic Subject's freedom, but also that they are a *praxis*, a result – which is sedimented but active (in return) – of the economic action process driven by this imaging and acting Subject consciousness.

Although economic freedom emerges naturally from the economic action process, it cannot be solely defined by the freedom to act or freedom of action since economic freedom is, ultimately, that which has to ensure that the action is optimal, i.e. achieves reasonable objectives, i.e. economic freedom is that which has to make the action better, of better quality, including all the meanings of the term "better quality" and which constitutes a source of reflection as such. Economic freedom is a *praxis* which aims to make the action better (which includes the economic action process's objective for a norm and regulation). It is by setting economic freedom, based on the practical result of the action which it represents, the objective of directing and improving the economic action as it develops from the Subject, that one may found an economic action process which is structured by a regulation which does indeed adopt an economic or financial content but, more generally, a normative dimension within the legal or political dimensions (political freedom, at an admittedly specific level, fundamentally forms part of such a general issue), and moral dimensions since, ultimately, the question of economic freedom in its widest sense (i.e. the question of freedom in the action relationship between the modern Subject and the world) is that of an action of quality (one dare not say a good action or an action which is right), a question which cannot be posed, in one way or another, without touching upon the issue of morality.

2. ECONOMIC FREEDOM AS SUBJECT AND AS COLLECTIVE FORM

2.1. *FREEDOM AND ECONOMIC FREEDOM*

§ 146.   We have advanced. We are seeking to establish a structure of the economic Subject and an economic action process which produces economic freedoms and which improves the action in return by exercising, from a quasi-external status, a normative and regulatory influence, the norm in turn being able to attach itself to a moral bedrock (transcendence).

Before going further, let us halt for a moment at the concept of economic freedom as it is formed and distorted within the economic action process. We have seen that economic freedom, as a concept, has the structural characteristics of a free Subject, the negativity of projection and creation whose *necessary* counterpart is action. This means that economic freedom, in the process which leads to the object with a (more or less) independent status and which has an external role as compared to the action process which it results from, is first and foremost an image with the status of an image-object, fashioned and conceived by the imaging consciousness which, we should note, is the first sequence of the acting consciousness within the economic action process, the first core of that which will later (non-linear sequences) become a financial image on the financial markets and then the hard core of positive action within the matter.

Economic freedom, within an economic action process stemming from the free Subject (*homo economicus*), is first and foremost an image-object produced by the Subject's imaging consciousness. This means that economic freedom is a *specific* design of the Subject-consciousness, that an infinite multitude of elementary forms of such image-objects are conceived and produced at any one time, that it is difficult to distinguish at this initial stage between the *other* forms of economic action (it is, however, essential to do so; we will come back to the question of finding out what differentiates the future standard economic action (project) within the structure and matter of the form of the image, from the form which contains the embryo of an economic freedom); that this multitude of conceptual embryos stemming from the imaging consciousness will (must) pass through a filtering process for selection and sorting (which we must describe; whose criteria in terms of structure and matter we must note). All of this must enable us better to identify the formation and path taken by economic freedom in order to obtain a *good* production of economic freedoms.

§ 147.   Economic freedom understood as freedom to act, freedom of action, mainly, is the accomplishment of a modern idea of economics, or at least of an interpretation of this concept, still in the modern era, since this is where the Subject as a force of action on the world asserts itself as the point of reference in man's relationship with the world, therefore as an economic Subject.

It is by trying to separate freedom from mere action and, accordingly, the economic elements from an (economic) Subject which is alone in the world (particularly since the solitary Subject, unaware of the Other, no longer takes much account of the world, the object of a design of appropriation and absorption) and which is moreover only defined by its acting character with regard to a technical act of capture. This is the task proposed in *Tractatus, Généalogie* and *Valeur et temps*, a task which involves in particular the consideration of the (economic) Subject over and beyond the individual (the Other) and within what is (being), directed towards the world in an active relationship which allows that which is to approach in order to encompass Subject, being and the world within one whole.

Economic freedom is not only freedom of action. One instinctively senses that the concepts of freedom and economics restrain and distort each other within such an interpretation. One instinctively senses that economic freedom can be defined alternatively in the context of a relationship with the world and with that which represents otherness, where a state of being is established which allows that which is to approach the Subject. Accordingly, it also involves considering economics in a different way from that in which they have been considered in their modern purpose. However, one senses that the concept of economic freedom accommodates a large space where a relationship is determined with that which is, has a relationship with time, and with that which, together with the Subject (but over and beyond the intrusive Subject), contains the issue of equilibrium in respect of the relationship with the world, its measure and its norm. Active thought cannot, on its own, encompass such issues.

The concept of economic freedom is not easily understood nor, as it were, pronounced. The Subject will say "I am free" before saying "I am free in economic terms", since, as we have stated, the essence of freedom precedes that of economic freedom. However, the word which states "I", and which expresses the Subject's pre-eminence, states that the Subject's structure governs the whole. And what does it mean "to be free in economic terms"? It is a much more intuitive matter – although not much easier to define – to state "I am free" than to state "I am free in economic terms". The term "economic" in fact qualifies freedom, while appearing to limit it, while also segmenting and fragmenting it: there would thus arguably be a way to be free in terms of economics, politics, sport and love, etc. – an infinite range of types of *practical* means of freedom (the term *practical* is important, since the modern definition of freedom as a *praxis*, as the action of the Subject on the world rather than as a relationship with or means of being in the world, is central to the construction of the modern concept of economics). By qualifying the concept of freedom, the term "economic" weakens and fragments it, by appearing to impose upon it a practical form or method ("economic" will state the practical relationship of a (free) "I" with the world). Since the person who states "I am free in economic terms" is implicitly stating "I am free *for something*", and sets freedom a design or objective.

It can accordingly be understood that to state "I am free in economic terms" expresses a qualification of the relationship of the Subject (I) with the world, such relationship being based on the development of freedom as defining the Subject. "To be free" and "to be free in economic terms" would therefore evidently not relate to the same conceptual matter. One might be free but not free in economic terms. This is important, since it may mean that freedom, a pure and fine concept, does not always (often) manage to impose upon the practical constraint constituted by the world and things (which involves distinguishing first the Subject – its freedom –, and second the world, which we fail to do); this may also mean, and we would lean more strongly towards this view, that the freedom which defines the Subject is indeed so pure, but especially so total and totalising, that it ends up contorting and dominating, within an apparent paradox, the very possibility of economic freedom, i.e. the possibility of a balanced relationship and a norm within and with the world.

2.2. THE SUBJECT'S OTHERNESS

§ 148.   Let us continue. When we think about economic freedom as a concept, we immediately think "*I* am free in economic terms": the concept of economic freedom is *in relation to the Subject.* At the same time, economic freedom is that which the Subject may, in certain circumstances, have access to ("I have acquired an economic freedom, economic freedoms") or which comes towards the Subject or to a certain extent from outside, in a manner which is less directly connected to the Subject ("it concerns a climate which is favourable to economic freedoms; there are economic freedoms"). One can thus see that economic freedom is both the structure which describes the Subject ("I am free in economic terms") and the object for the Subject ("to acquire an economic freedom"; "this economic freedom is good for me").

The concept of economic freedom includes a very pronounced structure which is for-oneself (for the Subject, for me, I) but the empowerment of the concept (in-itself), which is less evident but more real, opens up a field of investigation and research into the autonomous structures of economic freedom, in connection with the collective or constitutional forms which contain them. Since there is a link between the possibility of autonomous structures for economic freedom (the economic freedoms are then essential for the Subject and for the economic action process, which does not prevent them from also being the outcome thereof) and the possibility of collective forms of the Subject, in the same way as a link exists between the individualistic definition of the totalizing Subject and the difficulty, not in stating, obtaining or manifesting a certain number of "economic freedoms", but in distinguishing an ordinary action from economic freedom (everything becomes economic freedom). We shall assert that it is indeed certain collective forms of the Subject (State, public services, political parties, to cite just a few examples) which have, historically, borne the alienating structures of power negating the individual (the Subject as an individual) within its freedom. The negation of the Subject's freedom as individual freedom thus led to the negation of economic freedom; conversely, when left completely to its own devices, the structure of the free, individual Subject led to a system of appropriation and of actions (described as economic) which are potentially without norms or regulation; yet the possibility of such regulation depends upon collective forms, in particular institutional forms which are sufficiently autonomous to have an actual power of influence over the regulation, preservation and norm of economic freedoms as they emerge from the economic action process; economic freedom, as we have seen, can be described as a structure of action (an image-object transformed into a real object after impact), but also as the creation of economic freedoms with regard to the Subject, provided that the structures of the economic freedoms as objects are sufficiently autonomous to exist and to carry weight with regard to the Subject.

However, it can be said that it is not a simple matter to distinguish a collective form of the Subject which is inoffensive for economic freedom from a dangerous form. There will, on the one hand, be a set of institutions which frame the economic dynamic and which are involved in the attainment and preservation of its equilibria (we will return later to the definition of such equilibria); and, on the other, institutions which will, ultimately, negate freedom *and* economic freedom, i.e. both the freedom of the Subject and the very existence of economic freedoms as autonomous objects which standardise and regulate the whole of the economic system. How should such a distinction then be made? Any collective form which is economic or which plays a role in the economic action process (it may thus be a political form) contains a structure of the Subject (the Subject is an individual or a collective body). In both cases, it relates to a structure of the Subject, i.e. there is a definition through pure freedom, more particularly through the freedom of action. The collective form takes responsibility for the expression and exercise of freedom, understood as a force-will of projection and action. In the one instance, the collective form does not know how to take account of the Other, of other freedoms, the other consciousnesses which threaten at any moment to come into conflict, or takes account thereof by means of an elimination, suppression, a total and totalising negation of freedoms: the collective form, while being vested with the free force of a desire-to-act, will neither preserve nor produce economic freedoms (nor political freedoms). The totalising shift of the Subject, which lies at the heart of the risks of the modern era, now takes on a collective form and not that of the individual (in both cases, there is a contradiction with the preservation and autonomous development of economic freedoms). In the other instance, the integration of otherness (the Other as freedom-consciousness) is effected in such a way that the collective form manages to maintain an active role with regard to the economic freedoms.

Economic freedom is therefore potentially threatened by the free Subject as an individual (everything is economic freedom, every action is economic freedom right through to the disappearance of the concept within that of voluntary action); by the free Subject as a totalising collective form (the Other is ignored, gagged, integrated).

This means that the consideration of the Other, of the otherness of the Subject is one of the conditions for the perennial establishment of economic freedom and even more so for the production, in autonomous forms, of economic freedoms. This is a major condition of economic freedom: the resolution of the conflicts of freedoms-consciousnesses (of individual Subjects) by collective forms which do not lead to the negation of the economic freedom (economic freedoms) but reserve them by means of standardisation and by encouraging the production of institutions for such purpose (this is true of the totalising and dictatorial, collective form of the Subject, which captures the freedom-will). This concerns what we call the *condition of otherness*. It can be seen that an economic system may, at least in theory, do without Others, the Other, otherness, and in practice adopt a *laisser-faire* approach, if reality can be ignored on a long-term basis (one will then consequently come back to a coercive system dominated by the Subject-individual-king). Furthermore, and we will revert to this later, economic freedom is threatened within an economic action process which is governed by the individual, economic Subject when the conceptual structure of the (economic) Subject is only defined as a pure force of obliteration (of everything), a black hole of negativity-energy, a total and totalising action; one has, in fact, to manage to construct the Subject by introducing the time of memory and duration (and that of forgetfulness as well) within the Subject's structure, and thus within the economic action process. Memory and duration, as the raw material of the combustion chamber of the consciousness (in fact, the matter is made up of sections of the past which have been forgotten or recalled) constitute the second major condition, *the temporal condition.* We will demonstrate below, as in *La Dynamique boursière,* that the definition of a specific space-time reference frame for the economic Subject defined as a free consciousness offers not only raw material to be *obliterated* by the consciousness (projection, anticipation, from the image-object to action strictly speaking), which as a result can only as it were run in neutral, but also matter for the points and systems of equilibrium of memory and duration which may, in the manner of pillars, support the foundations of structures and systems of norms and rules. The existence of a specific temporal dimension of memory and duration, within a consciousness-freedom established as a specific space-time reference frame of a mental nature which produces energy (the energy which can be found within economics and financial), allows for an equilibrium of the economic and financial system and the economic action process to be constructed, and the norm can be based on the regimes of time provided by memory and forgetfulness, using matter-duration which is cut out and whose cut-out shapes will support the few fragile or precarious stabilities where norms and regulations may exist for a period of time.

§ 149.   Economic freedom, as we have seen, is a concept which is naturally for-itself in the sense that the subject states "I am free in economic terms"; but economic freedom cannot be defined without taking others into account and without resolving, in one way or another, the conflict of consciousnesses, which is a conflict of freedoms and of individual Subjects at the heart of the economic action process. As such, economic freedom is a concept for-others in the sense that the absolute freedom which may define the individual Subject and that Subject's economic action (without limits no less) will collide with the Other, an identical Subject-consciousness unfurling its own (economic) action, *ad infinitum,* for the same number of individual Subjects. Provided that nothing happens, the conflicting (economic) system has a good chance of cancelling or neutralising the economic freedoms. One can also see a particular, individual economic Subject impose *a* particular economic action process. Finally, one can see a collective form of Subject (party, institution, State, within those sectors which by their very definition extend beyond the economic threshold) resolve the question of the Other by means of the elimination or confiscation of economic freedoms, any amputation of economic freedom involving a reduction of the Subject's matrix structure, i.e. freedom. In the first case, and without any form of normative intervention, the economic system, if left to its own devices, may attain a sub-optimal competitive equilibrium where the freedom of individual Subjects does not prevent, although not without difficulties, the production of economic freedoms which have a certain autonomy in a collective form of competitive market of free economic Subjects defined as imaging and acting consciousnesses. In the second case, either (theoretical case) there only remains one individual Subject whose totalising action ultimately absorbs any economic freedom or, adopting a more realistic approach, the competition between individual Subjects ends up eliminating the economic freedom (economic freedoms) (an individual equilibrium which is non- or counter- optimal). In the last case, the totalising collective form deletes all or part of the economic freedom and the economic freedoms through constraint (the norm and regulation are obtained at the detriment of economic freedom), it can be said that there is a sub-optimal equilibrium which is not free.

The concept of economic freedom is not expressed as "I am free in economic terms" but, more completely, as "one is free in economic terms". Economic freedom may henceforth be approached as an action process directed towards and in respect of the world, which is initiated and governed by a Subject defined as a free imaging and acting consciousness, within the context of a specific space-time reference frame of a psychological, mental and/or moral nature structured by memory, duration and forgetfulness, incorporating the dynamic of others, of the Other, of otherness, in particular in order to resolve conflicting tensions, relating to a general economic system which produces economic freedoms, autonomous objects which assume inter alia collective forms and in particular institutional forms, which exude the conditions for the possibility of norms and regulations, the latter originating moreover in the existence of a temporal matter of memory and duration which allows for the existence of points of support and reference for sub-optimal systems of equilibrium or sub-equilibria, in any event forms which are sufficiently stable for at least the economic freedom (economic freedoms) to be preserved there. Furthermore, in addition first to the spatio-temporal reference frame of memory and duration, and, second, the possibility of constructing collective forms (institutions) which produce, and/or which act as custodians of, economic freedoms, in addition to these two major, connected elements which together contain the possibility of a norm and therefore of economic freedom (since, otherwise, the Subject's freedom if left to its own devices, tends to turn against freedom and the economic action tends to absorb economic freedom), one still has to try and separate the concept of economic freedom from the exclusive, modern link with acting and (economic) action for the purposes of possessing and transforming the world, i.e. to try and apply a broader meaning to the concept of economic freedom. The work, undertaken elsewhere, involves inter alia separating the more general concept of economics from that of the action and, at the same time, from that of freedom which is principally defined through action; this does not mean that action and freedom are excluded but, on the contrary, that an equilibrium is determined between Subject, being and world, which is, as such, the very meaning of *economics,* and that an economic action process is determined which provides a practice or *praxis* for a free, imaging and acting Subject which produces within the said process enough points of equilibrium in order for the action to maintain and renew the economic freedoms.

2.3. *TIME-MATTER AND THE NORM*

§ 150.   We have made some progress. Economic freedom tells us about the freedom of the Subject (I am free), whether individual or collective (we are free), the freedom to act or freedom of action towards and within the world in its modern sense (the action of transforming the world in the sense that the latter is literally "imagined" while in a state of not yet being, in the form of image-objects projected and fired onto the markets and which form the action matrix. Economic freedom therefore seems closely linked to an economic action process of the Subject. However, economic freedom cannot exist in other respects without the defined presence of a norm, and the economic action process itself cannot develop without such a norm. This is understood to be that which, within the economic action process and therefore within the very structure of the Subject and its action, enables landmarks to be placed as so many points of reference, as so many limited equilibria, which are of a secondary nature or relative, which give meaning and a sense of hierarchy to the order of image-objects in the same way as to the final, real actions.

The essence of such a norm can be sought within time-matter, within duration in the form of a block of cold wax, cut into sections in the same way as samples are bored in the earth's crust, in the same way as the rings of the past and of time are visible on thousand-year old tree trunks, duration therefore as an essential matter dulled by memory (and by forgetfulness, since they are the same thing). Economic freedom as an act, in action, is first and foremost within the act of consciousness (of), the design of the consciousness on the block(s) of duration which are more or less perfectly or imperfectly remembered (and therefore forgotten to a certain extent). The design of consciousness on the bands or blocks of duration, the design on the matter of duration, which obliterates such matter (negativity) in order to project it in a state of non-being (the project, the anticipation), an obliteration which produces the image, is the primary expression and the essence of economic freedom. It is this matter of duration which, like the DNA of any image and, ultimately, of any action in the true sense of impact with the world, leaves a trace and bears a trace, and provides, in the same way as the equipment of memory, the foundations for the norm.

Economic freedom is defined, in its essence, as the consciousness in action of an (individual or collective) Subject. Economic freedom does indeed constitute an act but it does not relate, at first, to the actual action of transformation of the world which may come naturally to mind (*praxis*). Economic freedom is the force or capacity of the Subject to take time-matter (which constitutes the structure of the space-time reference frame) in order to use it to make images and projections, i.e. forms which are inhabited by that which is in front of one, beyond the Subject, which is not yet (and maybe never will be), certain of these images, but not all, will indeed become complete actions, up to and including the exercise of transformation of reality (conversely, such real action stems from one or more images).

Economic freedom is the capacity of the conscious Subject to project beyond itself through the production of images which are all "negatives" of the world, i.e. the world as it is not, or is not yet. This means that economic freedom is not, in essence, *at first*, the action of impact with the real world as everything would seem to indicate (the majority of commentaries and discussions on the concept *commence with* the realisation, the practice/*praxis* and economic freedom is reduced and is worn out in its manifestations of impact, i.e. the common and general representation of the acting design of impact). On the contrary, the essence of economic freedom is located as closely as possible to the essence of economics as they are developed in the modern age, i.e. in the essence of the Subject's freedom which is merged with that of freedom, i.e. the project, which necessarily summons the action towards that which is not yet.

Accordingly, there is no economic freedom without imagination, which is an underlying motive of freedom. The final action and its result, which seem to define economic freedom after the event, are not of essential importance. Everything is decided within the vital and limitless energy of the Subject to obliterate *ad infinitum* in order to give birth to the project and then to the actions. The market of images, represented by the contemporary financial markets, only acts as intermediary within this global process where economic freedom produces images for final, practical actions which, effectively, aim to appropriate and modify the world's real matter. The financial markets have this necessary filtering role.

Economic freedom is therefore only freedom to act insofar as one bears in mind that the condition for possible action lies in the capacity of consciousness of the world, i.e. the capacity to think of the world as in a state of non-being (not yet being), to project it, to imagine it as it could or should be.

It is essential to note that this involves a modern purpose of economics. Within the context of this work, we will first pay attention to the modern conditions for the exercise of economics. Economic freedom as we know it, and which may seem to come from very far away, which may seem to have always been among us, is nonetheless ultimately a fairly recent concept. The concept of economic freedom has a strong historical background. The concept emerges with the emancipation of that of the Subject and there is not in fact any real prior trace of the concept. This leads one to wonder, first, if the Subject's capture of the concept of economic freedom does not lead to the negation or inversion of the meaning of the concept of economic freedom itself (the response is affirmative: delivered up to the Subject which paradoxically gives birth to it, economic freedom disappears within the Subject's design which is not subject to any norms); second, although the concept of economic freedom may, in certain conditions, be conceived beyond the Subject since the purpose of economics in the modern age requires one, in respect of a significant number of topics, to seek an emancipation of the Subject understood as freedom-will which wills itself *ad infinitum* within the endless appetite of real, practical actions, which are themselves limitless. This is a considerable task, the general terms of which we have established (*Valeur et temps* – Lettre sur l'économique). In the meantime, i.e. between a totalising reflection of the economic Subject which is without limits and an attempt to establish economics beyond the Subject, there remains a field of thought and praxis where it is a matter of demonstrating, from within the modern system itself as the same is and develops, that the Subject's economic action process can be standardised, i.e. that the process of production, guidance and perfection of images for the purpose of action is based, within its innermost structure, on a sufficiently stable matter (of duration, memory), in order to build the foundations for a norm and a regime. Second, it is a matter of demonstrating that the possibility of an emancipation of the norm, i.e. its capacity to assume a collective institutional form, to become an institution, by extracting itself as it were from the economic action process in order better to serve it, by challenging it in order to limit it, is based on such foundations (the economic norm, as emphasised in *La Dynamique boursière*, is at all times and in all places a function of a dense temporal dimension, i.e. of that which lasts and comes to us, through memory, without minimising the considerable uncertainty and volatility which accompanies it, and also the fragility, since chronic uncertainty and volatility are always the reflection of forgetfulness – there is an underlying analogy between uncertainty and forgetfulness, and also between risk and forgetfulness).

It is by means of this approach that we are trying to advance, principally, within the modern purpose of economics totally governed by the Subject, while searching for the means of radically reforming economics within the Subject and this process, establishing moreover some landmarks for a possible surpassment of the Subject within economics, which is no easy matter since economics and the emancipation of the (economic) Subject are one and the same within the development of the modern age and of the West.

§ 151.   The concept of economic freedom develops with the emancipation of the individual Subject as a process which exposes and suppresses that which prevents the Subject from showing the full *natural* extent of its relevant reason and its efficiency of action. Accordingly, the concept has, first, a tendency to be defined *as against* by means of a factor of resistance; that which gives it meaning can be found within that which opposes it or seems to go against its ability, its essence (it may be a matter, most of the time, of state forms of constraint, but ultimately, any adversity within the action process is eligible, partly in the name of an implied assumption of the fluid perfection of action and of a no less reasonable and reasoned perfection of the Subject itself in its approach). Second, economic freedom is conceived as a revelation and disclosure of a traditional (economic) Subject which naturally produces initiatives and perfect forms, provided it is able to express itself purely (one can see here, in part, the idealism of the conventional view of *homo economicus*). We emphasise the extremely idealistic notion of the Subject which dominates the construction of the concept of economic freedom, and which is totalising since the Subject's will, which has a tendency to colonize the concept of freedom (as will-to-live, a vital force of propulsion), asserts itself in the name of a purity and perfection of designs and action. Consequently, this acting and totalising conception of economic freedom asserts itself, despite the fact that the relevance of such a definition of the Subject, its realist nature and, above all, the worrying consequences of such a totalising conception are not really questioned. Such questions ultimately emerge, within the economic discipline or within finance, in the form of interrogations regarding the nature of the Subject's acting processes (animal spirits) and regarding the destructive consequences, for freedom itself and for the economic process itself, of a Subject left to its own devices, i.e. to the forces of a will-to-live and of development in the world.

Economic freedom is thus based, in its idealist and therefore totalising version, on an unsatisfactory conception of the economic Subject. This represents a significant line of work. This unsatisfactory conception of the Subject is either that of a Subject of rational, optimising perfection and total purity of calculation, or that of a limitless consciousness of projection through the action of trans-formation which is also pure in the sense that it lacks matter, density, memory or duration, a lightning speed of instantaneousness which reinvents the world at every moment. In both cases, one notes the absence of memory and duration, which as we have shown, constitute, together with forgetfulness, the fundamental elements of the specific space-time reference frame of the Subject and of the economic action process, and more generally of economics. In both cases, there is a lack of realism in the conception of the Subject, which is simply contradicted by observation. This lack of realism does not relate so much to the world, together with its unquestionable complexities which cannot be changed, but rather to the conception of the Subject itself, i.e. to the manner in which the impetus of the (free) economic action process is conceived, constructed and structured. The conception of economics itself is biased, from the outset, by the manner in which the Subject is constructed and explained. As a result, economic freedom, which is the very name given to the force of development by the Subject within and through action, is itself poorly defined. Accordingly, economic freedom will here represent the very dynamic of the action of a *homo economicus,* whose reason and calculation are optimising, and there that of a transparent consciousness, with no past, which advances by moments of lightning speed, whether rational or irrational, and without limit. In the one case, economic freedom will have a tendency to be defined by means of the suppression of all the barriers which prevent the perfection of *homo economicus* from showing the full extent of its efficiency and optimisation, and *the difficulties of understanding economics and the workings thereof will not be attributed to the infallible Subject, but rather to everything else, to all other matters.* In the other case, economic freedom will have a tendency to be defined above all by the infinite realisations of action and the actual impacts left on a transformed world, where technique plays an increasing role in the modern era. In this case, the economic Subject is a sort of black box, of vital forces and of will (it is already a more realist conception, accepting what is irrational and incomprehensible but the effort of understanding comes to a rapid halt at the borders of conventionality) and the difficulties of understanding economics are principally located within the analysis of the results of action, of impacts and not sufficiently within the Subject's operating mode. The concept of economic freedom is consequently sustained by the unlimited analyses of the modifications of things and of the world, the intensity and the number of practical impacts which may or may not expand the concept.

In any event, one notes the lack of a realist theory of the economic Subject, which will determine a relevant conception of economic freedom and of economics. We would counter the unsatisfactory conceptions of the economic Subject discussed above by a concept of freedom and of consciousness anchored in memory and duration and a reference frame of economic action structured by such dimensions of time; moreover, the conviction that economics and economic freedom, within the modern era dominated by the Subject, are determined, with regard to their concept and their definition, by understanding the Subject's structure. Economic freedom and economics are closely dependant upon the (economic) Subject's structure. This steers the research in two directions: the understanding of the (economic) Subject and the surpassment of the (economic) Subject. In both cases, a definition of economics is involved: modern economics (Subject); economics built on new foundations, going beyond the modern turn of events.

2.4. Provisional summary

§ 152. The contents of economic freedom are determined by the contents of the concept of the (economic) Subject, insofar as one agrees, at least temporarily in the analysis, to define the Subject through its freedom as action and therefore, by construction, to establish that, in modern reality, economics are themselves defined by a tripartite identity: between Subject, freedom (consciousness) and action. Once this economic identity has been established = f (Subject-consciousness, consciousness-freedom, freedom-action), it leads to a definition of an *economic Subject*, of *economic freedom*, of economic action.

By remaining within this modern context of analysis, we have demonstrated (*Dynamique boursière, Théorie du Sujet économique*) that, in order to obtain a more complete and, above all, a more realist understanding of this context, one had to establish that:

1) economics, in its modern purpose, was defined in its essence by the (economic) action process of the (economic) Subject (the surpassment of the said purpose towards a more original foundation for economics constituted by another approach, which is not the main focus of this work and which we initiated in *Tractatus, Généalogie* and *Valeur et temps*);

2) the Subject defined by means of a consciousness of freedom, understood as a force of negativity and obliteration of that which is in order to project that which is not yet, i.e. action, provided the definition of the *economic Subject* and, consequently, of *economic action*;

3) the Subject as consciousness and freedom was not an empty place but rather the place and mechanics behind a shock which liberated energy between the force of obliteration of the consciousness and the matter of duration, the distortions of this essential matter effected by memory and forgetfulness sustaining an energy and founding a dynamic, which accordingly deserves to define the *economic dynamic*;

4) the economic action was an action *process*, developing within a specific space-time reference frame structured by duration, memory and forgetfulness, the reference frame of the Subject itself, and constituted of sequence, the conception of image-objects (the internal phase of the economic Subject's consciousness), of selection, exchange and valuation of the image-objects as the matrices for projects and actions relating to that which is not yet (the internal-external phase of the financial market where one finds the co-existence of the image-objects represented by the projects-anticipations exchanged on the stock exchange *and* a physical form of the said image-objects, i.e. the financial market, the physical form of that which is in a state of non-being (not-yet-being), and lastly of the final organisation and impact of the real world, which fixes the action without its result and marks the end of the process, before the retroactive effect on an earlier stage of the process, through modification of the duration and memory matter.

In this modern context of analysis thus presented, the concept of economic freedom is defined by the economic Subject and, in general, by the *four premises of modern economics* which we have just noted above. Economic freedom is at once the economic Subject itself (which is defined through freedom), the economic action process and its outcome. There are, accordingly, at least three levels for the positioning of economic freedom. First there is the economic Subject, with which economic freedom is merged; economic freedom is the maintenance, the continuation in its being of the economic Subject as we have defined it above, from the innermost matter which constitutes and drives it (duration, memory, forgetfulness) up until its physical integrity as an individual or collective body or a distribution which is located in practice within the completion of the action process, acting physical realities. Economic freedom is the Subject (1st assertion) and the Subject is merged with freedom (2nd assertion). One means by this that (economic) freedom is embodied in, can be seen, and appears within the reality of an acting physical entity, whether individual or collective: economic freedom is the acting body of the Subject through which, within which it appears. At the same time, second assertion, the only Subject is active and the only active one is free, i.e. the very movement of the action forms one with the Subject which it defines *absolutely*. This identity, which seals the conscious Subject's infinite capacity to obliterate, is based on the energy of negativity, i.e. the permanent surpassment of oneself towards that which is to be done, is not yet and gives action substance. Finally, the two assertions "the Subject is freedom" and "the economic Subject is economic freedom" are equivalent and the term *economic* only serves to accentuate the modern achievement of an increasing identity between the Subject and freedom to act within, over and towards the world.

Within a second dimension, economic freedom can be understood as *action process*. Each term is important in its own right. Economic freedom can be described as a course of progress or sequential chain of events, without that meaning – on the contrary – a linearity or even rationality. Economic freedom, understood as a Subject's action, is a temporal process starting from an initial point of creation/freedom of energy (negativity/obliteration), of conception and then selection and organisation of image-objects up until their mutation into a body which produces an impact within reality. (Economic) freedom is a movement of a temporal essence (the energy resulting from the capacity to obliterate is sustained by a temporal matter of duration) and formative development of an energy to which a *form* is given. The process is a dynamic.

Finally, economic freedom is *impact*, i.e. that which allows itself to be more or less temporarily fixed as a product of the action process, which both provides the next matter in the action process within a perpetual cycle and also confers upon both freedom and the Subject a genetic or, rather, genealogical marker since the time-matter which sustains and constitutes the acting Subject-freedom is constantly increased by the impact of the action process. The impact has a retroactive effect on the process by increasing the time-matter of a new piece of information which may possibly modify its nature. It is the role of economic freedom, without this being a contradiction in terms, to produce what is necessary and necessity, since the action process is a machine which determines and selects that which is contingent and the Subject's impact comes back towards the Subject for which it constitutes the situation, in order to be surpassed.

All this takes place under the watchful eye of the Other, whose influence over the three dimensions discussed above gives economic freedom its definitive appearance.

Chapitre 7

FREEDOM AND THE MARKET
(with regard to Mr. Friedman)

1. THE COLLECTIVE FORMS OF (ECONOMIC) FREEDOM

§ 153.   When a certain number of liberal authors, of whom Mr. Friedman is undoubtedly the most emblematic, state that the market is, in a certain manner, a direct component of freedom, what do they really mean? They mean, essentially, in the specific terms of their own analysis, that the market prevents and contains coercion and that the market protects others. It is thus stated, impliedly, that the modern Subject as it is emancipated in the modern era, i.e. as absolute individual freedom, meets other Subjects and other individual freedoms and that the cohabitation and confrontation of their projects are naturally conflicting; economic freedom as conceived in the modern era (the Subject) requires that the otherness of the Subject, i.e. both the existence of other consciousnesses and projects, and the fact that the Subject, in its very structure is otherness (a projection beyond itself which is in a state of non-being), is also considered, at the same time.

We have shown that otherness constituted, in fact, an essential structure of the economic Subject in both the meanings discussed above. We have shown that the economic Subject projected itself within that which is not yet through the production of mental image-objects (we mean by this the production of the consciousness and of a specific spatio-temporal reference frame structured by duration and memory); that such image-objects were gathered together, for the purposes of selection, sorting, valuation and selection on the financial market, an external physical form of the production process of image-objects by the consciousness and a prefiguration of the final form of the practical action within the real world.

We therefore come back to the idea that the (financial) market constitutes, within the modern, economic action process (which is the name of the development of freedom in action, therefore of the Subject itself which becomes an *economic* Subject by means of this same development) an important sequence of the dynamic of modern economic freedom (and of simple freedom itself) as we have defined the same. The set of image-objects which is gathered within the semi-mental and semi-physical form of the financial market (which can be distinguished from the market of goods and services, the first gathering projects, anticipations, modes of being in a state of non-being, and the second gathering facts, events and things which result from the impact of the Subject's design aimed at the world); the distinction between sequences within the economic action process cannot mask the proximity of the issues; in both cases, the form of the market gathers the designs of the Subject-consciousness, at the stage of image-objects in the first instance (financial market), at the stage of actual goods and services in the second instance, and the market is, first and foremost, the place which *results* from the designs of the dominant, modern form, i.e. the individual Subject. One means by this that, spontaneously and at least initially, the market does not constitute a natural order for the clarification of the individual, economic Subjects' designs which are logically conflicting. On the contrary, there is nothing which spontaneously organises the set of image-objects which stem from the individual Subjects, which does not mean that the selection, valuation and transformation process of the image-objects cannot take place; it will take place and will produce its results, although the dimension of memory and duration which is essential for the determination of the value of the various projects is not, necessarily, correctly understood. The result of this is imperfect equilibria. This is why we emphasised the necessity, first, of fixing the possibility of a norm and of regulation within the matter of duration and memory, and, second, of considering that the collective (institutional) forms are able to contain the said norm and to bring it face to face with events. Such collective and institutional forms do not correspond to the form of the financial market itself, which is a collective form but which only manages in an imperfect manner to standardise itself and therefore requires auxiliary forms (which acquire independence) and which provide the norm (e.g. regulatory institutions).

There is nothing which, spontaneously and naturally, stops the vital force of the individual Subject in its development as a modern, economic Subject. There is nothing which prevents and organises with ease the conflicting productions of the various individual Subjects. An infinite number of image-objects will be produced at each moment.

However, this infinite number of images and projects will be captured in the form of the financial market which will ensure that they are identified and gathered together. Such images will continue to be conflicting but the conflict is confined to one form, the financial market. The financial market is a physical extension of the Subject's specific spatio-temporal reference frame before being a place or form for the resolution of conflicts between consciousnesses. The financial market is a place which reproduces the individual Subject's reference frame, a place of confrontation and of selection of image-objects (projects). The financial market, once one accepts the reality that the individual economic Subject is not alone but has been thrown into the middle of others (see *Théorie du Sujet économique*), may be described no longer as the physical form of the specific reference frame of a sole economic Subject producing an infinite number of image-objects in confrontation and selection, but as the *collective* physical form of the specific reference frame of an infinite number of economic Subjects which gathers together all their projects and action matrices; the structures of the forms remain identical.

The financial market is a place of gathering before being a place of "organisation", a confrontation of economic freedoms (in the sense of individual Subjects), a confrontation which is paradoxical (since it does not produce a spontaneous order) and which leads to a limitation of economic freedom itself. This collective form which constitutes the financial market may hope to achieve the production of a norm and order if, and only if, it manages at any given time to determine value on sufficiently solid grounds, and duration will dominate to a large extent in the determination of the dynamics of the sole random walks. As we emphasised in *La Dynamique boursière*, the practice of the financial market does not encourage this task, and the resulting dynamics are therefore far-removed from those which might include norms and rules. Furthermore, we have shown that due to the disturbances which are specific to the process (forgetfulness), optimal stability and equilibrium cannot be attained, even if a practice and analysis of the markets which incorporate such aspects would contribute to a significant improvement of the current situation. Consequently, the financial market requires collective and institutional forms which contain a norm and regulation.

The financial market is therefore a modern form of the economic Subject's action and, consequently, of economic freedom as the latter is expressed and develops, i.e. within the action process. The market is the physical form of extension of the mental activity of the production of images which are understood as matrices of the projects and anticipations. The market is the meeting point of the projects (images) for all the Subjects, which gives it the dual role of selection and valuation of the image-objects as between themselves for a multiplicity of Subjects (multiplicity of images, multiplicity of Subjects). As such, the market makes the conflicting diversity visible by organising it. The market therefore reveals the direct production of the economic Subjects and, at the same time, effects a selection which represents an order. This is the reason why liberal thinking can consider that the market channels and masks the violence of conflicts between the economic Subjects, which may prevent coercion. Adopting this view, the market itself becomes an (economic) Subject of a collective nature, producing image-objects which are transformed (from individual images), at a more advanced stage in the action process than the crude image-objects conceived by the individual Subject.

That said, the collective economic Subject represented by the market – and therefore as such the economic freedom resulting from the conflicting aggregation of individual freedoms and of their productions – is itself directly exposed to the risk of totalising appetite and lack of limits which have been identified for each individual economic Subject which is understood as pure and total freedom, and this is so even if, as remains true, the market effectively organises the violence and the conflict by confining it to the selective exchange and valuation of image-objects produced by the individual Subjects.

As such, the market is less a direct component of economic freedom than the visible form of the projects. This form is not disorganised organisation, an oblivious force, a random walk filled with incomprehensible matters which one occasionally seeks to describe (theory of the erratic market, which is incapable of producing a norm); this theory is merely an extension, in many respects, of the pure and totalising individual freedom of the Subject which is itself total, a freedom which is limitless within the action process. This is not the case, since the market constitutes an organised form which contains a norm, i.e. something which is comprehensible and which contains within it the possibility of regulation. This is indeed what we demonstrated in *La Dynamique boursière*; there is a specific reference frame which provides points of reference, of interpretation and of understanding of that which is determined and which occurs in the market at the time when the productions of image-objects of the individual Subjects come face to face in order to produce the collective form. We have also shown that it is only on the basis of this specific matter of the reference frame (duration, memory) that one can create a norm and regulation; that such norm, based on the innermost matter of the market, must be created *outside* the market itself, since the market cannot, or cannot adequately, simultaneously produce both the vital force of action and the norm which guarantees its reasonable, i.e. balanced continuity; that it is this very norm, for which other collective forms must be responsible (institutions), which *is the condition of economic freedom.*

When liberal thinkers state that the market constitutes a direct component of freedom, they seem to be saying that (economic) freedom cannot be conceived without the market component, for the principal reasons discussed above (protection against coercion, containment and organisation of the conflicting dimension linked to the existence of *other* Subjects). It is accordingly the dimension of the collective organisation of otherness which dominates the form of the market and there is an implied assumption that the (economic) Subject is incapable on its own of producing an individual norm which is sufficient to avoid conflicts containing something irreparable. We have shown, using a different approach, that the market originated in its entirety from the freedom of the (economic) Subject, that it constituted the physical and visible form thereof as a specific spatio-temporal reference frame which is strictly similar to that of the economic Subject defined as a consciousness which produces image-objects; that, as such, the market was fully integrated within the development process of the free Subject's action, the very name of economics in the modern era (economics, economic freedom and action of the free Subject-consciousness are equivalent terms within the modern understanding of economics); that the form of the market marked a differentiation, a new sequence within the action process, as compared to the individual Subject, first because it contains a necessity, a sedimentation phase of the image-objects produced by the Subject with a view to their selective purpose directed towards the final action (this necessity constitutes a form of dependence; there is no market without the prior freedom of an economic Subject conceived as such); second because it is a collective form which gathers together the Subjects' productions (it extends economic freedom, understood as the reasonable coexistence of the potentially conflicting projects of Subjects faced with the reality of others, by organising such economic freedom – as such, the market is the form of resolution of problems posed by the existence of others and of otherness in general for the individual Subject); that, accordingly, economic freedom as a development process of the individual economic Subject's action directed at the world in order to transform it (impact it) assumed a semi-practical form (halfway between the image-object produced by the consciousness at the project stage and the anticipation and the final form of action on impact with reality) and above all a *collective* form; the market is the formal response to the need of the individual economic Subject's action project to develop and the difficulty for a given project, i.e. for the individual production of images for the purposes of action, to develop under the threatening presence of others; that the market, as a formal, physical and collective extension of the Subject's essential freedom, is economic freedom in its very process and provided that one bears in mind that the economic Subject's economic freedom with regard to action constitutes an identity, i.e. that economic freedom is defined by action; that the market constitutes a (collective) Subject as such which acquires an undeniable identity and autonomy (*the* market, referred to as a person, or individual Subject), i.e. the market constitutes, as an economic Subject, a mutant form of economic freedom as the same is conceived in the modern era (the market *is* economic freedom, in its weak form as an extension and development of the individual economic Subject's freedom which it originates from, in its strong form as a collective form which acquires autonomy and an economic Subject in its own right, this economic Subject in its own right which is consequently able to produce in turn an autonomous logic of the free Subject whose structures are similar to those of the individual Subject but which, and this is only a paradox on the surface, may turn against the individual Subject itself); that the assertion that "the market constitutes a direct component of freedom" (which is an assertion of the need for the Subject's development through action) only acquires meaning in the narrow context, both in historical and conceptual terms, in which economic freedom is solely defined by means of the action process of a Subject which is itself free and whose freedom is merged within the action aimed at the world; this limitation of the economic concept, of Subject and therefore of economic freedom, contains the modern idea of the concept of economic freedom, which may and indeed must be criticised, over and beyond the Subject as it were; that the word used by liberal thinkers indicates that the market is already in the process of acquiring autonomy from the individual Subject.

The market cannot be considered, in genealogical terms, without the modern emancipation of the individual Subject as freedom to act. It constitutes its mirror image.

Freedom concerns the relations between men and it involves seeing to what point their activities may be coordinated. This means that the question of economic freedom is twofold, i.e. is presented under two aspects and the resolution of the conflicts between the two constitutes one of the principal challenges and one of the radical limits of economics. There is, first, the individual freedom whose essence is to persevere in its being and, in the case of modern economics, to act and continue to act in the assertion of a relationship of appropriation and transformation of the world which defines *individual economic freedom*. There is, second, the coordination of individual freedoms, i.e. the question of collective and/or institutional forms which propose a solution to the reality of the existence of others, of the Other, and therefore to the violence and conflicts which are intrinsically contained within the coexistence of individual freedoms. It relates to the *collective or institutional economic freedom*, which gathers the economic-financial (the market, the financial market) *and* political forms since the assurance, not solely of individual freedom, of individual freedoms, but also of collective freedom, of collective freedoms, involves the political form and creates the junction between economic freedom and political freedom. In this sense, economic freedom (collective form) preserves individual freedom by standardising it (by standardising the violence which is naturally expressed between individual freedoms) and accordingly such economic freedom contains a political dimension. Accordingly, the capacity to produce a norm which preserves the essential energy of individual freedom, by avoiding the collective, totalising forms (the market understood as a total expression of the dynamic of the individual economic Subject in action; a politico-economic form which establishes a "collective economic Subject" which is intended to effect the planning and above all to be totalitarian), constitutes a challenge.

As such, the market, and especially the financial market, cannot constitute successfully completed forms of collective economic freedom (of which they have a certain number of significant characteristics, i.e. the capacity to gather, select, value and coordinate the actions of individual freedoms) unless they are able to produce a norm *and* preserve individual freedom (the two are connected since, without a norm, individual freedom ends up negating itself by negating the freedom of others). Consequently, one is able to appreciate the type of problem posed (or to be posed) by a market which is defined as incapable of producing a norm, an uncertain force, which is random in its collective efforts or a force which destroys the individual by means of a totalising, collective market-Subject, and this inability to produce a norm (which provides meaning, something which is comprehensible) may result from a difficulty of comprehension which can be overcome in order to establish a norm or from the fundamentally chaotic and literally absurd nature of the market trajectories, even if such trajectories incorporate a certain degree of coordination of individual freedoms. We have stated that such comprehension was possible, using an interpretation of the appropriate reference frame of the financial market, creating the possibility of a norm and regulation, but based on an alternative collective or institutional form to the market itself, therefore an external and normative form. It is on this condition, in our view, that the form of the (financial) market and collective economic freedom, in the sense of the coordinated preservation of individual freedoms, are compatible.

In our view, this explains how the collective (institutional) forms which contain such norms of the economic action process of the individual Subject (i.e. the market, financial market as an essential sequence of the gestation and selection of projects, and the market of goods and services, i.e. image-objects which have become objects after the impact of the action on reality), are foremost in the development of modern economics, i.e. as action (= freedom) transforming the world (and therefore oneself), foremost for economic freedom itself understood as the identity between the individual Subject, the action and freedom.

The collective form of the (financial) market is precious within the modern organisation of the Subject's economic action process, since it gathers, sorts and values the matrices of future actions at the project stage, i.e. the projections and anticipations by means of which the individual freedoms are defined. Other collective forms are far less capable of doing so, at least on first analysis. Accordingly, of the two principal collective forms which are to some extent competing – first, the pure form of the State (by pure we mean the total organisation without any particular political tendency or politics), and, second, the political form of society (and often of the State, therefore a totalising, occasionally totalitarian form of organisation). In both cases, the collective forms do not play a natural role of the collective form of the market in the gathering, selection and valuation of the projects (image-objects) as demonstrated by us within the modern economic action process. However, these two forms may position themselves either as a normative organisation of the market (we will see that they are not the best placed to do so, which does not mean that they cannot inspire, under their impetus, collective forms of an institutional nature which, as distinct collective entities, are characterised by the possibility of containing a relevant norm for the market because such norm stems from an effective understanding of the market's specific reference frame, and therefore a regulation – it is a question, ideally, of collective institutional forms of regulation); or as a totalising organisation, i.e. containing the ambition (it is often a question also of an ideological and/or political project and such organisation is a collective economic Subject as such), within the economic action process as we have described the same, to replace the market in the sequence of the collection of image-objects, projects which are preliminary to the practical action (in the weak form), but also occasionally to substitute it, *as collective economic Subject*, for the individual economic Subjects, and in particular to produce image-objects in the place of the individual Subjects (imagination, anticipation and projection) or at least to try and forcefully direct their production by the same individual Subjects (strong form). The modern era, which is particularly contemporary (as if a form asserted itself within a sort of modern idea of modern economics), has shown numerous occurrences of totalising and totalitarian forms of this type, where the indoctrination of the production of image-objects, of the imaginary world, of the creation and of projects blocks to some extent the economic action process, action and freedom in general. There are many examples ranging from the artistic domain to territories which are very specific to the action of transforming the (economic) world and, often, *a* collective economic Subject which assumes an ideological and political form imposes upon the whole of the domains and territories, since the design of the said collective Subject, which empties individual freedoms of their contents, is so totalising. Since, and this is an important point, the totalising nature of the modern individual Subject, as the same is conceived within the action process over the world, which merges with freedom (individual economic Subject), without any norm or limit, which is naturally totalising, leads to the emergence of collective forms which themselves demand the same structure (pure and total freedom understood as a will to do and to act), and therefore of *collective Subjects* which negate (the paradox is merely on the surface) the individual freedoms which lead up to the reversal of the innermost logic of individual freedom (we have moreover shown that individual freedom, if left to its own devices, has a tendency to negate itself). One can therefore see that the collective form of a total, totalising and totalitarian Subject may come to replace the individual Subject, after first dissolving it, while at the same time creeping within both the essential structures of the individual modern economic Subject (action project directed at the world) and the sequences of development of the economic Subject's acting process (image-objects, selection, valuation of image-objects, actual impact and constitution of the economic fact and object). The totalising and totalitarian purpose of the individual Subject as it appears in modern economics therefore contains within it the appearance of totalising and totalitarian collective Subjects which end up negating the freedom which gave birth to them. Whether in an individual form or collective form, the modern structure of the economic Subject contains within it a total, totalising and totalitarian purpose. Accordingly, economic freedom comes in the end to negate itself, in an individual form or in a collective form, once the individual modern economic Subject is left to persevere in its being and its essence, whether alone or in the collective forms which are also political forms (economic freedom dissolves, at the end of its trajectory of essence and will, within a void of political freedom).

This consequently means that economic freedom only remains as economic freedom in certain conditions (we will demonstrate moreover that economic freedom may threaten freedom itself, the essence of which extends beyond that of modern economic freedom), in the same way that economic freedom and political freedom only form one whole in certain conditions.

We have stated that the peculiarity of the concept of economic freedom as it is defined and develops in the modern era within the action process is that it is of its very essence to negate itself, since its innermost structure is to be outside itself, directed at the world through the action of transforming the world, a dynamic of projection of will (freedom) which nothing seems, on first analysis, to be able to divert from a trajectory of insatiety and will which wills itself on an infinite unsatisfied quest. This peculiarity of the concept of economic freedom is inherited from that of the Subject itself (its freedom) whose modern emancipation contains, from the outset, in conceptual terms, the seeds of a negation through the consequences deployed by freedom itself through and within the action over the world which defines it in a quasi-unique (and, accordingly, limited) manner. We will return to the necessary possibility of reconsidering freedom in order to be able to adopt new points of view in respect of economics.

The concept of economic freedom – in its individual form (the Subject as freedom of the individual, whether pure and/or immersed in the reality of other freedoms and its conflicts), or collective form; the collective form – market, State, political organisation – which adopts the status of a collective Subject, within a normative and cooperative position with regard to individual economic Subjects, or, a more extreme view, within a position of conflict and of intention to eradicate and replace the individual Subject in the conduct of the economic action process (the latter remains intact in terms of its structure and sequences, there is a shift in meaning or substitution – for example when the shift of language shows it clearly, we talk of *the market*, as Subject, *the State* or *the party*) – therefore owes its own negation to its modern essence of will, in the extreme case scenario. It is therefore hardly surprising, contrary to what is most often asserted, that the link between economic freedom and political freedom is not automatic or systematic, indeed far from it.

Even though the concept of economic freedom is continually defined and collected in relation to the freedom of the individual Subject (an absolute value to be preserved and *increased* within a vision which is both ideal and worrying, since nothing stops the Subject; a relative value when it is a question of coordinating the individual Subjects, while preserving and increasing their scope, a coordination which occurs within/with collective forms and structures whose essential definition and assignment are to preserve/increase the Subject's individual freedom), accordingly even though economic freedom is filled with the individual economic Subject, in debate and in literature, *the essential part of the problems focuses on the concept of economic freedom in its collective form.* It is striking to note that the collective forms of economic freedom are all defined and position themselves by comparison with the individual, the individual Subject, irrespective of the objective with regard to such Subject (to coordinate, promote, guide, plan, transform…). The definition of economic freedom in its collective form, *as such*, therefore constitutes an objective.

One notes that the collective form of economic freedom may be directed at the coordination, the placing in contact and competition, for the purposes of organisation, of the individual freedoms and their projects (form of market) within an order which is fairly spontaneous (the specific dynamic of collection within the market of individual projects is enough for this spontaneous order). The collective form may also aim to standardise, frame and regulate the market (form of regulatory institution). It may moreover seek to replace the market, whether in part or in whole (form of State planning or of political tendency/coercion).

In all cases, one starts with the individual Subject and freedom. Consequently, the question of modern economic freedom is essentially that of the collective forms of economic freedom, since for a concept which is defined from the outset by its identity with the free acting Subject, and which must accept the existence of the Other (which is not easy and is not yet accomplished, since the whole of the economic theory is impregnated to such a large extent by the sole Subject approach; *homo economicus*, the figure of this sole Subject is finally less open to criticism for its framework of rationality – which is so rigid that it is not very realist – than for the absolutely astounding lack of the Other and of all the problems arising therefrom; one has to await the game theory, for a particular objective, in order to see the Other find a place within the strategy (or shall we say the design) of free consciousnesses which define the individual economic Subjects), accordingly for this concept which has to live with its otherness, with the other free and acting consciousnesses, the collective form constitutes a necessity, since once the question of (economic) freedom defined on the basis of a Subject which is alone in the world, involves at least one other person, the question is indeed one of knowing what becomes of economic freedom within a collective structure, moreover whose existence is in keeping with the need to coordinate, order and standardise such individual units within an economic action process which consequently has to be considered in a collective dimension. It must be borne in mind that not only economic freedom, as a concept, originates from the individual Subject considered as an absolute, unique and sole entity and, consequently, the same applies to the whole of the economic action process; but, furthermore, that this approach has hardly ever been questioned since the said origin of modern economics, which means that the emergence of collective forms which may or may not advocate economic freedom, whether rightly or wrongly (State, parties, totalitarian and ideological forms, markets...) occurred even though the theory continued, for the most part, to be based on the sole assumption of a total and unique individual Subject. This discrepancy between what was imposed by reality (various collective and/or institutional forms of coordination, coercion, planning... of individual economic freedom when confronted with the other, i.e. when confronted with individual freedoms) and a theory centred on an action process of the total individual Subject, which is moreover convincing, has encouraged numerous lacks of understanding and, above all, theoretical and practical biases. Accordingly, the majority of collective forms of action tend to be founded on the structure of the individual Subject, i.e. to copy the unique individual Subject, even though the collective forms remained intact and there was a conflict between individual and collective forms.

The principal question is therefore what happens to the economic freedom of the free, individual Subject, which is conscious and acting (identity) once the latter is not/no longer alone in the world. More specifically, what happens to the action process – i.e. the projects, anticipations, image-objects produced by each individual Subject – in an environment where others exist. It can be seen that collective forms appear in a fairly logical manner in order to organise and order all these productions of individual freedom. Accordingly, the collective form of economic freedom is first of all an organisation of the production of individual freedoms, the best known version of which is that of the market, the place and sequence of the economic action process where the action matrices are gathered (the image-objects, the projects) – this is the financial market – then a later, comparable sequence for the economic objects which are constituted after the impact of the action design within the real world – this is the market of goods and services. In its most traditional version, the market is presented as a consequence or extension of individual freedom. There is not, in fact, a particular definition of the market; the latter is entirely constituted by the individual freedoms which are coordinated and organised under the influence of a hand which is said to be invisible, the term being there to indicate that the *individual* structure of the Subject dominates the process (it is the individual reasoning of the Subjects which, in the market context, ensures the coordination and organisation). The market as a collective form is both easy to note (there is indeed a unit of collection) but hard to define, since the individual form dominates to such a great extent. To such an extent that, by adopting this interpretation, *the* market itself becomes the Subject and the invisible hand which is described in the traditional version makes one think of an individuation of the market, an individual form which extends and continues the individual Subject's action process. The market and the place of gathering of individual freedoms is itself an individual form, a superior individual which carries out, for the whole of the individual Subjects which produce action projects, image-objects and anticipations, the work of consolidation, selection and valuation, in the same way as the individual Subject which is alone in the world, carries out, within the action process, the sedimentation of the image-objects on the path towards the preparation of the practical action. The market is a physical form which externalises, for all the individual Subjects, this task of sedimentation. It requires more than sedimentation. It is a matter of selecting and valuing. This last word is important since the *value* does indeed emerge from the economic action process as a distinction and selection of image-objects which will constitute the matrix of actions transforming reality.

The market, in what we call the most traditional version is very deeply impregnated by the form of the individual Subject as total, pure and absolute freedom, and the market itself appears as a form of individual, of supra-individual, which diminishes in the presence of the individual Subject's dynamic. The market is not considered as a collective form but as a supra-individual (Individual). The "collective" form of the market extends the individual economic freedom by organising it, without contributing any particular collective content, since the spontaneous order attained by the collection of individual freedoms within the market context does not justify any special form of collective action. However, economic freedom, in the market context, continues to be totally that of the Subject-individual, of such Subject alone in the world, continuing its active design. In this context, the market moment has the appearance to some extent of a magical moment, where a spontaneous order is attained in a fairly mysterious manner, which seems to be due to the very nature of the individual economic Subject, in its active design, or to the very form of the market.

The traditional form of the market is based on a strong (total) interpretation of the modern individual economic Subject, which can be described as pure or totalising. As such, there is a strong initial assumption regarding the individual which will have consequences on the collective organisation of the individual freedoms. This strong assumption, which forms a large part of the essence of modern economics, of [Subject – freedom – consciousness – action], an identity which establishes the relationship with the world [action – transformation], is most of the time accepted without any discussion or challenge, once it seems to be definitively installed. The form of the market as a natural collective form of economic freedom introduced itself on the platform of a totalising view of the Subject. Such a view, which may or may not correspond to reality (we have moreover demonstrated that such a "purist" or "spontaneist" or "absolutist" analysis of the economic Subject would fail to take into account a certain number of specific characteristics of the economic Subject's reference frame, especially its spatio-temporal nature, and would fail to take account, in the formation of the action process, of the role of time-matter, duration and memory in particular), contains moreover – in a traditional version of the market which adopts without a great deal of discussion a certain view of the individual economic Subject, even becoming as it were a supra-individual form – the risk of an economic freedom which has no normative counter-powers and which is so total that it would end up negating itself in its capacity as freedom.

The paradox of modern economic freedom as the active freedom and will of a free Subject, the total and absolute consciousness of a world which is only appropriated in proportion to the transformations which ones makes to it and the traces which one leaves in it, is that it desires itself to such an extent that it ends up negating itself. The modern form of the market, particularly in its contemporaneous, financial component, is completely based upon two pillars, one of which, as we have just seen, was not realist and the other was dangerous, all of which bearing in mind this extravagant truth: that the whole system of economic freedom, *inter alia* in its collective and practical contemporaneous aspects (normative framework of the financial markets), could be based on such a totalising and decidedly unrealist assumption of the economic Subject (first pillar) and, consequently, on a tendency not to consider the *normative collective forms* of such a force if left to its own devices.

The excessive nature of the modern era and of the theoretical thinking which accompanies modern economics is due to the very manner in which the Subject's structure is established, which we have named the absolute and totalising aspect of such structure, which, as we are well aware, goes hand in hand with a vision and perception which are seductive (as a result of the purity which is a feature of this structure), angelic but decidedly unrealist; second, due to the manner in which, in the Subject's very structure and then in the practical forms of action as a consequence, the Other is neither present nor considered at the origins of the modern moment; the practical collective forms, which are strictly economic/financial (the market, the State) or political (the State once again, the parties, societies...) develop on ground which is dominated by the vision of the Subject which we have just discussed, in particular the presence of collective forms, even though the modern economic Subject is not considered in relation to the others; finally, the risk incurred from the outset by this total and totalising Subject, i.e. a shift of a totalitarian nature of a Subject which is so free that it is also free to negate its own freedom.

This excessive nature of the assumptions on which modern economics are based is absolutely astounding. It is a dual lack of realism of both the internal structure of the individual Subject (spatio-temporal reference frame) and the external structure of the economic Subject (relationship with others), which raises the question of the understanding and meaning of economics, of the Subject and of the economic action (failing which, there is a lack of understanding, chance, contingency or, on the contrary, a determinism which leads to the same result, the lack of desire to understand); a danger for the Subject itself caused by the absolute nature of the assumptions for the construction of the modern economic Subject. That represents a good deal of assumptions.

The work on economic freedom must, therefore, simultaneously include a realistic, descriptive analysis of the individual economic Subject (see *Théorie du Sujet économique*) and a definition of the collective forms which organise, extend and regulate the action process of the economic Subject amidst the *other* Subjects. In particular, it involves showing that which makes possible, within the collective or institutional form itself, the exercise of the collective assignment (coordination, selection and regulation). It is the general question of the conditions for the possible exercise of the roles of the collective forms in the context of economic freedom, i.e. the conditions for a possible economic freedom in its collective or institutional form(s) (norm, coordination...). Such conditions cannot be distinct from the very matter of the individual economic Subject in its innermost working (e.g. time-matter). The reunification of the collective forms of economic freedom and of a realistic, individual form, based on a common set of assumptions, creating within the same matter the interplay of individual active freedom and the collective conditions for its preservation, either with regard to those others, in respect of which there is a permanent need for coordination subject to the constraint of conflict, or with regard to itself, given the extent to which, if left to its own devices, the active economic freedom may harm itself to the point of elimination.

The form of the market is tautological in the sense that it constitutes, in the traditional, absolute vision, a summary (all the individual Subjects) which is transparent (the market itself has a tendency to adopt the super-individual form and dissolves within an extension of individual freedoms). From this point of view, the form of the market sanctions and confirms individual economic freedom and there is in fact no specific collective form of economic freedom. The market is a sequence (within the economic action process which forms an identity together with economic freedom) and a tool for the delivery of individual freedom. It does not contain any normative role or regulation.

Once it can be shown that the economic Subject (and therefore the concept of economic freedom) and the extension thereof represented by the market, are based, as we have stated, on such strong, absolute and pure assumptions, that they are unrealistic and worrying, since they confirm the analysis within a form of lack of understanding (a sort of magical determinism of chance and necessity of a spontaneous nature through the market and of unlimited will through the individual Subject's freedom to act), once such limits have been demonstrated, then there is a need not only to consider the individual Subject (and therefore the market) in a different manner, in a merely realistic design, in order to understand it better in order to satisfy the conditions for a possible norm and regulation (since the norm, in its very foundation, can only originate from the essential, well-understood matter of the Subject and the market in their operation within the economic action process), but also to satisfy the conditions for a collective (institutional) form which contains such a role with regard to the market. It is these collective forms which are most lacking in the modern economic action process as it has developed up to date, irrespective of what one may think of its relevance and purpose. The inability of this process to comprehend in its innermost matter (the Subject, the market) has resurfaced, by supporting excessive and absolutist theories on the theme of the Subject-market and by preventing the emergence of collective forms which contain economic freedom with and for the market by means of an ability to produce a norm. By doing so, the missing link of modern economic freedom is the collective form which produces a norm and regulation from the very innermost matter of the Subject and the market in their most realist operation, a collective form which must be embodied by the dedicated institutions (*the institutional structure of the modern economic action process* is the most important unthought-of matter, the origin of which lies in the spellbound fascination for an absolutist interpretation of the Subject and the market. This is the work which we referred to in *La Théorie du Sujet économique*), and it is within such collective forms and institutions that *positive* modern economic freedom can be found, that which extends the individual Subject in its project while protecting it from the danger which individual economic freedom exposes itself to, by being defined by the will-to-act which merges the Subject, freedom-will and action as a means of relationship with the world through transformation.

The missing link of modern economic freedom paved the way for other collective forms which were in conflict, for a variety of reasons, with the form of the market and, consequently, with the individual Subject as well. All such collective forms (State, clan, party...) have been criticised for hampering economic freedom, i.e. essentially the free, individual economic Subject and, also, political freedom.

Before coming to the question of these collective forms which might have seemed, from the point of view of economic freedom (at least from the aspect thereof which we have described as "traditional"), oppressive (from the point of view of political freedom) and/or ineffective (from the strictly economic point of view), we should note that as far as the market forms are concerned, there is a special collective form, namely the *company*. The company is special from the point of view of economic freedom: a form of collection (pooling) which goes beyond individual freedom (even if, as for other collective forms, there is a super-individuation, the company, or more commonly some brand or other, which is a sign of individuation) in the name of economic freedom, this collective form may (although not always) show coercive, ideological, vertical and appropriating biases, namely, when all is said and done, a collective form which may be fairly distant from the point where the theory would readily place it, purely from the viewpoint of economic freedom.

The company, like the market (but also, one might say, like all collective forms), first claims to coordinate the individual economic freedoms. *The function of coordination*, which seems to advance without concession or abandonment of individual freedom within the context of an idyllic presentation of the market (which as we have stated is absolutist and purist), may, as would be suggested by mere observation, be accompanied by *coercion* from within the company or as between companies. This means that one of the objectives of the function of the micro-economic coordination of the collective form of the company, i.e. to protect others from coercion is not always achieved. Although from the point of view of effectiveness, the collective form of the company is justified, in the sense of a strictly rational calculation, it must be able to be justified in principle from the point of view of the preservation of individual freedom, the means of channelling conflict and violence. However, this is not what can be observed, indeed far from it. What can be observed at the micro-economic level (coercion and negation of individual freedom within the micro-economic form; the monopoly or destructive confrontation of freedom as between entrepreneurial forms) cannot be easily reconciled with the macro-economic theory, which supposes an identity between the collective form of the market and economic freedom. The function of coordination (and undoubtedly, as a result, the function of reduction of direct violence and conflict between individual freedoms) performed by the company in modern economies – and on which the operation of the market is fairly generally based –, is obtained at the price of a certain concession of individual freedom (which may assume more excessive biases) and which we will call a *detour* (namely the stylised and theoretical development of the individual economic freedom of the free, conscious Subject whose actions are directed at the world in order to transform it, which is the foundation for the analysis of economic freedom and more generally of modern economics, both *de facto* and in reality takes the modern *detour* of the collective form which we can call *company* – the concept is a broad and diffuse one; the world is in fact only targeted by the economic Subject through this type of collective form, which means that the question of economic freedom must, once again, and from the point of view of the very vision of the market, be posed from the viewpoint of *the collective form* of economic freedom which intends or claims to embody or extend individual freedom). Such a detour may mean that individual freedom pursues its design by other means (the collective form, super-co-ownership) and that this collective micro-economic design (the company) ultimately forms part of the macro-economic analysis of the market, a collective form of economic freedom which is as it were supreme and which, as we have seen, over and beyond a purist vision of a spontaneous nature which is free and protects freedoms in their designs, does not know how to protect individual economic freedom (and its market interchange(s) by means of the detour which we have just discussed) from the risk of negating itself at the end of its action dynamic.

There is therefore a paradox between, first, a theoretical interpretation of the market which establishes that the interaction of individual freedoms which has been left to its own devices, in the context of a market seen as a collective form (individual freedoms) and transparent form (individual freedoms remain intact there in the absolute purity of their designs, the market being an invisible hand), produces a spontaneous order and an equilibrium (there is an identity between the collective economic freedom – provided by the market – and the sum of the unaltered individual freedoms) – and, second, the reality of observation of the market which sees collective forms insert themselves between the market as a global, collective form and the elementary individual freedoms, the company being one of them and one of the most important, and this entrepreneurial form modifies individual freedom, even going so far as to negate it in certain cases. We have stated that the unrealistic nature of the first part of the paradox and therefore the fact that, in reality, the question of economic freedom is lodged within the collective forms which all present themselves (from the market right up to the total, ideological, political form, including in passing the State, as planner) as boundaries for the coordination of individual economic freedoms (in the context of their own action design) and for the management of coercion which thus explains the problem that they have a tendency to be structured as superindividuations (collective individuals, the language of economics bears a trace thereof), and to extend the modern, individual economic Subject's project, which is original and pure, within the said structure (a design of active projection into a world which is to be transformed) and, in respect of certain of them, occasionally, to negate individual freedom itself. There lies the true paradox: the modern, individual, economic Subject's project contains the logic of a negation of the Subject's very freedom (in differing degrees which accordingly require a typology of the collective forms of economic freedom), even (and *a fortiori*) when passing through the filter of collective forms which are ultimately imposed by the existence of others, which imposes the functions of collection, coordination, selection (the monetary valuation of projects is its counterpart, in the language of money, which is the means of management of violence and interpersonal conflicts) and of reduction of coercion, which undoubtedly introduces a serious problem, since observation shows that this is not the case in a certain number of situations.

Individual economic freedom, which remains very theoretical, since the Other appears within the field of the action process, but which structures this process by means of its project dynamic (image-object) and the spatio-temporal matter of its reference frame (duration, memory), is therefore, in reality, immediately intermediated and therefore *transformed* by the collective forms which are structured by the same type of dynamic and the same matter and which enter into a process of individuation with interaction and retroaction with and over the individual freedoms. There is indeed an individual economic freedom but the question of economic freedom is posed immediately within the collective forms which intermediate individual freedom.

Consequently, the question of economic freedom is to know which of the collective and/or institutional forms are the most capable of tempering, standardising and regulating the necessary development dynamic of the acting Subject, which is all the more difficult since numerous collective forms assume this necessary dynamic as it were on their own behalf, by ultimately determining themselves as individuals as against the individual. Other collective forms will then be required in order to standardise such worrying collective forms. This is not an easy matter, since numerous forms, starting with the form of the market itself, voluntarily present themselves as security or protection for economic freedom. This is also true of planning or of authoritarian or totalitarian political forms. However, that which is then called "economic freedom" threatens to turn against freedom itself.

Economic freedom is therefore a collective or institutional form which confronts (in the sense that it does not, in fact, accept) the necessary dynamic of the active economic Subject, which may intervene because it understands this dynamic sufficiently to be able to aim to prevent it from destroying the individual itself and to lead the development process of this freedom, within the modern context of action in the world, to irreparable impacts within the real world.

One is led towards a definition of economic freedom which is not the most conventional. Economic freedom as a principal concept and issue is not that of the Subject (this is the most conventional and is of real importance, since it is the starting point for the logics of the economic action process) but rather that provided by a collective form which standardises this dynamic and this process. The production of institutions and collective forms which fulfil this task is the true guarantee of economic freedom.

Economic freedom is a process of development of the action in the modern age, as we have described. Economic freedom is also that which is attained within such process, when the latter does not turn against the individual Subject nor impose destructions upon the real world, a successful action process to some extent, and which cannot be so without friendly, collective forms.

Let us go back to the example of the entrepreneurial form. A company forms part of the collective forms which intermediate the individual economic Subject. For a certain number of reasons, individual freedoms decide to pursue their *individual* project through collective intermediary forms which constitute the market. It should be noted that this pooling largely results from a rational calculation which enables the production of goods and services to be optimised, which are the origin of the firm. However, by considering only the production and its efficiency with regard to a certain number of costs, one does not have an adequate vision of the *leap* which is required, from individual economic freedom (I project myself by choosing an image which will become an action within and over the world) up to an economic freedom which is understood collectively in the context of a particular form (that of the company) which itself expresses and makes choices (individuation, i.e. the assimilation of the company to the individual; we, entrepreneurial form, we project ourselves...). Although the structure of the action project hardly changes in terms of its dynamic and its matter, nothing states whether the collective form easily satisfies all the individual logics. A theoretical approach may make this assumption, once again adopting a pure view of the market (the collective form represented by the company transparently extends the individual freedoms and there is an identity between the collective form and the sum of the individual freedoms). However, once again, observation shows that, on the contrary, there is a leap or detour where overall, the individual freedom and its project are hemmed within a much wider project of a collective nature, which may be different and which may finally produce constraints for the individual.

A company cannot operate as a spontaneous order in which the *laisser-aller* attitude of individual freedoms would suffice to attain a natural optimum. Reality is very different. There is hardly any *laisser-aller* attitude on the part of individual freedoms but, on the contrary, their coordination (coercion) with regard to an action, the Subject of which is the company itself. The act of coordinating individual freedoms always leads, through collective forms, as an exception to the extension of the individual project, most of the time, to a *transfer* to an economic Subject with a collective structure which, *in return and not without risk*, modifies the individual and its projects.

2. ECONOMIC FREEDOM AND POLITICAL FREEDOM

§ 154.   The question of the relationship between economic freedom and political freedom requires first of all a clarification, in our view, that economic freedom is the name given, in the modern age, to the concept of freedom (we have discussed the identity between Subject/ freedom/action at length) in the same way that we have demonstrated that economics was the name of the modern relationship between the Subject and the world. This means that the question of economic freedom contains a strong historical background, the context in which it is understood here. Economic freedom is a certain modern interpretation of freedom where the emancipation of the Subject establishes the identity [Subject – freedom – consciousness – action] in the relationship with the world which is to be transformed. We consider that freedom may and must be reconsidered over and beyond this identity and consequently over and beyond economics, over and beyond the Subject. Economic freedom is not part of freedom but rather an aspect of the historical background of the concept of freedom and, also, of the relationship with the world.

The position of political freedom is somewhat different, since the historical background of the concept is not the same (it is longer) although, unsurprisingly, the question of a link between economic freedom and political freedom emerges in the modern age, which shows that the concept of political freedom itself mutates and draws closer to the guarantees and protections provided to a free Subject, itself called *homo economicus*, whose emancipation coincides with the development of an imagined and reasoned action directed at the world. The question of the link between economic freedom and political freedom is a modern one. From a conceptual viewpoint, political freedom is under the influence of the sudden appearance of modern economics.

There is a misunderstanding regarding the necessary connections between economic freedom and political freedom. Economic freedom, as it must be considered in the modern age, that is to say as it develops in the active identity discussed above, i.e. as a necessary *desire to act* (which seeks to be itself), connected without difficulty to all the collective political forms – including the most totalising, which will not cause surprise, since the concept of modern freedom is total and totalising – from the market up to the totalitarian regimes and the Plan.

If one defines the modern moment in time as that of the Subject's emancipation, more generally as that of the Subject's centrality (the relationship of the Subject with and towards the world), one doubtless notes a similarity with a historic democratic moment which is concerned by, and which promotes, the individual, its rights, its place and its role in society and more generally in its relationship with the world, which is thereby enriched in a more active sense. There is therefore a necessity of this modern moment in time which establishes man as an individual, Subject and actor, not to mention a special causality of economics with regard to politics, or the reverse. The individual and collective forms of *market* are facilitated and accelerated by a certain number of political developments which to some extent enable a societal or social creation of *homo economicus*, a citizen-consumer, citizen-producer/trader, namely the coupling of the functions of citizens which give the individual the legal and social tools for its new position and market functions (exchange, competition...). The dual affirmation of the individual as individual economic freedom and political acting Subject takes place in the context of a general reference to the market, a collective form which reflects new individual acting freedoms which are constituted by the modern moment in time.

We give, both here and in our other works, a special and wider meaning to the word "economics". Economics, in terms of both their perception and definition, remain widely marked by their stylised and theoretical view of a *homo economicus* whose two supports are individual rights and the market. Such a view is not strictly speaking false but modern economics (modern is defined by economics and there is an identity between the two terms) are in their essence the *Subject's* development in an exclusive sense and purpose (which is a liberation and an affirmation), the capturing (examination) of the world and of oneself. This purpose, which is the essence of economics (of the modern moment in time), extends far beyond the sole *sequence* of the installation of individual rights and the market within the democratic collective form, even though, as is the case, this sequence was the first and an important one. Since the development of the Subject as freedom acting on the world (which is desire to act), where the status of freedom conceals an ambiguity in its purpose (freedom is to desire and to act), means above all the absolute affirmation of the individual but also collective Subject (we have discussed the collective forces of super-individuation, of transfer and intermediation of individual freedom).

Once it is established that economics are above all, in their modern essence, the development of the Subject's dynamic, the development of a problematic and ambiguous force, since such force is absolute and without limits, borne by a freedom defined by the necessity of considering the world as in a state of non-being, i.e. of transforming it, a necessity which pushes the Subject to exist only outside and beyond itself, within the act of transforming the world, which is also a transformation of oneself (of the Subject itself), accordingly once economic freedom is established as a means of affirmation of the Subject over the world through action, as a means of progression of the world and of oneself, then one immediately sees that such an affirmation of the Subject may be embodied in collective forms which are potentially total, totalising and totalitarian.

Once the modern affirmation of the Subject is development and purpose, it is a matter of sequences, of a certain historicity of the said development and therefore of historic moments to which special political forms may correspond, within an overall development logic of the essence of the modern Subject (the Subject *creates* what we have called "modern", there is again an absolute identity). Accordingly the modern path, a mixture of democratic moments or sequences and also of totalitarian collective forms from among the most accomplished and frightening of human history, may become clear.

To establish the necessary link between economic freedom and political freedom, as is usually done, i.e. an economic freedom confined to the pure and unrealistic definition of the market and of individual freedom, and a political freedom which is itself solely confined to a definition of the democratic moment, does not allow one to account within the development of the modern age for that which was and which cannot not be considered; accordingly, a logic (a purpose) of the market form/democratic form pairing runs through the modern era but is not the only one since, on the contrary, other logics and purposes co-exist, undoubtedly with a link or necessity with the first pairing mentioned above. Only a view of the development of the Subject as essence of modern economics allows one to unify the various political forms which *necessarily* accompany the Subject's purpose of economics, around a homogenous interpretation.

In our view, there is accordingly a unitary interpretation of the pairing formed by economic freedom and political freedom, which includes a definition of the former as essence of modernity, and therefore sole point of reference (the Subject), and a multi-definition of the second, the forms of which are multiple. The development, which is not causality but rather necessity, starts with what we have named *economic freedom*, namely the essential logic (dynamic, matter) of the individual Subject which is, then, intermediated, transferred, extended and transformed by the collective and/or institutional forms (which may be super-individuations or collective forms which produce a standard and a regulation); certain such collective forms are political forms and, in our view, this is how the connection between economic freedom (development of the individual Subject) and political freedom (collective forms) occurs. We have stated that the question of economic freedom was generally that of collective forms of the individual Subject's dynamic; such collective forms being also political forms, the question of *political freedom* is determined by the manner in which the problem of modern economics is posed. *Political freedom must be approached through and as the analysis of collective forms of economic freedom.*

§ 155. It is not established *ex ante* that there has to be a necessary and logical link between economic freedom and political freedom and, consequently, between economic regimes and political regimes. Observation shows that combinations exist, certain of which may be optimal or preferable, provided that the standard of assessment is specified. One can observe the reasoning which founds economic freedom within general freedom, itself defined on the basis of individual freedom. Since the purpose of the democratic regime is to guarantee individual freedom, economic freedom is presented as a component of general freedom, economic freedom being guaranteed by the economic regime of competitive capitalism, a means of achieving the objective of political freedom. Adopting this approach, economic freedom is necessary, as defined, for political freedom and the (free) market meets this necessity, which creates an optimum. The regime of political freedom is consequently dependent upon the economic regime (capitalism).

This line of reasoning should be reproduced, in a refined version, since it permeates so many steps of so-called "liberal" theory, thinking and practices, in the manner of a quasi-truth. It is easy to see that it is possible to observe a capitalist regime co-existing with a lack of regime of political freedom, at least in static version (a dynamic version may lead one to think, in terms of sequences, that the presence of the free market regime ends up calling for the implementation of a regime of political freedom). A symmetrical line of reasoning may consequently hold that political freedom is the condition for economic freedom, by first establishing individual freedom as a principle and by guaranteeing its implementation within the sphere of action, which leads to the collective form of free market as an optimal form of political economic organisation. However, once again, it is possible to observe regimes which organise a satisfactory political freedom but are endowed with economic organisations which, although they do not strictly negate (individual) freedom, are involved in planning and prove to be interventionist in proportions which are occasionally significant (once again, in static version, one can always plead a sense of history and causality).

All things considered, the two pairings [economic freedom/political freedom] and [economic regime/political regime] – we repeat that the two notions of freedom and regime are distinct – maintain relations which are not very clear and in any event not unilateral.

Whether it is a question of economic freedom or political freedom, there is, as we have demonstrated, a high degree of tension between the individual form and what we have called the collective form, a *necessary* form of coordination of consciousnesses and conflicts. The *regime* is, to a fairly large extent, the collective form adopted by the two freedoms in order to resolve the innermost tension which inhabits them, in this context the market and democracy. However, it is by returning to the foundation of freedom, as it develops in the modern age, and to which economic and political freedom are supposed to be connected, and which are arguably only components thereof, that one can try to obtain a better understanding of the links, necessities or chances and coincidences (capitalism and democracy might thus turn out to have a contingent co-existence). Moreover, by noting that the collective forms of economic and political freedoms are the places where the true question lies, once the presence of the Other is accepted and considered within the horizon of the free individual consciousness, one tries to figure out how, on the basis of an original definition of economic freedom in politics, collective forms, whether or not different, could develop, with possible links. Since the question of a link between economic freedom and political freedom is that of the positions of the economic and political *regimes*, as compared to that which may unify the field, i.e. a unitary definition of that which represents freedom for the Subject in the modern age. The unitary or other nature of the field of collective forms (and such unity can only originate in a unitary source of approach to freedom and the Subject) holds the response to the question in particular of whether the explosion or fragmentation within the field of collective forms and the language of the *components* (*sic*) of freedom (whether economic, political, of morals, etc.) masks a profound unity or, on the contrary, the contradictory dissociation of the concept of freedom (and if there is a profound unity, is such unity due to the seizure of power within the field by a certain concept or *praxis* of freedom?).

What we are presenting is the invasion of the modern field by a doctrine of freedom, the triptych of identity [Subject-consciousness-action], i.e. the final equivalence between freedom and the action which transforms the world. This is the modern truth of freedom and, as we have demonstrated on several occasions, that which is called economic freedom becomes the name of the relationship between the Subject and the world through action. This means that, from the outset, the essence of the modern era develops from an essence of freedom which is itself special, and that, consequently, economic freedom thus established simultaneously reduces, exceeds and constrains the fields of individual freedom and political freedom. The field which we discussed above is unified by the triptych of identity of the free Subject/consciousness/action but this unification also contains within it the constraint which influences everything which, in the field of the Subject's freedom, is not in fact "economic".

A certain number of collective reforms containing freedom in its modern essence result from the above. Economic freedom, understood as a transforming act of the Subject in respect of the world, develops through the (free) market, which caries, selects and values the projects (image-objects) for the financial market, and the real impacts of action for the market of goods and services. The form of the market is supposed to resolve the question of the coordination of freedoms. Furthermore, one observes the development of political collective forms whose structure and objectives are those of the acting Subject but in a collective form which is strictly political or economic (the Plan, the party-State, etc.). The political field loses its autonomy in the sense that the collective form, after all, pursues the aim of modern freedom (the active appropriation of the world), by resolving the question of the coordination of freedoms and the question of the Other by means of a paradoxical surpassment of individual freedom in collective form, where there is an abandonment in whole or in part of individual freedom for collective goods (protection, well-being...). Such collective forms (of the Plan, in its various forms, is an important example thereof), of a political nature, are in fact inhabited by the modern economic design for a Subject, proving to be only slightly autonomous, as compared to pure economic collective forms such as the market. Let us be clear what we are saying: it is not that they are not different – they are profoundly different – but they are driven by the same essence, that of the freedom described above.

The field is dominated by the modern essence of the freedom which names the relationship of the Subject's transforming action with the world, within the term "economic". The essence of modern freedom develops from what is economic, within a field where the essence of what is political is constrained by the objectives of this modern essence, resulting in political forms which are only slightly autonomous (attempting to recover collectively on their own behalf the design of the pure, acting Subject or that of the market) and in competition or conflict with the collective form of the market.

One has, therefore, as a starting point, the development of the concept of modern freedom, which is that of the individual Subject, understood as an action project (a tearing-away from oneself and from the world, and therefore of liberation in this sense, for a projection *within the world* in order to produce an impact *on the world and on oneself*). It is on the basis of this source of modernity that *special* or specific freedoms and their collective forms must be understood, first because all such special freedoms are presented as components of freedom *itself*, second because the collective forms of organisation of individual freedoms are essential to the understanding of economic and political freedoms: the question of economic freedom or of political freedom is largely due to the resolution of the necessary conflict between the collective form adopted by the economic or political freedom and individual freedom.

The form of the (free) market is a means (we prefer the term "sequence") to an end, which is not political freedom but rather the accomplishment of the economic Subject's project, in this context a means to overcome the question of the conflict and violence due to the presence of others (the otherness of the economic Subject) and a sequence within the economic action process – refinement, selection and monetization of the projects before the actual sequence of *praxis* itself. The collective form of the market is supposed to permit an optimal accomplishment of the *individual* Subject's project, although, as we have noted, the individual Subject is in reality intermediated within the market itself by collective forms (e.g. the company) and, moreover, the market itself becomes a Subject-person (one talks about the "free market" as one talks about the free individual Subject) at the end of an empowerment of collective forms (of "market"). There is therefore a discrepancy between the theoretical (or ideological) description of the individual Subject defined as freedom and project and a reality of collective forms, including the market itself, which in fact continue the projects and actions (as such, the collective form of the market traces the structure of the individual Subject's project; i.e. continuation of the Subject's project with transformation of the collective forms into a Subject, which may become the aims of means or sequences). Whether the collective form of the market manages to preserve and assist with the individual Subject's project or whether it replaces it with collective forms, part of which takes over from the individual but which, increasingly, since this is its very essence, produces its own projects (independence of the collective forms of the market), there does not seem to be a necessary link with some or other political form. In fact, two possibilities can be distinguished, in a certain manner: a theoretical view which identifies economic freedom with the individual Subject and the (free) market as a neutral collective form (the individual's project is not constrained by the collective form), and the democratic form may seem to be a necessary link with this view; a more realist view in our view where, in short, there are in fact only collective forms, all inspired by a concept of freedom defined by the transforming action, certain of which may form part of the market and others not (centralised planning of the economy), associated with political collective forms, whether democratic or not. A considerable number of combinations is possible and in fact observed. Consequently, the optimal nature of such combinations is a legitimate question. Part of the response lies in the question itself: one senses a curve of efficiency and of *optima* in accordance with the situations (static) and over time (dynamic historic sequences). It is hard to risk defining an *optimum*. At this stage, let us remember that the question of economic freedom and political freedom is that of the collective forms by means of which each develops from a unitary point which is the source of freedom in the modern sense; that all such collective forms tend to become independent and to constitute themselves as Subject pursuing the action; that modern freedom is presented, with regard to the individual Subject, as transforming action; it is certainly possible to understand economic freedom and political freedom on the basis of that part of the collective form which constrains or amputates individual freedom but, once individual economic freedom (and just freedom itself) is defined as transforming action and taken over by collective forms on their own behalf which continue in their being (market, Plan...) *to the detriment of the individual*, it is very probable that we no longer know what we are talking about when we are discussing economic freedom or even political freedom, since the economic freedom which we are discussing in the modern and contemporary debate is contained in collective forms which develop over and beyond the individual and which are possibly unaware of it or are restricting it. This is one of the modern paradoxes, fanatical attention is paid to the individual, in its capacity as such, both in the definition of economic and political freedoms and, at the same time, as concepts which are, in reality, collective forms and which become liberated *as against* the individual; finally, that the field of the concept of the (principal) freedom which includes its modern components or special freedoms, is structured, i.e. dominated, by the modern concept of freedom, an identity [conscious Subject/freedom/action], which specifically forms the basis for economic freedom (and the economic Subject) as *special* notions and which is therefore imposed upon the rest of the field, including the political one.

§ 156.   If economic freedom is only understood to mean that which refers back totally, either to the individual or to the market (we have seen that economic freedom, or merely freedom itself, defined solely by the individual would have to come to terms with the reality of inter-mediations by means of collective forms, including, for example, the company), then the link between economic freedom and political freedom, the latter being itself defined on the basis of freedom of the individual and its objectives, then not only is the relationship in principle complex, non-unilateral and of uncertain causality but it can, moreover, be seen that the concept of political freedom has been colonised by that of economic freedom, understood as the development of the Subject's action. Numerous combinations can be envisaged, the optimal nature of which is open to discussion. In the modern era, i.e. in the context of the definitions adopted by the two concepts of economic freedom and political freedom, there is a trade-off curve which represents the *optimum* points. This *optimum*, if one notes the fact that economic freedom, in its modern definition (action of appropriation and transformation of the world) imposes upon the definition of the concept of political freedom, may acquire "optimal" forms, pairing, for example, market capitalism and non-democratic political forms. This means that, unless one questions the very concept itself of modern (economic) freedom, one is led to reason about the economic-political *optima* which may lead one far from what is commonly considered to be the case (economic freedom = democracy). The idea, which is relevant in other respects, of multiple combinations of the economic freedom/political freedom pairing, which are more or less relevant, is based on a *certain* idea of modern (economic) freedom.

Moreover, we have suggested that the link between economic freedom and political freedom was *indirect*, once the entire space which belongs to them is yielded to collective (and/or institutional) forms, which contain the possibility of a norm and which were analysed inter alia in *Théorie du Sujet économique*. The forms, for the most part institutional, and including even political forms, establish the link between the modern economic action process, as it develops from the Subject through the market and towards the impact within the world, and political freedom, understood as a structure which has a tendency to protect the Subject-individual from itself, including from its trans-formation into a political (restrictive) collective form setting itself up as a political Subject pursuing an objective. The collective forms of intermediation mean that there is a link between the two forms of freedom, which is indeed indirect, but this link does not authorise all the "optimal" combinations of the two forms of freedom, since these intermediary forms state the norm or recall it.

3. FREEDOM IS RELATED TO THE USE ONE MAKES OF IT

§ 157.   When a certain modern way of thinking asserts that *"freedom has nothing to do with the use one makes of it"* (Friedman), nothing more need be said. It is not possible to express more clearly the modern (economic) Subject's project for the projection, appropriation and transformation of the world, an oblivious force which is in a state of non-being, without limits, without standards. We have extensively described this modern economic action process where economics become the name of the relationship maintained with the world in this mode. Nothing more need be said in the sense that such a way of thinking does not consider the need for collective forms which we have called intermediary (which is in no way pejorative), whose purpose is precisely to remind the action process what it is, where it comes from (which explains the emphasis on memory, duration), i.e. to standardise *so that freedom is related to the use one makes of it*. This is the major issue: by leaving freedom, as it emerges in the modern age, to its own devices and its forces, one easily arrives at market/political combinations of collective forms which may be extreme since the *laisser-faire* attitude regarding freedom exposes one to such infinite processes of appropriation, including, and especially restrictive of, the world, people and things.

We refute the affirmation that "freedom has nothing to do with the use one makes of it". On the contrary, there lies the whole question. And, consequently, we refute the distinction drawn between a concept of freedom which governs two orders or blocks of values: the relations between men, where priority is given, in the so-called "public" *collective forms* to freedom; the *individual* exercise of freedom which contains private forms of the value of freedom, including ethics.

The principal consequence of such a distinction, in the construction of the concept of freedom, between the individual and the Other (the individual with the others), between therefore the individual form (which refers back to oneself, which is privative) and the collective form which is rendered necessary by the function of coordination when faced with conflicts, is to confine individual freedom to a narrow private sphere (a few philosophical questions, morality) and accordingly to return the whole of the concept of freedom (economic freedom, since this is our subject) to the collective forms, even though the concept of (economic) freedom arises in the modern era from the individual and continues to be presented as part of the concept of the individual. However, this is not the case. As we have demonstrated, economic freedom, although created in conceptual terms within the individual and its emancipation, is determined within the collective forms, through which it develops in the functions of coordination of individuals (*the freedoms*), with a more or less pronounced transfer of the function of Subject from the individual to the collective form (market, political entity...). The individual is in fact dispossessed, by means of this transfer, of a large part of the initial conceptual prerogatives of the concept of freedom which it contained, transferring them to the collective forms. One therefore makes the positive assumption that the individual's designs are pursued by other means, by the collective forms which have, however, as we have seen, a tendency to become independent.

There is therefore a breach between collective forms of freedom and individual exercise of freedom and the very fact of becoming or wanting to name this purpose indicates the breach in the concept of (economic) freedom and the difficulty in considering, first, the individual and (economic, political) freedom and, second, economic freedom and political freedom, together.

By returning individual freedom back to a private and privative, impenetrable sphere, i.e. in theory, cut off from a relationship with the Other, and at the same time, by dedicating a space of coordinations in order to define practical (economic, political...) freedom within a reality where the individual Subject *is constituted* by its relation to others, one undoubtedly has the impression of safeguarding/saving individual freedom, the concept of which, we repeat, dominates the modern view of freedom, in particular economic freedom. However, this is not the case, since behind this outward view, the individual dynamic is kept apart, or at least placed under collective supervision with regard to the reality of practical freedom which is that of collective forms. This is one of our principal theories. The tension which exists between the individual form and these collective forms, including with regard to the collective forms which seem to advance, equipped with the best possible assets for the individual, such as the (free) market, undoubtedly constitutes a dividing line between the various combinations [economic freedom/political freedom], of other collective forms (e.g. institutions which state the norm and regulation) which may help to relieve this tension. Furthermore, one cannot confine the moral dimension solely to the individual private sphere and send back, moreover, legitimately, the question of public freedoms to the collective forms, without realising the profound need to consider together, within the whole of the economic action process, the individual projection and the collective forms which manufacture the action, the individual and the norm produced by the collective forms.

In particular, the abandonment of the terrain of the norm (and, consequently, of that which may constitute the support for a moral approach) by the collective forms ("freedom has nothing to do with the use one makes of it") not only deprives the collective form sooner or later of its capacity to preserve and shelter the concept of freedom, but isolates/rejects the individual within a self-referencing moral code/norm, of which the much-criticised ascension of so-called individualism is a sign.

We have stated the extent to which, in its very modern foundation, freedom (the Subject, the action, this concerns a trinity of identities) contained the risk of its own negation; the extent to which the collective forms responsible for tempering this risk, whether economic or political, would themselves be running an even greater risk, that of confiscating the Subject's function (*the* market, *the* party...) for their own benefit, in order to pursue the same ambition of action but, possibly, to the detriment of the individual Subject itself.

Ultimately, the question of economic freedom is indeed that of the collective forms which are responsible for protecting the economic Subject from itself but whose persistence in being makes them (collective) Subjects themselves.

It cannot be stated that economic freedom is a component of freedom and, at the same time, that freedom has nothing to do with the use one makes of it, without leaving the development of the action process to its own devices and, in particular, without setting the individual aside from the concept of economic freedom. This is a question of pure desire-to-act, the total and totalising concept of Subject, freedom and action which, by merging, kick-off the modern age. The total aspect of this (economic) freedom is, in fact, impressive and unsurprising, once one understands the innermost structure of the (economic) Subject as a consciousness which is obliterating and acting. One has, on the contrary, to affirm that freedom *is* what one makes of it, for the same reasons; that the economic Subject is quite complete in its permanent projection outside itself and in the action of transforming the world and itself; that this action process, which is apparently without limits, must and may find the conditions for a possible norm and a moral code which is at least practical, if only temporary (see *Théorie du Sujet économique*). And this norm, because it is filled with duration and memory and the action itself of the individuals and collective forms, creates a link between that which must not be separated, the individual and the collective forms.

The emancipation of the collective forms – Subjects of the individual itself which gave birth to them to some extent, shows that the question of economic freedom is dominated by that of the collective forms and that it is ultimately a matter of saving the individual, despite certain appearances left by a contemporary omnipresence; second, that the practical forms have a tendency to be dominated by this economic question, with multiple combinations of economic freedom/political freedom, the optimality of which is open to discussion; finally that, since the sudden appearance of the modern, free and acting Subject, a logic does not cease to develop – through the collective forms – which endangers the individual itself, the latter hiding behind this modern (economic) Subject.

§ 158. Let us return to the theory according to which "freedom has nothing to do with the use one makes of it". We consider that the essence of the modern era can be found in this phrase and, within its core, which amounts to the same thing, the emancipation and development of the modern (economic) Subject, which is effected in a relationship of examination and transformation of the world, the whole of this movement specifically defining what is called economic in modern times. The limits of a "liberal" (and we use the term carefully) form of thinking can be found in this sentence. It is of little importance that this sentence was pronounced by Mr. Friedman, since, in our view, its essence brands *the whole* of modern economics, in its very purpose (see *Tractatus, Généalogie, Valeur et temps*), over and beyond the trends of thinking and theory which may traverse the field of the said economics.

One finds within this sentence both the idea – which defines the modern (economic) Subject – of a freedom as an open and *unlimited* field of a consciousness in permanent projection outside itself, which only exists outside itself, i.e. directed at the world, in image and action; and the more disturbing idea that freedom can be found beyond or set back from *doing*, from action. This second proposition, which creates the distinction between a private individual sphere of freedom and a "public" sphere, which organises the relations between men, is disturbing because modern freedom does, in fact, emerge from the identity between freedom, imaging/acting consciousness and action, i.e. freedom identifies with the Subject's *doing*, with the action and it could not be otherwise, given that the Subject-consciousness is presented as a total dynamic of projection outside oneself (freedom is *necessary*, the Subject cannot escape it, cannot escape from doing). It is this very identity between freedom and doing (action) which forms the basis of the concept of economic freedom.

This sentence therefore contains two problems: the unlimited, limitless nature of modern (economic) freedom, i.e. the difficulty of considering a norm for an action with an infinite field (we can add to this the question of morality, the conditions for the possibility of a norm within such an open field); the breach between the concept of freedom and action (doing) (which, inter alia, conceals the breach between the individual as absolute Subject considered as an entity alone in the world – which consequently bears the values of freedom and ethics – and, second, the universe of consciousnesses where the relationship with the Other leads to and produces collective forms where freedom (whether economic or political) is in fact determined). These two ideas contained in the sentence which we are commenting upon, apart from the contradiction which may exist between them, indicate the lack of reality which separates the private freedom of the individual from the collective forms of (economic) freedom, like a desperate attempt to save the individual, even though the reality of economic freedom is quite complete within the collective forms which contain and embody it and which replace the structure of the individual Subject's projection within the action, in the middle of others (the Other), since the question of economic freedom is found within action (what we have called the "economic action process") and within the collective forms which organise relations between the Subjects-consciousnesses; the immense difficulty of considering a norm and beyond that, a code of ethics, in the place where they should be considered, i.e. within the collective forms which contain economic freedom, once the Subject is presented as total and totalising freedom-action, replaced by the collective forms which inherit, as collective Subjects, this structure of DNA and which, as a result, may lead one to think, because freedom is not what one makes of it, that one might be able to do anything at all with freedom, i.e. the latter would be a movement of a desire-to-act which is impossible to stop (where freedom is a risk for freedom and the collective forms of freedom a risk for the individual).

Freedom does therefore, in its modern essence, have something to do with the use one makes of it, since freedom is ultimately *doing*, a modern identity which forms the foundation for economics in general and for *homo economicus* in particular. At the same time, the sentence which we have commented upon reveals a modern interpretation and purpose of the concept of freedom which we will call the *modern divide*, a modern divide of the initial concept which forms the foundation for the modern moment (emancipation and emergence of the individual Subject as freedom *and* action), a divide between, first, a freedom which we shall call effective, i.e. of reality and *praxis*, i.e. a freedom defined by doing, by action, which in fact adopts the name of economic freedom and, second, a freedom of values (in particular moral values) borne by the individual. Economic freedom, as we understand it in reality, while referring in both its views and its theory to the individual, is in fact borne by the collective forms which are distanced by the divide which we have discussed of a block of values confined to the private sphere of the individual. The principal theoretical (and practical) issue is therefore to re-establish the conditions for a fundamental unity of the concept of freedom, which consequently leads to considering the economic action process as unitary and sequential, from the individual structure to the collective forms which contain the expressions of economic freedom and political freedom, and to construct the possibility of a norm (and a moral code) within a *continuum* which incorporates the individual and the collective forms.

The issue of economic freedom as progressively posed in the modern age is the issue of collective forms (market, etc.) which are empowered or more independent and which distance themselves from the issue of the individual Subject. There lies the paradox: even though it is established that freedom has nothing to do with the use one makes of it, the concept of *economic freedom* is in fact emancipated through doing and through action (economic freedom is separated without valid reason from a concept of freedom). In certain aspects, the concept of *political freedom* follows a similar path to that of emancipation and automation within this general process which can be described as the description of freedom, with regard to the various means of doing and acting (economic, political), with economics dominating the field. It can be noted that the confinement of the concept of freedom solely to the individual sphere and only to "values", including morality, is unrealistic for two reasons, since the modern (economic) Subject is defined by action and develops with and against the Other, the Other constructing it as an individual and requiring that the coordination of individual freedoms be considered within collective forms.

4. INTERDEPENDENCE. THE INDIVIDUAL AND THE COLLECTIVE

§ 159.   The individual exercise of freedom and the relations between men do not constitute two separate levels, as assumed on a methodological basis by contemporary "liberal" tradition (Mr. Friedman), introducing a divide between the private sphere and the collective sphere, the mental and practical form of the individual's exercise of freedom (religion, morality...), and moreover a collective form of the coordination of projects (market, institutional and/or political forms). In fact, the modern individual, as an economic Subject, is defined by the projection beyond oneself within the transforming action project, which means that the individual, as freedom, cannot be defined, or at least not uniquely, on the basis of private practices linked to values and morals (the latter only acquiring sense by comparison to the action which constitutes the Subject as freedom, possibly by clarifying them). The economic Subject cannot be reduced to an isolated intellect which produces such resulting values and practices. The Subject is profoundly distinguished by the action or project which is what makes it an *economic* Subject. *The individual exercise of freedom is the exercise of action, of projection outside oneself and directed at the world.*

Second, the individual exercise of freedom is effected under the watchful eye and action of the Other and the individual's practices, within the sphere of the actual action itself or within that of private practices, in particular the moral ones, are profoundly influenced and structured by this general (economic) action process which we described in *Théorie du Sujet économique*.

Consequently, it can be seen that this so-called individual exercise of freedom is a form of *continuum* with the relations between men, an essential collective place, in fact, of economic freedom, but by way of an extension, and not an interruption, of the initial energy and structure of the individual (economic) Subject. The collective, and its various forms, inherit the structure of the individual's project/action, which prolong the latter up until its impact within the world through collective forms which select, value, eliminate and improve the individual projects. From this point of view, the (free) market is this form which gathers and coordinates the individual freedoms (there is accordingly an organic link between the individual exercise of freedom and the relations between men and there is no cause to separate them). However, there is an individuation, an empowerment of the collective form of the (free) market whose structures become (collective) Subjects, the market being the first thereof: when we say "the free market", we are no longer talking about individual freedom and the exercise thereof, but rather about freedom as a collective form (we have established, as an important part of our theory, that economic freedom could be found within collective forms); this is legitimate, but consequently reveals the inconsistency of the divide, within the very concept of (modern) economic freedom, between the individual exercise of freedom and the "relation between men" (collective forms of freedom which we have seen became independent as Subjects), and even leads to suspecting the project of removing the individual from the effective *praxis* of economic freedom, which is, generally, that of collective forms, which have become Subjects at the risk of the individual ("the free market" is an aspect thereof).

For their part, the "relations between men" form part of the individual exercise of freedom which develops as a global action *process* in the middle of the others. Freedom as a collective form and freedom as an individual form are one and the same concept, the unity of which must be affirmed and defended. What is at stake with collective (sometimes called "social") forms is to affirm and in fact to accomplish a mission to defend and protect the individual. This unitary affirmation, which often leads to presenting, at least in the views expressed, the freedom of an individual as a reference for the collective (social) regime, constitutes at the same time the principal risk, that of autonomous collective forms which are presented as Subjects and which dispose of the individual. We have emphasised that this is where one of the principal threats for freedom lies, occasionally under the banner of freedom itself. And the theoretical divide established between the individual exercise of freedom and the relations between men does not help reassure one, since it seems to endorse the independence of collective forms and a marginal, isolated status for individual freedom.

The majority of collective forms are indeed presented as reconciliations of interdependence and individual freedom, whether in relation to the (technical) form of the market or the centralised and later coercive management (the latter may, at a certain point, negate individual freedom or limit it). In both cases, one has a tendency to see individual freedom not simply as claimed or asserted, within the views and practice of the collective forms, but above all presented as a private and privative individual exercise, as stated above. It should be noted that the form of the "free market" is presented as a *technique*, and consequently distinct from the political or institutional collective form (that which sets the rules and meets what is often called a "requirement for government"). The free market provides protection from coercion through a voluntary exchange, which is informed and is beneficial for all those involved; it provides the best form of direct representation of the individual and its project and not that of the group or of the collective form which represents it or is supposed to represent it. Finally, and here the concept of economic freedom can be found in such an approach, the free market guarantees *diversity* (in the sense of representation as a proportional system) which, when associated with the collective form which is the best placed to ensure *conformity*, constitutes the fundamental connection of the modern concept of economic freedom, at the cost of a certain separation of powers as between economics (the market) and politics, the market removing the right of politics to inspect the economic organisation and excluding the risk of coercion, at least within the economic sphere (voluntary exchange without coercion).

These various elements constitute what can be called the modern liberal position. Let us reconsider some of them. The market is presented as a *technical* collective form for the reconciliation of interdependencies and individual freedom. The term is there in order to state the mechanistic evidence of the solution provided by the market in order to minimise (Keynes plumbing [system]) and not to cause concern. At the same time, the term *technical* refers back in a more worrying register to the (technical) appropriation by the (economic) Subject which transforms the world, a movement which defines economics as such in the modern period. This is the manner in which we interpret it. The economic action process, which defines the (economic) Subject, is a transforming projection of a technical nature, or at the least, the technique which permeates all its sequences up until impact. From this point of view, as we stated in *La Dynamique boursière*, the market constitutes a sequence of the economic action process, a sequence of sorting, selection, valuation (monetization) of the individual projects, an extension of the individual (economic) Subject's structure, all within a (technical) plan for the mobilisation of resources for impact (final sequence). The market constitutes a *technical* sequence.

This means, to our mind, that there cannot be, on the one hand, individual freedom and on the other the question of the Other (that of interdependencies), between which the market opens a bridge. On the contrary, we have shown the deep-set unity of structure (i.e. imaging and acting consciousness-project as a fundamental expression of modern freedom) which exists between the individual Subject and the (free) market, which constitutes a form of "physical" extension thereof. Here lies the first difference, which has implications since, consequently, individual freedom cannot be cast out into a privative or private marginality by distinguishing it, as if to protect it (this would in fact result in excluding it, by leaving the economic and political field completely free for the collective forms of freedom); individual freedom is literally mixed up in the collective forms and its fate is determined therein. The market is in its essence a (technical) clone of the individual Subject's structure.

This continuity of structures (concepts-images at the stage of the imaging consciousness; organised technical procedures at the stage of the market sequence) conceals a far more important mutation, since the market acquires independence as a (collective) Subject, which constitutes a threat for the individual Subject, for individual freedom. The position of privative or private sheltering of individual freedom (values, moral code...) is not fortuitous: it expresses this empowerment of the market as Subject without actually stating it, which, in passing, invalidates any theory involving the minimisation of the market as an element of plumbing (first version of the technical term), of no real interest. On the contrary, the market constitutes an essential collective form, inscribed within the technical nature of the economic action project/process, the paradox of which is that it stems from the same unitary structure of the individual (economic) Subject, the essence of which is rightly worrying (the essence of the Subject lies in the projection outside itself, beyond itself, within the transforming quest through action, which is infinite and infinitely unsatisfied, which means that the individual Subject/Subject of freedom is a danger for itself), and it is therefore a paradox to stem from the same unitary structure as the individual Subject and yet to constitute a threat for it.

The market is therefore anything but an anodyne collective form, especially since its innermost structure extends that of the individual Subject. The question of the individual Subject and that of individual freedom are connected to the collective form of the market. This is one of the characteristics of the modern period. It is on this basis that the question of the other collective, political and/or institutional forms must be posed, since such forms face two issues, namely to take responsibility for the requirement for governance of the market as (collective) Subject and to take responsibility for the protection of individual freedom (if one were to exaggerate, one might say that it is a question of saving the individual Subject, and consequently individual freedom, from itself, i.e. from the consequences of its collective development, in this instance within the market's technical sequence).

The individual Subject is neither *set aside* (from the market, understood as a technical body for the coordination of relations between men, political or institutional collective forms) nor is it *sheltered* within the collective form of the market.

§ 160.   The attempt to reconcile the interdependent (i.e. the taking into consideration of the problematic presence of others) and individual freedom (i.e. the taking into consideration of the presence within the world of a total and absolute free consciousness) lies at the heart of each of the concepts of economic freedom and political freedom, and accordingly of their relations. Economic freedom, as we have shown, must be considered on the basis of the economic action process, *as* an economic action process, which defines not only the Subject as an individual but also and especially the interdependence of individual Subjects as (a) collective Subject(s). There is, and this is essential, a continuity of process from individual freedom up to the collective forms of economic freedom. This implies, first, that one must consider and construct individual freedom by incorporating the Other (others constitute an active element of the innermost structure of each individual's free consciousness – there is no divide or breach between the strict dimension of the individual and that of the others); second, the collective forms of economic freedom, which extend the primary structure of the individual's imaging and acting free consciousness, are necessary (in the sense that the consideration of the Other is a necessity, and therefore the organisation of interdependence) and must be assessed in the light of their capacity to preserve the continuity of process, as between individual freedom and collective forms of interdependence, especially since the collective forms of the Subject (market or others) have such a tendency to become independent that the individual is at risk as an individual, and also because the modern essence of the free (economic) Subject (the acting and transforming projection) is sufficiently total and totalising to include the project within its development (the risk of its own negation (destruction). The relevant collective forms of economic freedom will also, therefore, be those which will preserve freedom from itself during its development, whether or not such forms are those of the market or political/ institutional forms in interaction with the market, in particular in regulatory mode. The capacity (possibility) of the collective forms, or certain of them, to produce a norm in this sense is crucial to the general equilibrium of economic freedom, understood as an economic action process of the Subject.

Before discussing political freedom, we should note in passing that interdependence constitutes one of the fundamental structures of the economic Subject, and therefore, at this stage, forms part of its essence. Interdependence, which is the foundation for the various collective forms which we have discussed (market, political structures, institutions which produce a norm), cannot be reduced to a *technical* question or dimension solely of the (collective) organisation of the coexistence of individual freedoms. Consequently, the collective forms of economic freedom (and we have seen that the latter constitute the most significant emerging face of the question of economic freedom) cannot be reduced, in the manner in which we may name and describe them, to technical external appearances and their essence reduced to a technique of arrangement and organisation. The essence of interdependence and the collective forms of (economic) freedom is located beyond the technical appropriation of the world, which is constituted by the modern economic action process. The very fact that interdependence, which is an ontological structure of the Subject, may be captured and examined by the organisational technique and forms of organisation shows the extent to which the modern purpose of economics, which leads that of the Subject into a relationship of projection which transforms the world, continuously runs the risk, in its essence, of being captured by a technical reality. It can therefore be noted, at the same time, that the capture of economic freedom through the technique of collective forms (the market being described as a simple organisational technique) stems from a certain modern purpose of the Subject of economics, within the link which the term economics designates between the Subject and the world and, also, that the essence of interdependence, of the Subject itself (whose innermost structure and organisation include the relation with others) is located beyond this technical force of attraction which runs through the whole of the economic action process. This force of attraction of the technique constitutes a danger for the collective forms of economic freedom, since there is located the individual's forget-fulness and the tipping point of the concept of economic freedom from the direction of the total and totalising action. It is accordingly the very meaning of the concept of (economic) freedom which is determined around this tipping point, where that which is economic (in the sense of acting and technical appropriation) and which expresses the constitution of the modern Subject and its emancipation, in its capacity as freedom, threatens to dissolve the Subject itself. The modern concept of economic freedom and the modern concept of (economic) Subject are traversed by this paradox. One must therefore consider the collective forms of economic freedom, starting with that of the (free) market beyond their form and their technical manner of organisation.

It can be seen that economic freedom can be defined principally as a continuity of structure as between individual freedom and the collective forms which do indeed extend it (there is neither a breach nor what we have called a divide, and divides are the primary sources of economic, social and political crises). There are accordingly two zones of tension (and therefore sources of crises): first, as between individual freedom and the collective form of freedom (the divide); second, even though continuity seems to be established, dissolution of individual freedom (absorption) in/through the collective form, which often comes together with a political form of constraint and coercion. In the former, the collective form is divided from individual freedom and the latter is cast out into a privative sphere of spiritual exercise of values, while being, formally, claimed by the dominant collective form (Mr. Friedman's theory of the free market and distinction between the collective freedom provided by the market's organisational technique and freedom which is to some extent private); the political form which we will call "democratic market capitalism" often accompanies this divide but cohabitations with more coercive forms are possible. In the second case, it is once again claimed that individual freedom is organised by the collective form, which becomes independent to the extent of acquiring the status of Subject; this is the case of the market in certain circumstances, whether or not coupled with democratic or coercive political forms, or interventionist collective forms. There are numerous combinations.

Political freedom, as a concept, describes the collective forms of organisation of the interdependence of individual freedoms more directly (than economic freedom). Political freedom is, from the outset, for-others in the sense that the very meaning of politics, for the modern individual Subject which becomes emancipated is, first of all, the management of the potentially conflictual relationship with others and of coercion. As such, political freedom may be understood, in the same way as the collective force of the market is occasionally understood, as an organisational *technique* for placing individual acting freedoms in contact. Consequently, by comparison with the Subject's economic action process the question is as follows: does the political collective form allow this action to develop in the best possible way? Does it provide continuity of structure as between individual freedom and the collective form of interdependence? Once again, the political collective form cannot be described solely as an organisational technique but rather as that which does or does not provide continuity of structure as between individual freedom and the collective form. Once again the collective form shows an astonishing propensity to become independent as a (collective) Subject and to convey the individual Subject in weak or strong forms, from the formal display of individual guarantees to the proclaimed and totalising coercion.

A parallel can be drawn between the forms and issues of economic freedom and political freedom. Both share the issue of a paradoxical continuity, as between individual freedom and a collective form of organisation of interdependence, based on a modern concept of the Subject which, however, being essentially defined by the transforming action of oneself and of the world, which is the very definition of what is called economics, introduces economics in a dominant position. One can therefore simply expect politics to manage to accommodate the development of this essence of action in the best possible manner *irrespective of* the political form (the democratic political forms will maintain, sometimes in a formal manner, a link with the individual Subject; the others, which are more coercive and interventionist, will incorporate it within a collective independent Subject).

When all is said and done, the modern concept of political freedom is considerably reduced by the definition adopted by the modern Subject, an acting, conscious freedom. The modern Subject, in its development, is *homo economicus* rather than *homo politicus*. Consequently, it is hardly surprising that numerous political forces are shaped, from the inside, by the economic question, which finds it difficult to obtain independence. The political question, within the purpose of the modern Subject and despite initial appearances, is dominated – which means that it is exploited, in the sense that the political form of organisation of interdependence is considered to be a *technique* for completing the (economic) action process, whether it is a matter of democratic or totalising/totalitarian forms, proclaiming the individual, the market or promising a new man at the end of a collective process which constitutes a collective Subject in its capacity as such – by the economic question. The tension and balance of power which may exist between the economic question and the political question, i.e. between economic freedom and political freedom, express the very purpose of modern man in his capacity as Subject.

§ 161.   It is one of the characteristics of modern times that the majority of collective forms of freedom, whether economic or political, are described as *techniques*, whether relating to the market in the context of a voluntary cooperation or a centralised management within the context of a coercion. This means that economic freedom (but the same is also true of politics) is not considered other than as a technical form, the means of organisation, in this instance, of the functions of coordination and interdependence. It is consequently economic freedom which makes the coordination take place.

This technical coordination of men as between themselves presupposes a function of cooperation, which is an individual and voluntary undertaking of the Subject, such Subject being defined as free (this freedom guaranteeing/acting as the foundation for the voluntary exchange), and the private form of the company, which ultimately ensures that the contracting party is indeed the individual. There is therefore an idea that one only has recourse to exchange, if one is a beneficiary (there is a *detour* of production for an indirect satisfaction of needs, a separation of functions and a division of work), since otherwise there would be a direct production by the individual. The company is the intermediary form between individuals, which provides the coordination between those individuals which supply and which acquire.

Let us return to each of the major assumptions, which form the platform for the dominant form of analysis, which is often described as "liberal". The legitimacy and efficiency of the collective form adopted by economic freedom, i.e. the function of cooperation, is based on the full and complete adherence (voluntary approach) of an individual Subject which is said to be free. The freedom of the individual Subject, the modern essence of which is the action of transforming projection directed towards the world, therefore includes, first, the realistic and legitimate consideration of the presence of others (functions of coordination and interdependence are therefore necessary), and, second, the necessity of considering the extension of individual action within the collective forms which organise economic freedom. There is indeed a coherent approach in the Subject's economic action process, which progresses from the purely individual sphere up to the collective forms. However, one important assumption remains, which is made in order to guarantee the link: the voluntary adherence to the collective function of cooperation, which even seems, according to certain authors, to form part of the essence of the free Subject, at least in theory. This first assumption may and must be examined critically. The voluntary abandonment of the free Subject's sovereignty is not so obviously the product of freedom itself and the identity established between the concept of the free Subject and the voluntary adherence to a collective form does not seem to be ratified by reality (the sudden emergence of others within the field of free consciousnesses is conflicting), always seems to contain a certain degree of coercion or *incentive* (motivation) which allows for different options of collective forms, in particular political ones, and therefore different combinations of economic freedom and political freedom, to be distinguished. Furthermore, a second assumption, which is no less serious, is made: the continuity of structure between individual freedom and the collective forms of economic freedom, and therefore the extension, the transfer of the project from one structure to the other, are effected without the dissolution (which may result from various forms of coercion, which are more or less visible or detectable) or disappearance of the individual Subject (replaced, for example, by a collective form which adopts the rank and status of Subject). Once again, such an assumption comes up against reality and covers a field of distinctions between several collective forms and also several combinations of forms (economic/ political). That which is called a *detour*, an important notion (the abandonment of the direct satisfaction of the design objective, which is the foundation for a circumvention or detour, within the economic organisation, e.g. a production detour), does not receive sufficient critical analysis: the collective intermediary, coercive (interventionist) or softer (corporate) forms, on which the detour is based do not, in principle, guarantee the free Subject's voluntary adherence (assumption 1) nor the preservation of the integrity of structure of the Subject's individual freedom, or of the Subject itself (assumption 2).

§ 162. The passage from the *individual* dimension (individual preferences) to the *collective* dimension (aggregation of individual preferences) can be found at the heart of the question of economic freedom (from individual freedom to collective forms of economic freedom) while constituting a serious obstacle to it. One finds, first, the individual's choice, presented as a pillar of individual freedom, which defines the individual Subject through the sum of its realisations or actions. Although, in theory, the choice of individual is total and pure, expressing a complete freedom (all the potential or instrumental freedoms are at work or accessible to the Subject), two sorts of limits emerge. The choice of the individual is considered to be distinct from that of any group which is supposed to represent it and to be preferable within a market context (and by comparison to a centralised framework); however, the insurmountable presence of the others, of others, imposes the collective form, the collective forms, even when such forms are refused or refuted (libertarianism); the collective form, even the most informal kind, remains a collective form and to struggle collectively for the cancellation of collective forms remains a collective effort. More generally, the individual Subject is intermediated in its realisations and actions, whether the abandonment of mediation (the *detour* of production or other *detour*) is granted, imposed or is invisible/unconscious. Furthermore, freedom which is presented as total may be described as effective, real or substantial, i.e. more limited (A. Sen). The first limit referred to above means both that the Subject's individual choice is necessarily constructed through the encounter with others (the regard, the conflict, the retroaction of the presence of the other or of the contact with the other), and, from this point of view, the individual choice is *already*, through its presence with regard to others, a choice which incorporates or engages a certain collective dimension (the pure individual choice is a purely theoretical view and individual freedom and individual choices must be considered as structures which are indeed individual in terms of their form but also structures for-others); that the individual preference, while remaining an autonomous form (the individual) cannot remain insensitive to other preferences, which are individual or collectively structured (group); that the individual preferences coexist at least (minimal collective form of aggregation); that such individual preferences also have to cohabit with collective preferences of groups, such groups, such as companies, intermediating (the detour), the development of the action (the realisation) of the individual Subject. Therefore, there is no pure individual choice, since the individual Subject is, from the outset, for-others. Second, the individual preferences have to coexist with the collective preferences of groups which extend and intermediate them in the realisation of their projects and actions in a more or less coercive manner, or which impose upon them more suddenly. The question of the aggregation of individual preferences in fact very often becomes that of the aggregation of collective forms which intermediate the individual (detour), and which continue to interact with the individual and its preferences. The history of individual choices is that of *detours* of action and of realisation imposed by the presence of others, and therefore that of collective forms of freedom. Economic freedom must be understood as a collective form aggregating *collective* preferences (collective forms of groups) which are supposed to extend the individual choice. The leap of this individual choice to the collective form of groups is scarcely evident, in the same way that the existence of an *optimum*, which corresponds to the aggregation of such collective forms, is not self-evident.

The individual Subject is for-others. It is freedom defined as the realisation and action process. The total and totalising nature of the concept of individual freedom, as a potentiality which is absolutely open, goes hand-in-hand with the limitations of this vital energy in real or effective terms. The capture of this totalising energy by collective forms, in various forms (group detour structures, interventionist or centralising, economic and/or political coercions), may help explain that freedom in action may be limited. What we may call *detours of freedom*, in order to indicate that free individual choices develop in the world through realisations and actions, which proceed by means of collective detours (or which are themselves collective detours). Economic freedom is a process of collective detours and the aggregation of such collective detours, therefore of the forms and structures which contain them, provides the possibility for estimating a sort of *optimum*. The *detour* (the fact that the individual pursues, whether voluntarily or involuntarily, its action and its realisations through the intermediary of collective forms) and the *transfer* (the fact that the question of individual choices is a question of the aggregation of collective forms, since only collective forms can be aggregated, since the individual-Subject is, from the outset, for-others, from its innermost structure up until the manner in which it develops in the world through its realisations), constitute two operating concepts of a theory of economic freedom.

We have moreover stated that freedom (and consequently economic freedom, which is an instrumental category of freedom, in the same way as other specific freedoms, even if economics, as we have emphasised, invade the concept of freedom through action and realisation in the modern era), is presented as total within the modern emancipation of the Subject (which merges with the economic Subject) but that freedom, in its appearances and manifestations, may be observed and described as being finally fragmented, reduced and limited. There is therefore a first paradox at work within economics, a paradox of freedom which witnesses the coexistence of a principle of energy which is vital to the very principle of the Subject's innermost structure (total freedom) and the heterogeneous manifestations, which are very unevenly distributed, of that same freedom in its various instrumental forms (e.g. elementary rights, what could be called "primary freedoms"). The difficulty in basing the conceptual foundation of the idea of collective preferences other than through the aggregation (– which is itself not easy) of the individual preferences adds to the paradox (if there are no collective preferences, then real, effective, substantial freedom – A. Sen – threatens to disappear).

It is therefore necessary both to try and understand the sources of this paradox of modern (economic) freedom and, moreover, to create the concept of collective preference *as such,* with sufficient autonomy so that it does not depend excessively on the conceptual trap which may be constituted by the idea of aggregation of individual preferences.

When the modern Subject is defined by freedom, why are so many holes found within the actual, effective map of freedom? As an initial response, one might say that the diffusion of freedom comes up against a certain number of obstacles, which will end up being removed by an enlightened and practical persistence: this is the idea of obstacles to the diffusion of freedom, a natural process frustrated by delays (this relates to a theory in favour of Progress), by inadequate forms of organisation, by a perfectible education... It would be a matter of time. And if, on the contrary, the actual, real, substantial obliteration of freedom were a consequence of freedom itself, as the same is conceived in the modern era, freedom constituting a danger for freedoms, the principle constituting a threat for the instrumental manifestations and appearances, freedom ultimately at risk from itself. The freedoms which are at issue within the instrumental manifestations of freedom (the initial freedoms, in the same way that certain authors have spoken of initial assets) do not have an essential conceptual core of freedom as a structure of the modern Subject, an obliterating, imaging and acting freedom, which continuously projects and transforms insatiety *ad infinitum.* That freedom, which forms the Subject's innermost structure of negativity (to be in a state of non-being, the driving force itself of action and realisation) supports economics in their modern essence of action and realisation. This structure of essential freedom, as we have emphasised, develops within an economic action process, one of whose features is precisely not, in the natural course of events, to attach great importance to instrumental freedoms (which explains the necessity for creating the possibility of collective forms which contain a norm, regulation), to transfer the Subject's status and structure to collective, economic forms (a centralisation of planning) and/or political forms (coercions), and ultimately to put itself at risk by becoming a danger for itself. The initial freedoms which are often at issue, whether political or economic, are *acquired* on the wave of vital energy of acting freedom which we have just discussed, *acquired* (through the norm, regulation) and not produced, moving back up an adverse flow.

There is an issue of instrumental initial freedoms *because* there is a development of the Subject's essential acting freedom. The said initial freedoms are *acquired* on the back of this development and not as a result thereof. One therefore has to distinguish freedom as a force which defines the Subject and the instrumental freedoms, which are no less important, by bearing in mind that freedom in its modern essence is action or realisation and that all the other freedoms undergo this force until certain of them are negated because they impede the development of this action process. Certain of the initial (effective) freedoms are under the threat of total and occasionally totalising development of freedom (the will) to act and to realise, within a context of individual freedoms which develop their preferences through the intermediary of collective forces (the groups, whose contours may differ), the aggregation of such collective intermediate forms (together with the form of the company) represent a sort of approximation of the collective preference; in fact, we have not adopted the concept of the collective preference since we consider, first, that individual preferences are at all times and in all places intermediated by collective intermediate forms and that there are at all times and in all places group logics (intermediate collective forms) and that the identity which establishes that collective preferences are equivalent to the aggregation (the sum) of the individual preferences is incorrect, since they are collective intermediate forms – which have to be added together or aggregated (the individual preference is not presented in a pure and naked fashion – the pure individual preference is a purely theoretical view); second, we consider that the concept of collective preference itself, which may legitimately seem to be founded on the collective economic and/or political forms (the groups) is a more or less unitary aggregation of intermediate collective forms and, all things considered, the idea *of an aggregation of intermediate collective preferences* (bearing in mind that there is no supreme or superior collective preference) seems to us to be the most relevant concept.

Chapitre 8

THE PRACTICE OF FREEDOM

(with regard to A. Sen)

1. REALISATION AND SITUATION

§ 163.   The question of economic freedom can be found within the possibility of collective choice as an aggregation of individual preferences which are each understood as a choice of that which was desired, wished for within the context of life. For certain persons, this choice, which corresponds to what was desired, constitutes effective freedom, although one is not truly aware of that which enables one to make this individual choice (which we have for our part, called a projection, a project) a reasonable choice (is not the individual wish, on the contrary, for a permanent and infinite insatiety, an unreasonable appetite which does not naturally find its norms?). Consequently, it is difficult to found (for concepts of public interest or social well-being) the collective choice (with regard to an economic freedom understood in its collective form), since nothing states that individual preferences, even if founded on a concept of effective freedom or as a capacity of individual choice for that which is desired, rather than on a concept of utility, may be individually, and collectively, standardised whilst, individually, the energy of obliterating projection (action) directed at the world seems to carry along everything in its path, including even the conflict of consciousnesses and of economic freedoms, and whilst, collectively, individual freedoms, which found individual preferences (the preference – the choice) are based on freedom, as a voluntary force to go beyond oneself/outside oneself in order to transform and do, based on freedom rather than on utility; the absolute, oblivious, powerful force which propels, projects and defines the Subject is freedom, a vital energy which is merged with that which is the Subject (it is in a state of non-being), and this vital energy precedes everything, every object, every function of utility), since such individual freedoms, which are isolated from each other in silos, find it so difficult to form the links of the collective.

The collective in the sense used by Pareto must improve the utility of each individual, but this involves an approach which defines the collective level (the collective form) of economic freedom through the function of utility. However, in our view, the individual and collective forms of preferences and choices refer back first of all to the freedom which is identified with the Subject and its action, a freedom which precedes any function of utility, which, as a force of energy and movement, precedes a design of utility; this force *is* total and seems incomprehensible, before being this or that thing, for this or that thing. Consequently, the collective form (of economic freedom) is first the expression, the external appearance of an *additional* freedom (the freedom of a collective Subject which exists in addition to the individual freedoms and Subjects, at the end of a transfer and empowerment of the collective form), which must, as we have shown, protect freedom from itself. We have, in fact, shown that the form of freedom-desire which defines the modern individual Subject and, consequently, a certain number of collective aspects of the Subject (economic, like the market, political, like an interventionist or coercive form), that this force of freedom constituted a threat for the Subject-freedom itself. Consequently, the collective is not at first defined by the utility for the individual Subject, but rather by the force of pure freedom whose structure is shared by both the individual and by the collective; the collective may therefore constitute a threat for the Subject itself, when a collective/institutional form is not attached to it containing the possibility of a norm and regulation, in order to avoid the Subject constituting a threat for the Subject (which is what it fundamentally constitutes within the modern definition which we have given it), since the collective often adds to the individual preferences as an autonomous freedom-desire (and therefore Subject); the *reasonable* collective form (of economic freedom) will be that which does indeed preserve freedom from itself as a blind force. The economic or political collective form is defined by comparison to freedom and not, at first instance, to utility. Such a collective form, when relevant, protects freedom from itself, the Subject from itself, before attempting to increase the utility of each individual.

§ 164.　　The person and the individual are the sum of their realisations. Such realisations can be identified with the sum of the appearances of the Subject. It can be said that the economic Subject, defined as acting freedom, is the sum of such realisations and, therefore, of its appearances. The realisation exposes the Subject's being, that which it is being that which it does, and therefore that which it is capable of. Freedom is merged with the practice of freedom (realisation), that which A. Sen calls substantial freedom; an act of the Subject through which the realisation (more specifically the action process) arranges for freedom to approach the world, exposes freedom as "to be done", a future capacity, potentiality or possibility.

The design exposes and reveals (economic) freedom, since the Subject's freedom and the design of the object (of the world) are one and the same. We have advanced a strong modern identity between Subject (consciousness), freedom and action (design). The design itself, as such, together with the product of such design (the object, we have used the term *"impact"*), reveal freedom as a process and economic freedom is the sum of such designs and of its impacts. Economic freedom is exposed within the very movement which it represents as an action process, i.e. an imaging and acting projection, up until impact. We have established this in *La Théorie du Sujet économique*. Economic freedom is the movement and the impact.

However, the movement which drives the process and the resulting objects or impacts do not contain an end, nor limits and there lies the paradox of freedom which we have advanced; as an imaging and acting process, which exposes the concept of freedom through its realisations and its impacts as a total and totalising force, (economic) freedom may end up exposing, through its designs and the object of its designs (the transformations of the world), *its own negation* as Subject. Here one can distinguish Sen's concept of *substantial freedom*. If the sum of the realisations actually defines economic freedom, this leads to the possibility (the probability) of the negation of (the Subject's) freedom by itself, since the power of the designs of the process of freedom has such a blind capacity to adopt itself as the object of transformation. This design may often take a collective coercive form. Consequently, the issue will be to identify *other* collective forces which may contain the possibility of a norm, in order to protect and order freedom as an imaging and acting process of the Subject.

Economic freedom as a process is exposed through the realisation itself which defines freedom and which has to be understood as, both, the path towards what has been realised, whether new or transformed, and that which has been realised or transformed. Economic freedom is, *ex post*, that which made possible the path towards the impact and the realised/transformed object, it is the path itself. And economic freedom may be understood on the basis of the object of the design and the design itself, since there is an identity between freedom, design/Subject of the design (which is created/transformed) and Subject. This field of economic freedom thus defined is infinite and that which is exposed by the *realisations* (in the sense used by A. Sen, *action/impact* in our terminology), that which is called "substantial freedom", namely the realisations which a person may benefit from, certainly characterises a field of potentialities (here one is back in the presence of the essential structure of freedom as "future", i.e. which is in a state of non-being (not-yet-being)), but cannot however imply that all realisations expose what might be called a *positive freedom*, i.e. a freedom which benefits the (individual or collective) Subject in the sense that it increases the Subject, without destroying it, within a process where freedom does not become the prey of freedom. We know that freedom is a process of creation, transformation and destruction which constitutes a serious risk for itself. *Positive freedom* is located within this limit. Beyond that, there is always a development of the process of (economic) freedom but there is a production of designs and impacts which are dangerous for freedom and for the Subject themselves (*negative freedom*). As such, the concept of "substantial freedom" (Sen) does not manage to distinguish this limit and, more fundamentally, does not analyse economic freedom as an action process which transforms the world and which completely defines the Subject and, especially, as a total and totalising process which puts freedom itself in danger, the *paradox of freedom* which we ourselves have advanced. Consequently, the distinction drawn between "substantial freedom" and "affective freedom" or "real freedom" in the sense used by Sen, must be clarified and revisited. Furthermore, if the drawing up of the collective forms of economic freedom, including the institutional forms, has to be part of the field and extent of freedoms, of freedom, i.e. of the actual field of action and realisation as a possibility for choosing such an economic action process (once again we come across this theory with Sen) – the collective form intervening in an actual, real field, i.e. *ex post*, after the realisations – once again the intervention of the relevant collective forms of economic freedom has to be determined by the necessity of *maintaining* the limit between positive freedom and negative freedom. The collective (institutional) forms of economic freedom are drawn up by reference to the limit of the territory of positive freedom and in order for economic freedom not to become a danger to itself, i.e. to the Subject.

§ 165.   If economic freedom is the whole of the realisations (in the sense used by Sen) – that which is literally realised but also the movement of realisation itself –, the whole of that which we have called the *economic action process*, with its various sequences running from the image up until impact, the whole of that which is chosen and projected, the whole of that by means of which the Subject becomes part of the world and selects itself, the whole of the *designs* (the dynamic and the energy of the design-projection are of greater importance than the object or the impact since, as we have emphasised, economic freedom and also mere freedom itself, are realisation processes and not some or other thing which is the impact of such process), if economic freedom is therefore quite whole within that which ensures that there is a *choice*, intention (to), a dynamic which we have fundamentally linked to the energy of the consciousness (of), a power of obliteration and creation (trans-formation through negativity), if economic freedom therefore lies within such a process, the factual identity established between doing and the action in the sense of the process (the realisation) and, second, the Subject and its freedom, which in effect means that the economic Subject is the sum of its appearances/realisations and that its freedom is an act, such identity nonetheless ascribes two types of limit to the issue of economic freedom: the action process which depicts the free Subject is a danger for the free Subject and the drawing up of the institutions (the norm) which are to be preserved, which we have called *positive freedom*; second, it remains difficult (impossible) to account for the freedom of choice (freedom as a choice), of the dynamic energy which ensures that there is an obliteration and that the process of creative energy and will is set in motion; it seems that we can only account for economic freedom through its appearances (i.e. the movement of its process and its impacts), since it is a peculiarity of the free economic Subject that it seems to be caught up in its realisations and the movement which it underpins. Economic freedom, and the economic Subject, are, in fact, in the modern era, defined by action and it is within the economic action process that the question of morality is also determined.

The modern economic Subject is the sum of its variations, of its manifestations, which should be understood as the whole of that which can be seen in the economic action process. In fact, the economic Subject can be seen and therefore described within this process. What is not easy to see is the essence of this process, an infinite creative energy, which is total and totalising, an obliterating impetus which continuously transforms the world at any given moment by projecting an economic Subject into it *ad infinitum*, which consequently therefore becomes apparent both to itself and to the world. Economic freedom presents itself with the most immediate and the most easily describable face, that *of impacts* in our terminology (realisations for Sen), and yet it is a dynamic process of creative energy (see *Théorie du Sujet économique*) and infinite power, a source of choices and of the whole process, a source which at the earliest stage of this energy remains difficult to describe, since this source retains a significant degree of mysterious depth and obscure density, a force which is presented, to a certain extent, beyond that which can be easily or unilaterally understood and grasped.

§ 166.   Economic freedom as a concept is total and absolute, since nothing within the essence of the concept of economic freedom, conceived as a prospecting action of the Subject over and beyond itself, can reduce or limit this development. The *substance* of (economic) freedom, if one adopts the terminology of substantial freedom (Sen) is total and totalising (this means that the development of the free economic Subject occurs at the risk of the economic Subject and of economic freedom themselves – economic freedom as a substance or the property or capacity to negate oneself).

The absolute nature of the concept of economic freedom, which may also characterise the freedom of an individual economic Subject which is alone in the world, leaves room, without disappearing, to that which we have called the collective forms of economic freedom, collective forms where the real, effective question of economic freedom can be found, since the presence of others, for the individual structure of each economic Subject and for the collective structure which gathers the individual Subjects, introduces a reality (the others) which is also a limitation; with the existence of the others and the *practical* necessity of considering economic freedom on the basis of/or means of collective forms (economics-planning, market-political, institutional), economic freedom becomes a concept *in situ* and the collective forms of economic freedom are forms of *economic freedom in situ* (this concept intersects in part the field of the concepts of *effective* freedom or *real* freedom, as described by certain authors, e.g. A. Sen once again). The collective forms of economic freedom, while developing from the absolute structure of the initial concept of economic freedom – as witness the totalising temptations of numerous collective, economic and/or political forms, setting themselves up as it were as an absolute collective Subject – are forms *in situ*, marked by a logic of constraints (which are not merely budgetary), which characterise all the choices. The collective forms of economic freedom constitute *relative* notions. The tension, at the very heart of the concept of economic freedom, between the absolute nature of the structure of individual freedom and the relative nature (*in situ*) of the collective forms, forms the very issue of economic freedom. Although the substance of economic freedom (substantial freedom for A. Sen) is absolute and allows one to consider *all* the choices and all the realisations, within a process which progresses from the Subject towards the world of realisations and objects, many people consider that the *real* or *effective* nature of economic freedom is determined within the collective forms, which will, first, state the possible realisations (selection, valuation, elimination) and therefore ratify, *ex post*, as it were, as part of a logic which runs from the development (realisation) process of economic freedom in action/*in situ* towards the ratification of the specific contents of economic freedom (which A. Sen calls the substantial freedoms); second, certain such collective freedoms will state the norm and regulation by stating the extent of the concept of economic freedom, i.e. the field of freedoms *in situ* (effective or real for A. Sen), by preserving them or even by increasing their influence.

§ 167.   Economic freedom is *in situ*. Furthermore, the total and simultaneously insatiable nature of the concept of economic freedom (which merges with that of the economic Subject) exposes the process of economic freedom to a dynamic of creative and totalising energy, which will be all the stronger since this dynamic is and remains in a state of insatiety (to be in a state of non-being); and second, to the necessity, as a result, of tracing lines in order to protect the process from the very dynamic which inhabits it.

2. The utility of (economic) freedom

§ 168.   One would therefore have to account for the economic Subject's freedom to choose by moving backwards as it were from what becomes of the economic action process (the development of freedom) during the realisations and impacts, therefore by moving backwards from that which holds itself out as a *utility* and towards freedom (freedoms first of all, since the concept of economic freedom can be seen through its specific manifestations based on an initial, unilateral concept of economic freedom), a freedom which is therefore revealed by the action process, which mobilises the functions of utility. However, this does not ultimately tell us much about the choice of realisation itself, its extent, its determining factors (the realisation reveals the function of choice of realisation), nor whether that which is realised on the basis of the functions of utility still remains, within the context of an exercise of freedom or, on the contrary, exceeds the limit of *positive freedom* which we have discussed, where freedom negates itself (coercion, negative freedom).

With regard to the first point, we have already indicated the difficulty and the limit represented by the identity between the realisation (action) and the freedom of action (of realisation), since economic freedom, as a concept, can be seen through its appearances, i.e. in the very process of the development of action by the Subject. There is no access to anything other than that which can be seen through the process. *Economic freedom is, at any given time, the sum of its actions* (appearances). However, as we have stressed, (economic) freedom remains, at any given time, in its capacity as a concept, a source of energy, an absolute, total and totalising matrix, which means that, if it is true that we only have access (through knowledge) to that which is acted/realised/done, the movement which contains the action process does not for its part cease to persevere in its being, and therefore potentially, to open up new paths, new realisations, and therefore to reveal economic freedom in new definitions and extents. In passing, it can be seen that the functions of utility are to some extent *taken up* by the economic action process as by the flow of a river of ice and defined, within a pure identity once again, through the action and flow of the process. The utility is provided by that which can be seen within the economic action process, which as a result reveals the concept of economic freedom. (Economic) freedom is a paradoxical concept, in the sense that an accessible meaning is totally contained within its manifestations and, at the same time, it remains a form of primary energy, which is obscure and hard to access. As such, it is not the function of utility which triggers the Subject's economic action process but *there is a* trigger and then realisations which may be interpreted as utilities. The essence of economic freedom can be found over and beyond the utilities and, yet, only the product of the functions of utility provides an opportunity to go back upstream to the principle of freedom.

As for the second point, it can be seen that the practical identity between economic freedom and realisations (freedom of realisation and realisation) creates a considerable ambiguity, since everything that is realised, or more generally everything which may result from the Subject's action process, whether it relates to a movement of the process itself or objects which are targeted or "created", is to some extent identified with freedom or with a freedom, a systematic process of revelation. This latter process encounters a limit (all that is action reveals or indicates freedom, a freedom; all that is realised reveals or indicates a freedom of realisation). Such an identity ends up ratifying a totalising version of the Subject's action process as (economic) freedom and of economics in general. Such an identity can only be framed on the basis of relevant collective forms which may contain a norm and regulation, and the possibility of demonstrating a *limit* to the development process of economic freedom which, in fact, has no limits.

§ 169.   We have advanced the absolute, total and totalising nature of the initial concept of (economic) freedom which at first only applies, especially and solely for the Subject taken as an individual. This freedom is absolute, in the sense that *everything* may be projected, anticipated and realised within the economic action process as described by us (*Théorie du Sujet économique*). Freedom is without limits and the capacity to obliterate reality which characterises it, from the image to the object, from imaging consciousness to acting consciousness, is infinite in conceptual terms, which bestows upon it an unsettling nature, since it is totalising. This initial concept of economic freedom may be compared, even though it is different, to that of substantial freedom (the essence, the substance of economic freedom), since the essence of economic freedom lies in the limitless development of the creative energy of obliteration. The limits and the relative nature of the concept stem from the existence and the conflicting presence of others, which imposes collective structures and forms, certain of which contain a norm and state the limit between positive freedom and negative freedom (freedom negates itself). Consequently, adopting our approach, economic freedom and economic freedoms, which are selected in order to define a sort of collective optimum, within the framework of collective forms and the exercise of regulation starting with the norms borne by institutional forms, this set of economic freedoms (effective, real economic freedom) appears in our analysis as a result of the development of the absolute initial freedom up until the collective forms, where the real and effective forms of freedoms for optimality and well-being are located. These are *practical initial freedoms*, whose structure and extent will vary over time and in accordance with the action processes (we will return later to the spatio-temporal structure of economic freedom by demonstrating that its innermost practical matter is made up of duration, memory and forgetfulness, in coherence with the structure of the economic Subject described by us). Although the concept of "substantial freedom" (A. Sen) has certain similarities with that of the absolute and total initial freedom which we have described, by reference to an unobservable essence, an infinite time which is open to what-is-to-come and what-is-to-be-done (that which could be done, may be done, could have been done) and an individualistic reality (which precedes any question relating to the conflicting existence of others), the substantial freedom in the sense used by A. Sen is, however, limited in two ways, by the reduced number of substantial freedoms which are finally selected, through the selection mode (revelation through realisation), and finally by the moral content which it contains, an *optimum* of utility which reveals the substantial freedom, which the individual may benefit from, the substantial freedom incorporating *from the outset* an ethical content, a propensity to help contribute to well-being, and in general a capacity to establish a collective equilibrium of well-being and ethical code which A. Sen fails to explain (it is not stated *how* the process of revelation of substantial freedom, through the action process and the object, arrives at this final selection). This constitutes a serious obstacle.

For our part, the relative domain of practical (actual, real) freedoms selected by the collective forms of economic freedom (market or others), selected and framed both on the basis of a logic of utility for the action, realisation, impact and object, and on the basis of a logic of a norm contained by certain collective or institutional forms which state the limit of the development of freedom and the conditions for a possible moral code, which we have explained (see *Théorie du Sujet économique*). At the same time, we maintain an absolute and total initial freedom, the essence of freedom and of the Subject, which contains to carry the energy which develops within the action process and which constitutes the innermost matter of the Subject's structure (whether individual or collective), thus ensuring the structural continuity of economic freedom. Furthermore, the arrival of the question and of the contents of a moral code within economic freedom, which is heaven-sent if one adopts A. Sen's approach within the concept of substantial freedom, takes place with some difficulty, if one adopts our approach (since here it is a formidable obstacle) and subject to conditions, through collective forms and the structure of duration and memory, practical forms of economic freedom.

§ 170.   The concept of economic freedom contains a structure which is the same as that of the economic Subject (*Théorie du Sujet économique*), and in the modern age, the two are merged. The primary matter, which is the subject of the consciousness's obliterating design (the very definition of freedom), a design which enables the Subject to become apparent to itself and to form itself, is time. The time of the economic Subject is that of economic freedom and *duration*, which is obliterated by memory and forgetfulness. These operations of the consciousness, these *acts*, are effected within a specific space-time reference frame, which we have extensively described in *La dynamique boursière* and in *Théorie du Sujet économique*, and which is marked by duration/ memory/forgetfulness, as well as by discontinuities and dilations.

This means that the free economic Subject is a Subject which remembers and forgets and that the very fact of being located within this dimension of duration (there is no relevant distinction between the past, present and future), of memory and forgetfulness is enough to define economic freedom. There cannot on the one hand be an economic Subject and on the other economic freedom (freedoms), the Subject acquiring such freedoms in the same way that one can target an object at the end of a process. There is indeed an economic action process of the Subject directed at the world which corresponds to freedom in its development. However, *the economic Subject is economic freedom.* This fundamental identity implies that economic freedom *is not like an object* which is attained at the end of a design; economic freedom is the very movement of the design, a much more extensive meaning of realisation (over and beyond that which is realised). Consequently, it can be understood that economic freedom is duration, a mobilisation of time-matter of the Subject and of the action process, memory and forgetfulness, within the very movement of the process itself but also, if the impact occurred at the end of the action process, when, within the object, there remains a structure which bears a trace of the process.

Economic freedom is a *Subject*. Our language often transforms it into an object, with a plural form which accentuates the transfer of status (the freedoms). Economic freedom always bears a trace of a genetic heritage of duration and memory, since economic freedom does indeed emerge from somewhere. Real, actual economic freedom (in the sense used by A. Sen), which we have called practical freedom, freedom which may wrongly be assumed to be an object, such freedom (such freedoms) are always and at all times characterised by a DNA of duration and memory, which provides a genetic map and a territory for a norm and a moral code. Moreover, this is a question of living, conceptual organisms, for the same reasons, since duration, memory and forgetfulness are in discontinuous movement within the reference frame formed by all three, in order to define both the Subject and economic freedom.

Economic freedom, as energy of creation, i.e. of obliteration, starting from imagination and going up to the impact within the action process (imagination and action are the one and only reality of the process of economic freedom), is, in the final analysis, an energy, which has indeed emerged from somewhere and is thus sustained by that which lasts and which carries along with it, like a river carries along blocks of ice, like so many pieces of that which has occurred or rather which leaves a trace, a river of ice which appears to move slowly but which can race away. Economic freedom is like a flow of duration, driven by that which is remembered or is forgotten.

Economic freedom, specific economic freedoms (described by some authors as "instrumental") are always constructed on the basis of that which has occurred (*the situation* characterising any parametric transformation of action at a given moment in time), whether it relates to a vision of flows of (economic) freedom – understood as energy and surpassment of that which lasts and based on that which lasts, this energy being formed within duration itself and within the memory recalls and lapses – or the vision of a stock of economic freedom (some or other freedom, which is justified, *ex post*, as it were, by the action which makes it possible). In both cases, which are fairly distinct (*an* economic freedom, which is linked to a given action, *the* economic freedom, which is in turn linked to the Subject as it is), there is a link with the time-matter which constitutes the flow (the imaging and acting projection of the Subject-consciousness) and the stock (the object-freedom, *a* specific freedom whose structure incorporates duration, memory and forgetfulness). *The* economic freedom and *the* economic freedoms are developing processes, whose movement occurs within a specific space-time reference frame, in the same way as the individual or collective *preferences* contain an adaptive dimension, i.e. form part of a process structured by duration, memory and forgetfulness.

§ 171. The individual preference is foremost within an approach of economic freedom whose concept is absolute and total and for which the individual is the starting point. Without going back to this assumption which forms the foundation for the modern era, two essential elements complete the concept of economic freedom, understood as an expression of preference. We have already stated that the structure of the individual's choices and preferences (individual freedom) cannot, as it were, be alone in the world and must have emerged from somewhere; the structure of individual preferences is, from the outset, for-others, i.e. the existence of others and the conflicting and structural presence of others is, from the outset, within the constitution of the individual economic Subject. There is not, on the one hand, the individual and, on the other, a collective body which is made up of a sum or aggregation of individuals. There is, from the outset, a collective structure of the individual when one refers to the *individual* or to individual freedom, within the economic discipline, it involves, from the outset, a structure which is defined by its otherness, by otherness, its openness, in its essence (since the Subject is an openness towards that which is to come, which is in a state of non-being), which is not reflected by the usual analyses of the economic individual (*homo economicus*). The otherness of the individual economic Subject and its dimension for-others are the first element which must be incorporated in any theory of individual preference.

The second element, which is just as essential, is contained within the structure of duration, memory and forgetfulness of the individual preference (which stems from the very structure of the economic Subject, which we have described on the basis of a specific space-time reference frame and, in particular, from a time-matter of duration, which is stimulated and distorted by the memory/forgetfulness pairing (memory *recall*, memory lapse, since it relates to designs, intentionalities). There cannot be a consciousness or economic action design, a setting in motion of the economic action process *ex nihilo*, although there is, in fact, an indefinable form of ultimate creative design, which sets the movement in motion. However, this design (this creative energy) is always based on an accumulated time-matter, a memory of past action processes, of their realisations, a memory of that which, over all, has already been revealed and exposed to the economic Subject itself. And everything which surrounds and structures the Subject.

At each moment, the individual preference, the choice, i.e. the manifestation of the Subject's individual economic freedom, engages or involves a set of blocks of duration, pieces of wax which are animated (in the sense of *anima*) by memory and forgetfulness, through the designs of the Subject's consciousness which are located at the source of the economic action process, since memory and forgetfulness must be seen as vital forces, as creative energy of the economic Subject defined as a free consciousness (there is an identity, in our description, between consciousness and freedom).

The individual preference is expressed within the instantaneity of the act of the free imaging and acting consciousness, but starting from/with a substance of duration and memory. This substance, this level which sustains economic action and economic freedom, incorporates, from the outset, all the manifestations of freedom, the realisations of the free economic action and, therefore, all that which could already be seen of economic freedom and mere freedom itself. The individual preference, because it is launched from a level of duration and memory, incorporates from the outset all the appearances of economic freedom (specific or instrumental freedoms, if one adopts the terms which we have used), i.e. *the economic freedoms which the action process has revealed* (which A. Sen calls substantial freedoms).

It can thus be understood that within the economic action process, where the economic freedom develops (which is revealed in turn by the action process as specific-substantial freedom, to use A. Sen's words), it is not, at first, a matter of accumulation of assets, of things, of real objects nor of producing an actual impact of transformation or growth through action (although this is featured in full within the dynamic of the economic action process), but rather an accumulation of time-duration, of time-memory and through that an accumulation of that which has been realised and, by being realised, revealed as economic freedom.

The free economic action process is a revelation process of freedom. The individual preference is a memory recall or lapse of an accumulation of actions, of action processes and of manifestations of freedom. It is through such essential plans that the *function of utility* develops, which consequently acquires a new meaning. Utility cannot therefore be assessed solely on the basis of the *impact* (transformation, realisation of the object, increase of the object itself, i.e. growth) but rather that which is *useful*, for the individual economic Subject, within the action process which projects towards and in the world, literally takes "on board", takes account of and incorporates everything about the Subject and its freedom, which duration and memory keep a trace of. The function of utility is a *proprietary* function and is *for-others*, namely the two elements which we have stated above (presence, from the outset, of others within the structure of the individual preference and, more generally, within the constitution of the economic Subject; the proprietary and therefore adaptive structure of preference and of choice which therefore refer to the specific space-time regimes which we have described (*La dynamique boursière, Théorie du Sujet économique*), in particular through their discontinuities. The economic (individual) preference and the free individual choice satisfy a logic (process) of proprietary utility in the precise sense that that which engages a realisation (i.e. the economic action process), *recalls* that which engages economic freedom, to be qualified by the heritage of economic freedom itself. Economic freedom has, already, left a trace, is already revealed by the Subject's actions and realisations; this memory recall of the heritage of economic freedom (substantial freedoms in the sense used by A. Sen) is involved in the Subject's function of utility.

Utility reveals the economic freedom within the development of the action process which characterises the modern Subject. The pure design of acting directed at the world (imagination, conception, realisation, transformation, sedimentation of the impact of the object into an *object*) incorporates a function of utility (answering the following questions: for what utility does the economic Subject do this? What is the decisive determining factor of the design? Which element drives the Subject within this process?) but this function of utility cannot be solely and narrowly defined by the *impact*, as is often the case. If one indeed wishes to take an interest in the whole of the action process, as described by us, it then appears that utility is first of all the process and the realisation which enables the economic Subject to be understood as freedom, thus through the specific manifestations of some or other economic freedom. The initial force and creative energy which ensure that there is a design, rather than nothing, undoubtedly remain, in the final analysis, not very accessible and this energy constitutes the essential determining factor of the movement of action which reveals freedom. This leads to a certain paradox where, in a certain manner, the initial force of freedom and action remains obscure and difficult to reduce to a useful reason; human action is involved. The economic Subject acts beyond any explanations of a useful reason, even if the latter enables one to understand the motives for such action.

Utility is that which reveals, within the same movement, that which can be done (which A. Sen calls effective freedom) and that which might be done (freedom as a future potential) within a given framework of possibilities (freedoms) of realisation.

Any action process of the economic Subject which establishes, through the act of revealing, a capacity/possibility of doing is called a function of utility. Utility encounters the limits of (economic) freedom itself, when freedom, as we have shown, constitutes a danger for itself. *Disutility* then appears.

Such a function of utility is founded within the structure of individual preference (the choice). The choice (the individual preference) is a revelation of freedom (as a potentiality) through the revelation of specific (effective, real) freedoms, whose structure is a negative of the action itself (acting reveals what is possible for free action, therefore the freedom of realisation itself). This is what we call utility, whose horizon is interrupted at the moment when freedom takes itself as prey or as target for the action, where desire (which wills itself) dominates the concept of freedom, where the completion of the acting projection ends up negating any future projection and the Subject itself.

Economic freedom does not target, in its capacity as action process, any object in particular, nor any object in general. Economic freedom is quite complete in the manifestation of preference, of choice, within utility as we have defined it, i.e. within the field of that which it is possible to realise, which has already been realised and therefore revealed as real specific (effective) freedom or which might be in the future (as such, we can see that economic freedom has a heritage, namely all the realisations/actions which have been effected and which have revealed the same number of specific freedoms; that economic freedom as a revelation process of that which has not yet been is not launched from nothing but from this heritage of effective freedoms which link, in a close and necessary manner, an action and the capacity of choice/preference; that economic freedom is therefore an adaptive process of memory and duration).

Economic utility is not defined by comparison with an object which it targets as a free economic Subject but by comparison with the field of action and of expression of preferences which is accessible to the Subject either immediately (because they are already realised) or potentially (because economic freedom is a cumulative hereditary process, where the effected/real freedoms, i.e. that which has been realised and revealed, the capacity, the choice to do, constitute the structure of that which might still be done, not *ad infinitum* but up to the limit of that which we have called positive freedom).

Even though the concept of economic freedom seems to be adorned with the instantaneity of *ex-nihilo* creations, it involves a hereditary and therefore proprietary and cumulative process (which does not mean that there is continuity, on the contrary) which is drawn up and constructed on the successive revelations through action or the realisation of the capacity of choice and preference to act.

§ 172.   For A. Sen, the object reveals freedom (which he calls "substantial") as a capacity of utilisation (function of utility) and of realisation of a certain number of actions which the Subject may realise. Freedom is presented after the event and is very close to utility, since freedom is the capacity to realise that which is useful for the Subject, i.e. to utilise its *relevant* environment (all objects do not contain the same internal *requirement* to be used by mobilising a freedom). (Economic) freedom is therefore presented *ex post* and the Subject is, *ex ante*, dominated/ crushed by a world of objects and effective or potential realisations which by their sole, absurd presence, summon a creation of meaning through the revelation of the freedom implied by their presence.

A. Sen's analysis contains a certain realism in the sense that it starts with the object and in fact points out from the start, involving a paradox which is also a weakness (the objects and realisations already present in the analysis stem from a concept of freedom and economic action process), that economic freedom is not necessarily fairly distributed (A. Sen makes an implied criticism of the absolute and total nature of the concept of freedom, of the idea that, despite an unequal distribution, the effective and real freedoms may always be based, for the purposes of their development and the extension of their domain, on a concept of unitary freedom – there are only realities, aspects or realisations, each of which conceals a freedom, in the same way one turns over a stone).

Such an analysis, by means of exaggeration, establishes that the object precedes freedom, that the realisation precedes freedom and, therefore, that the free economic Subject can only be revealed by starting with objects and realisations. Economic freedom is that which, *ex post*, gives meaning to a *certain* number of objects and realisations, which must be stated, formalised or *acquired after a brave struggle* in respect of the object, the world. A. Sen's view is that of an economic freedom of struggle, where the economic Subject is finally effaced, appears not to be very powerful, where it is a question of tearing the meaning of freedom out of the world of objects and realisations in order to create the Subject. And yet such objects which, if one adopts A. Sen's approach, are our starting point, *already* bear witness to the Subject's economic action process, continuously and *ad infinitum*. Accordingly, this analysis ultimately fails to state - even if it clearly contains the concern of a realistic pessimism to restore a greater degree of equity in the distribution of freedoms, based on the possible freedoms revealed by the objects and realisations, - the logic of proliferation of such objects and realisations, which nevertheless however to contain the concept of freedom and of action and, at the same time, the limit of freedom.

A. Sen does not therefore go back to the unitary concept of freedom which, in our view, determines the logic of realisations and objects, where the difficulties legitimately raised by A. Sen are located. The realist (or fatalist) view, which involves commencing the search with the object in order to establish a freedom, leaves intact the question of the formation of objects and economic action processes which, in our view, involve the economic freedom and Subject from the outset and at a very early stage.

In our view, as we have demonstrated, freedom (i.e. the Subject) is the source of the action process (which reveals/uncovers the freedom), which leads to the impact (and to the objects which totalise the impacts). The free Subject dominates the world, which it transforms and distorts until it negates freedom and until it negates itself. Freedom thus remains a paradoxical matter and only the appropriate collective institutional forms which contain a norm and regulation can state the limit, in order for freedom to remain positive. Economic freedom is determined within the collective forms which face, or even organise, the otherness of the Subject (of freedom), i.e. the presence of others and the difficulty in gathering the individual preferences, which may seem not to have any bridges between them. In our view, the concept of (economic) freedom is unitary, total and absolute and provides the principal structure for the individual preference, the choice (which does not mean that it does not stem from a heritage, on the contrary, since duration and memory constitute the innermost matter of the concept). The unitary, total and absolute nature of the Subject's concept of freedom (and therefore of the individual preference, which allows one to understand the difficulty in aggregating the individual preferences, not because they are different, which they are, but because they express an absolute and totalising structure; consequently, there is therefore a difficulty in creating aggregated social choices, public interest or social well-bring), this unitary nature remains present throughout the whole of the economic action process, of which it constitutes the framework, up until impact and the formation of objects. However, manifestations (apparitions) of economic freedom (the specific, i.e. effective or real, economic freedoms) are determined (i.e. are constituted) within various collective forms (market, Plan...) which do more than aggregate the Subjects and individual preferences (the collective preference is not a sum or even a function, in principle a stable function, of individual preferences but something else, of a specific nature, since there is an empowerment of the collective form in its capacity as Subject, which can consequently be found in interaction with the individual Subjects). The economic freedoms are determined here, within this tension between the individual and the collective, which is arbitrated by the institutional, regulatory and normative forms.

Although freedom remains absolute, the effective economic free-doms are the product of collective forms, whose very existence and constitution create and impose a function of constraint on individual choices. The effective freedoms contain both a limit (they only partially reflect an absolute freedom, of which they are manifestations or apparitions; but the concept of initial freedom remains absolute) and a constraint (contrary to what is often stated, the specific (effective) economic freedoms are collective and not individual structures, since they are produced by autonomous collective forms which are often structured like (collective) Subjects).

Utility is determined within the tension between the individual Subject and the collective form when, in one form or another (market, Plan...), economic freedom appears as the issue at stake. It is not the object or the realisation which reveals the freedom, whether such freedom is said to be effective (established, perennial and reproducible capacity to act) or potential (substantial, i.e. future force of action, latent strength). Freedom is uncovered within the action process itself, which reveals the Subject as Subject. The economic freedoms are revealed by the collective forms which face the individual preferences and the preservation of the individual field of capacity of choice and of preference subject to the constraint of the collective form and the limit which distinguishes positive freedom and negative freedom (when the potential force of freedom produces realisations and objects which negate freedom and the Subject themselves). The utility lies in the preservation of this individual field and the *optimum* is defined on the basis of this utility.

The *optimum*, in our approach, therefore progresses from freedom towards the object (impact) through utility, which is a function of the collective forms, the latter containing the real or effective freedoms, which are of a collective and not an individual nature. If the individual, in its capacity as economic Subject, is characterised by a total and absolute freedom, which structures its action design towards the object (and this freedom is force, a creative energy, a sudden appearance, which resists explanation and reason, or understanding), the effective (economic) freedom of this same economic Subject can be found in the collective forms which are constructed on the basis of/beyond individual preferences and individual economic Subjects, and the function of utility defines which part of the force of the initial individual freedom which targets the object is as it were "acceptable", or one could say "worth trying", in the sense that such design, when faced with other designs within a collective field (market, plan, collective economic and/or political forms), manages to express itself, without crushing or being crushed by other individual designs or the collective form itself (which is often endowed with a structure of the economic Subject, which contains its own design). An *optimum* therefore exists, which defines this playing field of what is "acceptable", which incorporates the institutional forms which contain the possibility of a norm and regulation (see *Théorie du Sujet économique*). It is within this field of tensions between the individual and collective that the *optimum* can be found. The objects of the economic design cannot by themselves reveal the utilities and, by the same route, the freedoms, since all the objects do not in fact correspond to impacts of design originating in an "acceptable" field, and therefore do not correspond to what we have defined as utility, which means that they do not reveal an effective freedom (a positive freedom, if one adopts the terminology used above), and on the contrary correspond to different forms of coercion and constraints, which negate the economic Subject as Subject. The concept of *positive freedom* which we use does not correspond precisely to that of essential fundamental freedoms but rather to a group of associations [individual designs/collective forms] which constitute a field where trade-off can be considered "acceptable", the whole of such associations corresponding to the possible *optima* for the economic Subject within a collective framework, i.e. incorporating within a unified field, first the individual preferences and, second, as if superimposed, one or more collective preferences, constructed as the empowerment of a group design, the group becoming economic Subject as a collective form.

It remains difficult to define and express a collective choice or a collective preference. What do we mean when we talk of a collective choice? We come up against, first, the individualistic nature of the concept of freedom (defined by individual preferences and choices) and, second, the presence of a function of utility which encompasses an ethical dimension (which amounts to defining utility in a manner other than the usual one), and finally the temptation of identifying a certain number of "basic" freedoms as the platform for a collective choice (which at least links the individual and the collective) and also for a certain code of ethics (certain authors talk of a "good life").

We have shown that, although the concept of (economic) freedom does not, in fact, propose a principle of aggregation as such, the individual (economic Subject) is in fact for-others in its very constitution, the effective freedoms being defined within collective spaces, and that, finally, the collective forms produce collective Subjects, i.e. an individuation of groups.

3. CAPACITY, POSSIBILITY, PREFERENCES

§ 173.   Furthermore, the definition of collective choices (collective pre-ferences) must incorporate, first, the absolute and totalising nature of the concept of freedom (which makes it necessary for there to be collective forms which contain the possibility of a norm) and, second, a time-matter made up of duration and memory (and forgetfulness), which explains the adaptive and persistent nature of the (individual and collective) preferences, the said persistence providing a key to the comprehension of "moral values", and finally the presence within the concept of freedom of two sources of choice, *capacity* (a total and absolute *possibility*, to be understood as counterparty for the nature of projection of freedom, which is still to come, rather than an effective, established, technical, social or political capacity: the Subject is, in its essence, pure possibility, and therefore *all* possibilities), and *realisation* (that which has actually already been realised, i.e. that which we called the *impact* of the economic action process in *Théorie du Sujet éco-nomique*), the realisations constituting the innermost time-matter of duration and memory, which structures the concept of economic freedom and produces persistence, adaptability and, in general, ensures that economic freedom is a concept which remembers, a concept which is *in situ*, i.e. which takes on board blocks of duration and realisations, where freedom is experienced, which defines the effective/real fields for economic freedom and the specific freedoms, endowed with memory – there is a close link between such memory and that which we call moral values, feelings – while leaving completely open the field of *possibilities* for economic freedom, such possibilities being based, at all times and in all places, on a heritage of realisations (duration/memory), which constitutes their DNA.

One therefore has to distinguish between economic freedom as a *possibility* (or *total and absolute capacity*, which defines the economic Subject's essence – which we have called *initial freedom*), which forms the foundation for the economic action process, with which economic freedom and the economic Subject are merged, i.e. the process of realisation, of realisations (which we call *impacts*), of economic freedom as *effective realisation* (or, consequently, *relative capacity*, i.e. established capacity to have been able to effect or realise, at a given moment in time, and, therefore, capacity to repeat, to renew, to reproduce or to produce persistence, which explains the importance of the phenomena of duration and memory within the process of economic freedom). Economic freedom as relative capacity is the field of specific freedoms as realisations, even if the realisation never manages to achieve something in itself: economic freedom must be seen as a *process*, i.e. a flow structured by duration and memory/forgetfulness, within a specific space-time reference frame which is that of the economic Subject. Economic freedom remains fundamentally as *capacity*, both absolute and relative, and possibility, i.e. a projection of doing in the mode of to-be-done and its being is, in its essence, in a state of non-being; accordingly, even that which seems to be fixed within the world, through the realisation and through the object, which produces an impact, therefore specific economic freedoms (some or other freedom), are not and never will of themselves be in-itself, but on the contrary, always shaped by the internal flow of duration, of memory or of the persistence, which enables the continuities and the proprietary origins to be identified, but also with spatio-temporal discontinuities, which are specific to the economic Subject's reference frame. The effective economic freedoms (i.e. effective, realised at least once), therefore form part of a heritage, which will or will not be recalled by the function of memory/forgetfulness, within the economic action process.

As such, economic freedom can be described as a flow of duration with persistencies and discontinuities, a duration sustained by the realisations and impacts and, ultimately, a total and absolute action capacity of infinite possibilities, which define the concept of freedom, with regard to *situations*, which are in turn completed. The principal such finitude is the existence of others, which imposes the effective, i.e. real, field of economic freedom, therefore of specific economic freedoms (the capacities realised, effected or manifested): the collective forms. The *collective form*, plan, market, political or other entity, constitutes the effective field of real development of economic freedom.

The collective form therefore forms the foundation for the collective choice (the collective preference), because it constitutes the effective/ real field of development of economic freedom, i.e. the *situation* of the economic Subject and of its freedom (a situation marked in particular by the formative presence of others, by phenomena which are hereditary, i.e. persistent, cumulative and supported by a non-linear function of memory). Individual freedom does not seem to propose a principle of aggregation of preferences but, at the same time, the *individual economic Subject is condemned to the collective form*, as the situation for the development and constitution of its freedom (the individual Subject, as we have stated, is, from the outset, for-others; purely individual freedom is a fiction; the notion of for-others requires the collective form; economic freedom can only be manifested through collective forms).

Economic freedom is incorporated within the field of the collective form as a process of action/realisation which, before even producing objects (this is not the essential issue), produces specific economic freedoms, which define the *optima* for the pairings [individual-preferences/collective preferences] (i.e. choice of the collective body, of the group as Subject). Such *optima* cannot be attained without the existence of collective forms which contain the norm (itself a hereditary function of duration and memory, which incorporates that which may be concealed by the term "feelings and moral values"), since the collective forms, if left to their own devices within the natural tension which exists between individual preferences and independent and individuated preferences of groups (collective choice), do not manage, in a spontaneous manner, to prevent the risk of the negation of freedom by freedom, of the negation of the Subject by the Subject. This risk includes the difficulty of the process of economic freedom to attain, in a spontaneous manner, the *optima* which establish the principles of equality of freedoms, of definition of basic, effective freedoms or of justice before freedom.

There is accordingly a foundation for the collective choices and preferences but there is no natural path towards a spontaneous social equilibrium (*optimum*).

§ 174.   Freedom is defined as *capacity* (*effective capacity* by A. Sen, i.e. the individual's capacity to exercise a freedom in relation to one or more objects). The capacity to realise, i.e. the capacity to implement effectively in a given context is also important for A. Sen. Finally, the distinction between action and well-being (an action may well not procure well-being, a "good life") involves a reference frame of economic freedom which encompasses a moral code and a new function of utility.

We define freedom as a *possibility* (to be in a state of non-being), which involves a *total and absolute capacity*. The initial freedom is absolute and the fact that such freedom is distributed in a heterogeneous or unequal manner – this is the reality of observation – cannot prevent the individual as Subject from being defined as an energy of capacity and possibility (consciousness of projection and creation of oneself and of the world). The increase of freedom (i.e. of specific freedoms) is an objective of human society: such an increase (accepted by A. Sen) cannot be established without simultaneously establishing an absolute and total principle for freedom. And, moreover, how should one segment such a concept? By starting with the effectiveness of reality, with "substantial" freedoms, A. Sen constructs a partial, segmented concept of freedom, while founding a development logic based on the increase of freedoms, which amounts to advancing, at least *ex post* (but also *ex ante*), the theoretical element of an absolute horizon of possibility for freedom.

This does not mean, on the contrary, that such freedom is without constraint. It is and this is what we have called the economic Subject's *situation*. The economic Subject's *situation* includes all sorts of elements, which far exceed the few very simplistic variables of prices and budgets alone (such variables are said to be "economic", although economics express in the modern age the entirety of the Subject's relationship with the world). One therefore finds, within the concept of *situation*, as it were, *everything else* (in the sense in which we used this term in *La dynamique boursière*), i.e. blocks of time-matter made up of duration, adopting, like fossils, multiple realisations, points of view, moral judgements (...), a matter driven by the dynamic of memory and forgetfulness.

The free Subject is *in situ* and this situation is chosen (assumed) by the Subject at any time by surpassing it (to be in a state of non-being).

This *situation* constitutes a specific space-time reference frame structured by duration, memory and forgetfulness (see *Théorie du Sujet économique*). The theory of freedom is a theory of the situation. One can also find within this situation, from the outset, the others, a piece of information which structures the Subject and the freedom, which is the basis for the legitimacy of collective forms as the place of production of effective freedoms.

If economic freedom stems from freedom as a concept and in particular from the absolute possibility as total capacity which characterises the Subject, the adjective "economic" is there in order to state something else in a different manner, which is not strictly speaking only the concept of freedom. Many analyses of A. Sen thus hold true for the concept of freedom, before they are possibly (not always) applied specifically to *economic* freedom.

We have established, from the outset, that the *economic* Subject was defined by the *action* process directed at the world, from image to impact, in a logic of creation and transformation, which is total and absolute and therefore exposed, at any given moment, to the risk of negating itself. Economic freedom is therefore paradoxical, continuously running the risk of disappearing, together with the economic Subject, a victim of itself. This is the special nature of economic freedom and of the economic Subject. Economics stated in the modern age man's relationship with the world and the concept of the economic Subject is the impetus of freedom as an action process, with which it is merged. This process develops within a *situation*, which structures a reference frame of memory and forgetfulness, a reference frame which also incorporates the components of a moral code (see *Théorie du Sujet économique*).

We stress the disturbing strength of the modern concept of (economic) freedom, which is shaped from the inside by that of desire, a desire which wills itself. We stress the risk that economics pose to the Subject and its relationship with the world.

This means that the process of (economic) freedom must be protected from itself by collective forms which produce a norm and regulation. It is of its essence to persevere in its being.

Furthermore, and because we call "economic" a much wider field than that which is usually understood, the concept of economic freedom must itself be more widely understood and in any case well beyond the narrow understanding of an exclusive relationship between the Subject and the object.

The modern economic Subject remains absolutely free, choosing a situation at any given moment, in order to surpass it. The economic Subject has no other choice but to make this choice (it is condemned to do so). This active pessimism leads to a total freedom in conceptual terms and, also, to a theory of the Subject as action over the world, which contains a dynamic without limits, since the Subject or its environment are unable to produce a norm or a moral code.

For us, the economic Subject is absolutely free, so absolutely that it has no other choice than to surpass its *situation* by acting. The value attached to this action lies in the said surpassment, rather than in the object targeted or in the actual impact itself. Although the individual economic Subject has no other *fundamental* choice (initial choice) than to surpass its situation, such surpassment being effected in the context of collective forms (groups), paradoxically it very often remains far-removed from the actual exercise of basic freedoms.

§ 175.   *Freedom is freedom of choice.* Not to choose to act, in principle for a design of creation/transformation of an object, is another choice. Or to act for other designs or reasons than the object, is yet another choice. That which A. Sen calls the "arrangement of choices" in fact opens up a very wide field, ranging from no-choice to motivations, which seem far-removed from economics and accordingly design a function of utility, where the *impact* of the action, to the extent to which the latter can be measured technically and physically, yields way to what A. Sen calls "well-being", a concept which is not very clearly defined as between quality of life, self-satisfaction and moral judgement. If it is a question of stating that the economic action process incorporates other elements besides the sole "economic" and traditional, utilitarian design aimed at the object, i.e. it incorporates the whole of that which is represented by the economic Subject and also by the world, we can only express our agreement.

Economic freedom involves choice: the effectiveness of the fundamental choice over and beyond the *situation*; the range of choices for action is the realisation (what A. Sen calls "the freedom of arrangement"); the range of motivations, i.e. the participating elements, of the action process. Until the theory of choice has reunified all the motivations, over and beyond the sole, and finally limited, "economic and financial" variables, we will not have crossed a decisive stage. The choice, at any given time, involves the economic Subject, the group (collective forms) and the world, in order to surpass it.

§ 176.   Economic freedom does not state, in its capacity as an economic action process, whether such process falls within reasonable limits, within a certain moral code, whether the pure action (insofar as the same can be distinguished and isolated) is fully aware, in the general function of utility and satisfaction, of that which A. Sen calls "well-being" and others "the good life", which can be gathered within a function of moral utility and, also, of individual subjective utility. We have established in turn, as early as our *Théorie du Sujet économique*, that the economic action process encompassed, within a general function of utility, the motivations and satisfactions, which steer the action design, together with the moral dimension.

Even so, the concept of "freedom of well-being" (A. Sen) remains nonetheless very blurred. It is unclear whether it means the capacity of the exercise of freedom not to harm freedom and the Subject itself (what we have called "positive freedom"); a hedonistic satisfaction of the individual, which is not particularly precise nor objectivised; a function of individual satisfaction which could be compared to a moral code as we did in *Théorie du Sujet économique*, i.e. a moral matter which stems from a time-matter of duration and memory, which structures that which can and/or must be.

Nor is it certain that one can easily distinguish that which, on the one hand, forms part of action and, on the other, part of well-being, as A. Sen tries to do, a distinction which then enables an economic rationality to be sought, which accepts the dimension of moral values. There would therefore, in this approach, be a split-away or segmentation of the functions of utility (an "economic" utility, a utilitarian rationality steering the action in its design through the real impact sought within the world and through the object; a utility or satisfaction called "well-being" which, as we have seen, remains blurred but which can generally be described as *moral utility*) and of value ("economic" value again, a product of the pure action process; a moral value, moreover, for the individual dimension of the economic Subject). There is no such distinction in our view but, on the contrary, a unitary function of *utility* and a unitary concept of value, based on the action process, which we describe as economic (which is merged with economic freedom) and which involves the whole of a situation which has to be surpassed in the actual economic act itself (which establishes the link with the object), a situation which provides the action/realisation process of freedom with a wide reference frame of duration, where the multiple and infinite traces of past action processes, and of everything else as well, are registered, which in our view forms a specific reference frame of economic freedom, where the norm and moral dimension are produced.

Economic freedom, once defined by action, involves the totality of the elements and determining factors of the process, which creates a *global utility* for the individual within collective forms (once again, we stress the need to advance the question of economic freedom within the collective dimension and therefore to examine the individual preferences through the intermediary of such collective forms; too many analyses remain individualistic in the formulation of choices and preferences).

We have defined *utility* as the function which optimises the individual preference within collective forms (groups), producing specific economic freedoms, for a given stage of institutional forms, which contain the possibility of a norm and for a mobilisation of the whole of the individual and collective heritage, within a specific spatio-temporal reference frame whose structure is a hereditary function of the [memory recall/lapse] type.

There is no reason for us to distinguish that which forms part of freedom and well-being/happiness, from that which is free and moral, from that which is free and just. The *optimum* which we have defined corresponds to effective, *positive* economic freedoms which are associated with a moral satisfaction. The essence of modern economic freedom, as the Subject's action process, is to be total and totalising and to summon, through its absolute development, all the utilities and values, in order to define a *positive* field of exercise of economic freedom (which is always a collective form, within a *social field*, which may give rise, in fact, to a social contract), which is compatible with the individual preferences and functions of satisfaction, together with the norm and moral code, which the duration and memory of the exercise of freedom itself help structure and sustain.

4. THE EQUILIBRIA OF UNDER-FREEDOM

§ 177.   What can be the foundations for a collective choice or collective preference, on which a form of social or public interest contract could be based?

By using the term "collective", one places the collective from the outset in a position of dependence by comparison to that which forms part of the individual, which imposes an argument in terms of aggregation. Moreover, once one talks of a collective choice or preference, one introduces the question of "who" chooses or prefers, the problematic presence of a Subject, which is in principle absent. There is an initial paradox of the collective choice, since the concept of choice or preference inherits a structure which is that of the individual economic Subject and the collective choice seems to dissolve this individual structure. Consequently, the question of the collective economic Subject cannot be avoided, not with regard to its *a priori* existence (*a priori* no collective Subject exists, there are only individual economic Subjects) but with regard to its construction through collective forms, where we have distinguished the shape of *groups*, which *effectively* contain manifestations and representations of economic freedom, and the shape of *institutional collective forms*, i.e. forms which contain the possibility of a norm and of regulation.

From this point of view, the task of creating collective choices and preferences amounts first and foremost to the conceptual construction of a collective economic Subject, certain forms of which, micro-forms (company, party...) or macro-forms (the market, the Plan...) can be observed and therefore bear witness to their existence. *There are* collective forms which seem to contain and express choices but such forms literally seem to be *apart*, different from the individual choices which exist *in other respects*. Do such forms incorporate the individual or do they represent something else, a possibly conflicting super-imposition of a different dimension?

One needs to look within the elementary structures of the individual Subject for something which may shelter the collective or at least look towards the collective. The initial foundation of collective choices and preferences is the individual economic Subject's structure for-others. The otherness of the individual Subject summons the collective into which the individual projects itself, in its very essence. The concept of the collective is, at this stage, a shape of the Other, of the world in general and of other individual Subjects in particular.

It is because the individual economic Subject is for-others, and therefore has a structure which is turned towards the other individual consciousnesses, that *the collective* may be conceived and created (there is no individual economic Subject, which is alone in the world), i.e. that the need to consider the connection, the conflictual situations and the aggregation is legitimised. This does not suffice to explain what the collective *is*, although we already know that there is a basis for the organised co-existence of individual Subject-consciousnesses. As such, the two dimensions of the individual and the collective are not, in conceptual terms, impenetrable and separate. In this sense, the collec-tive, in its most unrefined concept, exists from the outset; there is, from the outset, a coexistence of individual economic Subjects whose structure is built through the existence of other Subjects and a constitution of the *group* as a structure. The *group* appears, from the outset, in what one might describe as an informal manner, in the sense that the coexistence of individual economic Subjects projected towards the others spontaneously produces dynamics for grouping and aggregation, whether the latter are offensive (the positive effect of the group through the increase of strategic means of union), defensive (reduction of the negative effects of conflicting coexistence), positive (the aggregation produces, in fact, the increase of positive freedom as we have defined it, i.e. an extension of the economic Subject's freedom for all individuals, which does not negate either the initial freedom or the economic Subject itself) or negative (effects of the reduction of the individual Subjects' freedom and of the negation of the economic Subject). There is therefore *a group function*, induced by the otherness of the individual economic Subject in its essence. This group function may progress to a formalisation stage, which we have called *the collective forms*, where *an analogon* of the individual form of the economic Subject is structured, what should therefore be called a "collective Subject". There is a finalisation of a design, of a projection, drawing from the same reference frame, which becomes independent (i.e. duration, memory and forgetfulness of collective forms, which have a retroactive effect on the dynamic of the collective form and which sustain or drive it), and this design is no longer expressed by an individual economic Subject but through the individuation of a *group consciousness*, as the design of that which constitutes itself as an economic Subject. Consequently, the two dynamics of the individual and the formalised group (which we shall henceforth call collective, but which is now no longer the crude collective) occupy distinct dimensions of different natures and the tension which exists between these two layers becomes an issue for the concept of economic freedom and the Subject. The collective forms (market, Plan...), which may have been extended by the political collective forms (especially when the latter are coercive), pursue a dynamic of their own, which is not necessarily that of the individuals which are present within the collective. There is no spontaneous equilibrium, which passes through a norm and regulation. The dynamic of economic freedom produced by the collective form may effectively extend or transfer an aggregation of individual projections; it can also produce a sort of *equilibrium of under-freedom*, similar to Keynes' equilibrium of under-employment, a situation where the tension between the individual and the group produces a reduction in the positive field of economic freedom and the status of the Subject; it may finally produce an imbalance, when the collective form takes the upper hand, without an alternative normative and regulatory form (the collective form takes the upper hand, by reproducing the structure of acting projection aimed at the world, which has founded multiple coercive, economic and political structures; which may lead to a situation of formal freedoms where that which is displayed corresponds to a design of the collective form (group) and not of individuals).

Let us return to the issue of an *equilibrium of under-freedom*. While maintaining the concept of initial freedom, as total and absolute possibility and capacity within the structure of the *individual* economic Subject, we place *effective freedom* (i.e. the *real* development of freedom through its manifestations, apparitions and realisations, i.e. *the* specific economic freedoms) in the territory of collective forms (the organised groups), where the concept of (economic) freedom is relative, i.e. the (economic) freedom reveals itself, together with its heterogeneities, inequalities, between groups, between individuals and between different types of specific freedoms (of freedoms which are sometimes called "basic" and which apparently have more inessential capacities); such heterogeneities, i.e. the impossibility for *effective* freedom to attain an *optimum* in real life, are produced by the tensions between the individual preferences and the collective choices, such as those resulting from the collective forms (groups) and, second, through what we have called the "paradox of freedom", i.e. the tendency of the concept of freedom, in its individual or collective form to negate itself (by negating the Subject), when left to its own devices. This means that, in real life, the effective freedoms (there are only effective freedoms in real life) constitute an infinite set of *optima* of inferior rank (sub-optimum) which combine, for a certain level of (economic) freedom – degree, nature, circulation within a group, between individuals and other groups-, an individual function of preferences and a function of choice of collective forms. This set of equilibria of under-freedom offers boundaries which are more or less efficient and unstable. Finally, such equilibria of under-freedom can only be stabilised with the introduction of a function of a norm and regulation of the collective forms, which we have called "institutional".

There is an equilibrium of under-freedom because the design, which results from the collective form of the group, does not take the individual preferences adequately into account, or at all; the aggregation of the individual preferences may be artificial (the collective imposes a coercive form, which may, rarely, satisfy the initial individual preferences or other preferences; the collective imposes nothing or very little and there is a conflicting coexistence with the individual designs); it may be effective (democratic forms or forms by referendum), and yet not result in optimal satisfaction. The collective form has the power to seek to extend the individual preferences (which leads to specific political forms), but also to impose other preferences on individuals (the collective then becomes independent as economic Subject).

Numerous situations exist, all of which are characterised by an equilibrium of under-freedom.

There is also an equilibrium of under-freedom, because the collective form of groups is not "corrected" by a norm and by regulation. The effective (real) freedoms are then limited, even if they can be displayed. The question of the reality of effective freedoms, of the reality of the capacities of the individual, is a central one. Such real freedoms and capacities often prove to be far more fragmented than that which, in the absolute, one might be led, by the concept of (economic) freedom, to hope for as a *possibility*; more modest than one might be led to believe, as a result of that which the collective form states and produces, in terms of freedom; more reduced, in its realisations, that that which one might be led to believe by the affirmation of its effective nature.

The concept of freedom therefore continues to be governed by non-fulfilment within its essence and the dissatisfaction for the Subject, which it defines. This is, *a fortiori*, the result of economic freedom, which owes its essence to the development of the action as a principal structure of the (economic) Subject. The elementary structure of the action is the obliteration of that which is, in order to project (imagine) that which will (perhaps) be done differently, alternatively, in order to negate that which was not. The concept of economic freedom owes its nature to this, its depression of being, being in a state of non-being, an internal instability which makes it rather difficult to establish and maintain an equilibrium, which is continuously at the mercy of a breach or an overstatement, which would lead the action even further, up to the negation of freedom and the Subject.

A certain number of elements may explain the existence of equilibria of under-freedom, such as an inadequate or inappropriate distribution and use of *information*. The element of information, and yet other elements, are rather more symptoms or indications of the imbalanced structure of free action, which lies at the foundation of economic freedom. The latter is permanently shifting and, because it leads, continually, to projecting the economic Subject beyond itself (whether it involves the individual or groups, which have become independent as Subjects), it constitutes a danger for itself at any given time. There is a conflicting coexistence of individual Subjects, of groups between themselves, of groups-Subjects with regard to individuals, because economic freedom as an action process continually projects further and *ad infinitum* any aspect of the Subject. Accordingly, the question of the circulation of information, of access to information, of its production can be understood from the point of view of such manifestations of the economic action process.

It is therefore of the essence of economic freedom never to be adequate for itself, always elsewhere, removed, set aside from that which is expected. Economic freedom is a concept in flight, insatiable and which therefore gives chase to itself and adopts itself as prey. Freedom can never reach a complete mode of being: (economic) freedom is not, strictly speaking, in being. This ontological imbalance should be borne in mind, in order better to understand the conflicting dynamic of the individual consciousnesses, to which can be added that of the collective forms. The development of total and absolute logics of the economic Subject quickly manage to restrict the field of effective freedoms, whether it relates to the populations affected or the nature of freedoms (equilibrium of under-freedom).

Moreover, the coexistence of individual and collective forms, which have the rank of economic Subject, even if organised, does not amount to an aggregation, in the sense of an integration, and only the coercive forms of economic and political power seem able to guarantee such an aggregation, through the construction of an *other* economic Subject. Here we touch upon another paradox of economic freedom, through which only the coercion imposed by a "collective form-economic Subject" enables the aggregation of individual preferences to be guaranteed. And, at the same time, freedom and the individual Subject are about to negate themselves. There remains the equilibrium of under-freedom, which is offered by the *ordered* and *regulated* coexistence of individual preferences and collective preferences of groups, ordered since freedom remains positive (no negation of the Subject) and regulated since a norm is produced which provides limits.

The equilibrium of under-freedom therefore includes something fatal, to which it is destined by the very concept of freedom, as it develops in the modern era, as action over and towards the world which is called economics. Economic freedom, because it continuously pursues its object, without ever attaining it, an innermost depression of being which lies at the very heart of the structure of the economic Subject, is condemned to non-fulfilment, which echoes the finitude of the Subject itself. (Economic) freedom will never attain its total, effective development. Within the cracks which pierce its being, unequal distributions of freedom or of formal freedoms creep in. Even worse, individual freedom and its preferences remain at the mercy of collective forms, which contain the specific effective freedoms, at risk of seeing the individual designs excluded or eliminated, by those of the groups which are formed into Subjects. And the concept of freedom in turn remains at the mercy of itself, the self-destruction of a will which wills itself and which invades the concept of freedom. To hold and support individual preferences, when faced with collective forms, without yielding to the illusion that the individual forms contain (economic) freedom by managing without groups; to protect freedom from itself. All this constitutes a set of combinations for individual preferences and designs of group existence (collective forms), a set which includes *optima* of a lower rank, or what we have called equilibria of under-freedom. Such sub-optimal equilibria define the regimes, which are inserted within more extensive regimes, in particular macro-financial regimes, regimes whose structure is provided by time-matter (duration) and the phenomena of memory and forgetfulness. Such equilibria may be admitted or judged acceptable according to the era. The equilibria of under-freedom can often only be attained and above all stabilised by the introduction of collective, institutional forms, which produce a norm and regulation, a normative matter made up of duration and memory, within a specific space-time reference frame of a psychological nature.

The triptych which identifies Subject, freedom and action founds the economic freedom, which develops in the modern age. Total and absolute power, as a concept which founds the individual economic Subject, but effective freedom and its manifestations are however determined within the collective forms and the specific freedoms, which are relative, since incomplete. Although it is supposed to be naturally directed towards well-being and the "good life", (economic) freedom remains a cold, limitless concept of energy for projection and creative imagination.

The concept of economic freedom remains paradoxical in many respects, with regard to this concept which has to be protected from itself, and the definition of optimal combinations as between individual preferences and collective designs of groups and the establishment of collective forms, which are able to produce norms, seem to be two (of many) significant means of improving the equilibria of under-freedom.

FREEDOM AND TIME

(with regard to F. Hayek)

1. TRADITION, DURATION, MEMORY

§ 178.   F. Hayek takes an approach to the concept of freedom, which allocates considerable importance to what F.H. calls *tradition* (from *tradere*, to transmit), i.e. also *culture*, intelligence of that which has been transmitted in time, intelligence of past time within selective experience, relevance of adaptive duration, of memory with a progressive function. We see in this an echo of our own approach which, as we have seen, accords an important role to duration and memory within the Subject's economic action process and within the development of the *Subject's freedom* within the *action*, three concepts which are merged by economics in its modern sense.

For F.H., not only the conscious Subject but also the various collective forms contain an innermost specific spatio-temporal structure, which originates in duration, memory and forgetfulness.

Freedom develops within a temporal dimension (structure) and the (economic) Subject cannot be reduced to pure consciousness without reference, pure reason without (historic) temporal depth, which does not mean that consciousness does not have a lightning effect on such matter (this is the theory which we have developed). For F.H., the architectural bedrock of *tradition*, this structure which carries the edifice, distances the claims of reasoning reason in the sense that freedom, if not held back or moderated by this *tradition* (duration and memory for us), would be mechanically carried along (F.H. distrusts a mechanical and mechanistic description of the Subject as reason) in a forward flight of projection and appropriation of the world in the shape of the Subject (as an individual but also, as we have shown, as a collective form, e.g. a State or private organisation).

Duration and memory confer upon freedom, and the acting economic Subject on the same occasion, a dimension of the process of apprenticeship and evolution, a temporal matter which makes up the very structure of facts (actions) and impacts but also the structure of rules and norms (this is an essential point of our *Théorie du Sujet économique*) even including morality. Freedom therefore assumes a dimension of practical philosophy (*praxis*), which confers a value upon that which lasts (duration); the value is fundamentally a compression of time (duration), which may then dilate (forgetfulness, memory). The economic Subject's freedom is a practice and the action which contains such practice is neither pure reason of a formal consciousness nor a lightning effect which is itself pure and which develops from nowhere and without any basis. Unsurprisingly, we find F.H. comparing the idea of justice (what is just) with what is done (action) by taking *tradition* into account, in the sense in which F.H. uses that term, i.e. a positive selection process (only that which has proved itself and has succeeded will remain), which constitutes a very strong assumption regarding which we remain prudent – in our view, the action process indeed forms part of a specific spatio-temporal reference frame, which means that any manifestation of the economic Subject's freedom within the context of action can be reduced to a temporal function of duration, memory and forgetfulness, but the process is cognitive, learns from its errors, and is non-linear, the memory recalls or lapses precipitating the distortions of the reference time-matter and, consequently, of the imbalances and weaknesses: *tradition*, in the sense in which F.H. uses the term, has a force of inertia and linearity in appearance only.

When we state that this *tradition* (F.H.), this duration (P.B.) constitutes the innermost matter of the structure of action, projects and of freedom itself, we mean that the Subject's (economic) freedom sees its action fall within the limits of that which F.H. calls *long-term principles* and which, in our terminology, means that the norm, regulation and morality originate in this long spatio-temporal structure with which we associate duration (matter) and the processes of memory recalls/lapses (design of the consciousness).

Consequently, it is easier for us to understand what F.H. intended with the concept of *spontaneous order*, which is a false-friend since it does not relate to an order which stems from nowhere or indeed from some lightning effect of reason or consciousness, on the contrary: order is organisation (F.H. will say *catallaxis*) of that which lasts, continues to bear witness, by coming to the consciousness as that which *is*, and is transmitted. The concept of *order* refers to the term *regime*, which we have used in order to describe a specific spatio-temporal structure, which contains a certain coherence from the point of view of references of duration, memory and forgetfulness, of primary time-matter, and therefore from the point of view of norms and rules which characterise this or those regimes. That which, in fact, holds itself out as spon-taneous, is that which *is* (i.e. that which has lasted/ lasts) and comes to the consciousness and which the consciousness allows to approach it in a sort of constructive passivity, which indicates, and it is worth stressing this point, that the economic Subject's consciousness is not solely a design but is moreover a patient design, which not only allows an underlying matter to approach it (that which F.H. describes as tradition) but also targets such matter (and does not target a vacuum), the very structure of such design being designed by the dynamic of memory and forgetfulness – since, in our view, consciousness is distinguished from reason, consciousness is design and expectation, the expectation of that which approaches it and which *is* (duration) and design (being in a state of non-being) of such matter, a creative and acting obliteration ,as one sculpts a block of uncut stone. The consciousness is, in our view, therefore, both matter and design, expectation of that which is/arrives and action aimed at that which is not yet. And that which arrives is that which is remembered, which is marked by duration, i.e. has marked action and minds, whether consciously or not and has also been transmitted.

And the *innovation* itself, contrary to F.H.'s assertions, remains, in its essence, a function of duration and memory; there is no opposition between *tradition* and *innovation*, provided that duration and memory form the innermost matter of the action process (and therefore of the energy of obliteration, imagination/action/reaction), and of innovation as well. There cannot be any conservative weakness but, on the contrary, a powerful temporal basis for the action and the innovation, which is a section of past, driven by the designs of a Subject's consciousness, which forgets and remembers.

Consequently, the novelty resulting from the economic Subject's action is always made up of a dense time-matter (although also unstable). As such, the notions of projects and of tradition cannot remain antagonistic.

F.H. gives the action process, which is thus founded on principles which can be described as hereditary, a purpose of selecting that which has "worked", succeeded, a creative evolutionism, which to a large extent leaves pure reason at the doorstep, since the process contains that which is incomprehensible, unconscious, collective (...), a manner for

F.H. to indicate that that there is a process within a specific reference frame. Although our approach only manages to find proximities of analysis in F.H.'s approach, we do, however, see, within the design of successful selection, a reduction in the ambition of design, which retains its complexity and, consequently, a reduction in the projection of the Subject within the world to the sole identification of *optima* of realisation and impact (we have stated that the notion of *optimum* should be revisited and defined in a more ambitious manner, for a Subject, even if economic, which contains within itself other projects and other complexities than merely the calculating maximisation of its initiatives). For F.H., there remains a tautological residue (that which has lasted has lasted because it was good and just and this was the case because the people who acted in this way became more prosperous, by so doing).

By making the economic action process a process of adaptive revelation and apprenticeship (going so far as the expectation of that which is/approaches, a passive expectation of the consciousness before the design), our approach incorporates the idea of selection (we have presented the market sequence within the economic action process as a phase of gathering, confrontation and selection of projects) but we could not state, as F.H. does, that it involves selecting the *best* solutions, even if we knew exactly how best to define such words, how best to define the *optimum* which is hinted at here and which, it seems to us, is a matter for considerations and criteria, which extend way beyond a calculating optimisation of the project, in order to embrace a notion of optimum which is more ambitious for the free economic Subject in its action aimed at the world. We have ourselves shown how the collective form of the market (which however acquires independence as an individual Subject, the modern fate of economics) could be effectively described as a selective process of discovery and improvement (see *La Dynamique boursière, Théorie du Sujet économique*). And, yet, the freedom of the (economic) Subject cannot ultimately be justified by the sole gain of prosperity, measured by a pure calculating reason; there are so many things and values which are involved each time an action of economic progress is set in motion.

The concept of the Subject's economic freedom has roots which go far back in duration and memory. Once again, whether it involves the notion of *connections*, at the heart of the manufacture of mental/ psychological facts of the consciousness, or a direct reference to the *physiological memory* in his opus called *The Sensory Order*, F.H. embarks on a wide path which calls for a new *optimum*, while not managing to extricate himself from an objective which is still too narrow. The attention given to the mental phenomena (as compared to the material phenomena), which are alone of real importance for the understanding of economics, shows the extent of the issue of capture by the economic Subject as consciousness, consciousness for-others, pure freedom choosing itself in a *situation* (F.H.'s *tradition*), determined by sections of duration, memory and forgetfulness. The comprehension of the economic act, in terms of mental structure and temporal structure (historicity), marks a significant step forward. The title (*The Sensory Order*) adopted by F.H., includes a reference to the specific spatio-temporal reference frame of a mental nature (*sensory*) and the mention of *Order* which is found in the concept of *Spontaneous Order*, in order to state the extent to which that which constitutes the determining structure within which the action develops, i.e. *the Order* for F.H., is made up of a matter which F.H. describes as "sensory", and which, in our view, includes everything which comes to the Subject within duration, or which is remembered/forgotten by the same Subject.

§ 179. We have shown that the concept of (economic) freedom was inhabited by a paradox, due to the perseverance of freedom in its being which is absolute, total and totalising. Accordingly, nothing can prevent freedom from threatening its own existence, by setting itself up as a coercive and totalitarian power, in the very name of freedom. Lined up within this paradoxical category, which has not escaped F.H.'s attention (F.H. considers that a dictatorship may be liberal, that an authoritarian collective form is the only one which is able to protect the democratic collective form from itself, i.e. from a drift by the concept of freedom towards totalitarianism – this example can be found in economic history, e.g. in the experiences of countries such as Singapore or Chile), are all the collective forms which set themselves up as Subject and which undergo a totalising evolution, i.e. a totalitarian empowerment (this is the extreme case, and one may simply find interventionist, authoritarian or economic planning reorientations). Such a total and totalising reorientation may be effected in the name of the individual's freedom as such (liberal dictatorship), in the name of freedom and therefore in the name of the emancipation of all or part of the population (the working class as Subject, Subject of history, in addition, since the independent and total form of the collective Subject "working class" is accompanied by a teleonomy, the purpose of history); more generally, as emphasised by F.H., the absolute and total forms of reason (scientism, teleology of history, constitution of a Subject of history, construction of the aims of history...) prove to be a continuation of temptation (of reason), of the paradox of what we might call a more voluntary freedom, while at the same time failing to account for the complexity and stability of the Subject's structure and action (there is a lack of realism in such descriptions and analyses – as well as in that of a cold, calculating *homo economicus*, which no doubt corresponds to a totalisation of its modern definition, as pure freedom, which is experienced through the action but which, at the same time, fails to account for all the motives and determining factors of the economic Subject, in particular those which constitute the specific space-time reference frame, which we have described and which is structured by the forms of duration and memory). That which F.H. calls *mechanics*, i.e. all these systematic forms of reason, design and teleonomy and which he denounces, in order better to protect freedom, such mechanics, which are described as being tacked onto the living (and the living here refers directly to the matter of duration and memory, which we have described and which is found in F.H. under the terms of *tradition* or *culture*, which he then contrasts with reason); that which is called *mechanics* therefore beckons towards the dangerous essence of freedom, the dark side of this sun. To denounce the dangerous temptation, which inhabits the concept of freedom itself, in order to protect freedom from itself; to demonstrate and construct the complexity of an economic Subject made up of time-matter, as a means of (re)discovering freedom by revealing it in another essence.

§ 180. The market and, even more generally, the economic action as a *process*, i.e. that which is done in the mode of "to be done", that which is in a state of non-being (not-yet-being). This is what we have continually demonstrated in our work, namely that the economic Subject's freedom should be described as a process (of economic action) and, more generally once again, that modern economics are based on the concept of negativity (summoning that which is not yet, which is to be imagined, to be created, to be made), and symmetrically, that the concepts of economic Subject, freedom and action assembled at the point of convergence of the Subject's obliterating capacity, an innermost structure of the space-time of consciousness, which is also that of economic and financial objects found in the market and more generally in the economic action process, as we have described it. The form of the market contains this instability, this non-linearity, whose nature is similar to that of the economic Subject and its space-time reference frame. We therefore end up with the idea that the description of economic freedom, the Subject and action as *processes* (and, we might say, one and the same process, since the three concepts are of one sole essence, that of modern economics) and, moreover, the strong affirmation of the existence of *a* general equilibrium constitute two propositions, which it is hard to render truly compatible. It is not that the endeavour to establish equilibria of lesser rank (equilibria which we have described as sub-X, X being able to assume any value relating to a variable or a concept, we have thus discussed the equilibrium of under-freedom in the same way that Keynes discussed an equilibrium of under-consumption) disheartens us, on the contrary; this endeavour is founded within the dynamic macro-financial regimes, which are defined, as we have seen, by a specific space-time reference frame of duration, memory and forgetfulness, duration and memory enabling one to establish the time of the regime (which ends up disappearing and giving birth to another regime), the norms, regulation and elements of morality, which are at least temporary and practical (what we have called practical morality). The regimes represent spatio-temporal sections of a mental/psychological nature, i.e. structuring the economic Subject as a consciousness of expectation (i.e. which allows that which is/which lasts to approach one) and of design, which obliterates in order to act). These spatio-temporal sections, which form the regimes, undergo eclipses, returns, disappearances (which are, however, never definitive), since the dynamic of memory and forgetfulness, which determines the distortions of the regimes, their memory recalls and lapses, plays the regimes as one plays a piano keyboard. Consequently, it can be understood that the notion of equilibrium finds its meaning – which is relative, i.e. relative to a regime and to its determining factors – within the framework of a given regime (or family of regimes), and, moreover, that multiple regimes, which are more or less *active* at any given time (i.e. more or less forgotten), cohabit, coexist like parallel (lives), which may intersect, in the same way that elements of several economic regimes intersect and sometimes mix or confront each other. From this point of view, the *regimes*, in the sense in which we have defined them, constitute variable elements of the spatio-temporal reference frame placed on parallel trajectories, which may however intersect each other.

The description of the (economic) [freedom-Subject-action] triptych as a process introduces an inner-world, a structure, a reference to that which sustains the process (our duration or memory), a reference to that which adapts in order to continue and to last. The reference (the equilibrium) is, consequently, provided by comparison to that which creates the norm and the rule, this temporal matter of duration, which comes from the Subject and which is taken over and surpassed by the latter, through its design of imagination, creation and action (there is no absolute, pure and mechanical design of the Subject), which would consequently enable an idea of a general equilibrium to be founded by the economic Subject, which is thus defined absolutely; we have demonstrated that the economic Subject was, on the contrary, in a *situation*, which approaches it and defines it or rather leads it to be defined; this situation will provide the basis for the definition of a relative equilibrium, the basis since the situation will be distorted by interaction with the Subject, or everyday action like memory recalls and lapses of that which is already there.

The difficulty in establishing a general equilibrium, within an approach which is in process and which assigns a more ambitious depth and a more modest role to the economic Subject, which was perceived and pointed out by F.H., is an open door to the consideration of that which is uncertain (in respect of time and, in particular, of the temporality of the action, which creates the obliteration, by means of the infinite projection towards that which is not yet in being), of a more complex idea of the economic Subject, which is less mechanical, less absolutist, whether the said Subject is an individual or a collective form such as the State (it can be noted that F.H. criticises the intervention of the State, a collective independent form, which becomes Subject (of history, of *X*), since the concept of Subject (of) underlines to such an extent the teleonomic and potentially totalitarian design objective, of a modern Subject considered *totally*, i.e. as totality and force, and therefore possibly totalitarian).

Since economic freedom, Subject and action are processes and to take account (i.e. give an account) of such processes contributes to the protection of freedom, Subject and action from the totalitarian design and self-destruction which threatens all three of them.

Freedom, Subject and action as processes means a modest definition of the triptych of knowledge, reason and certainty.

One therefore tries to dispose of two problems or failings, in the manner in which one tackles the concept of modern freedom, and therefore that of economic freedom, to which it may largely be reduced. First, the identity between freedom and pure reason, through a second identity between consciousness and reason (the design of consciousness is absolute reason and, in modern times, it is a question of a calculating reason), the most traditional figure of *homo economicus* as a calculating Subject and technical consciousness of the world; such an identity disposes of what is uncertain and unsure, what is incomprehensible, there is a clear consciousness of the world and of oneself. Second, the identity between freedom and pure will through, once again, a second identity between consciousness and a voluntary will to appropriate (freedom is, first of all, an oblivious and powerful force/energy, a profound in-itself and which, in a certain manner, cannot be understood, pushing the Subject without limits to *desire*, this desire acquiring an ontological status, as can be found in German thinking from Schopenhauer onwards).

These two problems cannot easily be disposed of since, in fact and by experience, these two dimensions are at work within the concept of (economic) freedom, as it develops in the modern period, linked to each other very often in the description which can be made of the concept of freedom (accordingly the absolute and total character of freedom is presented and understood both as an affirmation of the Subject's will and a certain reason for its objective and teleonomy of design, an inappropriate association, since the *desire* is indeed dual or is super-imposed upon the concept of freedom in modern developments, is a force in-itself, which is imposed upon the Subject rather than being produced by the latter, a force which the Subject does not understand, or at least does not easily understand, i.e. contrary to that which may be implied by the concept of a reasoning and calculating freedom, in respect of the Subject's control of itself and the world).

The fact remains that these two problems, which F.H. identifies as obstacles to be disposed of, are not easy to dispose of, since there is indeed a history of the concept of freedom (and, accordingly, one can infer a history of the economic Subject and action), which sees these two dimensions develop; one means by this that (economic) freedom is not simply understood (described) in this way but that the concept of freedom effectively also develops in this way within reality. This means that it is possible, legitimate and desirable to try to redefine the concept of (economic) freedom either in order better to describe/understand the effective operation of the Subject within the economic action (*praxis*, and the same is true of the consideration, within the understanding of the economic Subject, of a specific space-time reference frame, which does justice to uncertainty, non-linearities, asymmetries…), or in order to establish the foundations for a framework of the consequences of the concept itself (accordingly the concept is inhabited by limitless desire, which leads one to question the conditions for a possible norm and therefore for regulation). Any attempt to redefine, to frame or surpass the concept of modern (economic) freedom - since, and this is essential, the concept of economic freedom contains a historicity, a modern status in this instance – must form part of the approach of an archaeology of the concept of economic freedom, i.e. for us, the archaeology of the modern birth of the concept concerning, in particular, the two dimensions and identities of the concept, which we have just discussed, dimensions which form part of the genetic heritage of economic freedom. Unsurprisingly, the attempts to surpass this modernity (F.H. is a good example thereof) come up against the impossibility of disposal (one cannot dispose of something which is a component part) and the need to take on board and surpass.

The radical reform of the concept of economic freedom, which may constitute a surpassment, therefore involves the understanding (i.e. the taking on board, the integration) of the genetic elements of the modern concept of freedom, legitimising a genealogical (see *Généalogie de l'économique*) and/or archaeological approach. It is through such lines of argument that one finds and recognises the most productive thinking, F.H.'s thinking being one of the most precious.

2. ORDER, REGIME, REFERENCE FRAME

§ 181.   That which F.H. calls "spontaneous order" is the state of a process *at a given moment in time* (since the adaptive process is based on trial by error and the selection of that which imposes itself through a capacity to survive), which is not unrelated to our notion of *regime* and, in general, of a *reference frame*. The idea is that, because freedom is such a process, which carries with it a whole innermost matter of time and more specifically of duration, which carries with it a whole *tradition*, in the meaning given to such term by F.H., then everything which seems to close or conclude the possibility of such a process is harmful and must be fought. For F.H., this is true for the idea of a plan, economic planning and centralised planning, of interventionism as well. Hayek sees within the independent collective Subject represented by the Plan (or, more generally, the State) the negation of the trial process (therefore, using our terminology, the negation and lack of a reference frame of duration and memory), this process which is on the contrary at work in the individual and which F.H. also finds in the collective form of the private enterprise. There is an assumption that the collective form of inter-vention of an economic planning or state type is incapable of learning and therefore of placing itself within a process (here we are indeed within the collective form of design, with strong objectives, the independent transfer of the individual Subject, whose total and totalising freedom is identified with desire), unlike, for F.H., the collective form of the private enterprise or the market (which are, in our view, collective forms which are semi- or totally independent), i.e. have a status as Subject and as such impose themselves upon the individual Subject, until they are able to dissolve or eliminate it – here we find again the limitless force of will, which inhabits the initial concept of freedom. By confronting, at the two ends of the spectrum of freedom, planning (State intervention) and the individual (individual initiative), the one repre-sented in a closed world, the other in an open place, driven by the dynamic of the process, F.H. does not in our view truly do justice to, first, individual freedom, which, as we have shown, is inhabited by the desire to appropriate, to transform the world, which may create an interventionist and totalitarian temptation of the Subject – in other words, there is a sort of naïve optimism of the individual Subject in F.H.'s thinking, which does not see that the excess of totalitarian closure, which he denounces in the collective forms of centralised planning is not unrelated, on the contrary, in genealogical terms, to the structure of the individual Subject which, as we have seen, in fact contains a totalising and totalitarian dimension (which, in certain instances, is transferred to a collective form). Second, F.H. does not seem to see that the Subject as an individual leaves room, within the capitalism which he describes, for the collective form of (private) company which may, in certain instances, impose upon the individual Subject, while diluting it, as part of a specific desire for independent collective organisation as a Subject; in the same way, the *market* as an independent collective form, acquiring the status of (economic) Subject may not only impose upon the individual but, of greater concern in F.H.'s analysis, the market as economic Subject does not always seem, far from it, to be able to be described as a process, in the sense used by F.H., i.e. with the capacity to learn by experience and to adapt, to be able to produce a norm and regulation (which, according to our terminology and our analysis, forms part of the innermost matter of duration and memory, which forms the structure of the reference frame of any Subject), thus returning to the "closed" status which Hayek confers upon the idea of central planning. In fact, in our analysis, *any* Subject, whether in its individual form or its collective forms, may be described on the basis of a referential structure of duration and memory, i.e. the matter which F.H. calls *tradition*, and this is not peculiar to a special form of Subject. Any economic Subject, irrespective of its form, inherits such a genetic structure, whose possible failings and excesses have been described above, but, and this is important, each of these forms of economic Subject constitutes a process and a dynamic whose trajectory shall prove, ultimately, to be "open" or "closed", to adopt F.H.'s meaning, i.e. harmful for freedom and the individual or not, since the trajectories are not known, they remain uncertain in terms of their capacity, *inter alia*, to produce a norm and to protect the freedom and the individual Subject from themselves, and this is true whether one is dealing with an individual form of freedom or any collective form, including a planning, State and/or political form. Accordingly there is *a priori* no particular reason to exclude the collective form of state intervention, since such a collective economic Subject is not *a priori* incapable of learning from experience or of an adaptive and normative process. This represents a considerable difference with F.H.'s approach.

§ 182.   The collective forms, which contain the possibility of a norm and regulation within a regime, which are in fact institutional forms, draw their capacity to produce a norm and their regulatory function in respect of the free action process from the accumulation of layers of duration and time, where actions, facts and things have been imprinted, in the same way as plants leave their fossilised trace in stone. Such forms, which are often also the most precious institutions of modern economic and political systems, are as it were concretions of *habitus* of duration and memory, of processes. Such sets are in no way inert; there is, on the contrary, as we have emphasised, a true dynamic of such sets, driven in particular by the movements of memory and forgetfulness. Such forms are also collective in the sense that the *habitus*, these living accumulations of blocks of duration imprinted with signs – facts, things, actions… –, far exceed the mere field of individualities, in terms of their capacity of capture and knowledge. Such forms have occasionally emerged from long processes (F.H.'s "discovery procedures" are not very different), from adaptive trajectories, from errors, which gives them a certain legitimacy of success (to survive – for a time, since, as we have seen, the regimes have a strong capacity to evolve and adapt, they are often mortal) and, above all, radically differentiates them from the collective forms, which are provided "suddenly" as it were, a unique and demiurgic creation of an (economic) Subject serving as the central creative consciousness (accordingly nothing is more remote than the idea of a Plan or, in general, further from the idea of a total and central Subject). On the contrary, economic freedom, as we have shown, is a question which can be found within the collective forms and can only develop harmoniously, i.e. without constituting a danger for itself, if there are sets which are in fact based on a dense temporal matter, which structures the action.

The modern (economic) Subject is demiurgic in its essence, i.e. its design is absolute, total and therefore potentially totalising. Consequently, (economic) freedom must be considered, i.e. protected from itself, within an interaction of sets and collective forms, whose independent transformation into a Subject (whether it relates to the manager, the party, the Plan, the private company organisation…) does not generate a totalising structure of absolute and perfect consciousness, a limitless centre of decision-making and comprehension, a calculating head of reason, a conscious structure of design, which is not *a fortiori* based on an innermost matter of duration and accumulated time but, on the contrary, arises *ex nihilo* through sorts of lightning effect. These are the matters which we find a trace of and can track in F.H.'s approach, in the same way that one heads down a promising forest path.

We can therefore see two important dimensions. First, we affirm the essential character of the accumulation of temporal energy (duration, memory…), in the same way one charges a battery, within the structure of the Subject's consciousness, as an individual and also as a collective form, where one finds in fact the practical question of (economic) freedom (market, State, Plan, private company organisation…), without being naïve, since the paradox of freedom indeed means in fact that, when faced with this ambitious objective, which must constantly be reassigned, in particular to dedicated institutional forms, but also to all forms of Subject by recreating them, the absolutist and totalitarian temptations of reason, will and pure consciousness *ex nihilo*, which inhabit the modern concept of freedom, can therefore constantly be found. Accordingly, the modern concept of freedom is a source of permanent tensions between these two faces of freedom, which we have described and whose confrontation we have alluded to through the use of the expression *paradox of freedom.*

The essential character of the accumulation of temporal energy must not lead one to think of an inert stock of energy, since, on the contrary, the energy comes from a permanent bombardment of the initial time-matter (blocks of duration) by memory and forgetfulness, within the Subject's essential reference frame. This dynamic is specific to the dynamic of economic freedom and, consequently, of economics.

Moreover, the Subject is, in its very structure, this time-matter of accumulation, which does not mean that it is not an actor, since it is to a profound extent, nor that it is "acted" but rather that its action (and this is also true of collective forms, which acquire a status as Subject) always develops (one must understand that it must accordingly develop confronted with the other forces of the concept of freedom, which contain the totalising temptation and the, as it were, "spontaneous" generation – we realise the extent to which F.H. laid himself open to a good number of unfair misunderstandings, by using the concept of spontaneous order", which does not in fact mean what it seems to mean but quite the contrary, i.e. the state of accumulation of energy-time (duration, memory)), therefore always develops within what we have called a *situation* (i.e. the established fact of that which has been, at a certain moment, accumulated, in the sense that we have given to the term accumulation, such established fact corresponding in part to Hayek's notion of *order*), and this situation is in no way fixed, on the contrary, it evolves as a dynamic, as we have discussed (the dynamic of memory and forgetfulness, as well as that of regimes). We are not very far removed from the meaning of *spontaneous order*, as used by Hayek and understood in its proper sense, i.e. as a temporary established fact of a given regime of accumulation of time-matter, for the individual Subject or for a special collective form, possibly established as a Subject itself or through its managers; we are not therefore dealing with a fixed concept, as the notion of order might imply; in the same way, as we have just stated above, the *spontaneity* means that this established fact of the regime of accumulation comes to the Subject as a situation, a Subject which will unfurl an action on the basis of this matter and beyond it, by surpassing it, and cannot mean a creative design of the Subject *ex nihilo*, on the contrary: the economic Subject is a design of accumulation (situation) and the considerable genetic heritage constituted by the regime of accumulation, which is occasionally constituted beyond the individual or collective Subject in question, imposes upon the Subject in the manner of a matter to be discovered and appropriated, for the purposes of a surpassment, which is the essence of a free economic action process.

3. THE MOTIVATIONS

§ 183.   We have shown that the concept of modern freedom, in its essence (which we have called "initial freedom"), which forms the foundation of economic freedom, was absolute, total and totalising and consequently contained a temptation of a totalitarian nature (which became clear in the individual form of the Subject but, even more so, in the collective forms, which became independent as a Subject, whether economic and or political; among such collective forms, one finds those which have been the most sharply criticised by "liberal" or libertarian thinking, incorporating a strong dimension of intervention, of voluntarism, the State, the Plan, whether or not paired with totalitarian, political structures, by constituting the traditional emerging aspects; this can be seen, for example, in F.H.'s work). In particular, the concept of will is instinctively mistrusted by liberal thinking, whether it is a matter of voluntarism of planning or of any centralised vague desire of the State or of a party-State – such collective forms are seen as closed, without tradition (in the sense used by Hayek, or without genetic heritage of duration and memory, to use our terminology). Curiously, the individual desire and voluntarism are not considered by this thinking to be threats but are, on the contrary, analysed as being potentially threatened by the totalising collective forms.

However, and this is our first point, the structure of desire which inhabits the individual and the structure of desire which inhabits the collective form, which has become independent as Subject (collective in the name of an entity, irrespective of the medium, population, ideology..., or "allegedly" collective in the sense used by the liberals, i.e. expressing in fact an individual-managing Subject or several Subjects pursuing their own interest), these two structures of individual and collective will are of the same type and one of them (the conceptual structure of initial freedom, that of the individual) has been transferred into the other. There can be no surprise and the individual, even if threatened (as it is) by the collective forms of (economic) freedom, remains a desire in its capacity as Subject.

This leads us to our second point. In our view, the initial concept of modern freedom is inhabited by the Subject's desire, a permanent expression of projection towards that which is to be done, this being which is in a state of non-being (not-yet-being), which makes the Subject into an acting freedom (it is desire, which creates the modern identity between Subject, freedom and action, and, therefore, also creates the total and potentially totalitarian character of the Subject). We mean by this that desire inhabits the modern concept of freedom and that such desire is not external to the triptych structure of Subject, freedom and action. We do not agree on this point with F.H., who did indeed detect this risk of desire; we say that desire is the element of risk of modern freedom. We deduce that (economic) freedom and the Subject must be protected from themselves and that the collective forms which contain the possibility of a norm and regulation, these institutions whose innermost matter is adaptive, made up of duration and memory, which comes to the Subject and which prevents the Subject from being merely a pure and oblivious energy, a practical or calculating reason, that the construction, identification and preservation of such institutions constitute an essential task for politics and economics. In this, we concur with F.H. and liberal thinking.

We diverge once again, when we say that, in our view, it does not stand to reason, *a priori*, that desire and its totalitarian or totalising temptations only affect or principally affect the state forms, economic planning or centralised control. This is our third point. First, the state forms of support of economic planning are not *a priori* necessarily *closed* in the sense understood by liberal thinking, and may incorporate a matter of duration and memory and may even contain the possibility of norms and regulation, based on a relevant "tradition" in the sense used by F.H. (accumulation of knowledge, facts, actions, which are selected, remembered or sometimes forgotten, this time-matter which is so essential). Second, other private collective forms, the market or the company, which have been *a priori* spared by this liberal thinking, may also contain a total and totalising temptation, which bears some semblance to the concept of desire. Finally, the individual itself, which often seems to be depicted in an almost naïve manner, as a threatened, innocent freedom, contains within it, at the heart of the concept of initial freedom, which creates it, the total and, once again, possibly totalitarian temptation. The last two aspects, which we pay particular attention to, are absent from so-called liberal thinking.

§ 184.   By creating the concept of (economic) freedom in the individual (the individual form), which we have called "initial freedom", which is based on the convergence of identity of the economic Subject, freedom and action, by thus creating this concept of freedom, we have from the outset understood something extensive, fundamentally open, for better or worse, something absolute, total and totalising, going so far as a totalitarian risk, and it is within this opening that we have placed the free Subject's economic action process.

Therefore something extensive, much more extensive at first sight than that which methodological individualism as the foundation for "liberal" thinking ended up (or started by, since modern economics emerges from this reduction) meaning, i.e. considering that the economic actors act *as if* (we add voluntary emphasis, this is important, as we shall see later) they maximised the utility or profits. While sharing a starting point, which is that of the individual, a starting point which is not, far from it, only methodological but historical (archaeological in the sense in which we have used this term), since the modern age identifies absolutely with the sudden appearance of the Subject (free, acting, it is an identity), and yet our conception of economic freedom, as the Subject's action process, is more extensive, since its foundation is of an ontological nature (all our earlier work has sought to show that economic is the name given to the modern relationship of man, – the economic Subject, *homo economicus* – with the world and with itself as well and, therefore, that by economic, and consequently by (economic) freedom, we intend from the outset to capture an ontological reality of modern man's being-in-the-world (see *Tractatus*, *Généalogie*, *Valeur et temps*)).

The technical reduction effected by methodological individualism (*as if*) is undoubtedly not so far removed from the ontological nature of the modern (economic) Subject, since the *technical* design of the action of appropriation, creation and transformation of the world and of oneself forms such an innermost part of the essence of modern man. One can say that, by severely reducing the economic Subject to a design of action (to adopt our phrase, "the economic actors act", a tautology of action which encloses the Subject within an acting relationship with the world, which is precisely economics and the Subject is merged with the economic actor, the two notions being based on the concept of freedom, which is annexed or invested, the whole of which forms an identity between Subject-freedom-action), thus by reducing the economic Subject to a design of action, the modern concept of freedom incorporates a function of utility (the action platform) and a function of maximisation (we use the term maximum, which clearly indicates the total, limitless dimension of the Subject's design).

However everything is *"as if"*, i.e. results from a methodological reduction, which ultimately leaves immense areas of investigation and interrogation regarding the possible meaning of the "maximisation of utility". At this stage of our analysis, one can in particular see within this a sign, a trace of an absolute and total initial freedom of the Subject which, being experienced through the action, leads to an economic action process, which corresponds to an ontological requirement of the economic Subject, defined as a force of extraction from oneself and from the world, of surpassment towards that which is not yet (the action project). The "maximisation of utility", under its technical exterior, states the essence of the modern Subject and its freedom – which merges with the action – and the technique moreover forms part of the modern purpose of this action (it therefore acquires an ontological meaning).

"The maximisation of utility", also known as the acting opening, which can be found at the heart of modern freedom, action and Subject, this triptych of identity which forms economics as we know them. However, it does not state the action process, its determining factors or dynamic. More seriously, it seems that we have made it say things which are not confirmed by observation or reasoning (pure and perfect rationality of the Subject, acts of design of the consciousness *ex nihilo…*). Worse, it also seems that, having lent such absolute and totalising attributes to the free acting Subject, ideas and then realities of a totalitarian nature were able to exist based on such beginnings, without the dimensions of the norm, limit or moral code, for example, having been considered.

The methodological reduction of individualism is not therefore incorrect, in the sense that it stems from a concept of the free acting Subject, which does indeed emerge in this manner in the modern era. It remains extremely poor and limited, once it involves considering the consequences and risks, for the Subject and freedom themselves. This reduction does not catch one off-guard: it displays its caution (*as if*) from the outset. However, this caution has been forgotten and many lines of argument have resulted from an absolute and total interpretation.

Faced with the reduction of methodological individualism, one has to affirm the complexity of the thinking of the free economic Subject's action process. In one manner or another, the manifestation of initial freedom, within the economic Subject's action process, leads to an interest in the economic Subject's *motivations* and there is a very wide spectrum of possible approaches of motivation, ranging from certain psychological regularities up to sociological environmental conside-rations and passing through pure forms of optimising calculation. To be interested in *motivations* is to attempt to work out the determining factors and dynamic of the economic Subject (see *Théorie du Sujet économique*). In our view, even before analysing (micro-analysis) the economic Subject's attitudes and behaviour and confronting them with a few theoretical assumptions of multi-disciplinary origins (the game theory, sociology, history...), we should return to the ontological dimension of the economic Subject and, first of all, to the initial concept of freedom, presented as an *act* (the link with the action is formed from the outset) of the consciousness, which is a design (directed at) (consciousness of), i.e. the constitution of an object in a state of non-being (the obliteration of reality, which drives the consciousness and the Subject out of itself towards that which is other), a dimension of positive negativity (since it constitutes the action and the Subject) of (economic) freedom. This is the context in which the notion of motivation should be examined, in our view. *Motivation* can be found, in conceptual terms, very close to the source or determination of the design of consciousness, which constitutes the economic Subject and which we have just discussed. *Motivation* is what triggers the process, which will lead to the economic action and, in so doing, constitute the Subject (in the modern sense) and reveal/uncover freedom as an act (the action – which here is economic – is the revelation of freedom and as such constitutes the Subject, in the modern understanding of the Subject, which is that of economics from a historical, or more specifically genealogical or ideological, point of view).

We have shown that the ontological question of *motivation* was similar to that of the energy, the force (and that of its origin), which drove the dynamic of the freedom/Subject/action triptych. We have identified, in order to cut to the essential matter, two main options, within an initial family, which can be described as absolute or total. First, an (economic) Subject defined as pure and total consciousness, i.e. a focal and central link for a clear decision *ex nihilo*; a pure and absolute form, of which pure and calculating reason is a slight variation; one can see here many aspects of *homo economicus*, as the same is advanced within the theoretical and modern view, and the support for the totalitarian temptations, which we have described as inhabiting, from the outset, the concept of initial (economic) freedom. This first main line of interpretation, which is based on the initial reality of the concept of modern freedom – an absolute, total and totalising concept, with a totalitarian temptation – and enables other important notions to be constructed and understood (collective forms of economic freedom and action) does not seem to us to be the most operative, i.e. able to do justice to the notion of motivation, in its original sense, together with the reality of observation (accordingly the forms of pure, calculating and central reason, which may inspire certain real forms, rarely manage to restore the economic action process, the role of the Subject and the outcomes of the whole).

Moreover, still within this initial family of freedoms, which have absolute and total forms (the concept of initial freedom is always absolute – here one is dealing with the most radical interpretations of its origin and of the role, which the economic Subject may play therein), an actor subject (in the unaltered forms of the consciousness in action and of the reasoned decision) but also and above all "acted", as it were, through the form which A. Schopenhauer calls "will-to-live" and the principle of which, in particular, we adopt here, oblivious force and energy, which are *there*, and which constitute the Subject/consciousness/action block, elements in-itself (i.e. which are what they are, with a certain incomprehensible dimension, in any event a dimension which remains concealed from clear consciousness, from reason). We have retained this dimension in our theory, in a less radical form, by incorporating within the consciousness of the economic Subject a specific time-matter (duration, memory) which *comes to* the economic Subject and to which the design of obliteration/action is applied, within a space-time reference frame, a dimension which imposes upon the Subject like a *situation*, which it surpasses by appropriating it within the very act of consciousness, which is an act of imagination, creation, conception of the project, which then becomes the actual action itself. In our view, the source of energy at the origin of the Subject's *motivation*, of economic freedom and action resides within this time-matter.

We have thus placed the unitary function of economic freedom, Subject and action within a second family. Without coming back to the total and absolute nature of the concept of initial freedom, and therefore without calling the latter into question (we consider that modern initial freedom emerges, with the Subject and action, as a total and totalising project, it is a piece of information), we adopt a structure of the economic Subject linking a design (of consciousness) in respect of a time-matter, which *comes to* the Subject (it *is*, while distorting, in accordance with a dynamic of memory and forgetfulness); the consciousness is not therefore empty but constitutes a form of combustion chamber of time-matter (see *La Dynamique boursière*, *Théorie du Sujet économique*), a more or less settled accumulation of slices and dust of acts and facts, which form the original substratum, the original *situation* of the Subject and whose act of freedom involves surpassing determination. The consciousness in action, as an act (of design of time-matter) is the act of revealing the economic Subject's freedom; the consciousness in action and the time-matter of duration and memory constitute the fundamental structure of the development of the freedom/Subject/action triptych; the consciousness in action is the superior form of the decision-making process, which is not totally that of pure reason and *a fortiori* solely calculating; it involves incomprehensible, absurd, contingent and irrational substance, which stems from the dimension which approaches the Subject-consciousness as in-itself, a time-matter of duration and memory; this incomprehensible substance (which may recall in certain aspects the totalising "will-to-live" which we referred to above) may nevertheless in part be understood or cleared by a better understanding of what the Subject's specific space-time reference frame is, of what makes a difference, by comparison with the absolutist theories, and opens up a field of investigation, of understanding of that which may seem to be a simple act of "animal spirits", and of construction of norms and regulation.

§ 185.   The traditional (and liberal) "invisible hand" which guides the individual, *over and beyond its intention* corresponds, at the foundation of (economic) freedom and individual *motivation* which we have just discussed, to this energy or force which is to some extent exogenous and which will determine, with a necessity and contingency, while not allowing itself to be interpreted or understood, the (economic) Subject's *motivations* and *intentions*. We have taken this analysis of the Subject-freedom-action triptych, determined "from outside" by an oblivious force (Schopenhauerian willpower or will-to-live, duration and memory) which forms the platform for a *situation*, which determines the freedom in action, whose surpassment of the *situation* (F. Hayek's "tradition", which we interpret as an accumulation of fundamental time-matter – duration is the essence of this dimension, which is other, external or exterior to the Subject, which the latter surpasses, while taking it over within the action which bears its genetic trace and whose dynamic is provided by the evolutions in memory and forgetfulness, since there is no memory without forgetfulness in the understanding of economic and financial phenomena and their dynamic, i.e. their cyclical nature) through action and within action is the revelation of freedom, in order to form a genealogical family in its own right of the concept of (economic) freedom in the preceding section. We have, in a certain manner, incorporated this dimension of the economic Subject's freedom in our theoretical approach, by making the time-matter of duration the innermost core of the Subject's structure and, consequently, of the concept of freedom and the economic action process.

The concept of the economic Subject's freedom in fact contains a dual structure. There is a pure *design* – this is the best known dimension, the one which is most commented on and to which the operation of the Subject-freedom-action triptych is most often reduced – (*intention, motivation,* there are numerous terms to describe the decision *as such* of a *homo economicus*, i.e. as a capture-projection mechanism, terms which are often connected to the order of reason, which is itself pure). However, this pure mechanism of design has no reality or efficacy – i.e. remains a totally theoretical vision, which is unsuitable for a confrontation with the observation of the free economic Subject in action – within a second dimension, constituted by the innermost matter of freedom and the Subject's consciousness (the three concepts form the modern identity) and therefore the action process, innermost time-matter (duration) which is opaque and incomprehensible, in numerous aspects, for a given individual in its capacity as Subject (matter which extends widely beyond that which is, the matter which comes to it in order to constitute it), incomprehensible (on first analysis) rather than *invisible* in the traditional sense of the "invisible hand", but there is a proximity between the two notions: the *invisible* nature referred to by the traditionalists declares this substance, this in-itself which will give meaning to the design (intention, motivation ...) and will sustain it (freedom, action, the Subject are the meeting point of the act of capture and of this matter).

The freedom of the (economic) Subject is not therefore a sudden appearance *ex nihilo*, in the same way that the design of intention or the motivation is not *ex nihilo*, and finally in the same way that reason, which is *a fortiori* calculating reason, is once again not pure capture *ex nihilo*. Freedom, as a concept, is the revelation (surpassment) of that which *is* (the situation, in our terminology, or the "tradition" in that of Hayek) and it is in this context that the economic Subject's freedom is in action and not *ex nihilo*. It is precisely because freedom (consciousness, intention, motivation or reason) is not *ex nihilo* but in action, i.e. the production of energy-time by a design which operates on and on the basis of an innermost matter of duration that, quite often, certain economic and financial phenomena may appear irrational or incomprehensible; they only appear so by comparison with a framework of analysis of pure reason and of the moment (the "trend" to use M. Friedman's terminology) when, in fact, they continue to be determined in their essence by a space-time dimension, where duration, memory and forgetfulness permit many things to be explained, which may seem to be neither apparent nor visible (in the sense that the traditionalists talk of an invisible hand). The behaviour of the stock exchange is an example in point (see *La Dynamique boursière, Les fondements*).

FREEDOM, JUSTICE
AND THE DESIRE TO ACT TOGETHER
(with regard to J. Rawls and L. v. Mises)

1. JUSTICE AND EQUALITY (WITH REGARD TO J. RAWLS)

§ 186.   We have made time-matter, and *duration* in particular, together with the dynamics of memory and forgetfulness, the essential elements of our analysis of economic freedom, Subject and action. This time-matter, the innermost matter of a specific space-time reference frame of the economic Subject, as acting consciousness, is the fundamental source of the energy and dynamic of freedom in action, i.e. of the projection of the economic Subject within the action process. This time-matter means, at any given moment, at all times and in all places, that there is a *beforehand*, which does indeed determine, differentiate and discriminate but which is surpassed, and this surpassment is the very gesture of the revelation of freedom in action. In our view, this time-matter takes on a dimension of an ontological nature, in the very constitution of the economic Subject's structure and of freedom as a concept, and also of an empirical nature, incorporating in particular the contingency of that which is *beforehand*, the constraint of that which *is* and comes, as a being, to impose upon and constrain in order to call for a capture-surpassment which is the very movement itself of freedom.

Consequently, our approach remains different from that of J. Rawls and, in particular, from the methodological detour through the concept of the *veil of ignorance* used by J. Rawls. The *veil of ignorance*, in fact, systematically introduces forgetfulness as a method (admittedly at the starting point but it is essential, since it structures the concepts of freedom, action and the Subject from the outset. We assert, on the contrary, that the starting point, i.e. the essence of such concepts, and more generally, those of economics and finance, can be found within the time-matter of duration and memory, which are also, in our view, the structure of the consciousness which defines the economic Subject. The individual particularities are eliminated by J.R., in the same way as that which we call the *situation*, a contingent constraint exercised over the constitution of freedom, the Subject and the action (there is in fact an emergence of freedom, the Subject and action in our view *because* of this *situation*, this *tradition* to use F.H.'s words, this accumulation of prior facts, acts, social relations). The presence of this temporal reality (which seems to us to reinforce the realism of the approach, since observation shows the existence of such a contingent constraint of that which is prior) does not mean that there is full, pure and perfect knowledge of that which forms such matter, on the contrary; this time-matter remains partly opaque, pierced with forgetfulness and unstable memory recalls; there is, accordingly, no need for us to have recourse to this *veil of ignorance*, in order to impose a restriction on knowledge, even if merely methodological. In our view, this means that one has to agree to consider, when adopting an approach which intends to remain realist, the link between the individual Subjects, which are involved in the construction of a cooperation (exchange) structure and the *situation* of empirical contingency, which is specific to them, and that it is in this context that one has to achieve *the general* without eliminating the particular.

The individual multiplicities, in the sense of genetic heritages constituted of precedences which are accumulated individually and within the relations (in particular the social relations) between Subjects, are the active components of any collective form, irrespective of the process by means of which this collective form emerged (deliberation, conflict, cooperation...). In our view, it involves not only social objects, which can be observed within a realist analysis of (economic) life but, more fundamentally, elements of the ontological constitution of the Subject and, consequently, of its action.

Our approach, based on considerations of an ontological nature, first, and of empirical realism, second, complicates the constitution of the *general*, once we refuse the detour through the veil of ignorance, in the sense used by J.R. Our approach incorporates the accumulation of time-matter (duration), i.e. the *accumulation* of aspirations, trends, leanings, motivations and social relations (accumulation in the sense of "tradition", as the term is used by F.H., or "permanent", in the sense used by M.F.) as a *situation*, i.e. a set of data, which is not inert but on the contrary dynamic (the dynamic is largely provided by memory and forgetfulness). It is on this basis that the designs of freedom and action are expressed and on this basis that the collective (institutional) forms must be drawn up, which contain the possibility of a norm, regulation and the general (see *Théorie du Sujet économique*). This differs from J.R.'s approach, which imposes, from the outset, limits which must be respected through a system of purposes. This does not mean, in passing, that our approach remains a prisoner of the sole dimension of efficacy of means, within the development of designs (weakness of utilitarianism) but that the limit and the norm must emerge from the design as it develops, i.e. from an accumulation of individual and collective time-matter. It is in this regard that we have shown that the question of (economic) freedom could essentially be found, with regard to its practical and moral issues, within the collective forms, which contain the possibility of that which is normative and general. One of the obstacles is the reality of the collective forms, which assume the *general* by eliminating, forgetting or diluting the individual multiplicities, the *sui generis general*, which is disconnected from the individual dimensions, whether it claims to aggregate them or replace them. It will, therefore, ultimately be a matter of protecting freedom from itself (in particular from transfers to collective forms, which have acquired independence as Subject and which contain the *general* to the detriment of the particular) and of preserving the individual multiplicities, in the name of realism, by maintaining, above all, that the structure of the whole of the individual and collective interaction is based on the accumulated time of precedences, a *situation* which forms a necessary pairing with *freedom*.

§ 187.   We therefore affirm a certain number of points of disagreement with J.R. Among these, the reconciliation made between the concept of *good* (in the sense of the source of the individual motivation and interest) and rationality. At most, we only acknowledge a *limited* form of rationality, i.e. a form of intentionality and design, which is specific to the consciousness within the making of the decision, but, and this is an important point, for a *situation* of time-matter of (duration), to which the very existence of the design process (freedom, action) is necessarily linked. The project and the individual Subject as projection are indeed autonomous but within a specific space-time reference frame, which is, in principle, neither empty nor *ex nihilo* but determined to some extent by a time-matter, which represents its contingency, i.e. the contingency of the freedom of the economic Subject and action.

Furthermore, the idea of *initial* goods, of *basic* freedoms does not, in J.R.'s theory state its origin, its necessity, its legitimacy, its evaluation or its historicity (is it a static system *ad vitam aeternam*, as seems to be the case, or must one accept, quite rightly, that the original list of basic freedoms and initial goods will experience a dynamic and what will the motives of such a dynamic then be?). For our part, while refusing the idea of an absolute necessity located within the (economic) Subject itself (absolute rationality) or within a sort of external cause (transcendence), we place emphasis upon that which founds what we have called the *situation*, a temporal matter of accumulation, which imposes upon the Subject (for a surpassment) with a dimension which is both contingent and necessary (contingent, since the Subject does not choose such an accumulation, and necessary, since the choice of economic Subject cannot be constructed without it, which, consequently, is a limited rationality, freedom and action).

§ 188.   J.R.'s theory contains, at the foundation of the structure of cooperation, elements of tolerance, recognition, reciprocity and *forgetfulness* of oneself, both for and within the collective and the general (or, one might say, a partial or limited identity, or limited convergence between the project, which has a strictly individual motivation and the order of cooperation contained in a collective form; the collective form extends the individual project or the individual projects itself onto the collective objective, the collective design being, in fact, supported by an individual design; this individualistic or egoistic design of the collective form and its objectives, by aligning interests, would arguably guarantee a certain efficacy). Let us return to J.R.: (social) cooperation is made possible by *forgetfulness*, which is at first methodological forgetfulness, as we have seen (the original veil of ignorance), but which goes further, up until *forgetfulness of oneself*. We contrast this with the reality of duration and memory, the reality of the particular, of all that is particular (to the individual), and the reality of the temporal structure of the individual Subject itself (time-matter exists, whether in a conscious or unconscious form). We return to the elements of the *situation* which we stated above, a dynamic situation, since this time-matter undergoes distortions (it would therefore be barely realistic to draw up a list of fixed *initial* goods or freedoms without stating both their foundation and the dynamic process of their revision or adjustment, which must pass through the appropriate institutional collective forms).

More generally, as can be understood, the attempt to establish a form of transcendence in-itself, the foundation of the system of freedom and justice (and, especially, the necessary foundation of the structure of cooperation and therefore of social reality), an attempt which is advanced using a methodological justification ("the original position", "the veil of ignorance") but which, in fact, establishes a regime of an ontological nature, securing the freedom-Subject-action system, remains unsatisfactory. This region in-itself, evidenced by the terminology of J.R. (*original, homogenous*), by negating the particular and the multiple, also negates the reality of the accumulated time (duration) which, through memory and forgetfulness, forms a link with the constitution of the Subject, the only matter which, in our view, if one adopts a realistic approach, is capable of populating such a region, which to our mind preserves the contingency of the constraint, which it exercises over the Subject-freedom-action triptych and, above all, the consideration of cooperation and the social structures.

The principles of such a triptych may be achieved by disregarding the *contingency* of that which constitutes individual life and social life (the situation, the accumulation). We call *basic, initial*, that which, in fact, sets this spatio-temporal mass in motion, at the point of impact between the Subject's design and this matter.

Paradoxically, although J.R. intends to be precise and effective and to avoid generalist abstraction by providing a list of particular (*basic*) freedoms, this list is, however, provided on the basis of a set of assumptions which could not be more abstract and which are not very realistic (the original position, the veil of ignorance) and the *basic* freedoms stated, while proclaiming their status as founders, do not seem to be deeply entrenched or founded themselves (they might be so, within the duration and memory which they emerge from, in a certain form and for a time, relative and dynamic forms).

§ 189. The concept of freedom is, in its essence, an absolute, total and totalising emergence of the Subject in action (acting), a projection which is necessary (this is the very definition of the Subject as consciousness, which has become a project) and contingent (determined by an accumulation of contingent duration). As such, the concept of freedom (and of the economic Subject and action as well), as we have stressed, is limitless, an absolute space for the development of energy, wherever the source is located (will-to-live, time-duration etc.). This means that the freedom of the economic Subject in action cannot, *ex ante*, incorporate the dimension of *justice*. On the contrary, first the two concepts of modern freedom and of justice (and of equality, a distinct notion), are clearly apart from one another. Although J.R.'s freedom consists largely of attempting to create a norm *from the outset* (i.e. at the origin of the concept, at the time of its constitution, which poses what we consider to be considerable problems, which we have discussed above) for freedom, as part of a search for compatibility with justice (as equity in this instance), for our part we submit that freedom, in its essence, cannot be limited or restricted in advance to a precise list of particular freedoms, which have a status (consequently an ontological status of *basic*, *fundamental* freedoms, within a position, which is stated to be *original*, which is indeed the fundamental approach). Freedom is, in our view, a development-projection of an ontological nature, which lies at the origin of an (economic) action process, which is, in fact, a revelation of a freedom in action of the Subject, which is, itself, ontologically, *for-others* – which implies, from the outset, incorporating the Other in all the dimensions of the free action process, from conflict to cooperation, from individual forms to collective forms of the freedom-Subject-action triptych, a structure for-others which places the practical, normative and moral reality of (economic) freedom within the collective forms and therefore procures that the questions of justice, of the *corrective nature* of the process represented by justice, as a collective institutional form, responsible for correcting, in a very general sense, that which is not in fact a natural trend of freedom and, above all, for correcting/standardising, on the basis of a time-matter which, in our view, constitutes the relevant norm and forms a coherent link with the original structure of freedom and the (economic) Subject, which is based on the same time-matter of accumulation (duration), are posed. Adopting our approach, such important questions must therefore be posed *in advance* of the construction of the concept of freedom.

For this reason, *inter alia*, the notion of "equal freedom" used by J.R. seems to us to be contradictory in its very terms, or rather, we might say that, in our view, (economic) freedom is, in its essence, the *difference*, first because the Subject, as freedom, is outside itself, being projected towards that which is in a state of non-being and, second, the Subject is for-others, these two structures being, in our view, of an ontological nature. This means that freedom and the Subject (and, consequently, the action process) are differentiation processes, where otherness constitutes a constituent structure. This also means that freedom is, as we stated above, the limitless development of an absolute and total process-project, which involves *difference* (of the individual with itself and of individuals with others), and conflict, what is social and the issue of cooperation. Freedom does not, in its essence, contain either justice or equality. It is during (further along) the economic action process, which reveals the Subject as freedom, that one finds the questions of justice and equality, together with the possibility of a norm, regulation and correction (see *Théorie du Sujet économique*), since the concepts of justice and equality, as corrective processes must be founded in the realist matter of that which has occurred and has accumulated (duration).

Correction forms part of the nature of the concepts of justice and equality, which are therefore also corrective processes of the process of freedom of the economic Subject in action. This means that such concepts are found, where the conditions for a possible *corrective* must and may be reunited and considered, i.e. where collective forms, based on the same energy as that which steers the action process, are located, an energy which may consequently be implemented, in order to *correct* the action process, in the name of the essence of freedom, Subject and action. This means specifically that *justice* constitutes a normative process, the norm and principles of which must be defined within a space-time reference frame, which is that of the Subject, structured by duration, memory, "tradition" (F.H.), what is "permanent" (M.F.) and not the trend, which seems to lead the world and the visible process of economic freedom and action (and which effectively does lead it from time to time, which *a fortiori* explains the need for *correction*).

§ 190.   Contingency and difference are, from the outset, contained within the structure of the definition of the Subject-freedom-action triptych. Contingency in order to *locate* (in the sense in which we have discussed the *situation*, as an element involved in the concepts of freedom and Subject), i.e. in order to incorporate within the concept of freedom and Subject – and, by so doing, constitute them – a dimension of time-matter, described as *environment* by some, as *tradition* by others, which seems to be an external structure but which, in fact, constitutes the innermost matter of the Subject as consciousness and of freedom as the revelation of this situation. *Difference*, in turn, lies at the heart of all the important concepts (the Subject is difference, in the sense of being set aside from oneself, within dissatisfaction and the project, as otherness through the for-others, which constitutes it and propels it, outside itself, towards another version of itself and towards the others; freedom is difference, as an action process, which leads towards another, to be in a state of non-being).

We define the (economic) Subject, first, by means of the design of intentionality, which is specific to the consciousness, such cons-ciousness not being empty, as it were, since it is inhabited by the time-matter. The dynamic, which presses towards that which is other and different welcomes time within its innermost structure, since there is no difference, no making of a distinction without temporality. This difference, of an ontological nature, is found, in a more practical dimension, within the course of the action process, within the questions of inequalities and, consequently of justice. The foundation of such questions lies in the difference, as essence of the Subject-consciousness and freedom.

We distrust the concept of rationality. By rationality, we mean the structure of intentionality of the consciousness, which defines the (economic) Subject and we talk of limited rationality, in the sense that this structure of intentionality is neither pure nor *ex nihilo* but, on the contrary, contains a sort of substance constituted by time-matter (duration). The action is therefore always rational, in the sense used by L. v. Mises, in this strict definition. The structure of intentionality therefore incorporates a time-matter which does not constitute a determinism (*a fortiori* positivist), – on the contrary – since the freedom of the economic Subject is revealed in the surpassment of this "substance" of duration, within and through the action (see, in particular, *Théorie du Sujet économique* and *La dynamique boursière*).

§ 191.   In J.R.'s approach, the contract (justice, the search for equity) frames, *ex ante*, that which J.R. calls the "conception of good", which is the development of the free Subject within the action process, a modern definition of the Subject-freedom-action triptych, which we have advanced. This modern conception of *good* includes, in our view, in its essence, freedom as action, the revelation of freedom through action (freedom in action), which strictly constitutes the (economic) Subject. We have shown that this modern concept of freedom (and of the Subject) is paradoxical, in the sense that it is literally without limits, and that it is in its development, i.e. in the sequences which occur after its development, that the collective forms (institutions), which regulate it, may be sought, i.e. the conditions for a possible limit and norm, and not at an earlier stage or *ex ante*, i.e. within an original limitation or mutilation of the concept of freedom. Consequently, in our view, the concept of freedom cannot be standardised *ex ante* or, to use J.R.'s terms, one cannot impose certain limits through the contract on the conception of what is good, or assert the priority of justice over efficacy and of freedom over socio-economic advantages; these are J.R.'s terms, since, in fact, freedom includes, in its initial concept of absolute and total development, all the forms of appropriation of the world, including the notion of efficacy. Economic freedom as it is constituted and develops in the modern era cannot be cut or mutilated; it is and develops in coherence with the essence of the modern economic Subject (*homo economicus*). The acting freedom of the Subject, which is the essence of that which we call *economic freedom* in modern times, can only encounter and find the possible conditions for its own regulation (which is necessary, since such freedom constitutes a risk for itself and for the Subject, and there lies its constituent paradox), within a patient and precise analysis of its means of development, within the collective forms which essentially govern the process thereof. Justice, equity and justice as equity can therefore only be defined and constituted as concepts, on the basis of an analysis of the economic action process as revelation of economic freedom and the Subject (see *Théorie du Sujet économique*).

By pursuing this approach, we will not state that the economy is subject (*ex ante*) to politics (J.R.), since the essence of freedom, as the revelation of the Subject in action (acting), is in fact what has been called *economics* from the modern era onwards (see *Tractatus*; *Généalogie*; *Valeur et temps*). The conditions for a possible limit, norm and regulation, which form the structure of what can be called *politics*, lie within the revelation process of freedom in action itself, and, in particular, within the collective forms of economic freedom, which we have described above in this work.

(Economic) freedom, which is *in action* in its modern concept, can only be standardised by that which it produces, by its effects, by the accumulation of time-matter, which originally constitutes it and structures its development, as an action process. This is why we emphasise the innermost matter of duration, which constitutes it, and the need to consider the conditions for a possible norm – within the appropriate collective forms – on the very basis of this accumulated time-matter. The concept of justice, which does indeed unite the conditions for a possible norm, a limit and regulation, can only be constituted on the basis of this accumulation, which continues, always and at all times, to be dominated by the energy of the Subject's freedom, which in the act, in the action, surpasses a given state of accumulation, in order to give it *another* sense and, by so doing, reveals the economic Subject, while endowing it with its substance of freedom. Freedom is essential, its energy is contingent, the sense produced by its revelation in action will summon the need for a norm and justice, since, in fact, nothing limits freedom *ex ante* and freedom represents the principal threat for itself.

§ 192.   There are two questions, among those raised by the reflection on economic freedom, and more generally the (economic) Subject, which justify that we mark a pause, since they appear to be, and effectively are, formidable and capital. First, can one expand the concept of economic Subject to such a great extent that not only can the Subject not be solely reduced to the strict search for its own interest, understood as calculating and efficient optimisation and allocation of rare resources (a strict and limited conception of what is "good" in the traditional sense of *homo economicus*) but, moreover, can be constituted as a "just citizen", in the sense used by J.R., i.e. can it be considered, in its essence, as bearing a project for a cooperation space, to be implemented with others around a conception of what is just, over and beyond the specific project, which defines it as an individual Subject? Second, can we consider that a collective form, or particular collective form, contains or embodies an action project (therefore, in the name of the collective, of a space and project for cooperation and, often, for justice) and, if so, can we consider that such a form can exist on its own, independently from the individual Subjects, to the latters' detriment, together with them, subject to appropriate terms or, on the contrary, can such collective forms, which have become independent as Subjects, not claim a real role (over and beyond symbolic forms), within the action process, as advanced by L. v. M., a process which will, always and at all times, be the result of individual freedoms, Subjects and actions (the collective then becomes a sort of handicapping veil, masking freedom and its development and leading to bad decisions), finally, assuming one can recognise such a collective form, which has become independent as Subject, is it not, if one looks more closely, the result of one or more individual Subjects (the *managers*, in the sense of liberal or rather libertarian criticism) appropriating the so-called collective decision-making space and word (the collective form would, once again, be merely a sort of veil, masking in this instance the individual dimension, which would endure – thus indicating that the collective form, established as Subject, does not really exist or, at least, constitutes a trap, a ruse of the economic action process and of the development of freedom and the Subject in action)?

We have shown that the modern concept of the Subject emerges as a very open project, i.e. as absolute, total and totalising energy. This means several things: that the modern Subject is, in fact, constituted as a force of projection towards the world, for the purposes of transformation of itself and of the world (which may, in particular, take on the form of a technical examination), a force which is literally without limits (or which does not hold the keys to its own limits, a theme of the paradox of freedom, which we have discussed – freedom is a risk for freedom and the economic Subject), a force whose balance (of power) established with the world, which is one of our main arguments, assumes the name of economics in the modern era; that the force of absolute and total energy which constitutes the economic Subject is, indeed, as a result of this very fact, a force of the search for the Subject's own interest, by the Subject and for the Subject, a structure of design and intention, which is itself absolute and total (and, therefore, without "natural" limits, i.e. whose concept of freedom is dated *ex ante*), and this design includes the objectives of efficiency and optimisation, even if calculating; that, however, it is not a question, first, of a pure design which is *a fortiori* merged with a form of pure reason, in the sense of an intentional creation *ex nihilo* and, second, of a design which is solely preoccupied by rational efficiency and calculating optimisation, and these represent the two fundamental points of our approach; regarding the first, we note and affirm that the design of the free economic Subject is based on the "substance" of time-matter (duration), essentially we establish the existence of a specific space-time reference frame of a mental/psychological nature, which structures the consciousness of the (economic) Subject, which is itself merged with the structure of the concept of acting freedom, a time-matter which is admittedly incorporated, digested, surpassed and assumed within the action of freedom but whose presence implies a different nature and operating mode of the economic Subject, from those of the simple and simplistic, hallowed *homo economicus* (the intentional design is a spectrum of multiple motivations and objectives; this design, which is constituted by duration, memory and forgetfulness, does not always take the paths, which appear to be rational, since the motivations are themselves deeply rooted in spatio-temporal layers of duration, memory and forgetfulness, so that the operation of the economic Subject, as free consciousness, is surely not that of a reason *ex nihilo*, which is driven by the sole concern of efficiency); that there is accordingly an essential *complexity* of the free economic Subject (and therefore of the concept of economic freedom), which results from a more complex and more realist structure of the design of intention, which constitutes the Subject and freedom, a complexity which does not mean, on the contrary, that such concepts are incomprehensible (the work undertaken in *La dynamique boursière* and in *Théorie du Sujet économique* seeks to demonstrate that it is possible to understand phenomena, which are accused of being irrational, provided that the relevant space-time reference frame is described and used, which is structured by duration, memory and forgetfulness (the detour via complexity for the field of comprehension of economic and financial phenomena, which are unexplained or described as the product of animal spirits or as pure chance)); that, accordingly, the Subject continues to be driven by interest (the structure of intention and design) but its motivations form part of a range of concerns, which is much broader than the sole design of effective optimisation (even if this latter design is present) and that this design of motivation, because it is supported by a temporal stock of duration or an accumulation of "traditions" (facts, gestures, actions, things…), in order to surpass the same, is far-removed from the simplistic diagram of the traditional *homo economicus*, even if this

simplification is recorded within the constitution of the modern economic Subject; that, moreover, the free individual economic Subject is
for-others from an ontological viewpoint, which means that it is part of
its very essence to project itself towards the other, towards others, that
otherness constitutes its nature, that accordingly, the presence of others
(the regard, the conflict, the exchange, i.e. all forms of contact with
others) is necessary for the existence of the individual Subject as such;
that, accordingly, because the concepts of Subject and freedom (which
are consequently economic) are in their essence for-others, an
elementary structure of their constitution, the question of freedom
includes, from the outset, not only the question of the relationship with
others (ranging from conflict to social cooperation) but the terms for a
possible "acceptable" relationship with others (this notion retains a very
vague meaning, we understand it to mean something, which accepts a
limit, a norm, a regulation) but, and this is an essential point, it does not
mean, on the contrary, that the initial freedom, which emerges from the
individual Subject, contains, from the outset, the concept of justice,
which is not a constituent part of the initial structure of the free Subject:
it is within what we have called the "collective forms of freedom", at a
later stage of the action process, that the conditions for possible justice
can be satisfied, which leads on to our second question, since, if the
concept of effective (practical, realistic) justice can only be the result of
collective forms, are we not obliged to recognise that the said forms
have a complete reality, *together with* the individual forms and to
overcome the doubts and criticisms aimed at such collective forms,
which we have noted above (e.g. those of L. v. M., for whom the
individual form is the only real and relevant one, when describing the
Subject-freedom-action triptych, since all the collective forms prove to
be traps or veils over the individual's reality)?

It can be seen that the second question posed above involves two
issues. First, as such, it involves recognising (or not) that there is a *real*
autonomy of the collective forms of the triptych structure formed by the
economic Subject, freedom and action, i.e. something more substantial
and operative than a simple veil – which proves to be a trap or an
illusion – thrown by the collective form over the whole of the individual
forms of the Subject, of freedom and action, thus deceiving on two
counts, since there would not be a collective *reality* (in the sense of
reality of a Subject, notion or speech) but solely individual realities
(even the summation or aggregation of such individual realities could
not constitute a collective group, or rather the collective term would not
represent anything), and, furthermore, this deceptive veil would produce
harmful effects by removing, dissolving, masking and constraining the

free individual acting Subjects, which are the only real ones. Second, as we have shown above, the recognition of a real autonomy of collective forms of economic freedom governs the possibility for founding a concept of justice, within the economic action process, at the heart of those collective forms, which are able to contain the conditions for a norm, a limit and regulation. By undermining the very bases of the collective form, within the economic action process of the free Subject, it is the very concept of justice which is considerably weakened in terms of the very possibility of its *realist* development (i.e. to adopt our thinking, based on the very matter of freedom and the Subject, the accumulated time, of which duration is the principal form, and which is transformed into energy-force, whose dynamic is governed by the memory/forgetfulness pairing).

2. ACTING TOGETHER (WITH REGARD TO L. V. MISES)

§ 193.   There are affirmations within the pure, liberal line of argument, e.g. that of L. v. M., which may appear to be contradictory, when placed end to end, but at least they create a preoccupation and an interest. One understands, this is the fundamental argument, that the collective act does not exist (in the sense of a collective Subject having its own design, position and intuition) within the action process (according to L. v. M. there is an identity between reason and action, both of which only describe that which is individual) and that there are only individuals as far as (economic) action is concerned, i.e. individual designs, individual interests or, finally, that the collective group (in the sense used by L. v. M. – which represents an initial concession – who accepts a "collective group", to be understood as an intentional structure of cooperation, decided upon by a certain number of individuals) is, as it were, simply the *neutral* exterior for the pursuit of individual interests, or at least certain of them (the collective group is a veil of neutrality, one can talk of the *neutrality* of the collective group). Therefore, besides the affirmation of the non-existence of the collective group, one finds a form of existence of forms of cooperative regroupings for benevolent reciprocity, in the sense that the collective group will never diminish or handicap the individual project but, on the contrary, increase it (the collective group is at least neutral). The collective group is still not a structure of its own, endowed with a Subject's capacities of intention and design (contrary to the principle of transfer, which we have developed) and it involves a form of cooperation, which *completely* satisfies the pursuit of individual interests (no reduction of the individual substance, consistent with neutrality), which, in our view, is sufficient in itself for one to imagine the practical difficulties of such an approach, in particular in complying with a minimal principle of realism.

According to L. v. M., if individuals act together (recognition of the minimum collective group), it is because it is in their interest to do so (the collective group does not exist at any stage through itself) and the collective cannot diminish the individual. Using our terminology, there would seem to be a for-others structure of the individual Subject but not a collective structure, which could be described as Subject, i.e. having autonomous properties and capacities. However, at the same time, the individual Subject is recognised as having "a desire to act together" (L. v. M.) which procures the foundation of society. Admittedly, this desire to act together is immediately limited and reduced to the need to find the *means* of attaining (undoubtedly in a more effective, more optimal, more rational manner) the interests of the individual Subject's projects. The individual Subject continues to be the absolute *purpose*, the form of collective cooperation is *a means* without personality (in the sense of the status of a Subject). However, the concept of the *desire to act together* is so strongly asserted that one is forced to acknowledge its ontological nature, which L. v. M. would undoubtedly refrain from doing. It is this concept, which forms the bridge towards the concept of society, which is also immediately reduced to a dimension of means for individual aims. Everything occurs as if L. v. M. (and beyond him the whole of the liberal trend) could not, as it were, follow through to the end the intuition that the collective does not exist (which is the absolute initial intuition), even if only for obvious reasons of realism (the Other exists, the otherness of the Subject is a fact), and, consequently, reintroduced it, after being constrained and forced to do so, in order to save the concept of society (which would not exist without it) and to comply with a realism of observation, which does indeed see forms of cooperation. This reintroduction, in order to save in turn the initial intuition, is effected in a minimalist manner but, as a result, weakens itself, since this reintroduction is not at all minimalist, even if one tries to pretend it is instrumental (since they are simply the *means*, the desire to act together and society are unhesitatingly ranked in subordinate dimensions). However, this is unconvincing. We maintain that, despite appearances, i.e. the organisation of required thinking, the ontological dimension of *acting together* (*desire to act together*, which links the intentionality of the individual Subject as acting will/desire, which is absolute and total, and the for-others, the radical otherness of the individual Subject, which, as we have emphasised, is *difference* in its most innermost depths) is indeed what is advanced and, moreover, it could not be any other way, for reason of considerations which we will describe as methodological realism (the individual Subject is evidently not alone in the world).

Consequently, if our analysis is correct, this dimension of the *desire to act together*, which is ontological in nature and which therefore constitutes an elementary structure of the individual Subject, establishes the foundation for that which may be located beyond (set apart, elsewhere, above...) the sole, literal search for an individual interest. This opens up a means of constructing collective forms, which may be more autonomous (without perhaps going so far as to transfer the Subject's structure), in any event the collective form cannot be maintained by the minimalist barrier, within which it was imprisoned. Consequently, the same is true of the concept of society, which therefore finds the possible conditions for a more affirmative foundation and, also, for concepts adjoining that of justice, since justice is not necessary within the neutrality of the collective group (there is no injustice) but, on the contrary, within the recognition of a certain autonomy and an *action* (as compared to a neutral stance) of the collective group.

For L. v. M., the conflict, or simply the contact/coexistence between the individual form and the collective form, which we consider to be not only an act of observation, which must be admitted by a minimal methodological realism, but, moreover and above all, an essential dimension of the understanding of (economic) freedom – the question of which can, in our view, be found principally within the collective forms – and of the dynamic, which exists between the two structures, therefore, for L. v. M., such a coexistence cannot occur, since the collective form has no aim (a dimension, which we acknowledge in the collective forms, through the transfer of the individual Subject's characteristics – there is an automation of the collective form into a Subject); accordingly there can be no conflicts of purposes between the individual and collective spheres. One can undoubtedly hope that this will be the case one day, by vilifying the obstacles raised against this evidence, which hinders *optimum* and efficiency and hope, and by praying for changes in policy, and, yet, the fact remains, as can persistently be observed, that the reality of human action is made up in such a way that such autonomous collective forces do exist, i.e. which contain, in the sense used by L. v. M. and many liberal thinkers, a structure of consciousness and, therefore, of intention, and that the link between the two dimensions, which is sometimes conflictual, produces facts and economic history.

Our own approach lays a good deal of emphasis on the definition of the (economic) Subject as consciousness, i.e. as intentional design, which overlaps to such an extent that it merges with the concepts of freedom and action (the principle of identity of the freedom-Subject-action triptych), the identity of the three concepts (necessary complementarity) consequently leading to describe each of the three concepts, for the purposes of the modern period, which is characterised by this identity, as *economic*, since it is this very identity which founds economics in the modern sense, in which we use it (to say "Subject" and "economic Subject" amounts, to a very large extent, to saying the same thing; the same is true for the concepts of freedom and action; in the modern period, however, the surpassment of this modernity may led to the separation and clarification of the two conceptual families, together with certain differences between Subject, freedom and action which have been erased).

The very rich path of the Subject, as consciousness and intention, freedom and action (there is an identity), encompassed by the concept of rationality or reason in L. v. M.'s line of thinking (action is declared to be always rational – we have clarified this point and the definition of the concept of rationality above) comes to a halt, in the grand Austrian tradition, within the boundaries of the individual and this line of thinking, which is so preoccupied by realism, refuses to take the plunge. It does not fail to condemn the holism which impregnates these collective forms, which are abundant within history, but instead of trying to consider them as realities (that which *is*), it calls for one to fight them (that which should be), yet another paradox for a line of thinking, which has always sought to report the position as it was rather than state what it should be. This plunge is however recorded within the concept of will, of intention to cooperate, a structure which does seems to make the individual Subject into a social being, becoming aware of the question of the means of emergence, organisation and regulation of intentional cooperation (the concept of society cannot be considered without this), the sole affirmation, which is, moreover, legitimate, of an intentional design to cooperate – whether positive or negative, the face of conflict forms part of the general notion of cooperation here – not stating how such designs cohabit, *a fortiori* when the collective group continues to be the *benevolent veil*, which we have discussed above. The collective form must be considered as such and within the framework of subjectivity, which is particularly appropriate, in order to describe the individual (by subjectivity, we mean, once again, the triptych of identity represented by Subject-freedom-action and especially by Subject-consciousness-design). It is quite possible that such collective forms should prove to be questionable or even detestable but this is not the first question posed to the group, which is rather that of finding the means, in order to report upon the phenomena of collective forms, which have become independent, as a collective consciousness (at least formally), upon their relations with the individuals, the individual forms of the consciousness and of intention, to report upon the effects of the dilution/disappearance/subordination of the individual, through such collective forms, which contain a collective consciousness (– whether such collective consciousness may prove to be a trap, where only a few individuals capture this so-called collective consciousness, is another matter –), to report upon an observed reality, which witnesses a *paradoxical* freedom, threatened by such collective forms or at least provoked by and/or under the constraint of its own limitless force, which calls for a norm and regulation, finally to report upon the collective forms themselves, upon their structure and their development (our theory of the empowerment of collective forms as Subject – the principle of transfer – from the characteristics of an individual Subject itself, enables one to understand that which at least asserts itself as a collective consciousness and therefore exists in such capacity and produces effects on individuals, effects which are not neutral and may be all the more harmful for such individuals and society, if the structure of the collective Subject is constituted of the same dimensions of absolute, total and totalitarian, acting freedom). The benevolent neutrality of the collective group is a fiction. Its harmfulness does indeed exist, requiring a norm. Its positive character exists as well, not the least of which being to provide a series of more or less satisfactory, temporary solutions (unstable equilibria and *optima* – which we have called the equilibria of under-freedom) to the essential fact, which integrates the desire for cooperation and for-otherness into the individual Subject.

General summary

THE FUNDAMENTAL PRINCIPLES

§ 194.   One will have understood from our earlier arguments that we have already adopted a position on this question, by establishing a certain number of principles. We have established the principle, which places the question of economic freedom within collective forms at the heart of the development of the economic action process (*principle of the collective form of freedom*). We have stated that, if the question of economic freedom lies within the collective forms, it is at the price of an extension/shift of the structure of the individual form of freedom into the collective form (*principle of the transfer of individual structures*). We have consequently established the acquisition, by the collective forms, of independence as Subject, which follows on from the preceding principle (*principle of autonomy of the collective Subject*). We have identified the conflicting coexistence of individual forms, as between themselves, and of individual forms and collective forms, with respect to each other, despite the presence of for-otherness within the very essence of the concepts of freedom and Subject, the need to find within the appropriate, institutional, collective forms the conditions for a possible norm and therefore for regulation and justice, since the concept of freedom does not contain the concept of justice, *ex ante* or originally, freedom even being faced with a *paradox*, that of being the principal risk, both for itself and for the Subject (*principle of the otherness of freedom; principle of the normative collective forms of freedom; principle of paradoxical freedom*).

We have emphasised throughout this work the essential pillar represented by the modern triptych of identity of Subject-freedom-action. This pillar is itself based on a description of the (economic) Subject as free consciousness, as a design of intention. The Subject, as consciousness and intention, therefore constitutes, in our view, a precious means of understanding economics and its phenomena. The notion of an intentional consciousness, as we have stated, incorporates within one and the same thing all of the more or less traditional characterisations of intentional design (motivation, will…).

This intentional consciousness is not empty. On the contrary, it conceals a "substance", constituted of time-matter made up of duration. This matter constitutes the intentional consciousness and the very dynamic of the design (in particular the memory/forgetfulness pairing). This "substance" of the (economic) Subject's constituent consciousness, i.e. time (duration), houses the question of value, to which it holds the key, namely the modern triptych of identity, (economic) Subject-freedom-action. The value is value *for* the Subject's intentional consciousness and value only exists by comparison to a context of the Subject, by comparison to what we have called in our work a *situation*, i.e. a certain temporal density of crude temporal matter (duration), which is more or less memorised or recalled, more or less forgotten or effaced, finally there are no economic or financial objects or phenomena, which are not objects of consciousness and, which find therein all the subjective density of the "value judgements" contained in L. v. M.'s approach, even if there are clear differences with regard to the legitimacy, construction and recognition of collective forms of freedom, of the Subject and therefore of action. And this value, which is a value judgement engaging the whole of the consciousness, including its temporal substance of duration, is therefore also the (inter)-temporal link, within the specific space-time reference frame of economics, a link which is provided by money. Value, and in general that which forms part of economics, is not inherent to things, goods, products, facts and realisations, *as such*; it always involves an intentional design of the consciousness, a capture of *judgement* (L. v. M.), of decision, of motivation, and is always based on the spatio-temporal substance of the consciousness. It is this value, which money, when it is not corrupted, is instructed to transmit within space and time (the space-time which forms the reference frame). This subjectivity, originating in the consciousness, is admittedly individual but also inter-individual and collective in our approach (and, in particular, there is indeed value, which comes towards the individual from others), a value judgement (in the sense used by L. v. M.) of *others* (other individuals but also collective forms, which have become independent), which may be binding on the individuals.

We have referred to the full importance of intentional consciousness and its space-time substance structured by duration, the pillar of our approach. A second pillar, which is very closely linked, is that of the consciousness, and therefore of the free Subject, acting as *difference*, an ontological status – to be in a state of non-being, the depression of being or obliteration, where temporality creeps in. It is this ontological form of difference, which sustains both the Subject's fundamental dissatisfaction, as basis for the various modes of intention (desire, will, motivation…), modes which are gathered within the concept of limited rationality, which we have clarified above, and its surpassment.

We have, at each instant, emphasised the extent to which the keys to a good understanding of economic phenomena lay largely in the hands of a time-matter made up of duration, memory and forgetfulness. This presence of time-matter cannot mean some form of determinism, which is *a fortiori* positivist, nor a historicism, where statistics alone would produce regularity, a norm and meaning. On the contrary, this time-matter is always intended to be surpassed, within the act, which reveals freedom and the Subject, at one and the same time, since, once again, freedom, Subject and action are different words to describe the same modern reality, the sudden appearance of economics, to such an extent that the only possible freedom, Subject or action are economic ones.

Rueil-Malmaison, Tahaa

January/August 2010

We are grateful to Mrs Melanie Lanoe for the traduction.

Titre I was initially published in France, *Théorie du Sujet économique* (Economica, 2010).

Titre II was initially published in France, *L'économie sociale de la liberté* (Economica, 2010).

TABLE OF CONTENTS

Achevé d'imprimer en septembre 2011
dans les ateliers de Normandie Roto Impression s.a.s.
à Lonrai (Orne)
N° d'impression : 112917
Dépôt légal : septembre 2011

Imprimé en France